MORE MONEY, MORE MINISTRY

MORE MONEY, MORE MINISTRY

*Money and Evangelicals
in Recent North American History*

Edited by

Larry Eskridge *and* Mark A. Noll

WILLIAM B. EERDMANS PUBLISHING COMPANY
GRAND RAPIDS, MICHIGAN / CAMBRIDGE, U.K.

Wm. B. Eerdmans Publishing Co.

255 Jefferson Ave. S.E., Grand Rapids, Michigan 49503 /
P.O. Box 163, Cambridge CB3 9PU U.K.

Printed in the United States of America

05 04 03 02 01 00   7 6 5 4 3 2 1

Library of Congress Cataloging-in-Publication Data

More money, more ministry: money and evangelicals in recent North American history /
edited by Larry Eskridge and Mark A. Noll.

p.   cm.

"Originally presented at an invitational consultation on "evangelicals and finance"
held in Naperville, Illinois in early December 1998."

Includes bibliographical references and index.

ISBN 0-8028-4777-3 (alk. paper)

1. Evangelicalism — United States — History — 19th century.
2. Money — Religious aspects — Christianity — History of doctrines — 19th century.
3. Finance — Religious aspects — Christianity — History of doctrines — 19th century.
4. Evangelicalism — United States — History — 20th century.
5. Money — Religious aspects — Christianity — History of doctrines — 20th century.
6. Finance — Religious aspects — Christianity — History of doctrines — 20th century.
I. Eskridge, Larry, 1954-   II. Noll, Mark A., 1946-

BR1642.U5 M67 2000

261.8′5′0973 — dc21

00-063606

www.eerdmans.com

Contents

v

CONTENTS

Part II: Specific Studies

Contents

Part III: Concluding Observations

Acknowledgments

The chapters which make up this volume were — with two exceptions — originally presented at an invitational consultation on "Evangelicals and Finance" held in Naperville, Illinois in early December 1998. That consultation, and the project in back of it, was sponsored by Wheaton College's Institute for the Study of American Evangelicals (ISAE). The Institute's staff and student assistants — Bryan Bademann, Carmin Ballou, David Gioe, Sarah Nichols, Mary Noll, Joel Moore, and, especially, Jennifer House Farmer — made an indispensable contribution all along the way, from the first planning meetings to the final preparation of this manuscript. That manuscript has, in turn, greatly benefited from the ministrations and expertise of the people at Wm. B. Eerdmans Publishing. Many thanks to Jon Pott, Jennifer Hoffman, and Katie Vander Molen for their contributions to making this volume become a reality.

One early lesson we learned was that finances cannot themselves be studied without having finances. Thankfully, that backing role was graciously filled by a grant from the Lilly Endowment, Inc., which made this book and project possible. Special thanks go to Fred Hofheinz and Craig Dykstra at Lilly for their unflagging enthusiasm and interest in this project.

A project such as this rarely emerges fully formed either intellectually or structurally. Neither did this one. From its beginnings, the ISAE's work on evangelicals and finance benefited from the insights and expertise of a number of scholars who helped us target the appropriate questions, vital issues, and key personnel to make the project come together. Among those who must be thanked in this regard are Jim Bratt, Scott Cormode, Kathryn Long, Donald Luidens, James Moorhead, Mary Joyce Oates, and David Richardson.

One individual must be particularly singled out for his vision, enthusiasm, and knowledge in this subject area, former Lilly Endowment director Robert Wood Lynn. It was his interest in the way that American Protestants interact with the both the spiritual and material dimensions of the financial realm that served as a crucial backdrop and impetus to the ISAE's even considering this topic. Without Bob Lynn's insights, prodding, and bibliographic assistance this project and book would never have seen the light of day.

Introduction

The fear of the Lord is clean, enduring forever: the judgments of the Lord are true and righteous altogether. More to be desired are they than gold, yea, than much fine gold. . . .

PSALM 19:9-10 (KJV)

I n the summer of 1911, Almyra Alston was commissioned a missionary to India by the Oklahoma conference of the Pentecostal Holiness Church. Starting out for California on the first leg of her journey, she had but ten dollars to cover her trip, her provision and supply, and her future support. However, "God miraculously supplied her need" and in early January 1912 she set sail for Hong Kong, staying there until "God saw fit to provide passage to India" where the determined Okie preached and taught for several years.[1]

Not quite so dependent on chance provision was William Bell Riley, famed scion of Minnesota fundamentalism, who took more proactive steps to ensure the survival of his Northwestern Bible and Missionary Training School in the early years of the Depression. In his book *God's Empire*, Bill Trollinger tells of how Riley and his board placed ads touting the wisdom of investing in the "FAIR AND CERTAIN EARNING" of a Northwestern annuity that provided the side benefit of investing "for Christ."

---

1. Joseph E. Campbell, *The Pentecostal Holiness Church: Its Background and History, 1898-1948* (Franklin Springs, GA: Pentecostal Holiness Church 1951), p. 346.

One ad took graphic advantage of the disastrous financial news of the day, showing a distraught man outside a closed bank intoning: "I wish I had invested my money in a [Northwestern] Annuity!"[2]

These two anecdotes from early in this century illustrate two prominent attitudes that twentieth-century American evangelicals have displayed toward money and its role in believers' lives. At one end of the spectrum, the earnest Miss Alston and her turn-of-the-century Pentecostal Holiness brethren emphasized a dependence on supernatural provision of needs while displaying blithe disregard for the "prudent" concerns of routine economic planning. By contrast, Riley's marketing ploy and appeal to providential investing are evidence of attitudes firmly rooted in a this-worldly concern to work out God's provision for his kingdom and our needs through the normal mechanisms of business and finance in a capitalist market economy. That both extremes — and any number of variants in-between — survive among evangelical attitudes at the end of the century is evident. Promise Keepers' sudden 1998 decision to cut back staff in a bold attempt to walk by faith and rely on the giving of "God's people" to determine the outline and extent of their future ministry[3] was a universe away from the marketing strategies that the Raymond Group, a Seattle area-based evangelical advertising firm, touted in 1995 as "a better way" to approach fund-raising for clients such as the International Bible Society.[4]

But the divergent attitudes do not end simply with attitudes toward the funding of "ministry." Indeed, as one begins to examine evangelical thought and behavior on other questions relating to Mammon — whether personal finances, tithing, business ethics, materialism, or the global economy — it becomes readily apparent that there is no universal evangelical opinion on money and its use, any more than there is a single evangelical view on church government and structure. One could hardly expect otherwise from such a diverse family of denominations and groups, given the jumble of influences — biblical, theological, historical, racial, ethnic, regional, and class — that have shaped what the late historian Timothy Smith first described as "the evangelical mosaic."[5]

2. William Vance Trollinger, Jr., *God's Empire: William Bell Riley and Midwestern Fundamentalism* (Madison: University of Wisconsin Press, 1990), pp. 88-89.

3. See "Promise Keepers to Lay Off Paid Staff," *Christian Century,* (11 Mar. 1998), pp. 254-55.

4. See ad in *Religious Broadcasting* 27, no. 2 (Feb. 1995): 1.

5. For years Smith, professor of American history at Johns Hopkins University un-

Strangely, however, there has been little attention paid to the relationship between evangelicals and money. This is all the more peculiar because, in many ways, there is no segment of the modern American religious community where money has so frequently played such a major role in key aspects of its development (and public image) during the past century. A few more obvious examples, hardly exhaustive, are sufficient to demonstrate the point. The existence of traditional evangelical taboos against ostentation and worldly entertainments — and their gradual relaxation or outright disappearance — speaks volumes about evangelicals' views on the right use of money. It also says a great deal about their improving fortunes with respect to class, income, and total wealth over the century. The early fundamentalist struggles over the disposition of denominational seminaries and the subsequent creation of conservative alternatives, while defended in strictly theological terms, were also firmly tethered to concrete financial questions of de-facto divestiture and infrastructural development. Controversy over fundamentalist and evangelical access to radio air time, an issue that birthed both the National Religious Broadcasters and its parent National Association of Evangelicals in the early 1940s, was a squabble about the distribution of free "public service" air time, as well as over the right of the "Electronic Church" to buy time for evangelistic programs. The pervasive Gantryesque image of evangelists in the popular imagination, fueled by the flimflam antics of such figures as Marjoe Gortner[6] or Jim and Tammy Faye Bakker, is a foul stew in

---

til his death in 1997, and several of his graduate students labored on a vast project, "The American Evangelical Mosaic," the results of which yet remain unpublished. The attempt to define American evangelicals has led to something of a small historiographic and sociological cottage industry over the last twenty years. No wonder, given the fact that to some degree or other everyone from the black Baptist to the Catholic charismatic, and the holiness Methodist to the conservative Calvinist Presbyterian, can be classified as "evangelical." In terms of a working definition of what constitutes an evangelical, however, British historian David W. Bebbington's fourfold description of evangelicals as Christians marked by a tendency toward activism, with a particular emphasis on conversion, the Bible, and the work of the cross (D. W. Bebbington, *Evangelicalism in Modern Britain: A History from the 1730s to the 1980s* [London: Unwin Hyman, 1989], pp. 4-17), serves as a better field guide than many an intricate discussion of denominational, theological, or historic pedigrees.

6. Gortner, a reknowned child-evangelist in certain Pentecostal circles in the 1950s, had by his early twenties lost any semblance of faith as he continued to cynically milk the revival circuit. In the early 1970s he agreed to expose the whole "revivalist racket" for a

which the desire for "filthy lucre" contributes one of the most notable ingredients.[7] And the rise of the Religious Right in the late 1970s was not only a story of an awakened evangelical political sensibility, it was also testimony to a well-organized grass-roots fund-raising machinery and the willingness of many politically conservative Protestants to put their money where their ballot was.

This particular volume is meant as a first step toward understanding how evangelicals have thought about, used, and raised money during the twentieth century. It derives from a larger umbrella project, "The Financing of American Evangelical Religion," conceived and administered by Wheaton College's Institute for the Study of American Evangelicals (ISAE), and funded by the Lilly Endowment of Indianapolis as part of its extensive "Financing of American Religion" initiative.[8] Under the project, nearly

---

film documentary crew. The resultant 1971 documentary, "Marjoe," showed the drinking, womanizing, and pot-smoking Gortner in action, including scenes where he divided up the night's take with a host pastor, and another scene where he sang blasphemous ditties and cavorted on a motel bed strewn with money. Gortner moved on from the acclaimed documentary to a career in grade-B movies and occasional roles in television shows such as "Starsky and Hutch" and the "A-Team."

7. By contrast, the negative stereotype of money-grubbing evangelists has given rise to strenuous counter-efforts to overcome this image; one thinks of Billy Graham's innovative organizational structure that the Billy Graham Evangelistic Association adopted in 1952 to pay flat salaries to the evangelist and his staff as well as provide for financial checks and balances within the organization (see William Martin, *A Prophet with Honor* [New York: William Morrow, 1990], pp. 138-40), as well as the creation of the Evangelical Council for Financial Accountability (ECFA) in 1979.

8. The Lilly Endowment's initiative on "The Financing of American Religion" was a family of nearly thirty separate projects examining a wide-ranging number of special topics and areas such as diocesan funding in the Episcopal Church, costs involved in running Catholic parishes and schools, religious organizations in American law, and financing theological education. (For a summary of the various projects see the document *The Lilly Endowment's Initiative on the Financing of American Religion* [Indianapolis: The Lilly Endowment, May 1997]). Much important work on contemporary American financing of religious organizations and individual and congregational giving and funding has been completed because of this initiative, particularly regarding Catholicism and mainline Protestantism. Some of the particularly valuable works that have been funded, at least in part, by Lilly funds include Mark Chaves and Sharon L. Miller, eds., *Financing American Religion* (Keyport, NJ: AltaMira Press, 1998); Dean R. Hoge, Charles Zech, Patrick McNamara, and Michael J. Donahue, *Money Matters: Personal Giving in American Churches* (Louisville: Westminster/John Knox Press, 1996); Mary J. Oates, *The Catholic Philanthropic Tradition in America* (Bloomington: Indiana University Press, 1995); John and Sylvia Ronsvalle, *Behind the Stained Glass Windows:*

thirty scholars were commissioned to examine particular aspects of the historical interaction between evangelicals and the world of money and finance. The results of this research were presented at an invitational consultation in Naperville, Illinois in early December 1998. Part of the material from that meeting has gone into a volume edited by Mark Noll that examines more generally Protestant interactions with finance from the early days of the republic to just before the War Between the States: *Protestants, Money, and the Market, 1790-1860*.[9] That book examines a time when evangelical stances on such issues were nearly tantamount to being the embodiment of Protestant (and arguably, American) interaction with money and finance. By contrast, this book examines the evangelical understanding(s) of money for the period after which "evangelicalism" evolved out of the conservative-liberal split of the fundamentalist-modernist controversy and now exists as a variegated movement within a much more diversified American religious and cultural landscape.

The Shape of the Book

Setting the figurative table for all that follows is an overview of the larger American economy in the twentieth century by economists Robin Klay and John Lunn as assisted by historian Michael Hamilton. One of the dangers of a study of this type, especially when most of its contributors are historians of American religion, is an inattention to the larger picture of what was going on within the American economy and how evangelicals related to that greater fiscal reality. In this opening chapter, Klay, Lunn, and Hamilton anchor the story of evangelical development to the growth and evolution of the American economy in the twentieth century. The story they present of the "miracle" of American economic growth and the ever-expanding size and reach of the federal government also shows how evangelicals interacted with these changes. In addition, it provides a cultural and economic context for understanding the whys and hows surrounding evangelicalism's evolution from a denominationally based movement to

Money Dynamics in the Church (Grand Rapids: Baker, 1996); Wesley K. Willmer and J. David Schmidt with Martyn Smith, *The Prospering Parachurch: Enlarging the Boundaries of God's Kingdom* (San Francisco: Jossey-Bass, 1998); and Robert Wuthnow, *God and Mammon in America* (New York: The Free Press, 1994).

9. Mark A. Noll, ed., *Protestants, Money, and the Market, 1790-1860* (forthcoming).

one centered on a vast armada of corporately structured parachurch organizations.

One of the important developments that paved the way for the twentieth-century economy was the rise of modern advertising and a consumer culture in the late nineteenth century. In his chapter, Gary Scott Smith examines the dissonance caused by the conflict between the old "Protestant Ethic" and the rise of the new ethic of consumption in the period between 1880 and 1930. In his wide-ranging research Smith finds a mixed reaction — denunciations of greed and materialism; a general acceptance and adaptation of the principles of advertising by most evangelicals; faith in the upward trajectory of economic progress while failing to see the many casualties left in its wake; and an emphasis on the salutary benefits of proper stewardship. This mixture certainly illuminates the evangelical mindset of that period, but it also suggests a basic conflict in the evangelical heart-of-hearts that continues to this day.

Big-time revivalism has played an especially important role in the growth and image of evangelicalism down through the years. In the next chapter, Charles Hambrick-Stowe (who has written a biography of Charles G. Finney)[10] considers the pragmatic side of what revivalist Sam Jones called a "sanctified business." From the days of Finney down through D. L. Moody, Jones, Billy Sunday, Aimee Semple McPherson, Billy Graham, and the rise of the Promise Keepers, the range of attitudes and behaviors, methods, and structures Hambrick-Stowe uncovers is interesting in and of itself. More subtly, however, he points out how problematic it is to sever the connection between serving God and the inescapable need for serving Mammon that makes large-scale evangelism happen. In that light, the messy questions concerning the integrity of an evangelist's ministry will always be tied up with the money — and the politics — of their patrons, wealthy or otherwise.

Michael Hamilton is a sagacious student of recent evangelical history, and his overview covers the period from the end of World War II to the present day. His analysis of this "boom" period in the expansion of evangelicalism explicitly links the explosion to the prosperity that enveloped American society. Hamilton argues that evangelicals, buoyed along

10. Charles E. Hambrick-Stowe, *Charles G. Finney and the Spirit of American Evangelicalism*, Library of Religious Biography, Mark A. Noll, Nathan O. Hatch, and Allen C. Guelzo, eds. (Grand Rapids: Eerdmans, 1996).

with the currents of postwar prosperity, have provided the financial where-withal for the phenomenal growth of the evangelical institutional and organizational infrastructure by giving away a healthy slice of their prosperity. At the same time, evangelical organizations pursuing their call to evangelize and minister have modernized and streamlined their operations by adapting the techniques of modern management and fund-raising. The inherent danger Hamilton sees is the temptation to begin focusing on growth itself. Hamilton's bottom-line equation — more money equals more ministry — is both an empirical conclusion and the description of a debatable assumption that undergirds much of the frenetic fund-raising (and giving) that energizes the burgeoning evangelical parachurch network.

A number of more focused studies follow, the first being Peter Dobkin Hall's examination of evangelicals' role in the rapid expansion and refinement of the American economy in the decades surrounding the turn of the century. With a nod to Max Weber, Hall finds a parallel trajectory in the growing split between liberal and conservative Protestants and the religious affiliation and sentiments of America's national, regional, and local economic elites. As he raises the question of why religious beliefs and practices that were firmly identified with the creation of the modern American order in the 1870s could seem thoroughly lined up against that power structure by the 1920s, Hall highlights a fundamental question about the nature of evangelicalism: Is it compatible with wielding power, influence, and economic clout in a pluralistic society? His analysis of the situation at the turn of the century is instructive for considering the future direction of the resurgent evangelicalism of the late twentieth century.

One of the salient facts of twentieth-century American economic life has been the increasingly vital role of women as consumers, as part of the workforce, and belatedly, as managers of their own enterprises. Susan Yohn examines an important evangelical manifestation of this phenomenon with her study of the economic side of the Protestant women's missions movement. To date, much of the literature surrounding this movement has centered on the manner in which such organizations extended the social and political clout of women in the late nineteenth and early twentieth centuries.[11] Yohn's piece is a fascinating glimpse into the "busi-

11. See, for example, R. Pierce Beaver, *American Protestant Women in World Mission: A History of the First Feminist Movement in North America* (Grand Rapids: Eerdmans, 1968);

ness" of women's missions and the various fund-raising and management strategies — often borrowed from corporate models — used to grow their enterprises until such time as success made them targets for "takeover" by official denominational (and male-dominated) mission boards.

The savvy, homespun business expertise of Yohn's Protestant women's missionary efforts, however, is not the only model for the missions enterprise. Alvyn Austin examines what would become a very influential approach to money management among evangelical organizations as he tells the story of the "faith" approach modeled by the China Inland Mission (CIM). Austin's account of why Hudson Taylor and his successors were reluctant to ask for money — or even make their needs known to their constituency — until well into the 1950s is a wonderful example of evangelical exceptionalism. The story of CIM is also a benchmark from earlier times by which to measure the later evolution of evangelicals' money ways.

It is possible in a book like this to be carried away by the sheer might of the market, by a focus on the histories of institutions and organizations, or by the behavior of economic elites and the macro forces that shape the economy. It is important, however, to remember that much of the population defined as "evangelical" would find no place in such a treatment. This reality is especially true when considering the vast numbers of evangelical Protestants inhabiting the heartland of evangelical Protestantism — the South — in the days before the arrival of Sun Belt Prosperity. Ted Ownby examines the economic attitudes and behaviors of two groups with particular strength in the early twentieth-century South — the Pentecostals and the Churches of Christ. As one might expect of people living hardscrabble lives amid tough economic circumstances, Ownby finds that neither group had much time for developing anything like a fully articulated economic worldview. Still, the hodgepodge of antagonism to worldliness, hatred of debt, and relative lack of political activism in an era framed by the rise of the populist movement and the Great Depression is instructive for thinking about continuing evangelical attitudes in the United States; it also provides much fodder for comparative study, particularly with the recent rise of evangelicalism in Latin America.

---

and Patricia Hill, *The World Their Household: The American Woman's Foreign Missionary Movement and Cultural Transformation, 1870-1920* (Ann Arbor: University of Michigan Press, 1985).

The work of Joel Carpenter has been responsible for reversing the notion that the 1930s and 1940s was a period of quiescence for American fundamentalists and the emerging evangelical movement. In the next chapter, a revision of an article that originally appeared in the journal *Church History*,[12] Carpenter re-approaches this key period with an appraisal of the important financial and economic dimensions of the fundamentalist revival. This added perspective solidifies the previous thrust of his work, showing that fundamentalism was not only resilient in terms of its grass-roots activism and institution-building, but that it prospered financially even during a period of daunting economic troubles.

The rapid growth in the number and size of Bible schools, colleges, and seminaries has been one of the major stories of the postwar evangelical resurgence in the United States. Robert Burkinshaw's comparative essay on the very differing trajectories of funding for evangelical higher education in the U.S. and Canada, however, makes it plain that straight-line expansion was not a universal phenomenon. His examination is useful not only for pointing out the differences that national contexts can play in higher education, but also for showing how the power of the state — or in the American context, its relative lack of power — directly affects the ability of evangelicals to exercise their activist tendencies. This difference is a factor that can be readily appreciated as a backdrop for the following essay, Barry Gardner's insider account of the revolution in fund-raising among evangelical agencies between the 1960s and 1990s. A fund-raising advisor for several evangelical ministries, Gardner writes tellingly of the practical, day-to-day changes in doing business that are all too often unseen from the academic's ivory tower. He describes the increasing sophistication of computer, printing, sorting, mailing, and telecommunications technology, which, coupled with government breaks for nonprofit organizations on everything from sales tax to postal rates, has wrought a mighty work indeed. Yet Gardner's is not an uncritical appraisal; there are signs that do not bode well for evangelical fund-raisers. The gains in funding technique and technology have been offset, Gardner argues, by an increasing sense of "donor fatigue" and the steady decline in churches' and denominations' role as a

---

12. Joel A. Carpenter, "Fundamentalist Institutions and the Rise of Evangelical Protestantism, 1929-1942," *Church History* 49 (Mar. 1980): 62-75. Carpenter's work on this period is fully fleshed out in his seminal book *Revive Us Again: The Reawakening of American Fundamentalism* (New York: Oxford University Press, 1997).

filter for funding appeals. How these factors may affect the parachurch net-work in the future — to say nothing of the attitudes and pocketbooks of evangelical givers — remains to be seen.

As the chapters by Hamilton, Burkinshaw, and Gardner establish, evangelicalism has prospered in the postwar American bonanza even as evangelicals as individuals, families, and congregations have prospered. But what do folk at the grass roots think of all this? How do they view money, stewardship, and their participation in the consumer society? The next two chapters, Larry Eskridge's examination of the rise to prominence and the teachings of evangelical financial advice guru Larry Burkett, and Dean Hoge and Mark Noll's survey on giving in Canada and the U.S., help to fill out this dimension of our study. Eskridge's essay on Burkett is a window on the money-related problems and concerns that have beset John and Suzy Evangelical since the 1960s. Burkett's counsel, he contends, strikes a happy balance of conventional financial advice and stewardship for many middle-class evangelicals that steers between the extremes of "health and wealth" narcissism and the "prophetic" demands of simple lifestyle advocates. Yet the popularity of Burkett's pessimistic books on the future of the American economy, Eskridge suggests, makes it clear that many evangelicals are hardly secure in their — often first- and second-generation — middle-class status in the larger socio-economic order.

Hoge and Noll's piece provides a contemporary snapshot of Americans' and Canadians' views on money and giving attitudes. Based upon a phone poll of 6,000 U.S. and Canadian citizens conducted by Toronto's Angus Reid Group in late 1996, the unusually large survey sample offers clear confirmation of national differences in terms of evangelical strength, as well as evangelicals' marked tendency to outgive other Christians. Their analysis confirms the strong hold that evangelical views have upon their adherents' lives and the clear correlation between an active faith and giving.

Closing out the section of specific studies, Tom Berg's fascinating examination of the 1995 "New Era" scandal turns from the behavior of individual evangelical givers to the heady world of big-time evangelical high finance. Despite the size and sophistication of modern evangelical marketing and fund-raising mechanisms, Berg concludes that the uppermost circles of evangelical money still bear an uncanny resemblance to old-fashioned face-to-face market relationships. Lured by the promises of matching gifts from mysterious anonymous donors, more than two hundred evangelical entities ranging from middling-sized congregations to respected liberal arts colleges, denominations, and huge parachurch organizations fell prey to an elaborate Ponzi scheme — a scheme that also took in gilt-edged dupes like Laurence Rockefeller and the University of Pennsylvania. Berg's glimpse of the "good old boy" networks that lent credibility to the scheme, and the key role the injured evangelical parties played in cobbling together an extraordinary settlement package, is a compelling picture of how evangelicals operate in the midst of — and are adjusting to — the complex workings of modern finance.

Rounding out the volume are a pair of closing ruminations on evangelicals' perilous tightrope walk over the abyss of mammon. Joel Carpenter returns with some probing insights on evangelicals and money as explored in the contemporary scene through Berg, Burkinshaw, and Eskridge's chapters. John Stackhouse concludes the volume, fittingly, with an eye to the theological dimension of evangelicals' historic interaction with money. Using the example of a Ms. Evangelical "Everyperson," Stackhouse explores the complicated — and frequently conflicting — levels of economic operation and meaning with which a conscientious evangelical Christian of average means comes into contact on a regular basis. His meditation cannot, of course, provide any final or definitive answers to the tangle of tortuous connections that link faith and money. It does, however, provide a proper sense of depth for both believers and historians (to say nothing of the believing historian) as they continue to contemplate the varied treasures on which evangelical hearts have been set.

The end of the book leads us to wonder where we go from here. *More Money, More Ministry* is only a first step toward a clearer conceptual grasp of the many historic, economic, cultural, and theological connections in the bewilderingly complex junction of worldly and heavenly values. In bringing this volume to publication we have realized afresh how much more needs to be done. Despite our attempts to cover as much ground as possible within the space of one project/book, the list of self-admitted lacunae still looms large. Unfortunately, we have had little room to address any number of events, themes, and topics that deserve their own individual attention: televangelism, evangelicals and the Great Depression, the rise of evangelical relief and social service agencies, and the ever-growing professionalization of evangelical clergy and staff are just a few of the more obvious. The slices of helpful information and illuminating anecdotes the authors in this volume have ferreted out of widely scattered sources are testimony to the great need for thoroughgoing economic histories of key evangelical institutions, denominations, and organizations. In the same vein, more studies of individual congregations' (and their members') economic histories would certainly clarify the ways in which economic issues have — or have not — affected grass-roots evangelicals' social, cultural, and political attitudes.

But there are larger oversights as well. The unique economic and historic context of African-American evangelicals, their churches, and their organizations are only tangentially touched upon in this book. Worse, there is no attention at all to the expanding Hispanic and Asian evangelical communities in North America. And the economic dimensions of the history of evangelical women in the twentieth century extends far beyond Susan Yohn's examination of early women's missions organizations. What this book has only just begun will no doubt need to be continued.

PART I

OVERVIEWS AND ORIENTATIONS

CHAPTER I

American Evangelicalism and the National Economy, 1870-1997

ROBIN KLAY AND JOHN LUNN, WITH MICHAEL S. HAMILTON

> *. . . seek the peace and prosperity of the city to which I have carried you into exile. Pray to the Lord for it, because if it prospers, you too will prosper.*
>
> JEREMIAH 29:7 (NIV)

In 1982 Alan Trachtenberg published a history of the late nineteenth and early twentieth centuries he called *The Incorporation of America*. Trachtenburg argued that the rise of big business did more than change the economy. The managerial values of large incorporated enterprises also changed the way Americans thought about themselves, and the way they organized themselves in the non-business areas of their lives.[1]

Trachtenberg had little to say about religion, but structural changes in the American economy that occurred around the turn of the century profoundly affected the organizational patterns and fortunes of American evangelicalism. As the U.S. moved from an agricultural to a manufacturing and then to a service economy, the raw fact of enormous economic

---

1. Alan Trachtenberg, *The Incorporation of America: Culture and Society in the Gilded Age* (New York: Hill and Wang, 1982).

growth made increasingly large sums of money available to religious organizations. Consequently, first Protestant denominations, and then the large independent evangelical organizations, readily adopted the managerial methods, strategies, and values that had been developed by business corporations. In so doing they grew even larger. By the 1990s evangelical religion in American was thriving, and the evangelical world more closely resembled the business world than ever before.

However, beneath this simple story of growth lies the more complex story of the relationship between evangelicalism and the American economy. At the end of the nineteenth century evangelicalism was fully integrated within the old Protestant denominations. But just as the denominations were experiencing unprecedented growth of their national structures by adopting business values and techniques, the center of gravity in evangelicalism shifted away from the denominations. In the depths of the Great Depression, evangelicalism turned its organizational energies to independent nonprofit agencies. Despite being a stunningly inauspicious time to launch new organizations that depended heavily on direct fund-raising, these "parachurch" agencies thrived. In the end, these organizations would look more like business corporations than did the denominations.

The American Economy, 1870-1930

The most obvious characteristic of the American economy in this period was its impressive growth. High birthrates and high levels of immigration — from 1870 through 1920, one in every seven American residents was foreign-born — kept the U.S. population climbing at a rate of 2 percent per year. Yet the economy grew even faster, at an average rate of 4 percent per year, and workers' incomes were rising.[2]

The transition from agriculture to manufacturing fueled the nation's economic growth. Agriculture expanded during this period, whether measured by the increase in land under cultivation (up from 189 million acres

2. U.S. Bureau of the Census, *Historical Statistics of the United States, Colonial Times to 1957* (Washington, DC: 1960), Series C228. Richard A. Easterlin, "The American Economy," in *American Economic Growth: An Economist's History of the United States,* ed. Lance E. Davis et al. (New York: Harper and Row, 1972), p. 126. On national income, see Easterlin, "The American Economy," p. 74, Table 4-3.

in 1870 to 319 million acres in 1900) or by the number of people employed in farming, which increased by 150 percent between 1870 and 1930. Yet industry grew much faster. Railroads led the way, becoming the nation's first genuinely large corporations in the 1870s and stimulating the rapid growth of the iron and steel industries. Between 1870 and 1930 employment in the railroad sector increased by over 1,000 percent, while manufacturing employment increased by over 400 percent. Between 1860 and 1910 total manufacturing output increased by over 1,000 percent, and for the first time in its history the U.S. became a net exporter of manufactured goods.[3]

Most people employed in industry lived in cities, so naturally the urban population grew much faster than the rural population. But some cities grew not as manufacturing centers but as networks of service providers, especially for farmers and for domestic and international trade. The percentage of Americans residing in urban areas increased steadily throughout this period, up from 26 percent in 1870 to 56 percent in 1930.[4]

Yet the overall pattern of economic growth was uneven. Prices actually fell during the last thirty years of the nineteenth century, and in this deflationary environment debtors — which included most farmers — suffered greatly. Farmers also suffered from the fact that the federal government financed itself mainly through import tariffs. Tariffs helped develop manufacturing by keeping the prices of manufactured goods higher, but tended to lower farm prices by reducing overseas demand for American food products. Economic downturns were so frequent that nearly everyone believed in the idea of a "business cycle" — the notion that economic depressions are a regular and inevitable part of economic growth. The U.S. economy suffered through major depressions from 1873 to 1879 (10,000 businesses failed in 1878 alone) and from 1883 to 1897; lesser but still serious downturns in 1903, 1907, 1910, 1913; and another major depression in 1920-21 after the nation had demobilized from World War I. These depressions worked enormous hardships on countless lives, but none of them were as bad as the unprecedented economic free fall that began in 1929. In its first four years the Great Depression cut the nation's total economic

3. Cropland: Gilbert C. Fite and Jim E. Reese, *An Economic History of the United States* (Cambridge, MA: Riverside, 1959), p. 298. Employment: Stanley Lebergott, "The American Labor Force," in Davis et al., *American Economic Growth*, p. 187. Manufacturing output: Jonathan Hughes and Louis P. Cain, *American Economic History*, 4th ed. (New York: HarperCollins, 1994), p. 308.

4. U.S. Bureau of the Census, *Historical Statistics . . . to 1957*, Series 178.

output nearly in half, and left one-fourth of the nation's labor force unemployed.[5]

Not surprisingly, the unevenness of economic growth produced a good deal of social turmoil, especially in the late nineteenth century. When an economic panic hit, corporations' first response was to slash prices in order to keep production up (high production kept per-unit costs lower). When lower prices produced net losses, their next response was collusion with each other to fix prices. When the government finally intervened in price-fixing, firms began to eliminate competition by merging with each other, producing some of the large corporations that are familiar to us today. Falling prices, economic downturns, monopolies, and price-fixing by banks and railroads generated widespread farm protests. Out of these protests came new regional tensions and a new political party — the Populists. When the Populist Party fused with the Democrats and nominated William Jennings Bryan for President in 1896, the long-standing equilibrium between the Republicans and Democrats was shattered, and the Republicans reigned over the national government. Meanwhile, cities had grown out of control. And the nearly universal tendency of the industrial leaders to regard their employees not as human beings but as units of production, combined with general economic instability, stimulated several waves of mass labor protest. Between 1881 and 1905 there were nearly 37,000 labor strikes involving some 7 million workers. By the last decade of the nineteenth century, many Americans — Theodore Roosevelt among them — believed that economic turbulence had brought the nation to the brink of social and political anarchy.[6]

A partial solution, clear to twentieth-century Americans but far less obvious a century ago, was to increase government regulation of business and the economy. State governments pioneered most of the early forms of business regulation. In the 1870s several states passed "Granger Laws" regulating prices charged by railroads, grain storage facilities, and others who performed services for farmers. In 1893 Illinois became the first state to legislate an eight-hour workday for women, and in 1902 Maryland adopted the first law to compensate workers in case of injury. The federal government later followed suit, establishing the Interstate Commerce Commis-

---

5. Robert Higgs, *The Transformation of the American Economy, 1865-1914: An Essay in Interpretation* (New York: John Wiley and Sons, 1971), pp. 19-21.

6. Trachtenberg, *Incorporation of America*, p. 80.

sion in 1887, the Sherman Antitrust Act in 1890, the Meat Inspection and Pure Food and Drug Acts in 1906, the Federal Reserve Act in 1913, the Federal Trade Commission in 1914, and the Keating-Owen Child Labor Act in 1916.

The whole idea of federal intervention in the economy in general was, however, highly controversial. As Congress became more friendly to the idea of regulating big business, the Supreme Court became, from the 1890s forward, an aggressive champion of "laissez-faire" — keeping the government's hands off business. The Court repeatedly struck down both state and federal efforts to regulate business, using as their Constitutional rationale the "due process" clause of the Fourteenth Amendment — a clause that had been intended solely to prevent former slaves from being deprived of life, liberty, and property. When the Court did not strike these interventionist laws down, they usually either nullified their effectiveness by severely limiting their scope, or they turned the laws against organized labor. A good example is what the Court did with the Sherman Antitrust Act. The Court refused to allow the breaking up of the American Sugar Refining Company's 98 percent monopoly, saying the law was not intended to apply to manufacturing. But the Court did apply the Act to uphold injunctions against labor strikes. The Court decided that strikes were illegal "restraint of trade," even though the Act clearly was never intended to apply to organized labor.[7]

Behind the economic dislocations, social turmoil, and confusion over what to do about them lay the emergence of a new kind of business entity in America — the large modern corporation. Before the Civil War, corporations existed only when chartered (by state legislatures) for special public purposes such as education or transportation. Most businesses were organized as proprietorships or partnerships. But after the Civil War states set up procedures whereby corporations could be formed merely by application. This new kind of corporation was encumbered by far fewer restrictions than the old chartered corporations and as a result proved more attractive as a structure for business organizations. Gradually, for-profit corporations acquired legal status as fictional "persons."

The beauty of this new form of business was that it could amass far more capital for expansion than could proprietorships and partnerships.

---

7. Stuart Bruchey, *Enterprise: The Dynamic Economy of a Free People* (Cambridge, MA: Harvard University Press, 1990), pp. 346-74.

The owners (stockholders) were more eager to invest in a corporation because they were liable only for the amount of their investment — not for the liabilities of the corporation. In exchange for limited liability, owners yielded operational decisions to a new class of businessmen — professional managers.

In the last three decades of the nineteenth century, for-profit corporations thoroughly dominated the economy, building huge industrial enterprises in transportation, mining, manufacturing, and processing, and dwarfing the size of state and federal governments. By 1904, three hundred corporations directly controlled 40 percent of all American manufacturing, and indirectly influenced another 40 percent. By 1929, the two hundred largest corporations owned nearly half of all corporate assets.[8]

Because modern corporations dominated the economy, the ideas and values they developed also spread deep into the fabric of American life. The new armies of professional managers that ran the corporations developed a new bureaucratic ideology that explained what they sought to do. The chief tenet of the new ideology held that rational and systematic planning could solve any and all problems. The chief end of rational planning was efficiency — avoiding waste and duplication in order to maximize profit. The managers believed that the best way to promote rational planning and achieve efficiency was to put decisions in the hand of experts and specialists. Once rational decisions had been made by the managers, "education" and publicity were necessary tools for persuading workers, customers, owners, government, and the general public to go along with the managers' decisions. Once all facets of society — business, schools, government, the arts, families, churches — were put on this basis, the result would be a more ordered, rational, improved world.[9]

The Incorporation of Protestant Denominations

Up until the 1920s, most evangelicals were a part of the Protestant mainstream. That is to say, evangelical Protestants and non-evangelical Protestants both participated in the life of the major Protestant denominations.

---

8. Trachtenberg, *Incorporation of America*, p. 4.

9. Ben Primer, *Protestants and American Business Methods* (Ann Arbor: UMI Research Press, 1979), pp. 65-68.

Definitions of evangelicalism are much-debated, but for these purposes evangelicals might be thought of as orthodox Christians influenced by Bible-centered, revivalist modes of faith. The largest groups of these could be found in Methodist, Baptist, Presbyterian, Congregational, and Restorationist denominations. Using the term "evangelical" in this way, there were two large parties of non-evangelical Protestants. The first and larger body of non-evangelicals were those Protestants in confessional or ethnic denominations, such as Episcopalians, Lutherans, Dutch and German Reformed, and Anabaptist groups. The second and probably the smaller group were the folks whose theology was moving toward liberalism, whose signature characteristic was a de-emphasis of the supernatural aspects of traditional Christianity. These proto-liberals could be found in the same denominations as the evangelicals, as well as in their own denominations such as the Unitarians. But the key point is that in these years nearly every denomination with a preponderance of evangelicals had significant numbers of non-evangelicals in leadership positions.

Religion as a whole benefited from the nation's economic growth in this period. In 1870, the ratio of church income to Gross National Product (GNP) was about 1:211. Although the GNP was growing faster than the population, giving to churches was growing even faster. By 1916 the ratio of church income to GNP had risen to 1:153, and in the next ten years it took an incredible leap to 1:119. The Great Depression hit church finances hard, and in 1936 the ratio of church income to GNP had dropped back to 1:159. But even with this downturn, church income rose substantially faster than the GNP between 1870 and 1936 (see Table 1, p. 22).

For the last thirty years of the nineteenth century, church income also grew faster, proportionately, than did income for the federal government. In 1870 federal spending was still inflated from the Civil War and Reconstruction, and the ratio of church income was one dollar to every twelve dollars generated by the federal government. For the next eight years federal receipts actually shrank before starting a very slow upward climb. Still, overall church income grew faster than did federal income, and by 1916 the nation's churches took in half of the amount of the U.S. government. But World War I marked the beginning of the unrelenting expansion of the federal government, and federal receipts began to rise more rapidly than either church income or the GNP. During what was a decade of very rapid growth in church income, 1916-1926, federal income grew so fast that the ratio dropped to 1:5. While the Great Depression lowered

TABLE 1 Church Income, National Income, and Federal
Government Receipts, 1870-1997
(In millions of current dollars)

Year	Church Income	Gross National Product	Ratio Church Income to GNP	Federal Government Receipts	Ratio Church Income to Fed. Rec'ts	Ratio Fed. Rec'ts to GNP
1870	35	7,400	1:211	411	1:12	1:18
1916	316	48,300	1:153	761	1:2	1:63
1926	817	97,000	1:119	3,795	1:5	1:26
1936	519	82,500	1:159	3,997	1:8	1:21
1997	70,000	8,110,900*	1:116	1,579,000	1:23	1:5

*Gross Domestic Product Sources:
— Church Income, 1870: Estimated from figures of Herman C. Weber, *Presbyterian Statistics: Through One Hundred Years, 1826-1926* (1927), *Encyclopedia of Southern Baptists* (Nashville: Broadman Press, various years), and *Minutes of the General Synod* (Reformed Church in America, various years); as to correlated number of churches given in Edwin Scott Gaustad, *Historical Atlas of Religion in America* (New York: Harper Row, 1962).
— Church Income, 1916-36: U.S. Bureau of the Census, Religious Bodies (1916, Table 16; 1926, Table 15; 1936, Tables 13 and 15).
— Church Income, 1997: From Noll Table 5.
— GNP, 1870-1936: U.S. Bureau of the Census, Historical Statistics of the United States, Colonial Times to 1970, Bicentennial Edition, Part 1 (Washington, DC: 1975), Series F1, p. 224.
— GDP, 1997: Economic Report of the President (Washington, DC: 1999), 326.
— Federal government receipts, 1880-1936: U.S. Bureau of the Census, Historical Statistics of the United States, Colonial Times to 1970, Bicentennial Edition, Part 2 (Washington, DC: 1975), Series Y352, pp. 1105-6.
— Federal government receipts, 1997: U.S. Bureau of the Census, Statistical Abstract of the United States: 1998 (188th ed.) (Washington, DC: 1998), Table 537, p. 339.

both church income and the GNP, federal receipts continued to rise, and by 1936 the ratio of church to federal income was at 1:8 (see Table 1 above).

But should Christians support the increased involvement of the federal government in economic matters? As the economic and social crisis of the late nineteenth century worsened, differing opinions on this question sharpened and became more contentious. Most Protestants, of all stripes, tended to lean conservative on this question. Horace Bushnell may have been a theological liberal, but when it came to economics he was as conservative as his orthodox counterparts. In 1869 he opposed government intervention in women's working conditions: "There is no such possibility as a legally appointed rate of wages; market price is the only scale of earnings possible for women as for men."[10] A minority of theological liberals advocated government-sponsored reform; these are remembered as the ministers of the Social Gospel. But a large number of reform-minded evangelicals — mostly people from the Wesleyan holiness movement — strongly advocated government intervention in the form of regulation of business, child labor legislation, and wages and hours laws.[11]

There was far less debate among church leaders over how much the new corporate management ideology ought to affect Christianity. In the antebellum period, Protestant denominations were very modest organizations. The first strong national religious organizations were not denominations but special purpose agencies of the Evangelical United Front (EUF), such as the American Bible Society. The Civil War, however, drew off the reforming energy that had gone into the EUF agencies, and many of them languished. Also before the war, a number of agencies that were related to denominations — but independent of them — were created to further Christian work of various kinds. After the war, as the denominations rapidly added members and churches, they took their first steps to imitate corporations by taking over control of these independent agencies. This was done in the name of efficiency and centralized planning. Perhaps the largest example of that trend was the 1872 annexation of the Missionary Society of the Methodist Episcopal Church (founded in 1819), which placed the society into the hands of a special "Board of Managers."[12]

10. Horace Bushnell, *Women's Suffrage: The Reform Against Nature* (New York, 1869), pp. 11-12, as quoted in Henry F. May, *Protestant Churches and Industrial America* (New York: Harper Torchbook, 1967 [1949]), p. 56.

11. On Christian attitudes toward the economic crisis of the late nineteenth century, see May, *Protestant Churches*. On the theology of the Social Gospel, see Winthrop S. Hudson, *American Protestantism* (Chicago: University of Chicago Press, 1961), p. 137. On evangelicals, Norris Magnuson, in *Salvation in the Slums: Evangelical Social Work, 1865-1920* (Grand Rapids: Baker, 1990 [1977]), gives several examples of evangelicals calling upon an unconverted government to change social structures through interventionist legislation. See especially pages 45, 87, 95, 111, 117, 126, 128, 136, 140-41, 170.

12. Primer, *Protestants*, pp. 27-30.

Thus, in the same years that Standard Oil was growing by acquiring oil wells, refineries, railroads, brokers, delivery routes, and retailers, the Methodists, Baptists, Presbyterians, Congregationalists, Disciples of Christ, and other major denominations all expanded their national bureaucracies by acquiring or starting agencies that performed the specialized tasks that constituted their idea of Christian mission. And in the same years that John D. Rockefeller was figuring out how to wring ever more money out of his enterprises so that Standard Oil could continue to expand, the new class of denominational managers were doing the same thing.

They developed methods they called "systematic finance," which by the early 1920s were operating with great success. Gone were the old annual offerings taken up by churches for a given agency; in their place were well-organized multi-year pledge drives that coordinated the efforts of all the agencies within each denomination. Accompanying the drives were sophisticated "education" campaigns — often developed by secular advertising agencies — designed to persuade congregations and individuals to make hefty pledges. Membership surveys and canvasses, magazine and leaflet publicity, prepared sermon ideas for pastors, Sunday school materials, crusade dinners, inspirational speakers, and duplex envelopes (one side for regular local gifts, the other side for giving to denominational enterprises) all proved remarkably successful at drawing money into the central denominational headquarters. Between 1916 and 1926, per church income jumped from $1,602 to $3,783 per year — 29 percent faster than inflation and 35 percent faster than the GNP. The percentage of this amount transferred from local churches into denominational coffers also increased from 15 to 18 percent.[13] But not only the institutions became wealthier. Be-

13. Computed from U.S. Bureau of the Census, *Religious Bodies: 1916* (Washington, DC: 1920), Table 16; U.S. Bureau of the Census, *Religious Bodies: 1926* (Washington, DC: 1930), Table 15; and Primer, *Protestants,* Table 1, p. 112. For further evidence on the financial success of "systematic finance," see Primer, *Protestants,* pp. 104-13. Several historians, beginning with Robert T. Handy in "The American Religious Depression, 1925-1935," *Church History* 29 (1960): 3-16, have noticed that the denominations seemed to be on hard times in the 1920s. So how does this square with the evidence of rising income? The answer appears to be that the multi-year drives focused on pledges. When huge amounts of pledges came in, denominations counted their chickens before they hatched and increased their expenditures accordingly. However, actual giving fell quite a bit short of pledges, and this then forced financial cutbacks. Nevertheless, actual giving still repre-

tween 1919 and 1922, the average salaries of Methodist and Congregationalist ministers jumped by 31 percent, while comparable salaries of federal workers in the executive branch went up by 7 percent and clerical workers in industry by 8 percent.[14] In addition to the major campaigns, denominations also began setting up endowment funds, and promoting the annuity plans that funded them. This too was successful. In 1909, 4.6 percent of denominational agency income derived from endowments; by 1929, the figure was 10.7 percent.[15]

However, the financial successes of the denominations' new corporate mentality came with substantial costs. As they built their multiple-agency centralized bureaucracies, experts were added to the payrolls, hierarchy flourished, interagency rivalries sprang up, and administrative expenses soared. Increasingly the managers focused not on religious tasks but on the organizational task of maintaining the administrative machinery. In so doing they began to speak a secularized language borrowed from corporate boardrooms. During the nineteenth century, denominational agencies had clearly existed to serve the churches. But in the minds of early twentieth-century managers, the churches existed to serve the denomination. Increasingly the managers came to see churches as local production units whose purpose was to generate income for the real work of the denomination, which was being done by the central agencies. Bureaucrats evaluated which kind of local church produced the most income, and then developed plans to encourage more of that kind of church. Ministers' records were scrutinized for their ability to produce income for the central agencies, and the best producers usually received the best appointments.

Accompanying this change of attitude was a genuine shift of power away from local ministers and bishops and toward the central agency managers. On paper denominational conventions had oversight of the agencies, but in fact most authority lay with the managers. This is the period in which agency bureaucrats learned how to manage appointments, committees, and information flows to retain maximum autonomy for

---

sented a substantial increase over giving in previous years, and by this yardstick the new fund-raising methods were a resounding success. In other words, cutbacks were not forced by lack of income, which increased substantially; they were forced by poor planning and excessive expenditures. See Primer, *Protestants*, p. 100.

14. U.S. Bureau of the Census, *Historical Statistics of the United States: Colonial Times to 1970*, Part 1 (Washington, DC, 1975), p. 168.

15. Primer, *Protestants*, p. 104.

themselves and their enterprises. Local pastors increasingly complained about denominational insensitivity to local needs. But the managers, jealously watching financial returns to make sure that they were getting their share of parishioners' giving, responded with their own complaints about the "parochialism" of local churches for neglecting the "larger work of the Church."[16]

This "incorporation" of the Protestant denominations happened concurrently with two other crucial developments of the late nineteenth century and early twentieth centuries — the spread of liberal theology within the denominations, and the rise of independent, interdenominational evangelical agencies such as "faith" missionary organizations and Bible institutes. It would be a mistake to suppose that all liberals supported the bureaucratization of the denominations, or that all evangelicals opposed it. The most famous liberal of all, Harry Emerson Fosdick, lamented that in the new corporate order ministers were being "swept off their feet by the demands of their own organizations, falling under the spell of bigness, and rushing from one committee to another to put over some new scheme to enlarge the work or save the world. . . . [Ministers are] doing everything except their chief business, for that lies inside individuals."[17] Likewise, many evangelicals were deeply involved in, and supportive of, the growth of the denominations' centralized bureaucracies.

Nevertheless, it is certainly true that, in general, liberals found the new business model of Protestantism more congenial than did evangelicals. The proliferation of denominational agencies emphasized education projects, social service activities, and institution-building — activities with which liberals felt most comfortable. Sliding down the list of priorities was evangelism, which was still nearest and dearest to evangelicals' hearts. Moreover, like business corporations, the newly bureaucratized denominations were substantially less democratic than they had been before the Civil War. True theological liberals, overrepresented in the upper levels of the hierarchy, were thus protected from democratic oversight by the more evangelical rank and file.[18] The new business mentality also brought in a more secular way of thinking about the relationship between the Church

16. Primer, *Protestants*, pp. 93-175.

17. Harry Emerson Fosdick, "What Is the Matter with Preaching?," *Harper's* 157 (June 1928): 141, as quoted in Primer, *Protestants*, p. 168.

18. Primer, *Protestants*, pp. 155-75.

and God that was more off-putting to evangelicals than to liberals. In 1929 the Secretary of the Congregationalists' Laymen's Advisory Committee, an expert on endowments, boasted to a denominational conference on finance that in the fund-raising programs he had designed, "nothing had been left to chance. At no point have we trusted that the Lord will provide. He won't."[19]

No such mindset could have been farther from that embodied in the rapidly growing body of interdenominational, evangelical "faith" missions, like the China Inland Mission, whose leaders absolutely refused to engage in "systematic finance." The chief hallmark of these agencies was their insistence that in answer to prayer alone, God would directly and supernaturally provide for all their financial needs. "Faith" groups refused to ask for money, or even to make known their needs. Yet over the years the faith agencies accumulated innumerable stories of how the Lord, indeed, had provided their needs. And like the denominations, they grew ever larger in the early decades of the twentieth century.

For many reasons, most of which are beyond the scope of this essay, the differences between liberals and evangelicals rolled to a boil in the period between 1915 and 1940. The incorporation of the denominations helped turn up the heat substantially. Many evangelicals were convinced that the administrative bureaucracies controlled by elite managers nurtured and protected liberal theology, and there was certainly enough anecdotal evidence to keep this idea alive.[20] In the end, some evangelicals voluntarily left the old denominations for new denominations that were more exclusively evangelical; others were forced out of their old denominations by non-evangelical bureaucrats; and some evangelicals remained in the old denominations but turned their energies to the growing network of independent evangelical organizations. The sum total of these actions was a shift in evangelicalism's center of gravity away from the historic Protestant denominations and toward the expanding network of interdenominational, special-purpose organizations. With this shift came major changes in how evangelicalism organized and financed itself.

---

19. Quoted in Alfred Williams Anthony, ed., *Changing Conditions in Public Giving* (New York: Federal Council of Churches, 1929), pp. 81-84, as quoted in Primer, *Protestants*, p. 120.

20. Primer, *Protestants*, p. 169.

The American Economy, 1930-1997

After World War II, the economy again made a major transition — this time from manufacturing to services. The service sector, which had employed 30 percent of the labor force in 1900, grew to 50 percent in 1950 and 70 percent of the workforce in 1990. During this period the American economy grew fairly steadily as compared to earlier eras. Adjusted for inflation, the GNP grew at about 3.75 percent annually between 1950 and 1973. Although this was slower than most other North Atlantic economies, the U.S. inflation rate was lower, which kept the economy more balanced. In comparison with the period between 1860 and 1940, the most significant feature of the post–World War II American economy was the absence of the serious depressions and frequent recessions that struck the economy so often before the war. The first real postwar turbulence came in the early 1970s, by which time massive government spending for the war in Vietnam and the new Great Society social programs had sharply increased the money supply. This, combined with the 1973 oil embargo by non-Western producer nations, stimulated double-digit inflation. Making matters worse was high unemployment — which economists had previously thought would never accompany high inflation — caused by the rapid swelling of the labor force as baby-boomers and unexpectedly high numbers of women began looking for jobs. In 1979 the Federal Reserve System began to attack inflation with higher interest rates, and job creation — which had continued to be strong through the recession — eventually caught up with demographic realities. By around 1983 these factors ignited a long period of economic expansion.

Historians traditionally do not link social turmoil to economics in this period the way they do for the 1890s and 1930s. But one could argue that the one major social dislocation of this era, that of the 1960s, was in fact rooted in economics. The Civil Rights protests stemmed from the fact that African Americans were economically, as well as politically, disenfranchised. Likewise, the inability of the economy to cope with the huge numbers of working-age baby-boomers contributed to youth movement-related disillusionment and unrest.

The question of whether or not the federal government should intervene in the economy, so much debated in the nineteenth century, had been settled once and for all during the Depression of the 1930s. Attempts by both the Hoover administration to spend the country out of the Depression, and attempts by the Roosevelt administration to reform the nation's financial structures, were generally popular. Though it was actually the war that ended the Depression, the idea of an activist government taking steps to insure economic growth and stability, strong employment, and a favorable business climate are now unquestioned. Since the 1940s, the serious debates have not been about the fact of government activism, but about what form government activism should take. Even the deregulation of airlines, trucking, and financial institutions in the 1980s proceeded not on deep ideological convictions, but only far enough to attempt to obtain desired economic benefits. The regulatory apparatus for safety questions remained in place, and any strong evidence that the desired economic outcomes were not being obtained would immediately call forth new regulatory expansion.

Meanwhile, corporate expansion has continued, moving beyond national boundaries. By 1962 the largest 100 corporations owned 50 percent of American assets, and by 1974, of the 100 largest economic units in the world, 49 were nations and 51 were multinational corporations.[21] Globalization of corporate enterprises is the order of the most recent era, as U.S. ownership of foreign corporations and foreign ownership of U.S. corporations has proliferated. Reflective of this new reality, the industrialized nations set up several international quasi-governmental institutions designed to prevent global economic catastrophes in the years following World War II, including the International Monetary Fund, the World Bank, and the General Agreement on Tariffs and Trade (designed to prevent the kind of import-tariff trade wars that had inhibited recovery during the Depression).

Probably the most difficult question to answer is to what extent, and in what form, corporate and business ideas and values continue to influence non-business areas of American life. In the 1920s corporate captains were American heroes who viewed themselves as the leaders of social betterment. As President Coolidge put it in 1925, "The business of America is business. The man who builds a factory builds a temple. The man who works there worships there." The prevailing 1920s vision for a better world was that of corporate-government partnership in promoting social welfare, where government was the junior partner.[22] However,

21. Trachtenberg, *Incorporation of America*, pp. 4-5.
22. Peter Dobkin Hall, *Inventing the Nonprofit Sector and Other Essays on Philanthropy, Voluntarism, and Nonprofit Organizations* (Baltimore: Johns Hopkins University Press, 1992), p. 62.

because corporate leaders eagerly took credit for the prosperity of the 1920s, Americans saddled them with much of the blame for the Depression of the 1930s. Public displays of patriotic service during the war rehabilitated their image during the next two decades. Then in the 1960s and 1970s a host of new issues (from the faceless inhumanity of corporate culture to industrial air and water pollution) raised substantial doubt about the social value of large corporations and the managers who ran them. But by the 1990s the image of the corporate CEO had rebounded again to the status of cultural hero, marked by the international celebrity of people like developer Donald Trump and communications mogul Ted Turner. The recently improved image of business leaders has not, however, restored the 1920s confidence that for-profit corporations can lead the way in social welfare matters. Ever since World War II, even corporate managers have accepted the shift towards a more state-centered attempt to create a better social order.

The oscillation of the public image of corporate tycoons over the course of the century suggests that Americans are deeply ambivalent about the influence that huge business corporations have wrought in their lives. In the nineteenth century ordinary Americans were thought of as "citizens," but the corporate culture has redefined us as "consumers." Our chief value to society as a whole is that we purchase goods and services in sufficient quantities to keep the corporate machines running. This has narrowed the contemporary conception of the good life to material prosperity, though the details of what constitutes material prosperity naturally change with the fashions of which goods and services are desirable. More than ever, Americans appreciate the products and services corporations produce. But at the same time all the suspicions about corporations and their bureaucratic structures that have been raised during the century linger on. The persuasive techniques of advertising have become ever more sophisticated and effective, yet they have also produced a powerful countercurrent of cynicism about contemporary media image-making. The corporate values of rationality and efficiency are still with us, though there is generally less confidence that these will by themselves produce a better world. Perhaps this is because efficiency is now often linked in the public mind with the quest for ever-higher profitability, and profit-seeking is widely regarded as a pernicious social force.

Perhaps this deep-running tendency to associate profit with profiteering has contributed to the recent rise of nonprofit corporations in

America. In 1940 there were only 12,500 secular charitable tax-exempt organizations; by 1992 there were over 700,000 — over a fiftyfold increase. Most of this expansion took place after 1960.[23] By contrast, the number of for-profit corporations rose during the same period from 473,000 to three million — a sevenfold increase. Moreover, it has only been since 1950 that support for nonprofits has broadened beyond corporations and wealthy individuals to include a substantial majority of the American public.

The national growth rate of the income passing through the nonprofits between 1977 and 1994 was 3.7 percent, as compared to 2.3 percent for government and 2.1 percent for business.[24] In the early 1990s, the nonprofit sector employed 6.8 percent of all employees in the U.S. compared to 4.2 percent in France, the next highest country. In the U.S., the nonprofit sector accounted for 6.3 percent of the Gross Domestic Product as compared to the next highest, the United Kingdom.[25] When isolating donation income only, Americans in 1970 donated $16 billion to nonprofit organizations of different kinds; by 1992, the figure had climbed to $105 billion. This increase of 556 percent outstripped the increase (over the same period of time) in Gross Domestic Product of 503 percent.[26] The fact that these organizations are free from the taint of profiteering, and are widely regarded as acting in the public interest as opposed to the interest of stockholders, has kept them in a favorable position with government agencies. The government has also aided nonprofits directly through grants and contracts, and indirectly through tax incentives to donors, exemption from paying taxes, and favorable treatment such as lower postal rates.

23. Hall, *Inventing*, p. 13. The qualifier "secular" is used here because every church and synagogue is also a tax-exempt organization. Adding the long-standing existence of these masks the magnitude of the very real changes that have taken place in this sector.

24. Virginia Ann Hodgkinson, Murray S. Weitzman, et al., *Nonprofit Almanac: 1996-1997* (San Franscisco: Jossey-Bass, 1996).

25. Lester Salamon and Helmut Anheier, *The Emerging Sector* (Baltimore: Johns Hopkins Institution for Policy Study, 1994), pp. 32, 35, as quoted in Francis Fukuyama, *The Great Disruption: Human Nature and the Reconstitution of the Social Order* (New York: The Free Press, 1999), p. 325 n. 11.

26. George Barna, *The Mind of the Donor* (Glendale, CA: Barna Research Group, 1994), p. 1.

The Growth of Evangelicalism and the Rise of the Parachurch Network

As noted earlier, giving to churches increased faster than the GNP between 1870 and 1926, and then slowed during the Depression. After the Depression, giving picked up again. Discounting the Depression-era blip, giving as a ratio of GNP has remained virtually the same between 1926 and 1997 — 1:119 compared to 1:116 (see Table 1).

Just as the issue of whether or not the government should try to influence the economy was settled for the larger society, so too for evangelicals. It is true that there were pockets of anti–New Deal Republicans who sometimes employed portions of the old laissez-faire rhetoric. And it is true that some important evangelical leaders were themselves anti–New Deal Republicans, opposing "big-government socialism" in theory and practice. But hardly anybody in the 1940s believed in a God-ordained "iron law" of supply, demand, wages, and prices the way most nineteenth-century Protestants did. What little economic discussion took place among evangelicals centered on how, not whether, the government should be involved in the economy.

After the 1930s the mainline denominations continued to expand due to general economic growth and population increases, but this kind of expansion masked a serious weakness. In fact from the 1920s onward the denominations controlled by coalitions of theological liberals and theological pluralists attracted progressively lower percentages of American Protestants. By the 1960s this weakness finally became manifest as the older denominations started shrinking. Meanwhile, evangelical denominations and independent churches attracted ever larger percentages of American Protestants, and significant numbers of birthright Roman Catholics as well.[27]

27. Dean M. Kelley, *Why Conservative Churches Are Growing* (San Francisco: Harper and Row, 1972 [rev. ed. 1977]); William R. Hutchison, "Past Imperfect: History and the Prospect for Liberalism," in *Liberal Protestantism: Realities and Possibilities*, ed. Robert S. Michaelsen and Wade Clark Roof (New York: Pilgrim Press, 1986), p. 71; Roger Finke and Rodney Stark, *The Churching of America, 1776-1990: Winners and Losers in Our Religious Economy* (New Brunswick, NJ: Rutgers University Press, 1992), pp. 237-75; Dean R. Hoge, Benton Johnson, and Donald A. Luidens, *Vanishing Boundaries: The Religion of Mainline Protestant Baby Boomers* (Louisville: Westminster/John Knox Press, 1994), pp. 175-202; and Joel A. Carpenter, *Revive Us Again: The Reawakening of American Fundamentalism* (New York: Oxford University Press, 1997), pp. 31-32.

But the growth of evangelical denominations is only part of the story. It is important to remember that a majority of evangelicals remained in the old denominations in the period between 1925 and 1960, and many are there today. This was possible, in part, because the most visionary and energetic of the post-1920s leaders turned their talents to creating independent, nondenominational, nonprofit "parachurch" organizations. These could, and did, attract workers and increasing support from evangelicals in both evangelical and mainline denominations, as well as from the growing number of independent churches. Networks of these organizations quickly formed, cooperating with each other in sharing information, training workers, and legitimizing each other for the evangelical public.

Financial evidence confirms that evangelical parachurch organizations are able to draw strong support from evangelicals within the mainline denominations. A 1996 survey of members of the Presbyterian Church (USA) demonstrated that members who described themselves as theologically conservative gave an average of $494 per year to religious organizations outside the PCUSA, while members who described themselves as liberal gave $303. Total per-person giving by conservatives was also higher than that of liberals, despite the fact that liberals, on average, had higher incomes.[28]

It is now clear that by 1940 the center of gravity in evangelicalism had shifted away from denominations to parachurch organizations. At the time of transition, this seemed to evangelicals like a disaster — they felt they had been dispossessed of the historic denominations built by previous generations of evangelicals. Yet in retrospect, the timing of this shift was uncannily fortuitous. At the very moment the liberals and their allies came to dominate the old denominations, the very importance of denominations in American life was slipping into a decline that has continued unabated.[29] And on the other side of the balance, the importance of independent nonprofit corporations in American life was just beginning a period of expansion that continues to this day. American support for nonprofit corporations has broadened and deepened dramatically in the very period

28. For a discussion of this general phenomenon (which does not include the PCUSA survey data), see Richard G. Hutcheson, Jr., *Mainline Churches and the Evangelicals: A Challenging Crisis* (Atlanta: John Knox Press, 1981).

29. Robert Wuthnow, *The Restructuring of American Religion* (Princeton: Princeton University Press, 1988).

that evangelicalism reconfigured itself into networks of nonprofit corporations.[30]

The evangelical parachurch is so decentralized and dynamic, and information is so spotty, that it is impossible to know how extensive it really is. There are six major kinds of parachurch organizations — foreign missions/international concerns; domestic evangelism/outreach; social service; education; communication media; and politics/public affairs. Altogether, parachurch evangelicalism is an enterprise with at least $20 billion in annual revenues, and possibly a lot more. Evangelicals give perhaps $14 to $20 billion, and possibly more, to their local churches, meaning that just in terms of annual budgets, the evangelical parachurch may equal, or even eclipse, the evangelical churches in size.[31]

How has this happened? To be successful, evangelical parachurch leaders had to come to their constituency with new visions and directions that at the same time remained consonant with the constituency's core beliefs. This gave them tremendous advantages over the mainline denominations. It allowed them more flexibility in addressing unmet religious needs, more latitude in how they organized to accomplish their tasks, and more responsiveness to the religious values of their constituencies.[32]

An example of how this worked comes from the history of foreign missions in the U.S. After the Civil War, women formed female missionary agencies in all the major denominations. These agencies were much like modern parachurch organizations because they were completely detached from denominational support or control, even though they limited their constituencies to given denominations. Built on the back of these independent agencies, the movement grew extraordinarily large. By 1915 the movement had enrolled more than three million women in forty societies, making it larger than any other missions movement or any other women's

30. Hall, *Inventing*, pp. 58-80.

31. See Michael S. Hamilton, "More Money, More Ministry: The Financing of American Evangelicalism Since 1945," pp. 104-38 in this volume. These figures cannot properly be added, because an unknown, though probably substantial, portion of parachurch income is provided by churches.

32. Ralph D. Winter, "Protestant Mission Societies: The American Experience," *Missiology* 7 (1979): 152-57; Nathan O. Hatch, "Evangelicalism as a Democratic Movement," in *Evangelicalism and Modern America,* ed. George Marsden (Grand Rapids: Eerdmans, 1984), pp. 78-80.

movement of the day.[33] It did so because the agencies did an excellent job of hiring women with a vision for foreign evangelization, recruiting volunteers to go abroad, and drawing ordinary women into support activities.

Then things began to change. The leadership oriented itself more toward the central denominational bureaucracy and less toward the women in the churches. The activities of the organizations also shifted away from the original vision they so successfully inspired — that of evangelization and deep spiritual life in which ordinary women's letters and prayers were crucial — toward a despiritualized work in education, health care, and social betterment that only required members' financial support. Eventually the agencies had lost so much momentum that they were absorbed, with little protest, into the denominational machinery.[34] In response to these changes, women turned in ever greater numbers to the "faith" missions agencies, which were the earliest of the modern evangelical parachurch groups. Beginning in the 1920s the foreign missions efforts of the mainline denominations began to flounder, while the number of evangelical missionaries and sending agencies rapidly multiplied. In the early 1950s the downward curve of mainline missionaries met the upward curve of evangelical missionaries. These trajectories continued to hold steady, and by 1985 the number of evangelical overseas workers — most of them attached to parachurch organizations — was nearly ten times that of mainline groups.[35]

The largest evangelical parachurch organization (aside from the Salvation Army, with annual revenues of some $2 billion) is a missions/international concerns agency, World Vision, with annual revenues in 1998 of $304 million. Robert Pierce founded the agency in 1950 to care for orphans in Korea. He pioneered the child sponsorship technique of raising money from individual donors, and it proved to be a terrific success. The organiza-

33. Patricia Hill, *The World Their Household: The American Woman's Foreign Mission Movement and Cultural Transformation, 1870-1920* (Ann Arbor: University of Michigan Press, 1985), p. 3.

34. Hill, *World Their Household*, pp. 156-67. Hill rightly notes that external cultural factors also helped diminish the vitality of the women's missionary movement.

35. Dana L. Robert, "'The Crisis of Missions': Premillennial Mission Theory and the Origins of Independent Evangelical Missions"; and Joel A. Carpenter, "Appendix: The Evangelical Missionary Force in the 1930s"; both in *Earthen Vessels: American Evangelicals and Foreign Missions, 1880-1980,* ed. Joel A. Carpenter and Wilbert R. Shenk (Grand Rapids: Eerdmans, 1990), pp. 29-46 and 335-42.

TABLE 2 **World Vision Income Relative to
Gross Domestic Product, 1959-1995**

Year	World Vision Annual Income (millions of dollars)	% increase from previous figure	Gross Domestic Product (billions of dollars)	% increase from previous figure
1959	2.7		507.2	
1969	5.1	88%	982.2	94%
1979	38.1	649%	2557.5	160%
1989	153.6	303%	5438.7	112%
1995	269.0	75%	7245.8	33%
total		9862%		1328%

Source: World Vision, "Understanding Child Sponsorship: An Historical Perspective," unpub. ms., n.d.; and"WV History Briefs," unpub. ms. (March 20, 1998). Economic Report of the President (Washington, DC), various years.

tion expanded its work throughout Asia in the 1950s and Latin America in the 1960s. In the 1970s it committed itself to "holistic ministry" (meeting spiritual, economic, and social needs), plus it began serving as a pipeline for U.S. government international disaster relief efforts. Along the way it employed multiple communication media, both print and electronic, to raise money from individuals and churches. Currently, over 90 percent of its projects are concerned with relief and development; less than 10 percent are concerned with evangelism. As Table 2 above shows, in its first decade World Vision grew at the same rate as the nation's economy. Since that time, it has grown far faster than the nation's economy.

As with foreign missions, so with other areas of ministry. Nonprofit organizations had the independence and flexibility to make them ideal tools in the hands of entrepreneurial individuals. They could identify both client constituencies with unmet needs, and support constituencies that could be persuaded to support programs to help their less well-off clients. Then the managerial techniques pioneered by large for-profit corporations came into play, as organizations rationalized their operations and consolidated their position with their supporters.

However, operating without a protective denominational structure left parachurch organizations highly vulnerable to loss of constituent support.

The vulnerability of their institutions instilled in parachurch managers an ethos of survival, which made institutional preservation paramount. Eventually, most parachurch managers invested their organizations with a quality of inherent moral value. They were never quite able to shake the conviction that the success of the agency was a sign of God's approval, while its decline would mean a setback to God's work in the world.

Conclusion

The "miracle" of American economic growth included the dynamic growth of Protestant churches. From 1870 through the mid-1920s church income grew faster than the national economy, and thereafter church income kept up with the nation's economic growth. The federal government grew faster, however, especially in the twentieth century, which by itself is one important reason for the increase in church-state conflicts since the 1960s. With the federal government so much larger than before, it is inevitably elbowing its way into space previously occupied by other governmental entities, private business, and of course the churches.

After the Civil War large corporations powered the economy. Before World War II they did so by the leave of the federal government; during and after the war they did so with the direct assistance of the government. In the process, corporations changed the way Americans organized themselves and their activities, and this included the churches. The Protestant denominations eagerly adopted corporate ways of thinking and managerial models, which at first greatly expanded their size and range of activities. But in the end their commitment to management by experts generated a gap between the denominational bureaucracies and the people in the pews. As evangelicals left leadership positions and turned their energies to the more flexible form of the nonprofit corporation, the old Protestant denominations had unwittingly begun a long, slow slide into decline.

The new evangelical nonprofit organizations — the "parachurch" — were even more like business corporations than were the denominations. Among other similarities, they were able to adopt the persuasive communication techniques pioneered by corporations to sell goods and services to consumers. They used these to "sell" their ministry visions to their support constituencies. But because Americans increasingly accepted the idea that nonprofit corporations operated primarily not out of self-interest but for the public interest, parachurch organizations were kept free of the taint of profiteering that has made Americans so ambivalent about the corporate domination of their economy.

Some have argued that the proliferation of parachurch organizations has served to isolate evangelicals from their non-evangelical neighbors in unhealthy ways. In some respects, this may well be true. But in other, equally important ways the parachurch agencies have brought evangelicals into closer contact with their neighbors. Evangelicals in the 1930s, in their eagerness to evangelize nonbelievers and to defend the Bible, generally neglected the social welfare of their neighbors. But the expansion of the parachurch network has expanded evangelical social concern as well. Now six of the seven largest overseas parachurch agencies focus more on relief and development than on evangelism, and the domestic social service groups probably outbudget, and certainly outnumber, the domestic evangelism agencies.

The first great challenge for all nonprofits, including the evangelical parachurch, is to avoid the inhumane tendencies that large bureaucracies tend to foster. The second is to prevent the organizational goals from turning away from the client constituency inward toward self-aggrandizement and self-preservation. It is hard enough for individuals to develop the Christian virtues of humility and self-sacrifice; harder still for a large corporate bureaucracy. But the effort to do so is crucial. Failure will eventually, and inevitably, mean that the organization has lost its first love and no longer serves its first Master.

CHAPTER 2

Evangelicals Confront Corporate Capitalism: Advertising, Consumerism, Stewardship, and Spirituality, 1880-1930

GARY SCOTT SMITH

As goods increase, so do those who consume them. And what benefit are they to the owner except to feast his eyes on them?

ECCLESIASTES 5:11 (NIV)

Between 1880 and 1930 a major shift occurred in American society and values. American capitalism began to produce a secular business and market-oriented culture increasingly divorced from traditional family or community values, conventional religion, and political democracy. As William Leach argues in his 1993 monograph, *Land of Desire,* "the cardinal features of this culture were acquisition and consumption as the means of achieving happiness; the cult of the new; the democratization of desire; and money value as the predominant measure of all value in society."[1] The Protestant ethic was increasingly confronted by a new morality that taught that economic prosperity depended on citizens learning to consume at high levels. America's long-standing emphasis on strenuous work, frugality, civic responsibility, and self-denial was threatened by a new ethic that

1. William Leach, *Land of Desire: Merchants, Power, and the Rise of a New American Culture* (New York: Pantheon Books, 1993), p. 3.

exalted increased leisure, impulsive spending, political passivity, and self-gratification.[2] While work and achievement remained important to most people, various cultural factors powerfully promoted play, pleasure, comfort, affluence, and display.[3] For many, self-realization became more important than self-control, and the values of self-gratification and indulgence — crucial to high levels of consumption — replaced those of self-denial and frugality.

The morality of hard work, plain living, and self-discipline had been "deeply imbedded in the American psyche" as a result of childhood socialization patterns and centuries of religious teachings. At the same time as Darwinism, biblical criticism, and secularization assaulted traditional Protestant doctrine,[4] a new consumer ethic emphasizing materialism, extravagance, and recreation penetrated journalism, government, social relations, social science, and even religion. The clash of these conflicting values systems produced cognitive dissonance and psychic disease in many Americans.[5] Numerous authors, advertisers, ministers, social scientists, and physicians preached "a new gospel of therapeutic release" to millions of Americans who were troubled by anxiety and nervous exhaustion.[6]

In its efforts to market goods and make money, commercial capitalism strove to create a new understanding of the good life by awakening new de-

2. T. J. Jackson Lears, "From Salvation to Self-Realization: Advertising and the Therapeutic Roots of the Consumer Culture, 1880-1930," in *The Culture of Consumption: Critical Essays in American Cultural History, 1880-1980,* ed. Richard Wightman Fox and T. J. Jackson Lears (New York: Pantheon Books, 1983), p. 3; Leigh Eric Schmidt, *Consumer Rites: The Buying and Selling of American Holidays* (Princeton: Princeton University Press, 1995), pp. 8, 14; Grant McCracken, *Culture and Consumption: New Approaches to the Symbolic Character of Consumer Goods and Activities* (Bloomington: Indiana University Press, 1988).

3. Daniel Horowitz, *The Morality of Spending: Attitudes Toward Consumer Society in America, 1875-1940* (Baltimore: Johns Hopkins University Press, 1985), pp. xvii-xviii. See also Richard Butsch, ed., *For Fun and Profit: The Transformation of Leisure into Consumption* (Philadelphia: Temple University Press, 1990).

4. See Robert Wiebe, *The Search for Order, 1877-1920* (New York: Hill and Wang, 1967), pp. 19-21, 42-43.

5. Douglas W. Frank, *Less Than Conquerors: How Evangelicals Entered the Twentieth Century* (Grand Rapids: Eerdmans, 1986), p. 213; Fox and Lears, eds., *The Culture of Consumption,* p. xiii.

6. Fox and Lears, eds., *The Culture of Consumption,* p. xi. See also T. J. Jackson Lears, *No Place of Grace: Antimodernism and the Transformation of American Culture, 1880-1920* (New York: Pantheon Books, 1981).

sires and convincing people that a high level of consumption was the surest path to national prosperity and individual fulfillment.[7] Advertisers sought to liberate the middle class "from the tyranny of Puritanism, parsimoniousness, and material asceticism" and to convince Americans that desiring, purchasing, and enjoying material goods were salutary rather than sinful.[8] Greater consumption, it was insisted, was necessary to stimulate production, which in turn would insure increasing levels of employment and affluence. As new methods of mass production spewed out a surfeit of goods, advertisers heralded material goods as the antidote to loneliness, poor health, weariness, psychic distress, and sexual dissatisfaction.[9]

While the roots of this modern consumer culture lay in the eighteenth century, several closely connected trends made it much more powerful in the late nineteenth century.[10] Innovations in production, transportation, communications, and advertising firmly established a national market. The assembly line, an increased emphasis on speed and efficiency, the proliferation of products, and new schemes of marketing transformed the nation's economic structure. The rise of a more bureaucratic society, the spread of routinized, monotonous toil, and the entreaties of businessmen and advertisers led many Americans to seek immediate gratification and self-fulfillment through consumption and leisure activities.[11]

How did evangelicals respond to the rise of "consumptive virtues" — once the sins of the Protestant ethic — that urged people to yield to impulses, spend freely, and engage in conspicuous display?[12] As Leigh Schmidt explains, the relationship between Christianity and the new consumer cul-

7. Leach, *Land of Desire,* p. 9; Simon J. Bonner, "Reading Consumer Culture," in Bonner, ed., *Consuming Visions: Accumulation and Display of Goods in America, 1880-1920* (New York: W. W. Norton Co., 1989), pp. 13-54.

8. Otis Pease, *The Responsibilities of American Advertising: Private Control and Public Influence, 1920-1940* (New Haven: Yale University Press, 1958), p. 41.

9. Leach, *Land of Desire,* pp. 4, 7.

10. On the roots of consumer culture, see McCracken, *Culture and Consumption;* Colin Campbell, *The Romantic Ethic and the Spirit of Modern Consumerism* (Oxford: Basil Blackwell, 1987); Jean-Christopher Agnew, "Coming Up for Air: Consumer Culture in Historical Perspective," in *Consumption and the World of Goods,* ed. John Brewer and Roy Porter (London: Routledge, 1993), pp. 19-39.

11. Frank, *Less Than Conquerors,* p. 127; Samuel Haber, *Efficiency and Uplift: Scientific Management in the Progressive Era, 1890-1920* (Chicago: University of Chicago Press, 1964).

12. Frank, *Less Than Conquerors,* p. 139.

ture was "complementary and contested." On the one hand, Christians, including many evangelicals, "often encouraged and even celebrated the new patterns of display and the new therapeutic values of relaxation and self-fulfillment." On the other hand, numerous evangelicals denounced extravagant spending, self-indulgence, and the commercial exploitation of holidays, calling instead for the careful management of resources and sacrificial levels of charity.[13] While critical of some of the methods and themes of modern advertising, many evangelicals enthusiastically used it to promote their own religious and commercial enterprises. There were few complaints that the new approach to advertising encouraged a materialism in sharp conflict with biblical norms for living. In the period between 1880 and 1930 evangelicals by and large strongly emphasized the biblical concept of stewardship and insisted that Christians should earn and control as much money as possible to further the spread of God's kingdom on earth. They argued that the faithful practice of stewardship would enhance spiritual growth and the development of character.

Advertising and the American Dream

Advertising played an ever-increasing key role in America's shift to a consumer society by helping sell the plethora of goods American manufacturers generated in the years after 1880.[14] To entice people to buy, advertisers used the mass-market newspapers and magazines that arose in the 1890s and early 1900s as well as door-to-door demonstrations, free samples, posters, electric signs, billboards, and direct mail. They also employed illustrations, photographs, slogans, jingles, and brand names.[15] The rise of mail-

13. Schmidt, *Consumer Rites*, p. 14.

14. Expenditures on advertising increased from $30 million in 1880 to $600 million in 1910 — 4 percent of the gross national product — a percentage that remained the same for the next sixty years. Leach, *Land of Desire*, p. 42.

15. On the history of advertising, see Frank Presbrey, *The History and Development of Advertising* (New York: Greenwood Press, 1968 [1929]), esp. pp. 339-99; William Leach, "Strategists of Display and the Production of Desire," in Bonner, ed., *Consuming Visions*, pp. 99-132; James D. Norris, *Advertising and the Transformation of American Society, 1865-1920* (Westport, CT: Greenwood Press, 1990); T. J. Jackson Lears, *Fables of Abundance: A Cultural History of Advertising in America* (New York: Basic Books, 1994); Susan Strasser, *Satisfaction Guaranteed: The Making of the American Mass Market* (New York: Pantheon Books, 1989), pp. 121, 196-97.

order houses, most notably Montgomery Ward and Sears, Roebuck, expanded the use of national advertising by flooding the nation with catalogues, especially after the creation of Rural Free Delivery in the 1890s. So did the development of urban department stores and chain stores, which like the mail-order houses emphasized selling large quantities of goods quickly.[16] By the early twentieth century advertising was dominated by professionals who studied demographics, conducted rudimentary tests to analyze the effectiveness of advertising copy, and began to employ the principles of modern psychology.[17] Advertisers created a number of national organizations "to formulate and sustain the mythology, rituals, and rationale of advertising and of the economic structure which it served." They also sponsored huge conventions to extol the "universality, humanitarianism, virtue, honesty, and indispensability of advertising."[18]

During this period, advertising gradually shifted from providing information *about* products to touting their secondary values and benefits and promoting consumption more generally as a way of life.[19] "Passing gradually from simple methods of announcement to complex methods of emotional and nonrational appeal," advertising attempted more and more to sell the good life.[20] Advertisers did not simply seek to sell products ranging from automobiles to zippers; they promised consumers "such subjective experiences as sexual attractiveness, enhanced manliness, or social belonging." They marketed "leisure, enjoyment, beauty, good taste, prestige, and popu-

16. See Roland Marchand, *Advertising the American Way: Making Way for Modernity, 1920-1940* (Berkeley: University of California Press, 1985); Strasser, *Satisfaction Guaranteed*.

17. Three important early books on this subject were Walter Scott Dill, *The Theory and Practice of Advertising* (1903); Dill, *The Psychology of Advertising* (1905); and Earnest Elmo Calkins and Ralph Holden, *Modern Advertising* (1905).

18. Pease, *The Responsibilities of American Advertising*, pp. 10-11, quotations in that order.

19. Michael Schudson, *Advertising, the Uneasy Persuasion: Its Dubious Impact on American Society* (New York: Basic Books, 1984), p. 151. See also Neil Harris, "The Drama of Consumer Desire," in *Yankee Enterprise: The Rise of the American System of Manufacturers*, ed. Otto Mayr and Robert C. Post (Washington, DC: Smithsonian Institute Press, 1981), pp. 189-216; *In Behalf of Advertising: A Series of Essays Published in National Periodicals from 1919 to 1928* (Philadelphia: W. W. Ayer and Son, 1929).

20. For example, automobiles were marketed as a "great symbol of aspiration," almost invariably associated in ads with affluence, glamour, and country estates. See Pease, *The Responsibilities of American Advertising*, pp. 34-35.

larity," insisting that these satisfactions were an integral part of the American dream.[21] Advertisers sought to persuade people to buy and play "cheerfully-comfortably-confidently," to "loosen their purse string[s]," to pursue new experiences and thrills through consumption, and to cease drawing a line between essentials and nonessentials, between needs and wants, because the prosperity of America depended on it.[22]

While advertisements in the years from 1880 to 1930 rarely quoted the Bible or featured Jesus, Mary, the apostles, saints, or even well-known contemporary ministers, they were often "secular sermons" that exhorted readers to "seek fulfillment through the consumption of material goods and mundane services." Although advertisers recognized that invading the realm of the sacred or the numinous might provoke negative responses, they sought to provide people not simply with material goods but with spiritual fulfillment and to satisfy people's yearning for transcendence and exaltation.[23]

21. Marchand, *Advertising the American Way,* pp. 348, 24, quotations in that order.

22. Marchand, *Advertising the American Way,* pp. 158-60, quotations from p. 159. See also Paul H. Nystrom, "The Economics of Consumption," in *Economic Principles and Problems,* ed. Walter E. Spahr (New York: Farrar and Rinehart, 1936 [1932]), pp. 419-46. In contrast to the other authors cited in this secton, T. J. Jackson Lears argues that advertisers sought to manage desire as well as stimulate it. "In national advertisements, which were designed increasingly by educated Anglo-Saxon professionals, pleasure was subordinated to a larger agenda of personal efficiency" (*Fables of Abundance,* p. 10). Lears seeks to correct the "common assumption" that "advertising ushered in 'a hedonistic culture of consumption'." The consumer culture that emerged by 1910 was "less a riot of hedonism than a new way of ordering the existing balance of tensions between control and release" (10-11). Lears claims that the most influential ad agencies were staffed by a "remarkably similar group of Anglo-Saxon males," many of whom were sons of Presbyterian and Congregationalist ministers. These men "clung to a secularized version of their parents' worldview: a faith in inevitable progress, unfolding as if in accordance with some divine plan" (154). Lears maintains that advertising continued Protestant patterns of thought by reincarnating "religious longings for purification and regeneration" in "an ethos of personal efficiency" (183). Advertisers were convinced that they were providing consumers with "power, choice, and purposeful direction" (228). Nevertheless, Lears maintains that advertising "promoted perpetual, unfulfillable longings, and focused those longings on commodities" (274). Mass production and planned obsolescence led many manufacturers to "systematically surround their products with a magical aura," but "to render the old magic obsolete when next year's model appeared" (380).

23. Although they seldom used such words as "'worship,' 'pray,' 'bless,' 'revere,' 'bow down to' or even 'adore' to describe the attitudes consumers should take" toward their products, advertisers often conveyed these notions through their illustrations

Like liberal Protestants, most evangelicals saw modern advertising as a generally positive force in society and used it to promote their own causes. While they demanded that advertising be truthful and tasteful, and denounced the advertising of products — like cigarettes — of which they disapproved, few evangelicals complained that advertising promoted a materialistic way of life at odds with biblical concepts of stewardship and discipleship. Evangelicals usually accepted rather than questioned the methods and results of advertising and seldom protested that much of modern advertising offered substitute satisfactions for the gospel.

Some evangelicals, most notably the prominent Presbyterian merchant John Wanamaker, pioneered in the use of advertising. In 1876 Wanamaker, a former YMCA secretary, an elder at Bethany Presbyterian Church in Philadelphia, and already the nation's largest retail dealer of men's clothing, opened a huge department store in the city. To publicize his "new kind of store," Wanamaker originated large-scale advertising. He advertised wares in expensive, full-page ads in daily newspapers that were accurate, informative, interesting, and rationally compelling. The tremendous success of his store convinced many fellow businessmen that advertising paid, and soon merchants across the country were studying and copying his methods.[24]

The Church's Use of Advertising

R. Laurence Moore and Susan Curtis explain how liberal Protestants, especially Social Gospelers, enthusiastically endorsed and used modern advertising in the early twentieth century to publicize and extend the work of Christianity.[25] As Moore puts it, "the alacrity with which Social Gospelers

---

(Marchand, *Advertising the American Way*, pp. 264-65). See also Marghanita Laski, "Advertising — Sacred and Profane," *The Twentieth Century* (1951), pp. 119-25. Economist Thorstein Veblen denounced America's businesses in *Absentee Ownership* (1923) for employing all the devices and strategies of religion in marketing their goods. Through their use of signs and symbols, colors and lights and "gestures," advertisers had "invested their goods with 'sacred' meanings that mean nothing and go nowhere." See Thorstein Veblen, *Absentee Ownership and Business Enterprise in Recent Times* (New York, 1923), pp. 321-22 and Leach, *Land of Desire*, p. 345.

24. Presbrey, *The History and Development of Advertising*, pp. 330-36.

25. R. Laurence Moore, *Selling God: American Religion in the Marketplace of Culture*

embraced the slogans and tools of advertising, financial growth, and efficient scientific management assumed almost apocalyptic significance." Ignoring criticisms that the advertising industry created "phony desires" and elevated "lying to a science," most Protestants gave it their explicit approval and support.[26] Evangelicals seemed to be just as enamored with the principles of corporate management and the quest for efficiency as their more liberal counterparts. Both groups zealously sought to use business methods and advertising principles to improve the operation and outreach of churches and parachurch organizations.

In 1908 Charles Stelzle, an evangelical who directed the Presbyterian Church (USA)'s Department of Church and Labor, published *Principles of Successful Church Advertising*, which served as a standard reference on the subject for the next two decades. Explicating themes repeated by numerous evangelical and liberal Protestants in similar volumes written in the 1910s and 1920s, Stelzle insisted that the church must advertise to make its message known to the world, attract adherents, and fulfill the Great Commission. If churches used the same scientific advertising principles businesses employed, Stelzle believed they would achieve the same success businesses enjoyed.[27] Stelzle urged churches to use innovative, artistic, systematic, emotional appeals to gain people's attention. He counseled churches to investigate the communities they sought to reach, to carefully decide what features they wanted to emphasize, and to design persuasive, positive, specific advertisements.[28] In 1910 Stelzle opened the Labor Temple in lower Manhattan to minister to working-class people in the neighborhood. It pioneered in the use of electric signs, and following the example of vaudeville, the church featured continuous attractions, including

---

(New York: Oxford University Press, 1994), pp. 210-35; Susan Curtis, *A Consuming Faith: The Social Gospel and Modern American Culture* (Baltimore: Johns Hopkins University Press, 1991).

26. Moore, *Selling God*, pp. 211, 215, quotations in that order.

27. Charles Stelzle, *Principles of Successful Church Advertising* (New York: Fleming H. Revell Co., 1908). See also "It Pays to Advertise," *Christian Advocate* (hereafter *CA*), 10 June 1915, p. 769; "The Campaign for Church Advertizing and Publicity," *Current Opinion* 61 (Sept. 1916): 184-85; "Minus Advertising," *CA*, 25 Sept. 1924, p. 1175; George C. Shane, "Should a Church Advertise?" *Ladies' Home Journal* 33 (Jan. 1916): 19; "Church Advertising," *United Presbyterian* (hereafter *UP*), 27 Jan. 1916, p. 5; "Advertising Is Not a Waste," *Reformed Church Messenger* (hereafter *RCM*), 5 July 1917, p. 21.

28. Stelzle, *Principles of Successful Church Advertising*, pp. 34-49. See also "What Shall the Church Advertize?" *Christian Century*, 17 July 1924, p. 907.

speakers, discussions, and movies. Stelzle's church was not the only one to advertise its wares through large electric signs and to emphasize churches' "selling points." Daniel Weigle's Friendly Church in Philadelphia spelled out its name in giant electric lights and experienced great gains in both membership and revenues. Meanwhile in New York City, Christian Reisner constructed a four-million-dollar "skyscraper" church, topped by a thirty-foot lighted cross. At the same time, many churches also emulated the patterns of the secular media and culture. Entertainment became an important feature of church services as some congregations built aesthetic, comfortable auditoriums, created high-quality music programs, printed "programs," and even referred to attendees as an "audience" instead of worshipers.[29]

Others quickly followed the path Stelzle blazed. The Men and Religion Forward Movement, an interdenominational organization largely led by evangelicals, devoted one of its seven conference volumes to how congregations could use the press to publicize their activities and message.[30] In 1913 Methodist Christian Reisner, pastor of the Broadway Temple in New York City, published *Church Publicity: The Modern Way to Compel Them to Come In.* The volume offered advice on how to attract people to Sunday morning, midweek, and Sunday evening services as well as to Sunday School, Bible classes, and revival meetings. Reisner claimed that advertising attracted thousands to the church, widened the church's influence, and stimulated many to think about the gospel message.[31] "Men are hungry for Christ," he wrote. "They will fall in love with him if they can be brought into a warm, brotherly, spiritual atmosphere. We must indeed 'compel' them to come in."[32] Reisner surveyed the 150 leading Protestant ministers for his book to determine what qualities they deemed essential for effectively advertising religion. For revivalist W. E. Biederwolf, "A real acquaintance with the principles of advertising" was crucial. Mark A. Matthews, pastor of the 7,000-member First Presbyterian Church of Seattle, stressed the importance of having "a Holy Ghost–filled preacher" and "a church in

29. Curtis, *A Consuming Faith*, pp. 236-37.

30. See *The Church and Advertising*, vol. 1 of *The Messages of the Men and Religion Movement* (New York: Funk and Wagnall, 1912). See also "The Religious Press as an Advertising Medium," *RCM*, 3 July 1913, pp. 7-8.

31. Christian Reisner, *Church Publicity: The Modern Way to Compel Them to Come In* (New York: The Methodist Book Concern, 1913), pp. 68-69, 30-31.

32. Reisner, *Church Publicity*, p. 5.

which every member has a burning passion for souls." Daniel Marsh, shepherd of the Smithfield Street Methodist Church in Pittsburgh, insisted that "Aggressiveness, originality, aptness at phraseology, [and] a passion for the work of saving men" were the key ingredients. Respondents lamented that a large amount of church advertising was ineffective because it was "cheap, prosy, pointless, [and] unimpressive in language, form, and circulation."[33]

In 1917 W. B. Ashley published papers presented at the previous year's church advertising section of the Associated Advertising Clubs of the World as a book entitled *Church Advertising: Its How and Why*. Ashley explained at length how Jesus was the "first successful church advertiser."[34] Contemporary pioneers in the field of religious advertising, he added, were "performing the same great service" for other churches "as did those few bold and inspired congregations that defied custom and prejudice, and installed the organ and the choir in the church service."[35] W. R. Hotchkin, the former advertising manager for Wanamaker's in New York City, argued that the church should use the same advertising principles and methods as the distributor of any other commodity. Reasoning that millions of Americans had been stimulated to buy automobiles because they saw the pleasure others derived from owning them, he insisted that the most vital element in advertising the church to outsiders was to show them the "joy, satisfaction, comfort, and peace" church members experienced. He argued that the "selling points" of the typical church were its pastor, who hopefully was a magnetic orator and a sociable, likable, respected individual, and its facilities, musical program, warm fellowship, stimulating public worship, social activities, and service to the community.[36]

By the early 1920s advertising was being widely used to proclaim the gospel message and promote the program of the local church. The Associated Advertising Clubs of the World (founded in 1911) had formed a department of religious publicity in 1916. Several denominations employed publicity secretaries. The Chicago Church Federation established a com-

33. Reisner, *Church Publicity*, p. 82.

34. W. B. Ashley, "The First Successful Church Advertiser," in *Church Advertising: Its Why and How* (Philadelphia: J. B. Lippincott, 1917), pp. 93-109.

35. Ashley, *Church Advertising: Its Why and How*, p. 3.

36. W. R. Hotchkin, "The Dynamics of Successful Church Advertising," *Church Advertising*, pp. 83-89, quotation from p. 83. See also "Advertising the Church," *RCM*, 1 Dec. 1910, p. 4; "How to Advertise the Church," *RCM*, 10 Feb. 1916, p. 3.

mission to encourage the use of advertising, and ministers and laypeople in Philadelphia and St. Louis created church advertising associations.[37] In 1919 and 1920 two hundred New York ministers took courses in advertising and, in the latter year, the Gospel Advertising League of New York was organized.[38] In 1921 Francis H. Case issued the *Handbook of Church Advertising*. Based on addresses given at the 1920 convention of the Associated Advertising Club's Church Department by leading publicity experts from churches, denominational and interdenominational agencies, newspapers, and the business community, it argued that advertising was a major "weapon of the church militant."[39] The book explained why the church needed to advertise, how to apply general principles of advertising to the church, and who should direct the church's advertising efforts.[40] It discussed how to advertise the church, how to adapt the church's message to local conditions, and how to pay for advertising. It also delineated what congregations should advertise — benefits such as companionship, comfort, salvation from sin, inspiring ideals, instruction in Christian living, Bible study, and opportunity for community service.[41] Although the authors tended to numerically evaluate the success of congregations, Case concluded that church advertising should not primarily aim to fill pews and augment collections but rather to help people meet spiritual needs.[42]

In 1925 Case edited another volume entitled *Advertising the Church: Suggestions by Church Advertisers*.[43] Its contributors argued that congregations should advertise to increase their membership, inspire their current members, enhance their influence in the community, strengthen interdenominational cooperation, and challenge the thinking of the un-

37. "As to Church Advertising," *RCM*, 14 June 1917, p. 27.

38. "How to Advertise Religion," *Literary Digest* (hereafter *LD*) 67 (20 Nov. 1920): 37; see also "'The Lord's Press-Agent' and His Church Advertising," *LD* 65 (17 Apr. 1920): 73-74; "'Selling' Religion," *LD* 70 (20 Aug. 1921): 28-29; "The Church as an Advertiser," *LD* 76 (17 Feb. 1923): 35.

39. Francis H. Case, *Handbook of Church Advertising* (New York: The Abingdon Press, 1921), p. 186.

40. Case, *Handbook of Church Advertising*, pp. 13-48, quotation from p. 25.

41. Case, *Handbook of Church Advertising*, pp. 49-86. See also Richard Beall Niese, *The Newspaper and Religious Publicity* (New York: George H. Doran, 1925); J. Richard Olson, "The Pulpit and the Press," *Moody Monthly*, Jan. 1923, pp. 204-5.

42. Case, *Handbook of Church Advertising*, pp. 112-15, 184.

43. This book contained excerpts of addresses given at church department sessions of the conventions of the Associated Advertising Clubs of the World in 1923 and 1924.

churched.[44] The teachings of Jesus, they alleged, encouraged the church to advertise. As the Southern Baptist H. F. Vermillion put it, "Jesus commanded his disciples to advertise. . . . Translated into modern terms, he would say put your light on the lampstand of the newspaper and in the candlestick of the billboard. . . . Set your city of salvation on a hill of publicity so that it cannot be hid among the confusions and distractions of the godless generation."[45] The authors recommended that a minister and a publicity committee, advised by an advertising expert, take charge of advertising within each congregation.[46] The various channels of recommended publicity included the pulpit, radio, church calendars, direct mailing ads, bulletin boards, billboards, electric signs, newspapers, and movies.

In 1926 Charles Stelzle left the ministry to become the president of the Church Advertising Department of the Associated Advertising Clubs of the World. Under his direction, the organization mounted a nationwide campaign to promote religion through the use of radio, newspapers, magazines, and billboards. The department conducted conferences to teach ministers and church workers how to use advertising and to educate newspaper editors and advertising executives about the problems and needs of the church. It devised materials to exhibit the benefits and progress of Christianity, furnished books on modern advertising to ministers and lay leaders, and offered lectures on advertising in seminaries.[47]

An Assessment

Characteristic of the enthusiasm many evangelicals had for advertising, one advertising company president contended in *Moody Monthly* in 1928 that the Holy Spirit was the "Sales Manager," the pastor was the first assistant sales manager, and every church member was a "salesman of greater

44. Francis H. Case, ed., *Advertising the Church: Suggestions by Church Advertisers* (New York: The Abingdon Press, 1925), pp. 31-34.

45. Case, ed., *Advertising the Church*, p. 43.

46. In *How to Advertise a Church* (New York: George H. Doran Co., 1920), Ernest Eugene Elliott counseled congregations not to depend on their ministers to promote their work because they lacked the time and expertise to do so (41).

47. "Advertising Religion," *CA*, 29 July 1926, p. 935; "Publicity for Virtue, Too," *LD* 91 (Nov. 13, 1926): 36. In 1923 the Department conducted a nationwide campaign to increase church attendance. See "It Pays to Advertise," *RCM* 20 (Sept. 1923): 3.

or lesser efficiency," based upon how long they had been reborn, their "experience in handling prospective customers," and their "skill in handling the Word of God." The church was "the company of sales handlers and demonstrators" who met together periodically to receive instruction, encouragement, and fresh supplies and to "tell the Great Manufacturer how happy" they were in his service. He asserted that the Holy Spirit used "advertising methods to promote the spread of the gospel," advising congregations to advertise their preacher, their physical plant, and their message, and urged church members to pray about how to best advertise their wares.[48]

Although most evangelicals were positive toward advertising, some objected to specific practices. Many demanded that advertising be truthful, and a few criticized advertisers for making false claims and using dishonest methods.[49] Some evangelicals protested the use of famous athletes to advertise cigarettes and beer.[50] Others warned that "high-powered, competitive advertising" sought to achieve sales "at the expense of good taste, decency, and morality."[51] A few even insisted that the overall impact of advertising was negative and at odds with Christian values. The editors of the *Christian Advocate* complained in 1926, for example, that many ads militated against the "adoption of Jesus' way of life" in the United States by appealing to "practically all of the un-Christian passions and traits." Readers were "continually bombarded with attractive appeals to such motives as vanity, greed, pride, envy, snobbishness, and materialistic ambition."[52]

These criticisms included those of neo-orthodox theologian Reinhold Niebuhr, who denounced the widespread use of church advertising. In 1924, he protested that church ads were characterized by "vulgar self-praise and a cheap appeal to the crowd's love of novelty and sensation." He insisted that the newspaper's church page proved that the spirit of commercialism had invaded the church. The practice of announcing

48. Joseph A. Richards, "Spirituality in Church Advertising," *Moody Monthly* 28 (Jan. 1928): 225-26.

49. "Answers to Inquiries," *CA*, 10 Mar. 1898, p. 395; "Truth in Advertising," *Serving-and-Waiting* 19 (July 1929): 75.

50. "Posted Lies," *CA*, 3 June 1915, p. 736; "Another 'Framer' Garbled," *CA*, 29 July 1915, p. 1006; "In Cigarette Advertising It's Bunk," *CA*, 26 Dec. 1929, p. 1584; William K. Anderson, "Will They Force Us to It?" *Christian Century*, 18 Dec. 1929, p. 1568.

51. "What Are They Doing?" *CA*, 13 June 1929, p. 743.

52. "Jesus and the Advertising Pages," *CA*, 18 Feb. 1926, p. 199.

sermon topics forced pastors to devise catchy titles and contributed to the dearth of exegetical sermons. Niebuhr argued that newcomers attended church because of an "acute spiritual yearning" or because friends brought them, not because of ads. The widespread use of ads, he contended, indicated that most Christians no longer engaged in personal outreach.[53]

Despite this body of Protestant critique, the leading critics of modern advertising in the early twentieth century came not from the churches but from secular sources. Back during the Progressive years, the muckrakers had railed against the flagrant abuses of "marginal operators — rubber stock schemes, phony correspondence courses, patent medicine panaceas — " and, in a more generous spirit, labeled the practices of national advertisers as "pardonable exaggeration."[54] Another major source of protest was from the consumer movement that arose after World War I. Through the mid-1920s, the movement consisted primarily of local organizations of club women who investigated the sale of food and milk and occasionally led boycotts of high-priced goods. In 1927 the movement received a substantial boost with the publication of Stuart Chase and Frederick Schlink's *Your Money's Worth*, a best-seller that strongly criticized the marketing structure of American business, and particularly lambasted advertising for exploiting consumers' ignorance of specialized products.[55] Like Protestant ministers though, the professors, editors, retailers, physicians, government officials, writers, and consumer advocates who criticized advertising during the years before 1930 did not, in general, challenge the quest to increase consumption or America's prevailing economic values. They primarily denounced misrepresentation and advertising's role in the waste of economic resources. Advertisers confronted these objections by publicizing codes of ethical

53. Reinhold Niebuhr, "What Are the Churches Advertising?" *Christian Century*, 27 Dec. 1924, pp. 1532-33.

54. Lears, *Fables of Abundance*, p. 203.

55. To help consumers sort through the competing claims of commercial salesmanship, Schlink founded Consumers' Research, an independent testing facility, that by 1930 had 12,000 members, a national newsletter, and a staff of technicians to evaluate products. See Stuart Chase and F. J. Schlink, *Your Money's Worth: A Study in the Waste of the Consumer's Dollar* (New York: Macmillan Co., 1927). See also Stuart Chase, *The Tragedy of Waste* (New York: Grosset and Dunlap, 1925), pp. 27-52, 84-125, 265-86; Stuart Chase and Roy Durstine, "Are We Debauched by Salesmanship? — A Debate," *Forum* 79 (Jan. 1928): 22-45; P. W. Wilson, "Prosperity of the United States," *CA*, 21 Nov. 1929, p. 1418; Pease, *The Responsibilities of American Advertising*, p. 100.

conduct, condemning practices that harmed the public, and contending that the "self-regulating mechanism of a competitive market" would force unethical and irresponsible advertisers out of business.[56]

In the postwar period both mainstream and Marxist critics attacked advertising for manipulating consumers by appealing to emotions and irrationality, proclaiming false values, promoting a materialistic ethic, and prompting people to purchase unnecessary or overpriced goods.[57] By contrast, however, in the years between 1880 and 1930, neither evangelicals nor more liberal Protestants objected much to advertising's aims and methods. While evangelicals, as will be explained below, often inveighed against materialism, they said little about the role advertising played in expanding the tastes and desires of consumers, creating social envy, or making people feel ashamed of the way they lived.[58]

It is easy to understand why so many evangelical and liberal Protestants applauded and used the methods of modern advertising. They seemed to be producing marvelous results for many businesses in sales, profit, and growth. Moreover, businessmen often served on many church boards and encouraged the use of advertising. The cultural milieu of the early twentieth century pressured churches to operate with business-like efficiency, adopt aggressive strategies for growth, appropriate their resources wisely, and conduct campaigns to raise millions for kingdom causes.[59] As Leigh Schmidt puts it, "in America's voluntaristic milieu, the churches, like merchants, were immersed in the free market; the idioms of

56. Pease, *The Responsibilities of American Advertising,* p. 200. As early as the 1910s advertisers waged an extensive truth-in-advertising campaign to help win legitimacy for their practices. Their participation in the ideological moblization for World War I also gave them greater credibility. See Daniel Pope, *The Making of Modern Advertising* (New York: Basic Books, 1982), pp. 186-218.

57. See, for example, J. B. Fowles, *Advertising and Popular Culture* (Thousand Oaks, CA: Sage Publications, 1996), p. 65; Stuart Ewen, *Captains of Consciousness: Advertising and the Social Roots of the Consumer Culture* (New York: McGraw-Hill, 1976), pp. 31-39, 177-84; Stuart and Elizabeth Ewen, *Channels of Desire: Mass Images and the Shaping of the American Consciousness* (Minneapolis: University of Minnesota Press, 1992).

58. David E. Shi, *The Simple Life: Plain Living and High Thinking in American Culture* (New York: Oxford University Press, 1985), p. 220. Almost all religious periodicals accepted paid advertisements to help finance their publication. One exception was *Serving-and-Waiting,* which excluded all paid ads out of fear it might compromise its witness. See "The Matter of Advertising," *Serving-and-Waiting* 11 (Feb. 1922): 632.

59. Moore, *Selling God,* p. 209.

competition and promotion were widely shared across the culture."[60] "It pays to advertise is just as true of religion as it is of Uneeda Biscuits or Ford cars," declared the editors of the *Christian Advocate* in 1922.[61] These cultural forces, coupled with their belief in the efficacy of advertising, led many evangelicals to employ the language and techniques of advertising in their quest to convert souls and expand their ministries. In so doing were they cleverly adapting their presentation of the gospel to their historical context and shrewdly using secular concepts and methods to proclaim their message more compellingly and convincingly? Or were they accommodating the gospel to their culture and sacrificing their distinctive principles on the altar of expediency and efficiency? Were they making religion into another commodity and using advertising in an attempt to persuade potential consumers to buy it in the ideological and cultural marketplace? Was religion, like other consumer goods, being hawked for the benefits it could deliver, the psychic and material satisfactions it could deliver? "Was there any way," R. Laurence Moore asks, that religious leaders could have avoided a "market mentality — the imperative to expand, the association of growth with innovation, the reliance upon aggressive publicity? . . ."[62] Despite the protestations of Reinhold Niebuhr and a few others, probably not.

Evangelicals, Consumerism, and Stewardship

As discussed above, in the early twentieth century a new consumption ethic strongly clashed with the production ethic of the nineteenth century. The combination of new machinery and hard work flooded America with a deluge of consumer delights that threatened to destroy the nation's economy unless people increased their spending. Consequently, business lead-

60. Schmidt, *Consumer Rites*, p. 273. He points out that many congregations cultivated the promotional possibilities of the holidays in similar ways to "their compatriots in the marketplace" and even created a "web of 'stewardship' Sundays of one kind or another" to entice people to come to their services.

61. "Advertising Religion," *CA*, 19 Jan. 1922, p. 57. See also "Church Advertising," *CA*, 21 Nov. 1912, p. 3; "It Pays to Advertise," *CA*, 11 Feb. 1915, pp. 191-92; Christian Reisner, "It Pays to Advertise," *World Outlook* 4 (Oct. 1918): 8; Elliott, *How to Advertise a Church*, pp. 75-93.

62. Moore, *Selling God*, p. 119.

ers, salesmen, and advertisers strove to demolish the Protestant ethic's emphasis on frugality and moderation. They insisted that if Americans practiced plain living, the results would be economic disaster. Consumption was thereby transformed from a vice to a virtue, to a new necessity.[63] This shift, as we have seen, depended in part on public relations experts and commercial enterprises convincing Americans to want and buy more. But, it also depended on higher wages, shorter hours, and vacations for workers so that employees had the money and time to engage in consumption and leisure. Finally, it required the extension of credit to the masses and the creation of installment buying so they could afford to purchase the nation's new products. The widespread adoption of these practices in the 1920s led many Americans to abandon the long-standing emphasis on frugality and staying out of debt as antiquated and detrimental.[64] As a result, by 1930 many American homes had refrigerators, washing machines, and vacuum cleaners, and almost two-thirds of American families owned cars.[65]

63. Schmidt explains in *Consumer Rites* how shopping and gift giving became crucial to the celebration of Valentine's Day, Christmas, Easter, and Mother's Day as the "rituals of home and marketplace competed with church-centered celebrations." These "secular liturgies" represented a "new kind of faith in family and abundance" that displayed "a striking capacity both to absorb Christianity and to supplant it." At the same time, there was often a close connection, "however incongruous and paradoxical," between holiday shopping and Christian symbols as merchants like John Wanamaker consecrated the marketplace by creating "Christmas cathedrals" out of their department stores (159-67, quotations from 159). All the examples of criticism of the commercialization of Christmas and Easter Schmidt provides are either from more liberal Protestant sources like *The Outlook* or Social Gospelers like Edwin Markham and Walter Rauschenbusch, or from secular periodicals like *Harper's Bazaar* and *Ladies' Home Journal* (183-86, 234-36). My own research uncovered little evangelical protest during this period about the commercialization of Christian holidays and how the intensified consumption they stimulated forced many women and children to work long hours in sweatshops and factories. As Schmidt shows, evangelicals often participated enthusiastically in the proliferation of holiday souvenirs and mementos as the trade catalogues of the David C. Cook Company were filled with cards, candy, flowers, Easter eggs, booklets, and pins, and Sunday school teachers regularly gave these items to their students (232).

64. Shi, *The Simple Life*, p. 219.

65. The American diet also improved; Americans consumed much more fruit, vegetables, milk, and cheese, and less flour, potatoes, corn meal, and beef. See Horowitz, *The Morality of Spending*; Stanley Lebergott, *Pursuing Happiness: American Consumers in the Twentieth Century* (Princeton: Princeton University Press, 1993); Harvey A. Levenstein, *Revolution at the Table: The Transformation of the American Diet* (New York: Oxford University Press,

Biblical Stewardship

R. Laurence Moore argues that in the late nineteenth century theologically progressive ministers like Henry Ward Beecher helped make luxury and extravagance respectable by teaching that pious Christians contributed to the public welfare by consuming with refinement and good taste. In the early twentieth century, Moore adds, Social Gospel ministers sought to "demonstrate that God's material abundance, if managed correctly, left everyone in private possession of a comfortable share of the world's goods."[66] To what extent did evangelicals promote these convictions? What attitudes did evangelicals adopt toward money and consumption? How did they view the biblical doctrine of stewardship? To what extent did their Christian faith direct their approach toward earning, spending, and contributing money? What connection did they see between their standard of living and use of possessions and their spiritual lives?

Several themes stand out. By and large, evangelicals rejected the notions that possessions were a danger to be despised, a reward of righteous living, or an autonomous entity people could use any way they pleased.[67] Evangelicals, by contrast, insisted that possessions were a trust from God. They argued that the sovereignty and ownership of God and the stewardship of humanity were taught throughout Scripture.[68] One Southern Presbyterian

1988), pp. 194-97, 210-11; Daniel Boorstin, *The Americans: The Democratic Experience* (New York: Random House, 1973), pp. 96-155, 182-87, 206-13, 326-31, 352-65, 422-45; Robert H. Walker, *Life in the Age of Enterprise* (New York: Paragon Books, 1967), pp. 207-44; Laura Shapiro, *Perfection Salad: Women and Cooking at the Turn of the Century* (New York, 1986).

66. Moore, *Selling God*, pp. 208-9.

67. See John and Sylvia Ronsvalle, *Behind the Stained Glass Windows: Money Dynamics in the Church* (Grand Rapids: Baker, 1996), pp. 183-84.

68. Clementina Butler, *Ownership: God Is the Owner, I Am His Steward* (New York: Fleming H. Revell Co., 1927); L. B. Hartman, *The Business Aspect of Christian Stewardship* (Philadelphia: American Baptist Publication Co., 1907), p. 63; Charles A. Cook, *Stewardship and Missions* (Philadelphia: The Judson Press, 1908), p. 33; George E. Farrar, "Faithful Stewardship," in *Modern Stewardship Sermons by Representative Preachers,* ed. Ralph S. Cushman (New York: The Abingdon Press, 1919), p. 67; John M. Versteeg, *The Deeper Meaning of Stewardship* (New York: The Abingdon Press, 1923), p. 92; Ralph S. Cushman, *Dealing Squarely with God: A Stewardship Primer* (New York: The Abingdon Press, 1927), pp. 28-41; W. M. Weekley, *Getting and Giving or the Stewardship of Wealth* (Dayton, OH: United Brethren Publishing House, 1903), pp. 13-20; Ina Corrine Brown, *Jesus' Teaching on the Use of Money* (Nashville: Cokesbury Press, 1930), pp. 18, 38; Harvey Reeves Calkins, *A Man and His Money* (New York: The Methodist Book Concern, 1914), pp. 59, 191-92, 198, 344.

pointed out that the Bible referred to prayer about five hundred times, to faith fewer than five hundred times, and to material possessions more than a thousand times.[69] Other evangelicals emphasized that more than half of Christ's parables were about possessions.[70] In addition to explicit biblical teachings, the basis for stewardship also lay in the Golden Rule, the example of the early church, the needs of God's kingdom, the task of fulfilling the Great Commission, the conviction of conscience, and gratitude to God.[71]

Evangelicals repeatedly asserted that the biblical concept of stewardship involved all aspects of people's lives — their talents, time, knowledge, experience, opportunities, and possessions.[72] God was the ultimate owner of all things; He entrusted material possessions, including money, to individuals who were to use them wisely to accomplish His aims.[73] In a widely read and cited book published in 1918 to promote the PCUSA's New Era Movement, David McConaughy argued that "money was the acid test of stewardship."[74] Some evangelicals agreed that how people valued, earned, and dispensed money was the most important aspect of

69. Roswell Long, *Stewardship Parables of Jesus* (New York: Abingdon-Cokesbury Press, 1931), p. 138.

70. Albert McGarrah, *Money Talks* (New York: Fleming H. Revell Co., 1922), pp. 114-15; Ellen Quick Pearce, *Woman and Stewardship* (New York: Stewardship Department General Council, 1928), p. 36; Long, *Stewardship Parables of Jesus.*

71. Bert Wilson, *The Christian and His Money Problems* (New York: George H. Doran Co., 1923), pp. 58-60. See also George Louis Rinkliff, *Administering God's Gifts* (Philadelphia: The United Lutheran Publication House, 1928), p. 12; Ralph S. Cushman, *The Message of Stewardship* (New York: Abingdon Press, 1922), pp. 15-110, 151-201; Harvey Calkins, *Stewardship Starting Points* (Evanston, IL: The Epworth League of the Methodist Episcopal Church, 1916), p. 110.

72. Frederick Agar, *The Competent Church: A Study of Christian Competency and Church Efficiency* (New York: Fleming H. Revell Co., 1924), pp. 29-31; Traverce Harrison, *Studies in Christian Stewardship: A Church Efficiency Text-book* (Cincinnati: The Standard Publishing Co., 1922), pp. 30-31; Calkins, *A Man and His Money,* pp. 145, 277; "Consecrating All to God," *The Continent* 44 (Mar. 1913): 395; Altwood Collins, "The Tithe[,] the Beginning of Stewardship," *CA,* 19 Oct. 1922, p. 1307; William Rigell, *Investments in Christian Living* (Nashville: Sunday School Board of the Southern Baptist Convention, 1930); Long, *Stewardship Parables of Jesus,* p. 119.

73. Frederick Agar, *The Stewardship of Life* (New York: Fleming H. Revell Co., 1920), p. 13; Long, *Stewardship Parables of Jesus,* p. 135; Hartman, *The Business Aspect of Christian Stewardship,* p. 63; "Stewardship," *UP,* 24 Jan. 1924, p. 4.

74. David McConaughy, *Money, the Acid Test* (Philadelphia: The Westminster Press, 1919).

stewardship.[75] Others insisted that the use of money was *an* acid test of faithfulness in stewardship but that other activities were equally important.[76] Still other evangelicals disagreed with McConaughy, pointing out that some people were willing to give their money to the church but had no time for prayer, Bible study, witnessing, or community service.[77]

Money and possessions, many evangelicals argued, could be either assets or liabilities; they could contribute to either spiritual enrichment or spiritual impoverishment.[78] Roswell Long, the president of the United Stewardship Council of the Churches of Christ in the United States and Canada, maintained that money was potentially "spiritual in function and character."[79] As S. D. Gordon put it, money could be "the most faithful, intelligent servant" or "the most cruel, exacting tyrant." The moral dimension of money depended on how it was used.[80] Money should not be disparaged as "a necessary evil or filthy lucre," insisted Presbyterian Guy Morrill. Rather than reviling money, Christians should "treat it as a minister of God, [a] bearer of God's love and goodness."[81] Harvey Calkins, the Stewardship Secretary of the Methodist Episcopal Church, averred that the challenge of the present generation was "to recognize the spiritual content of money" and rescue financial affairs from "sordidness and greed."[82] To accomplish this aim, believers must "Christianize all the processes of money-making, money-saving, and money-spending."[83]

Because wealth was holy when used in accordance with the purposes

75. Cook, *Stewardship and Missions*, p. 32.

76. McGarrah discusses various reactions to McConaughy's thesis in *Money Talks*, pp. 165-76.

77. For example, see Agar, *Stewardship of Life*, p. 73.

78. Agar, *The Competent Church*, p. 31; Cook, *Stewardship and Missions*, p. 167; W. W. Scudder, "Christ and the Money Test," in *Missionary Ammunition for the Exclusive Use of Pastors:* no. 5, "The Money Test," (1918), p. 4.

79. Long, *Stewardship Parables of Jesus*, p. 139. See also Albert Vail, *Stewardship Among Baptists* (Philadelphia: American Baptist Publication Society, 1913), p. 74.

80. S. D. Gordon, *Quiet Talks on Service* (New York: Fleming H. Revell Co., 1906), pp. 135, 138, quotation from p. 135. See also "Mammon of Unrighteousness," *Serving-and-Waiting* 19 (June 1929): 56.

81. Guy Morrill, *You and Yours: God's Purpose in Things* (New York: Fleming H. Revell Co., 1922), p. 128.

82. Calkins, *A Man and His Money*, p. 349.

83. Alfred E. Waffle, *Christianity and Property: An Interpretation* (Philadelphia: American Baptist Publication Co., 1897), pp. vii, 27, quotation from p. vii; see also Julius Earl Crawford, *The Stewardship Life* (Nashville: Cokesbury Press, 1930), p. 117.

of God, Christians should usually seek to earn as much as they could through righteous means.[84] "The Bible," wrote Cortland Myers, pastor of Tremont Temple in Boston, "encourages men to make money."[85] "It is a good rule," proclaimed Methodist Ernest A. Miller, for people to make as much money as they could through sound economic and moral methods.[86] Good stewards, added Albert McGarrah, author of several books on church efficiency and an executive with the PCUSA's New Era Movement, had "a duty to produce wealth."[87] The fact that productivity and standards of living increased wherever the gospel was faithfully practiced, he contended, demonstrated God's approval of wealth. McGarrah argued that Jesus devoted so much of His teachings to the subject of money because it was a "sacred blessing" that was an essential ingredient in the divine plan for humanity. Money was like radium. A right amount used in the proper way would remedy many evils. But if used improperly or in the wrong amount, money would neutralize faith and destroy the "vitals of the Christian life — spirituality, vision, humility, sympathy, democracy, love and loyalty to Christ."[88]

God had so designed the world, evangelicals explained, that money was essential to the advancement of His kingdom. John Roach Straton, pastor of the Calvary Baptist Church in New York City, insisted that "the need of money in the affairs of the kingdom" was "urgent and imperative."[89] "The extension of the Kingdom of God," wrote Bert Wilson, Secretary of the United Christian Missionary Society, depended on Christians using their money-making talents for God's glory.[90] Christians should control the world's wealth as far as possible, declared Baptist Albert Waffle, and use it to promote the gospel.[91] The purpose of stewardship, asserted

84. For example, see Albert McGarrah, *Modern Church Finance: Its Principles and Practice* (New York: Fleming H. Revell Co, 1916), pp. 24-25.

85. Cortland Myers, *"Money Mad"* (New York: Fleming H. Revell Co., 1917), p. 11.

86. Ernest A. Miller, "God or Mammon?" in Cushman, ed., *Modern Stewardship Sermons,* p. 86. See also "Wealth of the Upright," *CA,* 22 Sept. 1898, p. 1537; cf. "Religion and Rich Men," *The Interior,* 26 Oct. 1899; C. Z. Weiser, "The Ethics of Wealth," *Reformed Quarterly Review* 9 (Apr. 1887): 139.

87. McGarrah, *Money Talks,* p. 70

88. McGarrah, *Money Talks,* pp. 115-18, 120-21.

89. John Roach Straton, *The Salvation of Society and Other Addresses* (Baltimore: Fleet-McGinley Co, 1908), p. 29; see also Cook, *Stewardship and Missions,* p. 81.

90. Wilson, *The Christian and His Money Problems,* p. vii.

91. Waffle, *Christianity and Property,* p. 25. See also Cook, *Stewardship and Missions,* p. 81.

Methodist Irwin Paulsen, was to build up the kingdom of God on earth.[92] Faithful Christian stewardship served as a testimony "to the power and reality of Christianity."[93] It often brought revival to congregations and their communities and would "lift the church to new levels of spiritual life and power."[94]

The practice of biblical stewardship, evangelicals frequently alleged, was crucial not only to the advancement of God's kingdom but also to individual spiritual growth. Baptist Frederick Agar contended in several books that faithful stewardship enriched people's spiritual life and enlarged their prayer concerns.[95] The Methodist Stewardship Creed stated that setting aside "a separated portion of income" was "an act of worship."[96] Giving and worship, averred Presbyterian John Simpson, were inseparable. A Christian's giving was "a spiritual barometer" of his zeal for God.[97] Baptist Charles A. Cook maintained that faithful stewardship depended upon persevering in prayer and relying on the assistance of the Holy Spirit.[98] Julius Earl Crawford, the stewardship secretary of the Methodist Episcopal Church, South, argued that stewardship was as integral a part of the Christian life as "praying, reading the Bible, testifying," and receiving the sacra-

92. Irwin Paulsen, *It Is to Share: A Guide to Stewardship Education in the Local Church* (New York: The Methodist Book Concern, 1931), p. 72; Morrill, *You and Yours,* p. 6.

93. Cook, *Stewardship and Missions,* p. 163; McGarrah, *Money Talks,* pp. 38-39.

94. Quotation from Morrill, *You and Yours,* p. 131. See also Paulsen, *It Is to Share,* pp. 35, 59, 61; Charles W. Harshman, *Christian Giving* (Cincinnati: Jennings and Graham, 1905), pp. 50-51; Edgar Lowther, "Efficient Stewardship Cultivation," *CA,* 20 Feb. 1930, p. 234; Ralph S. Cushman and Marth R. Bellinger, *Adventures in Stewardship* (New York: Abingdon, 1919), pp. 151-52; John Blackburn, "How to Have a Revival," in Cushman, ed., *Modern Stewardship Sermons,* pp. 20-21.

95. Agar, *Stewardship of Life,* pp. 75, 130, 133; Frederick Agar, *Church Finance: A Study of the Wrong Methods and the Remedy* (New York: Missionary Education Movement of the United States and Canada, 1915), p. 81; Frederick Agar, *Church Profit-Making: Is It Right? Does It Pay?* (New York: Fleming H. Revell Co., 1929), pp. 44, 49, 59, 60, 64, 80-81. Cf. Luther E. Lovejoy, *Stewardship for All of Life* (New York: The Methodist Book Concern, 1924), p. 130.

96. Cushman, *Dealing Squarely with God,* p. 46. See also McConaughy, *Money, the Acid Test,* p. 129.

97. John Simpson, *This Grace Also* (New York: Fleming H. Revell, 1933), pp. 27-34, quotation from p. 34; see also "A Study in Contributions," *UP,* 11 July 1907, p. 5; Pearce, *Woman and Stewardship,* pp. 61-62; William H. Leach, *Church Finance: Raising, Spending, Accounting* (Nashville: Cokesbury Press, 1928), pp. 199-207.

98. Cook, *Stewardship and Missions,* p. 152.

ments. It was "absolutely essential to the development of a normal, well-rounded Christian life."[99] McGarrah asserted that spirituality would become "more real and vital" as Christians used all their material resources in accordance with the teachings and example of Christ.[100] Stewardly management of all possessions, Albert Waffle contended, brought joy, peace, and comfort, and gave people a deep sense of God's presence.[101]

Many authors also insisted that the use of money was closely connected with the development of character, a very important concept in popular evangelical culture during this time period. This was evident in the frequent assertion that Christ's teaching about stewardship did not center on raising money for the church but rather on developing Christian character and advancing the entire kingdom enterprise. The primary purpose of stewardship, as Julius Crawford wrote, was not to increase church finances or to augment benevolence budgets but rather to develop Christian character.[102] "The entire end of Christian stewardship," opined Methodist Luther Lovejoy, was improving human character.[103] Guy Morrill insisted that all forms of property — land, houses, businesses, and stocks — were "God's appointed agency" for developing Christ-like character.[104] Other evangelicals averred that the greatest test of character was how people treated money and that the way people used their money affected their character.[105]

99. Crawford, *The Stewardship Life*, pp. 8, 136, quotations in that order. See also Andrew Murray, *Money: Thoughts for God's Stewards* (New York: Fleming H. Revell Co., 1897), pp. 16-23, 43, 51-59; Harvey Calkins, "Broader Conceptions of Stewardship," *CA*, 20 Feb. 1930, p. 233.

100. McGarrah, *Money Talks*, pp. 14-15, 42, 167, quotation from p. 14.

101. Waffle, *Christianity and Property*, p. 104.

102. Crawford, *The Stewardship Life*, p. 29. See also Chester Carwadine, "The Cost of Money," in Cushman, ed., *Modern Stewardship Sermons*, p. 31; Robert Colpitts, "Effect of Stewardship Upon Character," *CA*, 20 Feb. 1930, p. 235; Morrill, *You and Yours*, p. 6; Joseph Berry, "A Serious Movement for Christian Stewardship," *CA*, 20 Jan. 1927, p. 80; "Think on These Things," *CA*, 17 Mar. 1927, p. 326.

103. Lovejoy, *Stewardship for All of Life*, p. 125. See also Butler, *Ownership*, pp. 62-63.

104. Morrill, *You and Yours*, p. 12. See also "Business First," *UP*, 1 Sept. 1927, p. 5.

105. Paulsen, *It Is to Share*, p. 20; Cook, *Stewardship and Missions*, p. 165; Harrison, *Studies in Christian Stewardship*, p. 32; Perry W. Sinks, *About Money: Talks to Children* (Chicago: Fleming H. Revell Co., 1903), p. 37; "Business First," *UP*, 1 Sept. 1927, p. 5.

The Perils of Prosperity

While praising the positive potential of money, evangelicals believed that it could also have a detrimental effect on people's spiritual lives. They repeatedly declared that the love of money was the root of all evil and reiterated Christ's warning that people could not serve both God and mammon.[106] Expressing a common sentiment, William Evans, a professor at Moody Bible Institute, warned that while it was not sinful to be wealthy, it was dangerous.[107] Reacting to the rise of America's consumer culture, many evangelicals complained that "things were in the saddle" and denounced materialism. Cortland Myers argued that the phrase "'Money-Mad'" aptly described contemporary American life. Irwin Paulsen lamented that many ministers were openly declaring material prosperity to be "a sign of God's favor." Millions of Americans had adopted a "religion of prosperity" and feverishly pursued money and the things it could buy, especially expensive houses, fancy automobiles, and fashionable clothes.[108] Numerous evangelicals like Philip Howard, president of the Sunday School Times Company, warned Americans about the "perils of prosperity."[109] "The most determined enemy with which Christianity has to contend," wrote one evangelical, was "the almighty dollar."[110]

106. William Schaeffer, "The Teaching of Jesus on the Subject of Wealth," *Reformed Church Review* 11 (Apr. 1907): 154; "Material Wealth and Spiritual Worth," *Presbyterian Banner,* 19 Dec. 1929, p. 7; Cleland B. McAfee, *Studies in the Sermon on the Mount* (New York: Fleming H. Revell Co., 1910), pp. 111-34; P. E. Burroughs, *Our Lord and Ours: Stewardship in Missions* (Nashville: Sunday School Board of the Southern Baptist Convention, 1928), p. 42; Myers, *"Money Mad,"* p. 46; Horatious Bonar, "The Love of Money," *Our Hope,* Nov. 1924, pp. 297-300; "Can Rich People Be Saved?" *Sunday School Times* 75 (Apr. 1933): 290; Weekley, *Getting and Giving,* p. 80; Paulsen, *It Is to Share,* p. 20; Brown, *Jesus' Teaching on the Use of Money,* p. 150; Miller, "God or Mammon?" p. 85.

107. William Evans, *The Christian: His Creed and Conduct* (Chicago: Bible Institute Colportage Association, 1911), p. 67. See also "Prosperity," *CA,* 6 June 1929, p. 711.

108. Paulsen, *It Is To Share,* pp. 24-25.

109. Philip Howard, *Living Through These Days* (New York: Fleming H. Revell Co., 1930), pp. 105-9; "They That Will Be Rich," *CA,* 23 June 1898, pp. 1004-5; "The Perils of Materialism," *UP,* 2 Nov. 1916, p. 4; "The World's Mania for Material Good[s]," *UP,* 27 Nov. 1924, p. 4; "Material Wealth and Spiritual Worth," *Presbyterian Banner,* 19 Dec. 1929, p. 7; Cook, *Stewardship and Missions,* p. 16; Versteeg, *The Deeper Meaning of Stewardship,* p. 98.

110. William Thomas Moore, *Preacher Problems of the Twentieth Century: Preacher at His Work* (Cincinnati: Standard Publishing Co., 1907), p. 311.

Other evangelicals protested that Americans, including many Christians, spent too much on luxuries and squandered too many resources.[111] They complained that the bill for America's luxuries was staggering — about 20 percent of the total national income in 1920.[112] Evangelist Billy Sunday and other evangelicals frequently railed against wasteful spending. In his sermons, Sunday often reported the amount of the nation's annual expenditures for tobacco products, alcohol, jewelry, automobiles, candy, chewing gum, and pet dogs.[113] Bert Wilson criticized the wealthy for such extravagant purchases as a necklace that cost $600,000, an amount that could have "kept sixty missionaries on the foreign field for ten years." Numerous evangelicals contended that the rich were morally obligated to give much more than ten percent of their income to Christian causes.[114]

Evangelicals insisted that the spending patterns of many average Christians also failed to conform with biblical teaching on stewardship. Methodist Ralph Cushman claimed that in 1920 Americans collectively gave only ½₀ as much to churches as they spent on luxuries.[115] Other evangelicals insisted that "ostentatious display" of any kind contradicted biblical teaching and complained that many Americans were converting luxuries into necessities.[116] Ina Corrine Brown denounced the idea that middle-

111. "Immodest Fashions and Luxuries," *Our Hope* 16 (Oct. 1909): 249; "Lovers of Pleasure More Than Lovers of God," *Our Hope* 16 (Mar. 1910): 513-14; "Prosperity and Good Times Not in Sight," *Our Hope* 20 (May 1914): 691. The editor of the *UP* complained that Americans, including Christians, were too preoccupied with sports, evident in their spending of five dollars on sports for every dollar they spent on religion ("Are We Going Sport-Mad?" *UP*, 22 Dec. 1927, pp. 6-7).

112. Wilson, *The Christian and His Money Problems*, p. 88.

113. On Billy Sunday, see Frank, *Less Than Conquerors*, pp. 216-19. See also Morrill, *You and Yours*, pp. 210-11; Burroughs, *Our Lord and Ours*, p. 45; Brown, *Jesus' Teaching on the Use of Money*, p. 98; Straton, *The Salvation of Society*, p. 40; "Ye Have Lived in Pleasure on the Earth," *Our Hope* 17 (Oct. 1910): 342; "Enormous Sums Spent for Luxuries," *Our Hope* 27 (Jan. 1921): 420.

114. Wilson, *The Christian and His Money Problems*, pp. 107-14, quotation from p. 107. See also Charles A. Cook, *Money Power: A Study in Christian Stewardship* (New York: Fleming H. Revell Co., 1933), pp. 37-38. They argued that a family who made $100,000 a year could not properly tithe $10,000 and live luxuriously on the other $90,000. The affluent should give a much higher percentage of their income to the Lord's work and live modestly.

115. Cushman, *Dealing Squarely with God*, p. 18; Long, *Stewardship Parables of Jesus*, p. 150; "The American Dollar and How It Is Used," *Our Hope* 32 (Jan. 1926): 434.

116. Paulsen, *It Is to Share*, p. 27; "Wealth and Waste," *The Interior*, 18 Feb. 1897;

class Americans could spend as much as they wanted on themselves because their purchases were not as extravagant as those of the rich. Too many Americans, she protested, were indulging their children and living beyond their means.[117] These consumption patterns, several evangelicals complained, led American Protestants to collectively give only about 30 percent of what they should give (a tithe) to the church.[118] "The blight of avarice, covetousness, and materialism," bemoaned Baptist John Roach Straton, "is resting upon us." If Christians curbed their spending on luxuries and obeyed God's commands with regard to money, they could "evangelize the world in this generation."[119]

Christian Giving

While insisting that Christian stewardship involved all aspects of life and all uses of money, evangelicals argued about the mechanics of giving to the church and other Christian causes. Evangelicals agreed that the nature and character of God furnished the ultimate basis for giving, that the motive for giving was more important than the amount donated, and that Christians should give cheerfully, sacrificially, and systematically.[120] However, they disagreed about whether the tithe continued to be binding on contemporary

---

"Things That Make Christians Unfruitful," *UP*, 10 July 1930, p. 5; "Thanksgiving in 'Hard Times,'" *UP*, 20 Nov. 1930, p. 6.

117. Brown, *Jesus' Teaching on the Use of Money*, pp. 96-97, 159, 166.

118. Cook, *Stewardship and Missions*, p. 17; Cook, *Money Power*, pp. 75-76; Wilson, *The Christian and His Money Problems*, pp. 90-91. A UP pastor lamented in 1903 that the members of his denomination, acknowledged as one of the nation's most generous communions, only gave about 30 percent of what he calculated their tithe would be. See E. B. Stewart, *The Tithe* (Chicago: The Winona Publishing Co., 1903), p. 71. Julius Earl Crawford calculated in 1922, based on the assumption that the nation's 25 million Protestants had the average per capita income of $586, a per capita tithe would be $58.60, but per capita giving was only $17.82, less than one-third of what a tithe would be. See *The Call to Christian Stewardship* (Nashville: Publishing House of the Methodist Episcopal Church, South, 1926), pp. 46-49.

119. Straton, *The Salvation of Society*, p. 41; Stewart, *The Tithe*, p. 72; "The Great Wealth of the United States," *Our Hope* 33 (July 1926): 34.

120. "The Two Mites," *Our Hope* 10 (Dec. 1903): 394-96; Lewis Sperry Chafer, "Christian Giving: A Divine Grace," *Serving-and-Waiting* 17 (Nov. 1927): 203-5; Crawford, *The Stewardship Life*, p. 131; Murray, *Money: Thoughts for God's Stewards*, p. 11; Long, *Stewardship Parables of Jesus*, p. 151; Stewart, *The Tithe*, p. 78.

Christians. Supporters of tithing argued that it was commanded in the Old Testament, not rescinded in the New Testament; it had been endorsed by Jesus — proportional to individual resources, and was vitally necessary to both individual spiritual growth and the advance of God's kingdom. Moreover, it acknowledged God's ownership of all things and had been widely practiced in church history.[121] They scoffed at arguments that the tithe was too difficult to determine (the income tax showed the absurdity of this contention) and that poor families could not afford it (how could those who were utterly dependent on the goodness of God afford not to tithe?).[122]

Defenders of tithing also chronicled the stories of churches that had grown rapidly in financial resources, numbers, and spiritual vitality when their members committed themselves to tithing.[123] Hundreds of congregations adopted the Tithe Covenant Plan (originated at Wesley Chapel in Cincinnati in 1895) and many claimed to achieve amazing results.[124] Congregations that used tithing plans, advocates contended, engaged in aggressive local missionary work, supported foreign missions, experienced revivals, added many new members, aroused great interest in the community, developed a spirit of cooperation and harmony, abolished their debts, paid their pastors well, and demonstrated the power of the Holy Spirit.[125]

121. Frank Leavell, *Training in Stewardship* (Nashville: Sunday School Board, Southern Baptist Convention, 1920), pp. 63-76; John Wesley Duncan, *Our Christian Stewardship* (Cincinnati: Jennings and Graham, 1909), pp. 11-57; Straton, *The Salvation of Society,* p. 31; Simpson, *This Grace Also,* pp. 60-64; Cushman, *Dealing Squarely with God,* p. 56; "The Tithe Duty," *The Interior,* 4 Jan. 1906, p. 5; Otis Dale, "Financing the Kingdom," *The Interior,* 7 May 1908, p. 601.

122. Simpson, *This Grace Also,* p. 64; Rigell, *Investments in Christian Living,* pp. 83-87; Harrison, *Studies in Christian Stewardship,* pp. 106-8.

123. James L. Sayler, *American Tithers* (New York: Abingdon Press, 1918); Emma Robinson, *Stewardship Stories for Boys and Girls* (New York: Joint Centenary Committee, Methodist Episcopal Church, Methodist Episcopal Church, South, 1918); H. H. Moore, "The True Story of a Unique Experiment," *CA,* 6 Apr. 1922, pp. 417-18; Crawford, *The Call to Christian Stewardship,* pp. 41-46; E. G. Richardson, "Some Results of Organized Stewardship," *CA,* 23 May 1929, p. 647; "The Test of Those Who Have Tried It," *UP,* 27 Jan. 1927, pp. 9-11.

124. Stewart, *The Tithe,* pp. 74-75; William Roberts, "Experience of Wesley Chapel, Cincinnati," *The Interior,* 4 Jan. 1906, pp. 8-9; E. B. Stewart, *Tithe Covenant Plan for Financing the Kingdom of God* (n.p., n.d.); James Hensey, *Storehouse Tithing or Stewardship Up-to-Date* (New York: Fleming H. Revell Co., 1922).

125. Arthur V. Babbs, *The Law of the Tithe* (New York: Fleming H. Revell Co., 1912), pp. 208-9.

As an added benefit, tithing advocates alleged that many tithers enjoyed business success, personal prosperity, and the spiritual benefits of great joy and future treasure in heaven.[126] Southern Baptist Frank Leavell adamantly insisted that "tithing, if conscientiously practiced," as promised in Malachi 3:10-11 and Proverbs 3:9-10, "absolutely guarantees material blessings."[127] Although he did not advocate tithing as a means of gaining material wealth, no one did more to promote the thesis that they were connected than Thomas Kane, a Presbyterian elder and successful businessman. From 1876 to 1924 he issued a series of pamphlets that included biblical defenses of tithing, questions and answers on the subject, and thousands of testimonies about the benefits of this practice. Using the pseudonym, "Layman," Kane distributed millions of free and nominally priced tracts to the nation's evangelical ministers.[128] Around 1900 several societies were created to promote tithing, most notably The Tenth Legion, which soon came under the control of the Christian Endeavor Society, and The Twentieth Century Tither's Association of America.[129]

While acknowledging that tithing produced many good results, other evangelicals countered that this practice was not authoritatively sanctioned in the Bible and thus it could not properly be said to be *the* biblical standard for giving. To require tithing was to mandate legalism in the church, which was contrary to the spirit of Christ and the principle of grace.[130] Moreover, tithing could too easily become a substitute for the

---

126. Harshman, *Christian Giving*, p. 53; Leavell, *Training in Stewardship*, p. 81; Butler, *Ownership*, pp. 40, 74-75, 92-93; Mrs. Thomas Arnold, "The Benefits and Blessings of the Tithe," *UP*, 10 Mar. 1927, p. 11.

127. Leavell, *Training in Stewardship*, pp. 80-81, quotation from p. 80. Cf. Duncan, *Our Christian Stewardship*, pp. 103-11; Rigell, *Investments in Christian Living*, pp. 89-90.

128. By 1920 the Layman had published thirty-eight different tracts, including ones by Robert E. Speer, Bert Wilson, Harvey Calkins, A. J. Gordon, and H. Clay Trumbull. On the theme of tithers receiving blessings see, for example, Layman, *Tithing and Its Results* (Chicago: The Layman Co., 1916), and Layman, *Adventures in Tithing, 1919-1920* (Chicago: The Layman Co., 1920).

129. Henry Lansdell's *The Sacred Tenth, or Studies in Tithe-Giving, Ancient and Modern* (New York: E. S. Gorham, 1906) contained a bibliography with almost 600 books and pamphlets on stewardship. On these tithing organizations, see George Salstrand, *The Story of Stewardship in the United States of America* (Grand Rapids: Baker, 1956), pp. 41-46.

130. Versteeg, *The Deeper Meaning of Stewardship*, p. 74; Chafer, "Christian Giving," pp. 203-5; "Is Tithing 'God's Plan'?" *Christian Century*, 1 Dec. 1927, pp. 1415-16.

stewardly management of all possessions.[131] Hugh Martin, the Literature Secretary of the Student Christian Movement, argued that giving should be proportionate to people's means. For some the tithe was too much; for others it was too little. He and other evangelicals pointed out that neither Jesus nor Paul said anything about the tithe.[132] Paul simply instructed individuals to give as God had prospered them. People must decide how much to give, said Martin, "in light of conscience, intelligence, and the prompting of love."[133] Similarly, Irwin Paulsen counseled Christians to commit themselves to giving a definite proportion of their income to God's work, whether it was 5, 10, or 50 percent, as it would require greater sacrifice for some to give 5 percent of their income than for others to give half of their income.[134] Some evangelicals also objected to the frequent connection of material and spiritual blessing with tithing. If tithing automatically brought material benefits, many people would tithe for the wrong reason. They did not believe that God made bargains with human beings.[135] "Let's quit telling folk," declared John Versteeg in 1927, "that if they will tithe, they are sure" to become prosperous.[136]

The Management of Resources

While they discussed the importance and general principles of biblical stewardship at much greater length, evangelicals did offer Christians some concrete advice about how to administer their resources. Because they wanted to avoid legalism, prized Christian liberty, and recognized that circumstances varied as a result of the size of people's families, the local cost of living, the need for reasonable savings to meet future obligations, and other factors, most evangelicals were reluctant to prescribe how Christians should disperse

131. Versteeg, *The Deeper Meaning of Stewardship*, p. 63; Versteeg, "Rescuing Stewardship from Materialism," *Christian Advocate*, 6 Oct. 1927, pp. 1202-3; Leavell, *Training in Stewardship*, p. 77.

132. Hugh Martin, *Christ and Money* (New York: George H. Doran Co., n.d.), p. 105; Robert E. Speer, *The Principles of Jesus, Applied to Some Questions of To-Day* (New York: Fleming H. Revell Co., 1902), p. 109.

133. Martin, *Christ and Money*, pp. 105-6.

134. Paulsen, *It Is to Share*, pp. 114-15.

135. Paulsen, *It Is to Share*, p. 117; Vail, *Stewardship Among Baptists*, p. 75.

136. Versteeg, "Rescuing Stewardship from Materialism," p. 1203.

their money in very much detail.[137] As David McConaughy put it, "God's stewards are allowed large liberty to use their own sound sense in determining what is requisite, provided only and always that they 'seek first his kingdom' and be ready at any time for an accounting."[138] Most evangelicals agreed with Albert Waffle that Christians should be guided by the words and example of Christ, inferences from the law of love, and the leading of the Holy Spirit (and other relevant scriptural passages, many would have added).[139]

While rejecting asceticism as unbiblical, most evangelicals argued that a "happy medium between poverty and riches" was "best for the welfare of the soul" and that the ideal for property was "modest sufficiency."[140] This lifestyle would avoid the perils of prosperity and the problems of poverty, although most evangelicals agreed with Princeton Seminary professor Robert E. Speer that there were more spiritual dangers in wealth than in poverty.[141] Ina Corrine Brown maintained that Jesus endorsed "the effort of every man to provide those things necessary for the normal balanced life and the highest all-round development of the individual and the family." She insisted that every family should have nutritious food, a comfortable, attractive, pleasant home, books, music, and adequate recreation. People had a duty to spend some of their income on these things, but they had "no right to spend all or an undue amount" of their income on these things. Every man had an obligation to his family "to provide the necessities of life, conveniences where possible, and to add to that as he can comforts and simple luxuries that make life beautiful and pleasant."[142]

137. F. B. Meyer, *Steps Into the Blessed Life* (Philadelphia: Henry Altemus, 1895), p. 231; Brown, *Jesus' Teaching on the Use of Money*, p. 17; Vail, *Stewardship Among Baptists*, p. 113; Martin, *Christ and Money*, p. 106.

138. McConaughy, *Money, the Acid Test*, p. 60; see also Waffle, *Christianity and Property*, p. 63.

139. Waffle, *Christianity and Property*, p. 61. See also Schaeffer, "The Teaching of Jesus on the Subject of Wealth," pp. 145-61.

140. Crawford, *The Stewardship Life*, p. 114. See also Edward Tallmadge Root, *"The Profit of Many": The Biblical Doctrine and Ethics of Wealth* (Chicago: Fleming H. Revell Co., 1899), pp. 106-26; McConaughy, *Money, the Acid Test*, p. 58; Christopher Hazard, "Make Less Money and Have More Life," *Moody Monthly*, Nov. 1925, p. 110.

141. Speer, *The Principles of Jesus*, p. 102.

142. Brown, *Jesus' Teaching on the Use of Money*, pp. 89, 108, 111, quotations in that order. Cf. Waffle, *Christianity and Property*, p. 149.

Presbyterian David McConaughy provided more specific guidelines for consumption. He insisted that faithful stewards should regulate their spending in light of their basic necessities for themselves and their dependents, their needs of "higher development" such as education and music, their "care and repair of the mind and body" through medical provision and recreation, their obligations to government and public institutions, and their business-related expenses. He advised readers never to borrow, never to purchase anything they did not need, and always to buy the least expensive item that could serve their purposes. He distinguished among necessities (things indispensable to well-being), conveniences (things that made living easier), comforts (things that brought satisfaction without extraordinary expense), and luxuries (things that afforded self-gratification in "an unusual and costly manner"). He contended that Christians must not spend money on luxuries, but he argued that people's motives determined whether purchases were permissible and insisted that luxury can be defined only according to geographical location and social class.[143] Neither Brown, McConaughy, nor other evangelical authors explained what Christians should do if they could not provide these things without spending all or almost all of their income on them. Few acknowledged the reality that the limited income of most working-class families made it impossible to achieve this goal. Moreover, few of them emphasized the problem of maldistribution of income and resources whereby, according to one evangelical, in 1930 more than 50 percent of the heads of American families earned less than $1500 a year (the Bureau of Labor Statistics calculated the subsistence level for the average American family at $1386 in 1918) and 2 percent of the nation's population owned 60 percent of the wealth.[144]

A few evangelicals exhorted Christians to adopt an austere lifestyle of "soldierly self-denial and abounding sacrifice." Presbyterian Albert McGarrah writing in 1922, for example, insisted that "food, recreations, clothes, education, culture, [and] beauty" were "good or bad exactly to the degree" that they made people more God-like and that they promoted or

---

143. McConaughy, *Money, the Acid Test*, pp. 61-65, quotations from pp. 61, 65. See also William Cunningham, *The Use and Abuse of Money* (New York: Charles Scribner's Sons, 1891), pp. 212-19; Harrison, *Studies in Christian Stewardship*, pp. 85-86.

144. Paulsen, *It Is to Share*, p. 106; U.S. National War Board, *Memorandum on the Minimum Wage and Increased Cost of Living in the United States* (Washington, D.C.: GPO, 1918), p. 10. See also Horowitz, *The Morality of Spending*, pp. 120-25.

hindered "the plan and program of God for the world."[145] Pointing out that everyone felt poor and could easily spend their entire incomes on their own interests, he challenged church members to limit their personal expenses to a moderate amount and to engage in sacrificial sharing rather than surplus giving to aid God's work. He urged Christians not to use the rationalizations of keeping up with the times or the "high cost of living" to prevent them from giving generously to Christian causes.[146] McGarrah argued that compared with the incomes, pleasures, and comforts of their great-grandparents and with those of 90 percent of the world's people in the early twentieth century, most American Christians lived in luxury. He castigated church members for spending substantially more on luxuries, recreation, and needless items than they gave to the church.[147]

Evangelicals offered financial counsel about other specific matters. Several argued that successful stewardship depended on devising and following a budget.[148] Some congregations, like the Delaware Street Baptist Church of Syracuse, devised a sample family budget, which was printed in its bulletin and discussed by members at a meeting. The United Stewardship Council of the Churches of Christ of the United States and Canada prepared a chart people could use to construct family budgets.[149] Other

145. McGarrah, *Money Talks*, pp. 65, 117, 68, quotations in that order. See also Root, *"The Profit of Many,"* pp. 253-57.

146. McGarrah, *Money Talks*, pp. 72-73, 97. See also "Stewardship," *UP*, 24 Jan. 1924, p. 4; "Self-Denial for the New World Movement," *UP*, 15 May 1924, p. 5; "Our Possessions," *UP*, 17 Apr. 1930, p. 7; Lewis T. Guild, "Hard Facts and Easy Money," *CA*, 9 June 1927, pp. 714-16; cf. "The Drift of American Life," *The Christian Century*, 25 Nov. 1929, p. 1599.

147. McGarrah, *Money Talks*, pp. 155, 162-63, quotation from p. 155. See also Vail, *Stewardship Among Baptists*, 112-13; Cook, *Stewardship and Missions*, pp. 75, 108; McConaughy, *Money, the Acid Test*, p. 129; "Money and Happiness," *CA*, 13 Aug. 1903, pp. 1303-4.

148. Brown, *Jesus' Teaching on the Use of Money*, p. 99; Crawford, *The Stewardship Life*, p. 124; Paulsen, *It Is to Share*, p. 110; Long, *Stewardship Principles of Jesus*, p. 150. Not surprisingly, all these books were published in 1930 or 1931. See also Pearce, *Woman and Stewardship*, pp. 47-55. The Stewardship Department of the General Council of the PCUSA issued a book with columns for expenses, saving, and giving entitled "Budget Book with a Conscience." The YWCA published a personal budget book for single and self-supporting women.

149. Leach, *Church Finance*, pp. 43-45. The Delaware Street example was based on an income of $2,000 per year and apportioned 25 percent for rent, 25 percent for food, 15 percent for clothing, 10 percent for charity, and 7 percent for savings. The United Stew-

evangelicals urged Christians to live within their income and to avoid going into debt.[150] Borrowing was often the first step toward calamity. Christians should not buy on credit or the installment plan because doing so was uneconomical and potentially harmful to spiritual life.[151] Writing in the *Christian Advocate* in 1927, J. George Frederick, the former manager of *Printer's Ink,* denounced the widespread practice of installment buying as "destructive of spiritual values" because it obscured the difference between necessities and luxuries and enticed people to overspend.[152]

Numerous evangelicals endorsed saving. Cortland Myers counseled newly married couples to "make a holy resolution together to save money" and urged Christians to save money to establish businesses, to provide financial security in old age, and especially to promote God's kingdom.[153] McConaughy argued that saving obviated waste, conserved resources, and prepared people for the future. He insisted it was legitimate to save to provide for self-improvement, buy a home, enlarge or repair a house, set aside money for retirement, or start a business.[154] Crawford labeled saving a "Christian duty for those whose income" was "sufficient to permit it." It was a "mark of sagacity, foresight, independence, and self-denial."[155]

Evangelicals, though, warned people against hoarding, miserliness, and greed as well as seeking to be so personally provident that they ignored God's sovereign control of the universe. For this reason, some evangelicals objected to insurance and pensions on the grounds that they displayed a lack of faith in God's provision and hoarded money that should be

---

ardship Council chart ranged from monthly incomes of $100 to $400 and family sizes of one to four and prescribed a sliding scale of giving, ranging from 10 to 13 percent based on various combinations of income and family size.

150. F. B. Meyer, *Religion in Homespun* (New York: Fleming H. Revell Co., 1904), p. 169; Meyer, *Steps Into the Blessed Life,* p. 232.

151. Martin, *Christ and Money,* p. 94.

152. J. George Frederick, "'Five Dollars Down and a Dollar a Week: Mortgaging Body and Soul to Instalment Luxuries," *CA,* 17 Feb. 1927, pp. 200-202, quotation from p. 201. See also J. George Frederick, "Obsolescence, Free Spending, and Creative Waste," in his *A Philosophy of Production, a Symposium* (New York: The Business Bourse, 1930).

153. Myers, *"Money Mad,"* pp. 37-50, quotation from p. 41.

154. McConaughy, *Money, the Acid Test,* pp. 78-83, quotation from p. 81.

155. Crawford, *The Stewardship Life,* p. 125. Cf. Edwin A. Kirkpatrick, *The Use of Money: How to Save and Spend* (Indianapolis: Bobbs-Merrill Co., 1915); Martin, *Christ and Money,* pp. 93-94; Moore, *Preacher Problems of the Twentieth Century,* p. 297; "The High Cost of Living," *The Congregationalist and Christian World* 101 (Oct. 1916): 493.

used to evangelize the world, but most leaders defended these practices as prudent, practical, and consistent with scriptural teachings.[156] Few evangelicals said anything about the morality or wisdom of investments, despite the fact that in the 1920s numerous religious periodicals regularly featured investment columns and ran ads from investment houses, trust companies, and banks.[157] One exception was Irwin Paulsen, who urged Christians not to invest in corporations that prohibited labor unions, bribed politicians, paid insufficient wages, employed children, or made no provision for laid-off or retired workers.[158]

The Church: Finances, Efficiency, and Stewardship

For many evangelical and liberal Protestants, Christian stewardship required high levels of efficiency in all areas of life including religious organizations. The Men and Religion Forward Movement of 1911-1912, for example, entitled its official history, *Making Religion Efficient* (1912).[159] Some evangelicals urged congregations to model biblical stewardship for Christian families and to practice business efficiency in their own management of resources. In *Modern Church Finance: Its Principles and Practice* (1916), Albert McGarrah claimed that the financial methods used by most congregations were scandalous and hampered God's kingdom both spiritually and materially. He rejoiced, however, that more and more congregations were seeking to implement business methods that were scriptural and therefore bound to be successful.[160] His book was based on his visits to over two thousand congregations and his leadership of hundreds of interdenominational conferences and institutes on stewardship and finance, and it was

156. For example, see R. E. Porter, "Pensions versus Faith," *UP,* 8 May 1930, p. 4; R. W. Burnside, "Pensions and Faith," *UP,* 8 May 1930, p. 4. See also Boorstin, *The Americans,* pp. 182-87.

157. Moore, *Selling God,* p. 217.

158. Paulsen, *It Is to Share,* p. 26. See also J. E. Baker, "The Ethics of Investment," *CA,* 8 Sept. 1927, p. 1095. E. Benjamin Andrews, the president of Brown University, discussed this subject at some length in *Wealth and Moral Law* (Hartford, CT: Hartford Seminary Press, 1894), pp. 69-75.

159. See Gary Scott Smith, "The Men and Religion Forward Movement of 1911-1912: New Perspectives on Evangelical Social Concern and the Relationship Between Christianity and Progressivism," *Westminster Theological Journal* 49 (1987): 110-12.

160. McGarrah, *Modern Church Finance,* p. 5.

produced with assistance from the Laymen's Missionary Movement, the Methodist Commission on Finance, the Baptist Forward Movement, and the Presbyterian Every Member Canvass Committee. McGarrah argued that successful church finance included honest and prompt payment of all bills and obligations, the avoidance of debts, the adoption of wise and ample budgets, the use of effective fund-raising methods, and the collection of contributions from all members.

Among the keys to congregational financial success, he maintained, were having an active congregation, democratic leadership and decision making, social and missionary vision, an "efficient" pastor, faithful and competent financial officers, securing written subscriptions and weekly pledges, using an every-member canvas, and educating parishioners in scriptural principles of stewardship. McGarrah also urged each congregation to raise all the money parishioners could give, rather than simply raising more than it had previously, or as much as other congregations, or even all that it needed.[161] He insisted that congregations must procure funds by using scriptural methods — tithes and offerings — not by pew rents, annual fees, or schemes such as bazaars and suppers, a point also hammered home by Baptist Frederick Agar in several books and by other evangelicals.[162]

By the 1920s business methods had begun to permeate the church, promoted by the *Journal of Church Management,* which began publication in 1923, and by a spate of books.[163] Some evangelicals, however, protested the widespread use of business methods in the church, the church's increasing dependence on large gifts, and the growing tendency to measure the success of congregations by their revenues, endowments, and facilities

---

161. McGarrah, *Modern Church Finance,* pp. 7, 11-18, 67-77. See also Versteeg, *The Deeper Meaning of Stewardship,* pp. 172-80; Leavell, *Training in Stewardship,* pp. 90-97.

162. McGarrah, *Modern Church Finance,* p. 64; Agar, *Church Profit-Making;* Agar, *Church Finance;* Agar, *The Competent Church,* pp. 63-65; Agar, *Stewardship of Life,* p. 126; Harshman, *Christian Giving,* p. 25; Paulsen, *It Is to Share,* p. 53; Weekley, *Getting and Giving,* pp. 70-71; Helen K. Wallace, *Stewardship in the Life of Women* (New York: Fleming H. Revell Co., 1928), pp. 49-53; "Church Suppers, Fairs, Etc. Are They of God?" *Serving-and-Waiting* 12 (Jan. 1923): 425-27. Many evangelicals objected that these fund-raising methods were unfair to businesses in the community, sometimes were unprofitable, kept Christians from carrying out mission in the world, cheapened the church, and gave some Christians an excuse for not tithing.

163. These included *How to Make the Church Go* (1922), *Business Methods for the Clergy* (1923), *The Competent Church* (1924), *The Technique of a Minister* (1925), *Church Administration* (1926), and *The Practical and Profitable in Church Administration* (1930).

instead of by their conversions, baptisms, tangible fruit of the spirit, and social outreach.[164]

Increasing Commitment to Stewardship

The amount of attention Protestants devoted to the subject of stewardship increased significantly between 1880 and 1930. Especially after 1910, the number of books, periodical articles, and pamphlets discussing steward-ship multiplied. More and more Sunday School classes and Bible study groups used stewardship materials, and stewardship campaigns — espe-cially every-member canvasses — became common. Contemporary ob-servers reported that greater numbers of sermons discussed the responsi-bility and rewards of stewardship.[165] Several organizations were created to advance Christian stewardship. In 1917 the Laymen's Missionary Move-ment appointed a Stewardship Commission that based its program on the principles of God's ownership of all things, people's duty to wisely manage all that God entrusted to them, and setting apart a definite proportion of income for the extension of God's kingdom.[166] In 1920 the United Stew-ardship Council of the Churches of Christ in the United States and Canada was created to teach Christians how to be good stewards in all areas of life.[167] Several denominations conducted major campaigns to raise money to expand their mission: the Men and Millions Movement of the Disciples of Christ (1913), the New Era Movement of the PCUSA (1919), the New World Movement of the Northern Baptist Convention (1919), the 75 Mil-

164. "Is Religion to Succumb to Business?" *CA,* 24 Apr. 1930, p. 519; "Money," *CA,* 13 Nov. 1930, p. 1393; Ray Allen, "Money and Methodism: Does the Dollar Speak Too Loud in the Methodist Chorus?" *CA,* 2 Dec. 1926, p. 1628. See also "The Money Menace and the Church," *Christian Century,* 2 July 1925, p. 849; "Church Commercialized, Minis-ter Charges," *Christian Century,* 5 Aug. 1926, p. 997.

165. For example, see Leavell, *Training in Stewardship,* p. 29; Harrison, *Studies in Christian Stewardship,* pp. 7-8; Leach, *Church Finance,* pp. 43, 63-67, 209-14.

166. Among those who served on the commission were Frederick Agar, Harvey Calkins, Ralph Cushman, David McConaughy, Robert E. Speer, and Bert Wilson.

167. Ralph Cushman played an especially important role in promoting steward-ship. He first served as the Secretary of the Department of Stewardship of the Methodist Episcopal Church, then as the Secretary of the Department of Stewardship in the Inner-Church World Movement, and finally as the first president of the United Stewardship Council.

lion Campaign of the Southern Baptist Convention (1919), the Centenary Celebration of the Methodist Episcopal Church (1919), and the New World Movement of the United Presbyterian Church (1920).[168] The most ambitious scheme of all, the Interchurch World Movement, launched in 1918 to promote world evangelism and social reform, failed miserably (raising only a fraction of its goal of more than $300,000,000), in part because of intensifying theological conflict within Protestantism.[169] At the same time, however, numerous denominations created stewardship departments, Protestants sponsored dozens of conventions and assemblies to promote the biblical concept of stewardship, and many women's societies made stewardship a major focus.[170] This emphasis on stewardship was especially strong among evangelicals.

How much impact did this outpouring of concern about stewardship have upon the attitudes and practices of evangelical lay people? While little systematic data exists, denominations that held financial campaigns in the 1910s and 1920s did raise considerable amounts of additional revenue for local, national, and foreign missions.[171] While the evidence suggests that fewer than 50 percent of evangelicals tithed in the early twentieth century,

168. Salstrand, *The Story of Stewardship,* pp. 59-61. In an earlier effort to promote stewardship, the Methodist Episcopal Church issued a series of pamphlets on the subject in 1915 written by leading pastors and seminary professors. See Harvey Calkins, "Stewardship Campaign of the Commission on Finance," *CA,* 16 Sept. 1915, p. 1257.

169. See E. G. Ernst, *Moment of Truth for Protestant America: Interlude Campaigns Following World War I* (Missoula, MT: Scholar's Press, 1974).

170. See Pearce, *Woman and Stewardship;* Wallace, *Stewardship in the Life of Women.* In addition, the United Stewardship Council adopted "A Business Man's Stewardship Platform" in 1928.

171. See Charles H. Fahs, *Trends in Protestant Giving: A Study in Church Finance in the United States* (New York: Institute of Social and Religious Research, 1929). From 1913 to 1927 total per capita benevolences for eleven leading Protestant denominations increased by 89 percent while inflation increased by 62 percent (31). Per capita total giving in the PCUSA increased by about 75 percent between 1913 and 1926; in the Reformed Church of America it almost doubled between 1913 and 1926; in the Southern Baptist Church it increased by almost 130 percent during this period. For the two Methodist, two Baptist, and three Presbyterian bodies included in this study contributions to religious colleges and schools increased by 62 percent from 1906 to 1916 and 103 percent from 1916 to 1926, a sizable increase even allowing for inflation and population growth (35). George Connell, "Stewardship in Several Conferences," *CA,* 18 Sept. 1924, p. 1143. See also Ralph S. Cushman, *Studies in Stewardship: A Centenary Textbook* (New York: Joint Centenary Committee, 1918).

evangelical attitudes toward stewardship seemed to be more positive during the period under investigation than they are today.

Conclusion

William Leach argues that by 1915 "much of the United States was becoming a Land of Desire" as the corporate money economy, drive for profits, and "new economic institutions — department stores, national corporations, hotels, theaters, restaurants, and commercial and investment banks — were beginning to reshape American culture." The nineteenth-century goal of material comfort was being superseded "by the idea of possession, by being through having . . . by desire rather than fulfillment." Leach maintains that many prosperous evangelical and liberal Protestants as well as many middle-class Catholics and Jews endorsed the idea that the new consumer culture was not antithetical to religion. They believed instead that the two were "moving forward together hand in hand toward a kind of American millennium." As a result, organized religion joined businesses, government, universities, and advertising agencies in sustaining and supporting the new capitalist order.[172] Leach contends further that evangelical Protestantism (although he often uses this term loosely), because it was "more upbeat and liberal, less dogmatic, unsure about divine sovereignty, . . . more concerned with how people behaved than with how deeply they thought about God and sin," was "far more compatible" with a commercial economy than Calvinism was.[173] Leach accuses Christian entrepreneurs, most notably John Wanamaker, of wanting both salvation and earthly success, of desiring God's blessing and heavenly reward as well as commercial gain, affluence, power, prestige, and material progress. While supporting revival meetings, institutional churches, interdenominational ministries like the Salvation Army and the YMCA, and many civic, educational, and humanitarian enterprises, these businessmen promoted a very different set of values through the commercial and industrial organizations they built. Although they often praised simplicity, thrift, and spirituality, they lived luxuriously, paid low wages, and sought to entice Ameri-

172. Leach, *Land of Desire*, pp. 190-92, first three quotations from p. 190, fourth from p. 192.
173. Leach, *Land of Desire*, p. 195.

cans to buy the products they manufactured and sold. They supported the social side of religion both to aid the poor and develop more productive, moral, docile workers. They gave much of their fortunes to Christian institutions, and they practiced personal piety. But they also helped create and defend the new pecuniary culture and economy, both because of the benefits they believed it bestowed on society and because of the rewards they personally enjoyed. Meanwhile, Dwight L. Moody and most other revivalists found it difficult to criticize the new commercial culture because capitalists paid most of the bills for their crusades.[174]

However, the situation is not as simple as Leach makes it sound. Evangelicals neither had the power to shape the new consumer culture to the degree Leach suggests they did, nor did they have the power to prevent its development. To a large extent, consumer capitalism was "a giant and unrelenting economic mechanism" that met "its requirements for continued growth and health by its own historical logic and with blatant disregard for human sentiment."[175] As this culture became more dominant in America, many evangelicals strongly promoted a doctrine of biblical stewardship. Moreover, some of them critiqued consumerism's underlying philosophy and its effects on American culture.[176]

After 1900, various forces made it increasingly difficult for evangelicals to direct cultural life as they had done during much of the nineteenth century. Theological battles diverted Protestants' attention from cultural issues, sapped their energy, and reduced their effectiveness. They were forced to combat biblical criticism's attack on historic Christian doctrines, Darwinism's assault on the divine creation and providential direction of the world, and numerous secular philosophies' onslaught on ultimate standards for moral life.

Meanwhile, secularization deeply penetrated many facets of American society, influencing people's presuppositions about politics, economics, education, social activities, marriage and family, and recreation. While

174. Leach, *Land of Desire*, pp. 197-209, 214, 220.

175. Frank, *Less Than Conquerors*, p. 33.

176. Evangelicals did not mount as significant a challenge to consumer capitalism as did Edward Bok, the editor of *Ladies' Home Journal*, nature enthusiasts John Muir and John Burroughs, proponents of the Arts and Crafts Movement, author Sinclair Lewis, social philosopher Lewis Mumford, New York social critic Ralph Borsodi, the Nashville Agrarians who wrote *I'll Take My Stand* (1930), or some Social Gospelers like Walter Rauschenbusch. See Shi, *The Simple Life*, pp. 181-232.

most evangelicals unintentionally or unwittingly abetted the secularization and commercialization of American life in some ways, many of them staunchly resisted these trends, at least to the extent they understood their incompatibility with biblical values. The new consumer culture offered numerous attractions, many of which were desirable from a biblical perspective: an unprecedented level of productivity, a higher standard of living, shorter working hours, better working conditions, more material comforts, labor-saving devices, increased leisure time, a proliferation of choices, greater cleanliness, and more mobility. No wonder it was so appealing to most Americans.

Through their practice of stewardship, their critique of self-indulgence, and their emphasis on moderation, evangelicals offered substantial resistance to the consumption ethic, which modern advertising presented so enticingly. Nevertheless, they often failed to recognize, or at least respond to, three things. The first was the power of advertising to shape people's perceptions, desires, and lifestyles. While often denouncing extravagant spending and conspicuous display, evangelicals rarely recognized advertising's prominent role in promoting these practices.

Second, most evangelicals ignored the fact that millions of working-class people did not share many of the benefits of the new culture. The majority of those who worked for wages continued to struggle in the early twentieth century to pay for food, shelter, clothing, and other necessities. Overlooking aspects of their own heritage and the message of the Social Gospel, most evangelicals emphasized the importance of individual initiative and effort and neglected the institutional forces that kept many people mired in either subsistence living or poverty.

This neglect led to a third shortcoming: most evangelicals did not seem to understand that social and economic forces were making it very hard for all Americans to practice biblical stewardship, to tithe, to forsake covetousness, and to avoid extolling money and possessions. They provided little analysis of structural and institutional developments that contradicted Christian values and made it increasingly difficult for individuals to follow the teachings of Jesus.[177] To the extent that they did think about larger economic forces, evangelicals usually believed that the free enterprise system ensured the most technological progress, the greatest productivity, the highest standard of living, and the best way of life. They believed

177. Frank, *Less Than Conquerors*, p. 203.

that its worst features could be mitigated by Christian paternalism, philanthropy, and the practice of biblical stewardship. Moreover, like conservatives today, many evangelicals were convinced that some of society's expanding wealth would "trickle down" to the indigent and help raise many of them to a middle-class lifestyle. Evangelicals were also reluctant to criticize the structure and practices of the American economy because thousands of affluent businessmen gave large sums of money to their congregations, parachurch organizations, and revival campaigns. As a result of these factors, evangelicals, like liberal Protestants, were not nearly as outspoken about the enticements and problems of the new consumer culture as were some secular critics.

Evangelicals sought to offer guidance to people who had lived through both a technological and a psychic revolution, but they had little understanding of the nature of the transformation that had occurred. They rarely acknowledged that "rapid and seemingly uncontrollable change in the material realm, in social and economic conditions," had a major impact on people's inner life and spirituality.[178] Between 1880 and 1930 the pace of life accelerated dramatically, societal guidelines for individual behavior became less clear, rationalization and bureaucracy more and more dominated political and economic life, clock time came to govern daily life, efficiency became a prized goal, and personal success increasingly served as the chief criterion for evaluating individual worth. Many of the evangelicals who struggled to adjust to these new developments embraced a pessimistic premillennialism that rejected the possibility of ameliorating social and economic conditions and focused instead on rescuing souls from a shipwrecked world. Because their eschatology encouraged them to act in ways that sharply contrasted with their productive and consumptive pursuits, it contributed to great discomfort, tension, and guilt among many of those who took their faith seriously. Nevertheless, during these years most evangelicals, including many premillennialists, vowed to work diligently at their vocations to glorify God, earn as much money as they could to support their families and finance God's work on earth, and to wisely manage all their resources. However, because of the countervailing pressures we have described, their performance often did not measure up to their intentions. It is easier to see the impact of these catastrophic

178. Frank, *Less Than Conquerors*, pp. 40-46, 123-29, quotations from pp. 46, 124. See also Wiebe, *The Search for Order*, pp. 19-21, 42-43.

economic and social forces in hindsight than to have recognized them while living through them.

In the final analysis, how effective was the evangelical response to the rise of modern advertising and consumerism? Is it a model that today's Christians can emulate or a source of the troubles we experience as we confront contemporary consumer culture? Is the biblical doctrine of stewardship an adequate approach for dealing with the practices, possibilities, and perils of this culture? The shift from a productive to a consumptive culture has been a mixed blessing. In some ways it has enriched our lives; in others it has impoverished us. As a result, we have better health, longer lives, improved nutrition, mass education, more knowledge, greater opportunities, and many material comforts. On the other hand, advertising and the availability of extensive credit have prodded people to pursue "an ever-elusive good life defined in material terms," "to chase constantly after pleasures" that remain just beyond their reach.[179] And the proliferation of things has made it more tempting to worship the creation instead of the creator and to lose a sense of what is truly important in the midst of our frenzied life. Christians should practice stewardship by recognizing God's lordship over all life and our responsibility to use wisely and creatively all the resources He has entrusted to us to advance His kingdom. At the same time, however, we need to critically analyze the nature, structure, and impact of consumer capitalism. We also must strive to redesign economic and social life, including the practices of advertising, the meaning of work, patterns of consumption, and attitudes toward possessions, in accordance with the biblical ideals of justice, shalom, and compassion.

179. Horowitz, *The Morality of Spending,* pp. 162, 147, quotations in that order.

CHAPTER 3

"Sanctified Business": Historical Perspectives on Financing Revivals of Religion

CHARLES E. HAMBRICK-STOWE

What then is my reward? Just this: that in preaching the gospel I may offer it free of charge, and so not make use of my rights in preaching it.

1 CORINTHIANS 9:18 (NIV)

Promise Keepers' financial crisis of 1997-1998 illustrates the challenge that has faced large-scale evangelistic work since the days of Charles G. Finney. The amount of money required to produce such special revival meetings — involving vast auditoriums, transportation of people and equipment, use of the latest communications technology, and often generous honoraria for speakers — is of a different order of magnitude than the annual operating budget for most local churches. An exploration of the funding of revivalism opens windows onto the generally cozy, but sometimes prophetic, relationship between religion and American commercial culture. As southern Methodist evangelist Sam Jones once put it, revivalism is "sanctified business." He and Sister Aimee Semple McPherson saw no conflict between evangelism and enjoyment of wealth, and Billy Graham created an operation that is described by his biographer as "Evangelism Incorporated." Yet Charles G. Finney, one of the inventors of the modern evangelistic machinery, argued for simplicity in living and identified "the national love of money" as one of America's besetting sins. And Billy Graham, aware of mammon's appeal and the risk of scandal, found ways to separate evangelism's big money from the evangelist himself.[1]

The evangelical Christian men's ministry Promise Keepers (PK), inaugurated in a 1990 meeting of University of Colorado football coach Bill McCartney and seventy-two other men in Boulder, subsequently attracted 22,000 to the University of Colorado stadium in 1992 and 50,000 in 1993. PK burst onto the national scene with an attendance of 278,600 at seven stadiums in 1994, peaking in 1996 with 1.1 million men at 22 stadium rallies. Scholars from a previous generation like William Warren Sweet would be stunned at the response of men to this new packaging of the old revival formula. In his *Revivalism in America: Its Origin, Growth and Decline*, published in 1944 just prior to the ascendancy of Billy Graham, Sweet concluded that revivalism had "run its course in America." Although Sweet acknowledged the rise of "numerous new revivalistic sects," and that these flourished in the 1920s and 30s while the liberal churches languished, he believed their appeal was limited primarily to the rural poor. Yet Promise Keepers represents the continued vitality of sophisticated urban revivalism and of the tradition's place in American society more broadly. Speakers at Promise Keepers meetings have often alluded to the movement's perpetuation of the revival tradition, a fact reinforced by worship music that includes rocked-up versions of classics like "Stand Up, Stand Up for Jesus," the theme hymn of the 1858 Businessmen's Revival that swept America's northern cities. If the rise of Promise Keepers in the 1990s demonstrates that the revival tradition's vitality has not waned, the movement also illustrates the ongoing difficulty of serving God and needing mammon.[2]

1. Kathleen Minnix, *Laughter in the Amen Corner: The Life of Evangelist Sam Jones* (Athens, GA: University of Georgia Press, 1993), p. 59. William Martin, *A Prophet with Honor: The Billy Graham Story* (New York: William Morrow, 1991), p. 123. Charles E. Hambrick-Stowe, *Charles G. Finney and the Spirit of American Evangelicalism* (Grand Rapids: Eerdmans, 1996), p. 201.

2. William Warren Sweet, *Revivalism in America: Its Origin, Growth and Decline* (New York: Charles Scribner's Sons, 1944), pp. 174-76, 182. Edward E. Plowman, "What Went Wrong? The Inside Story of Policy Decisions and Economic Conditions that Pushed Promise Keepers to the Brink of Financial Ruin," *World*, 21 Mar. 1998, pp. 12-16. On the survival of revivalistic conservative evangelicalism, see Joel A. Carpenter, *Revive Us Again: The Reawakening of American Fundamentalism* (New York: Oxford University Press, 1997).

Promise Keepers did differ from all previous efforts in funding its work by charging admission to events. However, several decisions caused the organization to run out of money. PK poured its resources into the massive 1997 "Stand in the Gap" assembly, which brought the largest crowd in history to the Mall in Washington, D.C., at an expense of almost $10 million. In March of that year PK also aired a national TV special that cost $4 million and brought in under $3,000 in gifts. Meanwhile, registration at fall 1996 and 1997 stadium conferences, and hence PK's major revenue source, declined seriously. Reasons for the decline may have included the ticket cost, interest saturation, reaction against PK's racial reconciliation message, and plans to attend the free Washington assembly instead of a stadium event. At the Stand in the Gap assembly itself, the last-minute attempt to receive an offering was botched badly. Despite the financial crisis, PK decided to offer subsequent events free of charge in order to attract more seekers in need of salvation. In 1998, therefore, PK began funding its work in much the same ways its predecessors have done for more than a century and a half. Sustained operation must now depend on steady donations from many thousands of faithful supporters, income from revival-related books and merchandise, and the patronage of wealthy believers.[3]

These methods of funding revivals of religion go back at least to the Great Awakening, when the free-wheeling Anglican evangelist George Whitefield established the principle that to influence all of society such work must be interdenominational or, better yet, nondenominational. Although many denominational agencies have supported evangelists throughout American history — a noteworthy example being early-nineteenth-century Connecticut Congregationalism's Asahel Nettleton — most have moved in wider circles than their denominational origins and have attracted independent financial support. The need was exacerbated when audience sizes exceeded the ability of any church building, court house, or school house to hold those who waited to hear the evangelists. Such was the case in Philadelphia in 1739 when, as Benjamin Franklin noted in his *Autobiography,* "arrived among us from England the Rev. Mr. Whitefield" and "it seem'd as if all the World were growing Religious."

3. "Promise Keepers to Lay Off Paid Staff," *Christian Century,* 11 Mar. 1998, pp. 254-55. Art Moore, "More PK Downsizing," *Christianity Today,* 5 Oct. 1998, pp. 20-21. On the marketing of Christian merchandise, see Colleen McDannell, *Material Christianity: Religion and Popular Culture in America* (New Haven: Yale University Press, 1995), chapter 8, "Christian Retailing."

Whitefield loved to preach outdoors where he could reach thousands rather than hundreds with the gospel, but, "it being found inconvenient to assemble in the open Air, subject to its Inclemencies," leading citizens organized to plan a special building. In a display of philanthropy that would become emblematic of many American preachers' future campaigns, "it was no sooner propos'd and Persons appointed to receive Contributions, but sufficient Sums were soon receiv'd to procure the Ground and erect the Building . . . about the Size of Westminster Hall; and the Work was carried on with such Spirit as to be finished in a much shorter time than could have been expected." While Franklin ascribed the success of the program to the generosity of public-spirited civic leaders, evangelists in the generations between the Great Awakening and the present would not hesitate to identify such events as miracles.[4]

George Whitefield set a pattern for later evangelists with his personal ability to raise money for his work, especially for his orphanage in Georgia. Franklin describes in comic fashion his resolution not to give when at "one of his Sermons I perceived he intended to finish with a Collection." Not even the practical Franklin could resist his appeal, however. "As he proceeded I began to soften, and concluded to give the Coppers. Another stroke of his Oratory made me asham'd of that, and determined me to give the Silver; and he finish'd so admirably, that I empty'd my Pocket wholly into the Collector's Dish, Gold and all." Whitefield was not the last evangelist to be suspected of "apply[ing] these Collections to his own private Emolument," but Franklin "never had the least Suspicion of his Integrity" and defended him as "a perfectly *honest Man*." Franklin's knowledge of Whitefield stemmed not only from objective and secular-minded observation ("we had no religious Connection") but from their business dealings. Franklin printed the evangelist's sermons and journals, which were so popular that they built excitement for future campaigns and brought added income into his ministry. Whitefield and Franklin discovered that there could be a *market* for religion and learned "how to exploit these new [market] forces." As Harry Stout put it, "both exhibited a precocious appreciation for the art of promotion and the consequent power of popularity."[5]

4. Leonard W. Labaree et al., eds., *The Autobiography of Benjamin Franklin* (New Haven: Yale University Press, 1964), pp. 175-78. Harry S. Stout, *The Divine Dramatist George Whitefield and the Rise of Modern Evangelism* (Grand Rapids: Eerdmans, 1991), p. 223.
5. Stout, *Divine Dramatist*, p. 223.

When Charles G. Finney began to preach in the North Country of New York State in 1824 he was licensed and then ordained by the Presbytery of St. Lawrence. But he was never bound by denominational constraints. His early financial support came from the Female Missionary Society of western New York, which stipulated only that he "labor in the Northern part of the County of Jefferson and such other destitute places in that County as his discretion shall dictate." Finney's commission thus allowed him to move freely among Presbyterian, Congregational, and even Baptist churches and to preach at public buildings, such as schools and court houses, in meetings designed for the entire community. Finney maintained his ecclesiastical independence by relying on independent financing throughout his career. When he did receive a salary from a local institution — New York's Broadway Tabernacle, First Church in Oberlin, Oberlin Collegiate Institute — it was always with the proviso that he could travel for significant portions of the year.[6]

The largess of wealthy patrons was indispensable to the financing of Finney's meetings. In 1825 Ogdensburg attorney John Fine, who had once proposed to completely fund the evangelist as his personal missionary in the North Country, provided him with what he needed to shift his ministry to the boom towns of the new Erie Canal in Oneida County. Fine sent a tailor to outfit him with a new suit of clothes and gave him sixty dollars in cash, with which Charles and Lydia Finney bought a carriage. When the Finneys were in a city for weeks and months at a time, they generally lodged as guests in the homes of the most prominent citizens — judges, lawyers, merchants, and manufacturers. This pattern, established by Finney in smaller cities like Utica, Rome, and Rochester, was replicated when he moved to the large urban centers of Philadelphia, Boston, and New York. Over the decades of his career, not only hospitality but substantial financial support would be forthcoming from the rising business class of antebellum Yankee America, from evangelical philanthropists like Anson Phelps, the Dodge family, and Arthur and Lewis Tappan of New York, Josiah Chapin of Providence, and Willard Sears of Boston. Finney, and many evangelists who came after him, moved easily among such folk. He did not come as a poor backwoods revivalist with his hand out to his so-

---

6. Hambrick-Stowe, *Finney*, p. 34. Garth M. Rosell and Richard A. G. Dupuis, eds., *The Memoirs of Charles G. Finney: The Complete Restored Text* (Grand Rapids: Zondervan, 1989), pp. 63-68, 379-89.

cial superiors. He did well among lawyers in Utica, mill owners in Rochester, and business tycoons in New York City because he was cut from the same cloth as they were. With a professional self-identity from his experience as a school teacher and a lawyer, with his uncanny ability to express the gospel of new birth in the language of democratic hope, and ingrained with the American promise that upward mobility was linked with geographical mobility, Finney embodied — and shared with his wealthy patrons — the evangelical ethos of the New Republic.[7]

Finney gave larger place to human agency than did the Calvinism of his Puritan forebears and his Old School Presbyterian critics, but his gospel was not just a religious expression of self-interested Jacksonian can-do individualism. In fact, Finney described sin as each individual "setting up his own interest in opposition to the interest and government of God." Jacksonianism was for Finney the apotheosis of sin, "each one aiming to promote his own private happiness, in a way that is opposed to the general good." Sin could be defined simply as selfishness, and the love of money he considered a national sin. Finney's support for such causes as temperance, women's rights, fair treatment of American Indians, and the abolition of slavery stemmed from his belief in the Edwardsian doctrine of "disinterested benevolence": that personal salvation meant commitment to the common good. The drive to make money, Finney preached, must be subordinated and harnessed to the work of evangelism and the moral reform of society. In the extraordinary case of Rochester in 1830-1831, the revival of religion meant actually closing schools and businesses when meetings were being held. "If we do our business for God," Finney preached, Christian businessmen will close their doors, send employees and customers to the meeting, and "consider it in the light of a holiday." For converted shopkeepers during that charmed campaign it meant smashing barrels of liquor in the streets and dumping the contents into the canal.[8]

When Finney preached in Boston that penitents must renounce their worldly wealth it made his host Lyman Beecher squirm. Beecher stood up and quickly assured his people that when they did so God would "give it right back" to them. Finney believed evangelical philanthropy flowed from

7. Hambrick-Stowe, *Finney*, p. 45. Rosell and Dupuis, eds., *Memoirs of Finney*, pp. 134-35, 285-89.

8. Hambrick-Stowe, *Finney*, pp. 88-93, 110-11. Rosell and Dupuis, eds., *Memoirs of Finney*, pp. 299-327. See Paul E. Johnson, *A Shopkeeper's Millennium: Society and Revivals in Rochester, New York, 1815-1837* (New York: Hill and Wang, 1978).

hearts that were disinterested — spiritually detached from possessions and committed to benevolence. Finney's career depended on the willingness of some of these believers to commit their resources to his ministry. An evangelical "association of gentlemen" first brought him to New York City in 1829, and, after Rochester and Boston, tried to lure him there on a permanent basis. They purchased and renovated the Chatham Garden Theater, including "a dwelling house, contiguous to the theater, *for the minister,*" and hinted at the eventual construction of a vast revival cathedral (Broadway Tabernacle) for his use. Finney was beginning to look west, but Lewis Tappan argued persuasively that "very soon Railroads will bring all the business men to this city twice a year." How could Ohio compare with the "moral influence" that could be "exerted . . . in that thoroughfare where 30,000 walk daily?" Finney's portrait, painted twice in New York, shows him as an urbane sophisticate far removed from the early caricature of him as "the madman of Oneida." An early Mohawk Valley supporter complained that Finney's preaching manner had changed — "Not so much point. Not so much unction. More regard to niceness of diction." His unpolished brother George wrote from upstate to warn, "When I look at your elivation in society I allmost shudder." He pushed his famous brother in prophetic fashion: "Why is it that [your] enemies are becoming [your] friends and the opposition of the church and the world is dying away — is it because every body is becoming better — is it because the world are less inclined to hate and persecute a man that aims at a high tone of piety?" He concluded with the plea, "May God keep you humble." Charles Finney was in fact deeply impressed with the piety of his benefactors, having seen them on a daily basis as a guest in their homes. But George's point was well taken, and the tension between wealth and holiness could never be eliminated.[9]

At least two problems loomed in Finney's ministry because of his reliance on the patronage of the wealthy. First, the financing of his evangelistic ministry was linked with his patron's political views. When the Tappan brothers agreed to support Oberlin Collegiate Institute in 1835 it was on condition that it become a beacon of abolitionism and a pioneer in the education of blacks and women together with white men, and that Charles G. Finney become its professor of theology. Eight professorships

9. Hambrick-Stowe, *Finney,* pp. 121-22, 129-36. Rosell and Dupuis, eds., *Memoirs of Finney,* pp. 347-49, 356-67.

were endowed by "the friends in New York." Arthur Tappan promised Finney privately, "I will pledge to give you my entire income, except what I need to provide for my family, till you are beyond pecuniary want." Finney replied, "That will do." But when Finney refused to take a radical position on the immediate abolition of slavery, would not elevate anti-slavery to primacy among the issues of the day, and even continued to seat blacks separately in worship, Lewis Tappan accused him of "sinning against conviction." Financial support from the Tappans was in grave danger of drying up. However, the second problem made it a moot point, for the brothers lost their fortune. First came the December 1835 fire that raged through New York's business district. Hundreds of structures, including the Tappan Building, were destroyed. Then came the financial crash and national depression of 1837. Among the major companies that went bankrupt were the firms that had supported Charles Finney's ministry and Oberlin Collegiate Institute, including Phelps and Dodge, Arthur Tappan and Company, and Finney's publisher Leavitt, Lord, and Company.[10]

Finney and Oberlin survived the crisis as new patrons came forward. On Thanksgiving Day 1837, after preaching an especially satisfying sermon, Finney returned home to find his wife Lydia smiling. "The answer has come, my dear," she said. She had in her hand a check for two hundred dollars from Josiah Chapin of Providence, Rhode Island, with a promise of more to come. A businessman who had weathered the financial collapse, Chapin would pay Finney's salary of $600 a year until 1846, when Boston entrepreneur Willard Sears joined the Oberlin board and assumed that responsibility.

The fact remains, however, that evangelism can be separated from neither the vicissitudes of the business cycle nor donors' whims and sociopolitical convictions. In a similar fashion, the evangelist's charisma is also indispensable from the viewpoint of the institutions with which he is affiliated. When Finney toured in Britain for long periods, sponsored by wealthy merchants of the same sort that had supported him from his earliest days in upstate New York, Oberlin faced repeated financial difficulties. Letters from the boards of both the college and church implored the evangelist to return. Not only was Finney needed in the pulpit and in the classroom but the institution required a fresh infusion of funds from what they

10. Hambrick-Stowe, *Finney*, pp. 160-61, 172-73. Rosell and Dupuis, eds., *Memoirs of Finney*, pp. 379-89.

called "your rich friends." Finney's fund-raising for his meetings and the institutions with which he was connected never achieved for him an especially high personal standard of living. He and his wives (widowed, he married three times) lived in simple comfort in the house provided by the college. He always eschewed luxury and even attempted to foster a movement for "retrenchment," or more simple living.[11]

Dwight L. Moody, who succeeded Finney as America's premier evangelist after the Civil War, shared his predecessor's aptitude for raising funds, ability to easily make friends with business leaders, and self-identification with the commercial culture of the northern states. As a young salesman in Chicago devoting every waking minute of his spare time to YMCA and other evangelistic work, Moody secured a free pass from the railroad superintendent — "the first recorded beg of the man who was to draw vast sums into Christian enterprise" — and a larger, rent-free hall for his Sunday School from the mayor of the city. In 1860 he refused a salary from the YMCA, living off his savings, thereby giving him, in the words of a biographer, "a moral right to beg for mission causes."[12]

Still in his twenties when he became president of the Chicago YMCA, Moody was able to move in extraordinarily high circles because the wealthy had adopted that institution as their own. Cyrus McCormick and George Armour were trustees; businessman John Farwell became an exceedingly generous benefactor. On one occasion McCormick gave Moody a check for double the amount he was asking for because, "I began to think of the noble work he is doing in our city, and what a splendid fellow he is." Moody and his philanthropists found one another to be of mutual benefit. McCormick, as the manufacturer said, "became sure of Mr. Moody's great worth" in advancing the evangelically based civic work he and his friends were eager to fund. Farwell so responded to his leadership that he financed the new YMCA building (twice, as the first structure was demolished by fire), designed by a premier architect as a grand public building and named "Farwell Hall." Moody and his wife, meanwhile, were frequent guests at the McCormick mansion and Farwell presented them with a "gift house" on State Street. When Moody began to emerge as a lay

11. Hambrick-Stowe, *Finney*, pp. 177, 240-41. Rosell and Dupuis, eds., *Memoirs of Finney*, pp. 389, 401-2.

12. J. C. Pollock, *Moody Without Sankey: A New Biographical Portrait* (London: Hodder and Stoughton, 1963), pp. 34, 37, 43.

preaching evangelist, these philanthropists set him up with a tabernacle, organ, and furnishings. Evangelistic meetings in New York City and during the first British tour yielded funds from the same type of wealthy patrons for the building of a permanent tabernacle in Chicago, which Farwell soon undertook at LaSalle Street and Chicago Avenue. Recalling one of McCormick's early donations, Moody once said: "God gave me the money that day because I needed it. And He has always given me money when I needed it. But often I have asked Him when I thought I needed it, and He has said: 'No, Moody, you just shin along the best way you can. It'll do you good to be hard up awhile'." There were few times when Moody had to "just shin along." Preparing for his second British campaign, he was asked, "Are you going to preach to the miserable poor?" The evangelist replied, "Yes, and to the miserable rich, too."[13]

The 1873-1874 campaign in the British Isles brought the issue of dealing responsibly with revival-generated income into focus. As usual, the meetings were financed by groups of businessmen organized as patrons. Although Moody admitted that in Scotland he had accepted personal gifts "to myself for my own use," he was soon overwhelmed by the outpouring of donations and the potential for more to come. He wrote home that "for the last three months I have had to refuse money all the time." His caution stemmed from charges that he was nothing but "a speculating Yankee" and rumors that the tour had been organized by P. T. Barnum for the sole purpose of raking in money. Moody responded by eliminating collections from his meetings — which for his first four and a half months in London's Agricultural Hall came to £28,400 — instructing committees to raise all funds for the campaign privately. In this Moody returned to the practice of Charles Finney, who did not receive offerings from the masses attending his meetings but relied on patrons and local committees. Meanwhile, Moody let it be known that he and his song leader Ira Sankey received no honoraria for leading their meetings but relied entirely on royalties from their revival song book, *Sacred Songs and Solos,* for living expenses. Sankey's gospel songs like "The Ninety and Nine" were so popular in Victorian England that when an enlarged edition came out in January 1875 it was clear that royalty income far exceeded their personal or professional needs. Moody and Sankey directed the publisher to give all royalties to "one of your leading citizens" for distribution among charitable causes. Upon their

13. Pollock, *Moody Without Sankey,* pp. 62-63, 69-70, 82, 86, 92, 96.

departure from England, the evangelist did accept a substantial gift of money, which he used to purchase the farm in Northfield, Massachusetts, that would become the site of future educational and evangelistic work. Collections at meetings were simply not necessary, for, as has been said of Moody, he "need only lift his finger for money to flow."[14]

Returning from the triumphant British tour as a celebrity, Moody chose Philadelphia as the site for his first American evangelistic crusade of grand proportions. It was an ideal location because the bond between religious organizations and the business community had been solid since the Businessmen's Revival following the Panic of 1857. The YMCA was at the heart of the work, promoting noon-hour meetings at locations throughout the city and, in the spring of 1858, in a portable "Union Tabernacle" tent that accommodated 1,200 people. Among the saved was young John Wanamaker, who acted on his new faith by relentlessly evangelizing the city's children and youth and organizing Bethany Sunday School. At age 20 he became America's first full-time paid YMCA secretary — and used his savings from the $1,000 salary to launch himself in business. Wanamaker and other rising Philadelphia business leaders like George H. Stuart brought aggressive advertising methods to their religious work, using the secular newspapers, and communicated with one another daily about Sunday School and prayer meeting matters by telegraph. Dwight Moody insisted on three conditions in his negotiations with the Philadelphia committee: united support among the churches, with endorsement by at least two hundred ministers; an adequate facility; and no competition — churches must suspend their own activities during the hours of his meetings. Committee chairman Stuart, who had known Moody during the Civil War when they both worked for the United States Christian Commission, assured the evangelist there would be no problem. The ideal Tabernacle location was the old railroad depot across the street from where Philadelphia was building its new city hall. Wanamaker, in London at the time, had an option on the property as the site of what was to become America's first department store. A cable to London brought an immediate positive response, and upon his return Wanamaker purchased the property and gave it to the committee rent free.[15]

14. Pollock, *Moody Without Sankey*, pp. 116-17, 122-24, 139, 150, 155.
15. Pollock, *Moody Without Sankey*, p. 162. Marion L. Bell, *Crusade in the City: Revivalism in Nineteenth-Century Philadelphia* (Lewisburg, PA: Bucknell University Press, 1977), pp. 169, 176-77, 185-88, 209, 212-13.

Moody's Philadelphia revival from November 21, 1875 to January 16, 1876 depended entirely on the support of the business community. This support came in the form of cash, services, and materials. Not only upstart merchants like Wanamaker but the city's wealthy elite, including bankers Jay Cooke and Anthony J. Drexel, signed on as patrons. A prominent architect donated his services for refitting the depot. Companies installed equipment for heat, gaslight, and other necessities for free or at a discount. Special trains were added to the schedule and tickets were sold at special rates. Hotels were bursting at the seams and church members opened their homes to out of town visitors, while the evangelist himself stayed in the home of John Wanamaker. A committee of thirteen ministers oversaw the spiritual side and a committee of businessmen managed the practical arrangements, with subcommittees for fund-raising, expenses, publicity, usher and choir recruitment, and tickets (which were free but necessary for crowd control). Meetings were advertised on the amusement page of newspapers; 50,000 posters were printed weekly; hundreds of thousands of circulars were distributed; and, following Finney's earliest technique for producing a crowd, house to house visits were organized. The cost of the revival was reported to be $29,538, raised entirely from private contributions, but this does not include the value of donated services and materials. When it was over the furnishings were sold off to finance the construction of a new YMCA building. The proceeds came to more than $100,000, although the value of certain items (Moody's chair, President Grant's chair) was inflated by virtue of their use in the revival. Both in terms of the crowds that gathered day after day and of its organizational sophistication, it was, in the words of Marion L. Bell, "a revival the like of which Philadelphia had never before witnessed."[16]

Moody followed the same formula for financial success in his next campaign in New York City and throughout his career. In New York the committee, with J. P. Morgan serving as treasurer, rented Barnum's "Great Roman Hippodrome" for the meetings. Adequate funding was assured by the support of such magnates as Cornelius Vanderbilt, Jr., and manufacturer William E. Dodge, whose family had supported Charles Finney more than forty years before. The marriage of business and religion brought benefits to both in ways that raise questions about mixed motives. Although Moody was known in Philadelphia to be preaching freely, not for a

16. Bell, *Crusade in the City,* pp. 215, 226-29, 209.

fee, Marion Bell concludes that "it is probable that Moody and Sankey received an honorarium privately from generous patrons. Sums were not disclosed, but Moody's style of life implies an adequate income." Moody did accept private financial gifts and honoraria in connection with his American campaigns. But Bell's assessment may be unduly harsh. In September 1875, just prior to the Philadelphia campaign, Moody and Sankey had Dodge set up a trust into which all royalties from their song books would be deposited and then dispersed for YMCA and other evangelical charitable work. In the next ten years more than $357,000 came into the trust, an amount that would have made them rich. Moody seemed to relish the experience not of accumulating wealth but of having it pass through his hands and into the community. He enjoyed, he said, "getting things started" — and most notably the Bible Institute that bears his name. The problem was not that the evangelist was greedy but that he identified himself uncritically with American business culture. For his part, John Wanamaker certainly benefited materially from the revival. In May 1876, as Philadelphia was beginning to celebrate the centennial of the Declaration of Independence, Wanamaker opened his department store on the site of the Tabernacle. The area around the old railroad depot had been on the edge of town just a few years before, blocks from the commercial district to the south. Moody's evangelistic meetings had brought many people there for the first time, paving the way for future shopping trips and the rise of this new part of the city. The twin association of the store's location with Moody and Wanamaker was good for business. Conversely, the gulf between the commercial and the working classes widened in the Gilded Age as the Finneyite link between revival and social reform weakened. Moody, taking the side of his wealthy friends, opposed the rise of organized labor, denouncing unions as a threat to the nation. As Marion Bell has observed, evangelists like Moody were so "bound to the business culture, they could not question it."[17]

Few evangelists have been more wedded to the culture, and unembarrassed by the acquisition of wealth, than the southern Methodist Sam Jones, who was at his peak from 1885 through the 1890s. Like Finney, Jones had been a lawyer before his conversion, and he moved with ease among business and civic leaders. Early in his career, preaching as an agent for an

---

17. Pollock, *Moody Without Sankey*, p. 164. Bell, *Crusade in the City*, pp. 229, 237-38, 249, 19.

orphan home in Decatur, he attracted Atlanta businessmen to its board —
including R. A. Hemphill, whom he called "one of God's bankers," and tobacco magnate General Julian Shakespeare Carr of Durham. Supported by
agrarian populist Tom Watson, who lionized Jones as "the greatest Geor-
gian this generation has known," the evangelist expressed racial views that
might charitably be described as benevolent white supremacy (one black
reported that in his sermon Jones "called me a 'nigger,' and a 'dog,' and a
'brother'"). Jones's greatest convert was Nashville riverboat entrepreneur
Tom Ryman, who built his famous auditorium (later home of the Grand
Ole Opry) to serve as Jones's Union Gospel Tabernacle. Ryman, of whom
Jones said "there has been no more wonderful convert to God in the nineteenth century," went to far as to refurbish his riverside saloon as "Sam
Jones Hall" and rename his best riverboat "The Sam Jones." Jones also
made friends with railroad men — for example, when he preached in New
York City he stayed in the home of the president of the Delaware and Hudson River Road — and rode their trains for free, sometimes in their private
cars.[18] Another wealthy backer was Confederate hero General W. H. Jackson, who had experienced conversion in a wartime camp meeting but later
backslid as a wealthy horse farm owner and was convicted anew when
Jones preached: "There's many a man here that's going right straight to
hell on a blooded horse." He immediately raised ten thousand dollars to
build a home for the evangelist in Nashville. When Jones declined on account of his wife's love for their mortgaged, partly built cottage in
Cartersville, Georgia, Jackson insisted he take the money anyway. According to biographer Kathleen Minnix, "Jones used the money to pay off his
creditors and began furnishing his home in the sumptuous Victorian style
for which 'Roselawn' would become known." At home in elite society, enjoying his status as a kind of "priest of the New South," Jones anticipated
many twentieth-century evangelists who equated material and spiritual
blessings.[19]

Ordinary people were also a significant revenue source. In 1884, a

18. Walt Holcomb, *Sam Jones: An Ambassador of the Almighty* (Nashville: Methodist
Book Publishing House, 1947), pp. 114, 130. Sam Jones, *Sam Jones' Own Book: A Series of
Sermons, With an Autobiographical Sketch* (Cincinnati, 1886), pp. 34, 47-48, 50. Minnix,
Laughter in the Amen Corner, pp. 8-9, 73.

19. Minnix, *Laughter in the Amen Corner*, pp. 59-60, 84. James Lutzweiler, *The Unex-
amined Revival of Rev. Sam Jones in Charlotte, North Carolina, 25 April 1890 to 2 May 1890*
(Jamestown, NC: Schnappsburg University Press, 1995), pp. 5, 12, 16, 22.

Waco journalist gave Jones "all honor," as a "wizened little Georgia corn-cracker," for his ability to attract a crowd and reach the hearts of the masses. In a typical aphorism, he preached, "God bores through the top of a man's head to his heart and on down to his pocket." And as with evangelists going back to George Whitefield, when Jones gave his pitch people emptied their pockets for him. The modest three-hundred-dollar offering from one Los Angeles meeting, for example, included seventy-five dollars in nickels. Much of Jones's appeal lay in his ability to employ the common language of plain-folk southern culture, and it worked in Boston, Toronto, and Chicago as well as in the old South and the Southwest. People loved to sing "welcome songs" in "darky dialect" like "Sam Jones is comin' . . . In de name of de Lawd." Tom Watson recalled how "he abused us and ridiculed us, he stormed at us and laughed at us, he called us flop-eared hounds, beer kegs, and whiskey soaks. . . . For six weeks the farms and the stores were neglected, and Jones! Jones! Jones! was the whole thing." With his coarse, down-home humor, it was said that "there is no getting around him in a collection." Jones preached, "Don't worry about your money. God bless you, bud, they'll haul you off in a shroud without a pocket — and if it had a pocket your arm would be too stiff to get into it." Or: "You little stingy, narrow-hided rascal . . . a fly could sit on the bridge of your nose and paw you in one eye and kick you in the other." He laid down the rule, "Give till the blood comes."[20]

The expense of a Sam Jones revival was borne largely by the community. Preparing for the 1885 revival in Nashville, which proved to be his breakthrough to national fame, Jones stunned the local committee by demanding a three-thousand-dollar tent, claiming that in "the city of churches" no building was large enough. Early attendance at a Methodist church proved his point and he got the tent. On a tour of Texas cities, cotton warehouses were made over or large wooden tabernacles, seating five to ten thousand people, were constructed wherever he went. While major expenses like these were often underwritten by leading citizens, organization of the revivals as "union meetings" insured broad local support. In Memphis, for example, Jones was able to bring together thirteen pastors and congregations representing five denominations to sponsor his meetings. Jones described these January 1883 meetings as "the first revival I ever

20. Holcomb, *Sam Jones*, pp. 57-58, 81. Minnix, *Laughter in the Amen Corner*, pp. 60, 95.

held which gave me newspaper notoriety." He always looked to the press for advance publicity and extensive revival coverage, often including transcriptions of sermons. "It's the devil doing my advertising free," he boasted, readily admitting that "to the newspapers I owe much."

Not only did Jones garner support for his work, Jones personally received big money for his efforts. An early four-week effort in Brooklyn, New York yielded a personal honorarium of $1,000. Always insisting his services were free, soon the evangelist was receiving up to $500 for a single appearance as a free gift. He generally received $800-$1,000 for an eight-day revival, although on occasion it could be double that amount. He would use his own generosity as a stimulus for the offering in order to leave the local committee in the black, and perhaps generate a substantial gift for himself. In St. Louis in 1895, for example, he announced: "The rent of this hall . . . is $2,000. . . . You can take your choice. If you don't pay [it], I will." As the ushers began to move among the crowd, someone shouted out, "We won't let you, Brother Jones, not a cent!" Jones kept the cost of his operation low, so a high proportion of his honorarium became net personal income. He maintained a modest and ever-changing staff. His informal organization included advance men to coordinate publicity and ushering, a chorister to lead large combined choirs and congregational singing, and other evangelists to share preaching and other duties. His best-known chorister, E. O. Excell, would employ pianists, an organist, and often an entire band. Excell's meager five-dollar-a-day salary from Jones was augmented by substantial royalties from his song books. Jones's financial records were sketchy at best but, according to Raymond Rensi, notes in his appointment book indicate an annual income of nearly $30,000 from 1885 to 1898, with a third of this from book royalties. By 1906 he claimed to have "made over $750,000 with my tongue" as "the best-paid preacher in the United States." When challenged by a New York reporter on the propriety of such wealth he replied that he "was not getting paid more than the people thought him worth."[21]

Sam Jones lived in genteel luxury back in Cartersville. With his wife as business manager he invested heavily in local banks, factories, businesses, and real estate. He could have made even more — declining for ex-

21. Minnix, *Laughter in the Amen Corner,* p. 66. Raymond C. Rensi, "Sam Jones: Southern Evangelist" (Ph.D. diss., University of Georgia, 1971), pp. 16, 279, 301-2, 314-15, 327.

ample to participate in the mass marketing of his photograph, of which thousands were sold without permission at a dime a piece. Jones also prided himself on giving away a large portion of his accumulated wealth. Much of his charity went to needy individuals — including poor blacks and whites of his acquaintance, underpaid pastors, and, ironically, given his anti-intellectual posturing, scholarship support at Vanderbilt, Mercer, Emory, Scarrit, and other educational institutions. At one point he indicated that he had given away $275,000 of the $300,000 he had earned. For all that, he died a rich man, with his estate valued at a quarter of a million dollars. With Sam Jones the gospel of wealth found a home in the revival tradition. "I used to be a preacher on the poorest circuit in Georgia and had many trials," he said in 1899, "but I preached the truth and now I am the best paid preacher on the continent."[22]

Jones paved the way for twentieth-century evangelists in another way as well, by making the revival a form of entertainment. While revivals had no doubt always functioned as a pastime, a Sam Jones revival was just plain fun. "I have seen preachers who looked as sad and solemn as if their Father in heaven was dead and hadn't left 'em a cent," he quipped. He augmented the customary organ with a brass ensemble or, preferably, a full band with horns, winds, and drums. In place of an "ag-o-o-o-nizing altar call," Jones reduced the moment of decision to a raised hand or a handshake. "Now while we sing," he invited, "come give me your hand and let's settle it." This "clown of conservative evangelicals," as Minnix has called him, did more to create the environment for Billy Sunday and those who followed than did the more seriously businesslike Dwight L. Moody. Certainly, the early twentieth century witnessed a proliferation in the number of professional evangelists, Gypsy Smith and Wilbur Chapman being perhaps the best known, itinerant preachers whose livelihood came from the revivals they produced.[23]

Sam Jones was unfettered by the ethical restraints that had kept evangelists from Whitefield to Moody from using their calling to turn a big profit. Although every successful revivalist was an exceptional fund-raiser, most used that skill to support charitable and missionary institutions. After Jones,

22. Rensi, "Sam Jones," pp. 324-33, 155. Minnix, *Laughter in the Amen Corner,* pp. 106, 129.

23. Jones, *Sam Jones' Own Book,* p. 383. Rensi, "Sam Jones," p. 305. Minnix, *Laughter in the Amen Corner,* p. 243. William G. McLoughlin, ed., *The American Evangelicals, 1800-1900* (Gloucester, MA: Peter Smith, 1976), p. 186.

however, many evangelists aspired to personal wealth and considered its acquisition a sign of blessing. Billy Sunday, who rose from an impoverished Iowa childhood to play major league baseball before accepting a call to become a YMCA evangelist, came to exemplify the new stereotype. In the early years he never took more than a freewill offering on the final night, but then Sunday began to insist that the Midwestern towns in which he was preaching construct ever-larger wooden tabernacles. This expense, and Sunday's addition of musical and administrative staff, required frequent and larger offerings from the crowds. When he moved up to the nation's mid-sized and major cities in the mid-1910s, total offerings over the course of a revival were bringing in tens of thousands of dollars. According to Lyle W. Dorsett, even though Sunday donated his entire New York City collection of $120,500 to the war effort and Chicago's $58,000 collection to the Pacific Garden Mission, "from 1908 to 1920, the Sundays earned over a million dollars . . . when the average gainfully employed worker would have earned a total of less than $14,000 for the same period." Sunday's wife Nell, who had assumed the role of business manager, added such key staff as music director Homer Rodeheaver and effectively "transformed the tabernacles into entertainment establishments as well as preaching halls." As requests for both Billy and Nell to speak "came in by the thousands," they were "inundated with money received from offerings and through the mail." During this period Billy Sunday also became friends with millionaires like John D. Rockefeller, Jr., and enjoyed hobnobbing with movie stars and politicians. Sunday's "obsession with money," however, brought grief in his family life, personal unhappiness — "once they succumbed to gathering it in, there was seldom enough" — and scathing criticism from both the secular and religious press for "selling the gospel."[24]

Sister Aimee Semple McPherson, at her height in the 1920s as one of America's best-loved evangelists, was also noted for her flamboyant manner of living. Although early engagements, under the auspices of various Pentecostal missions, were a hand-to-mouth operation, by 1919 she was renting prestigious halls like Baltimore's Lyric Theater for three hundred dollars a day and receiving travel advances from local committees. In addition to freewill offerings, campaigns were financed by contributions from

24. Lyle W. Dorsett, *Billy Sunday and the Redemption of Urban America* (Grand Rapids: Eerdmans, 1991), pp. 63-66, 80, 91, 94, 99, 101, 118, 139. See also Roger A. Bruns, *Preacher: Billy Sunday and Big-Time American Evangelism* (New York: W. W. Norton, 1992).

local churches and other groups (including, despite her remarkably progressive work among blacks and Hispanics, the Ku Klux Klan) and the selling of subscriptions to her magazine, *The Bridal Call,* and pictures of "Sister" at a dollar each. With her mother Minnie Kennedy as her business manager, Sister staged her revivals as lavish musical and dramatic productions, often appearing in costume — as a police officer on a motorcycle, for example — to drive home her point. Her most ambitious evangelistic work was accomplished with the construction of Angelus Temple in Los Angeles and her pioneering work on radio, including her own station KFSG (Kall Four-Square Gospel). With impeccable timing, the station went on the air during the city's Radio and Electrical Exposition. In similar fashion, Sister dedicated her Temple on January 1, 1923, the same day her float won a prize in the Tournament of Roses parade. All was done "on faith," with money appearing when it was needed. She preached in the St. Louis Coliseum and they gave $16,000 for Temple construction; at the Denver Auditorium they gave $13,000 plus $5,000 for chairs. The business organization and staff of her Four-Square Gospel Association, and then the International Foursquare Gospel Lighthouses, grew increasingly sophisticated. But conflict with her mother and disillusioned employees brought on a series of crises. Allegations of financial irregularities, lawsuits over a number of improbable business schemes that fizzled, sexual escapades, and melodramatic faked disappearances discredited her in the eyes of many. But Americans found it hard not to love her.[25]

Young Billy Graham, as a student at Florida Bible Institute (FBI) in the late 1930s, had witnessed the preaching of a number of evangelists. His father had taken him when he was only five to hear Billy Sunday in Charlotte, and it was under the respected Southern Baptist revivalist Dr. Mordecai Fowler Ham in 1934 that he experienced a quiet conversion. One of the touring evangelists that appeared at FBI made an impression on Billy because of his expensive clothing and extravagantly comfortable style of living. He handed Billy a fat one-dollar tip and gave him some worldly advice — that "there is more where this came from" and Billy could get his share if he worked hard and learned to preach the gospel. Shortly thereafter, the

25. Edith L. Blumhofer, *Aimee Semple McPherson: Everybody's Sister* (Grand Rapids: Eerdmans, 1993), pp. 147-48, 167, 266-67, 233, 244, 310-12. See also Daniel Mark Epstein, *Sister Aimee: The Life of Aimee Semple McPherson* (New York: Harcourt, Brace, Jovanovich, 1993).

school's president had the students pray for FBI's financial survival, as ten thousand dollars was needed immediately. Miraculously, a telegram suddenly arrived announcing a gift in that very amount. As William Martin notes, "This experience moved Billy far more than the old evangelist's generous tip, but the lesson was the same: 'There is more where this came from'."[26]

Graham was uneasy about the Elmer Gantry image of the American revivalist when he began his work with Youth for Christ (YFC) after World War II. Certainly he and his colleagues — George Beverly Shea, Grady Wilson, and Cliff Barrows — were nothing if not flamboyant in dress and performance. "We used every modern means to catch the attention of the unconverted — and then we punched them right between the eyes with the gospel." But since they were salaried employees offerings went straight to YFC and they were free from the temptation to fill their own pockets. When the team began touring independently the traditional freewill "love offering" system of funding revivals troubled Graham. Evangelists typically collected the money and, after expenses were paid, were accountable to no one for the balance. Of course, with the advent of federal income tax, Internal Revenue Service scrutiny was beginning to make wholesale profiteering by revivalists more difficult. At Modesto in 1948 Graham and associates pledged to keep themselves financially above board by arranging for local committees to handle the payment of bills and the honoraria for the team. After the triumphant 1949 Los Angeles crusade Graham preached in Boston at Park Street Church, which had been Finney's chief Boston pulpit a century before. Skeptical reporters asked how much money he expected to make in Boston. According to William Martin, "The evangelist explained that the Northwestern Schools [where he was then president] paid him eighty-five hundred dollars a year . . . that he would receive no income from the crusade, and that a committee from the Park Street Church would release a full, audited financial statement when the meetings ended."[27]

The Billy Graham Evangelistic Association (BGEA), created in 1950, was the means by which Graham achieved career-long financial stability and accountability. Graham had been stung during the Atlanta crusade

26. Billy Graham, *Just As I Am* (New York: Harper San Francisco, Zondervan, 1997), pp. 18, 21, 29. Martin, *Prophet with Honor,* pp. 71-72.

27. Martin, *Prophet with Honor,* pp. 93, 107-8, 124-25.

that year when the committee took up "a substantial love offering for him and his team at the closing service." Newspapers ran side-by-side photos of ushers with bags of money and a smiling Graham. On the advice of Jesse Bader of the National Council of Churches, Graham and his team went on fixed salaries and never again accepted an honorarium for crusades. Furthermore, through BGEA he was able to finance wide-ranging ministries in radio, film, magazine and book publishing, the television program *Hour of Decision,* and a pavilion at the 1964-1965 New York World's Fair. Purchase of an office building and the hiring of staff (eighty employees by 1954) made it possible to manage a vast direct-mail operation that generated income far beyond what could be collected in an arena or stadium. The financial strength of BGEA also made it possible for Graham to tour parts of the world untouched by large-scale evangelistic efforts. The Graham organization covered all expenses of the team, leaving committees only with local costs, which in Third World nations were often met with volunteer labor. In addition to millions of individual contributions, Graham, like most of his predecessors, sought and received substantial donations from wealthy patrons for special projects. Controversial right-wing oil-rich industrialist Russell Maguire gave him $75,000 to begin the film ministry; J. Howard Pew of Sun Oil pledged $150,000 to guarantee the start-up of *Christianity Today* and $100,000 to begin the television ministry on ABC (which was not needed because of viewer donations); and a veritable Who's Who of the New York City financial establishment "found it relatively easy to raise a large portion of the projected $600,000 budget" for the massive 1957 Madison Square Garden crusade, sponsored by the Protestant Council of New York. Several of the key New York City families had supported Finney, Moody, and Sunday before Graham.[28]

Billy and Ruth Graham are certainly well off financially but no one would accuse them or any on the BGEA team of living in luxury. The only real hint of impropriety within the organization came in 1987, the year of Jim and Tammy Bakker's fall. It appeared that the Bennett agency, which had always handled Graham's media work, was profiting unfairly from some of its business arrangements. The fact that Graham's daughter Bunny had married into the Dienert family which ran the agency, and that the Dienerts were known for their aristocratic tastes, cast a poor light on Graham and BGEA. As always with Billy Graham, steps were quickly taken to insure that his min-

28. Martin, *Prophet with Honor,* pp. 134-41, 212-15, 225-26, 231, 405.

istry would continue scandal-free. This, of course, was not true of all evangelists in the 1970s and 1980s. The Bakkers' PTL empire, including the television program and Heritage USA theme park, took the gospel of wealth and entertainment that had found a home in pentecostalism to the extreme; thousands of people were bilked out of millions of dollars. The high cost of television made the regular appeal for funds more important than ever. When Jimmy Swaggart's sexual conduct was reported to the Assemblies of God and made public, it was announced that his ministry lost $200,000 a day for a month. Oral Roberts has often been criticized for pleading for money for a worthy project and then using it to plug the holes in some other aspect of his ministry. The model of financial accountability that Dwight L. Moody and Billy Graham sought to exemplify remained at odds with the temptation to profit from the celebrity status evangelists have enjoyed since the days of George Whitefield.[29]

Billy Graham told an International Conference for Itinerant Evangelists that they "need to be transparently honest" in their financial management. The Graham organization, World Vision's Stanley Mooneyham, and others in 1979 established the Evangelical Council for Financial Accountability (ECFA) to help ministries achieve this goal by opening their books to the public and adhering to a set of standards. In the words of a *Christianity Today (CT)* editorial, the time had come to counter long-standing complaints that religious ministries are run by con men who are "just in it for the money." They were also paying attention to Senator Mark Hatfield's admonition that regulation was necessary — and "if you don't do it, Congress will." Evangelistic ministries, *CT* stated, "can now prove to the public that they have nothing to hide." The fact that ECFA failed to detect the criminal behavior of PTL, a member from 1978 to 1986, did not detract from the importance of its standards for the management of evangelism. As Tom Berg's article in this volume shows, ECFA played a major role in the resolution of the early 1990s New Era scandal. In the late 1990s, Promise Keepers leaders emphasized that they were working with ECFA in that organization's struggle to continue its work on the massive scale it had achieved. The combination of astronomic operating costs in the electronic

---

29. Martin, *Prophet with Honor*, pp. 556-58. Randy Frame, "$8 Million Worth of Unanswered Questions"; "PTL: A Year After the Fall"; "More Trouble on the Broadcast Front," *Christianity Today*, 18 Mar. 1988, pp. 36-38, 44-47. See also Steve Bruce, *Pray TV: Televangelism in America* (London: Routledge, 1990), and Carol Flake, *Redemptorama: Culture, Politics, and the New Evangelicalism* (New York: Anchor Press/Doubleday, 1984).

age and high-profile scandals related to the abuse of power, sex, and money have brought matters of ethical responsibility to the front burner for evangelists and evangelistic ministries.[30]

No critic of Promise Keepers has had grounds to accuse its leaders of financial malfeasance. But opponents on the religious and political left point with great concern to the high level of support from wealthy, politically savvy power-brokers of the Christian Right, insinuating that the Promise Keepers revival is a Trojan horse for right-wing politics. Critics of Promise Keepers on the extreme fundamentalist right, on the other hand, denounce the ministry for its broadly evangelical ecumenism, and some are perhaps uncomfortable with its witness for racial reconciliation. Those who have experienced blessings through their participation in the Promise Keepers revival, meanwhile, began receiving a steady barrage of mail pleading for regular contributions. They had to adjust to the image of Coach Mac begging for offerings as if he were just another televangelist. Promise Keepers had seemed to many of them to be above all of that, although fund-raising and teaching the importance of Christian giving had been part of PK from the start. Historically, evangelists who engaged most successfully, and perhaps most faithfully, in big-time revival ministries in America found ways of soliciting operating funds from wealthy patrons and masses of believers in a dignified manner, without the appearance of avarice, with the focus on Jesus Christ and evangelical social institutions that were thought to advance his kingdom. It has never been easy, however, to separate the personality of the evangelist from the plea for money, or to separate the politics of patrons from the management of the ministry. It now seems likely that the days of the large-scale evangelistic meeting are far from over. The revival tradition, which some saw as having "run its course" before the 1940s, is still deeply rooted in American culture at the dawn of the twenty-first century. If this is true, then the tensions between serving God and the need for mammon — between preaching the gospel and fitting into the commercial culture, between the call to "do the work of an evangelist" and the impulse to seek out friendships with business leaders — will continue to characterize those ministries that come after Promise Keepers.

30. Billy Graham, *A Biblical Standard for Evangelists* (Minneapolis: Worldwide Publications, 1984), p. 91. "Accountability in Fund Raising," *Christianity Today*, 6 Apr. 1979, pp. 10, 48. "Cleaning House: ECFA Expels Members," *Christianity Today*, 7 Oct. 1988, pp. 44-45. "Fund Raising Ethics: ECFA Celebrates Ten Years," *Christianity Today*, 20 Oct. 1989, p. 44.

CHAPTER 4

More Money, More Ministry: The Financing of American Evangelicalism Since 1945

MICHAEL S. HAMILTON

But who am I, and who are my people, that we should be able to give as generously as this? Everything comes from you, and we have given you only what comes from your hand.

I CHRONICLES 29:14 (NIV)

When John F. Walvoord took on financial responsibility for Dallas Theological Seminary in 1945, he had a big job on his hands. The seminary was deeply in debt, including unpaid salaries amounting to more than two years of the school's budget. Yet many of the seminary's leaders had a strong aversion to an active fund-raising program. Walvoord remembers, "The theory was that if we were worthy and were faithful in prayer, no fund-raising activity would be necessary."[1]

---

1. John F. Walvoord, "Guidelines for Organizations to Develop a Christian Philosophy of Fund-Raising," in *Money for Ministries,* ed. Wesley K. Willmer (Wheaton, IL: Victor/Scripture Press, 1989), p. 107 [106-16].

Unless otherwise noted, founding dates and annual budgets for evangelical parachurch organizations are taken from Evangelical Council for Financial Accountability, *Member Profile Directory* (Washington, DC: ECFA, Jan. 1998).

This sentiment is immediately recognizable to anyone who grew up in evangelicalism (but undoubtedly mystifying to anyone who did not). It had its origins in the prayer philosophy of George Müller. After converting to evangelical Christianity, Müller emigrated from his native Germany to England, where in 1835 he established an orphanage. His primary reason for doing so was not, oddly enough, to care for orphans. It was, rather, to establish a visible proof — to weaker Christians and to unbelievers — that God was alive and would sustain those who depended upon him solely by praying for their needs. Müller's method for relying entirely upon God was never to speak of the orphanage's current needs, even if asked, and never to incur debt. He was, however, an aggressive publicist. For fifty years he wrote copiously and traveled widely, telling Christian groups about the way God had always provided for the orphanage through answered prayer — frequently in dramatic, nail-biting, last-minute fashion.

Müller's ideas were taken up by two British missionaries, J. Hudson Taylor and Amy Carmichael, and all three became extraordinarily famous and admired in American evangelical circles.[2] In short order many North American evangelical institution-builders also adopted Müller's practices. Between 1880 and 1940 several organizations — most notably foreign mission agencies such as the Africa Inland Mission (1895) and the Latin America Mission (1921) — were founded on these "faith" principles. They resolved never to take on debt and never to ask directly for funds, in order to prove God's existence to an unbelieving world.[3]

It was not long, however, before these voluntary principles hardened into *de facto* regulations. By the early part of the century a large segment of the evangelical public not only admired those organizational leaders who relied solely on prayer; many had come to believe that it was morally wrong for a ministry organization to make its needs known or to ask directly for money. W. Cameron Townsend, founder of Wycliffe Bible Translators (1934), once asked one of his large contributors when it was acceptable to go beyond prayer and ask people directly for help. The contributor

2. Elisabeth Elliot, *A Chance to Die: The Life and Legacy of Amy Carmichael* (Old Tappan, NJ: Fleming H. Revell, Co., 1987), p. 153.

3. Richard Ostrander, "The Life of Prayer in a World of Science: Protestants, Prayer, and American Culture, 1870-1930" (Ph.D. diss., University of Notre Dame, 1996). On the Latin America Mission, see Elisabeth Elliot, *Who Shall Ascend: The Life of R. Kenneth Strachan of Costa Rica* (New York: Harper and Row, 1968), pp. 90-91.

replied: never.[4] This was the obstacle Walvoord encountered at Dallas Seminary.

However, despite the popular mythology that evangelical institutions were built solely on prayer, Müller's "faith" model was not the only example parachurch ministries inherited from the nineteenth century.[5] The other was the entrepreneurial model that Dwight L. Moody pioneered just after the Civil War. Being a lifelong layman, Moody was a product not of the seminary but of the marketplace. What is most noteworthy about this is *not* that he attracted the support of businessmen — seminary-trained ministers had been doing this for decades. Nor is it unusual that he used business methods of organizing religious activities — the connections between market techniques and religious enterprises run in both directions and go back at least to the period of the Early Republic.[6] The pioneering characteristic of Moody the businessman is that he was, in every respect of the word, an entrepreneur. He developed a vision for innovative methods of evangelization, laid plans to carry out the vision, and then sold the vision to backers and workers. He thus marshaled resources, financial and human, into independent organizations that would produce the religious product — be it education, publications, or revivals — that would embody the vision. Like Müller and those who imitated him, Moody avoided debt and plowed publication royalties back into his enterprises. But unlike Müller, Moody was bold as the winter wind when it came to asking for money. He regularly and enthusiastically buttonholed America's corporate barons to ask for large gifts, and spent much of his time personally signing thousands of typed "begging letters" sent to potential supporters.[7]

Both the faith model and the entrepreneurial model had their backers in the first half of the new century, but the faith model possessed the

4. Paul Fischer to W. Cameron Townsend, 10 Nov. 1945, Townsend Archives #904041, JAARS Center, Waxhaw, NC. (Thanks to William Svelmoe for this reference.)

5. Parachurch ministry organizations are independent, nondenominational, special purpose, nonprofit corporations organized to do particular kinds of religious work such as evangelism, foreign missions, international development, broadcasting, publishing, education, and so forth. Parachurch organizations are the institutional backbone of North American evangelicalism.

6. R. Laurence Moore, *Selling God: American Religion in the Marketplace of Culture* (New York: Oxford University Press, 1994).

7. J. C. Pollack, *Moody: A Biographical Portrait of an Evangelist* (New York: Macmillan, 1963), pp. 296-98.

presumption of higher spirituality. Charles Blanchard, the long-time president of Wheaton College who spent most of his adult life asking for money, once described his methods as spiritually inferior to those of Müller and Taylor. Said Blanchard, "God did not give me that faith."[8] Thirty years later, John Walvoord also personally struggled against this presumption before finally admitting that the faith model simply was not working for Dallas Seminary. He persuaded the leadership to begin communicating the school's needs to the constituency, and "after sending out a letter approximately every six weeks for several months, the flow of income for the first time in the history of the organization began to equal its budget." The seminary was never again substantially underfunded.[9]

As it turned out, most evangelical organizations would soon cast aside Müller in favor of Moody. A postwar economic boom remade North America: in the U.S. between 1945 and 1993, annual per capita disposable income (in constant 1987 dollars) climbed from $8,281 to $14,569.[10] In the process, American evangelicalism was remade along with it as the leaders of evangelical organizations scrambled to lay claim to as much of the new American wealth as they could. Only echoes of the faith model now survive, and those usually in smaller organizations. Since 1945 the entrepreneurial model has prevailed, and even the symbolic remnants of the faith ideology are fast disappearing. For instance, the Sudan Interior Mission (1893; now SIM International) recently changed its corporate slogan from "By Prayer" to "People . . . Reaching People . . . Reaching Others." It must be remembered that evangelicals first adopted faith principles as a way to demonstrate God's presence and power, not because faith principles were an especially efficient way to raise money. Since World War II, evangelical entrepreneurs have shown less interest in proving God's existence through their fund-raising strategies than in growing their ministries. Increasingly, ministry leaders came to feel handcuffed by faith principles, which seemed to place arbitrary limits on the amount of money they could raise. The mindset now locked into place in the evangelical parachurch world is the assumption that "more net income . . . translate[s] directly into more min-

---

8. Frances Carothers Blanchard, *The Life of Charles Albert Blanchard* (New York: Fleming H. Revell, 1932), p. 114.

9. Walvoord, "Guidelines for Organizations," pp. 107-8.

10. Calculated from data in John L. and Sylvia Ronsvalle, *The State of Church Giving through 1993* (Champaign, IL: Empty Tomb, 1995), p. 123 (Appendix C). The Ronsvalles' data was taken from figures published by the U.S. Bureau of Economic Analysis.

istry."[11] This essay explores how American evangelicals have, since 1945, gathered the money they needed to do more ministry.

The Structure of American Evangelicalism

As an entity, evangelicalism itself can be conceived at three different levels: the individual, the denominational, and its existence as an interdenominational movement. Employing each of these three angles of view yields complementary insights into how evangelicals have financed themselves. Each angle of vision is helpful in certain ways; each also has limitations.

One conception is thinking of evangelicals as individuals who share certain beliefs and experiences, such as belief in the authority of the Bible and the necessity of salvation through faith in Jesus Christ, and the experience of individual conversion to Christianity as the starting place of the Christian life.[12] Here pollsters can be the most help, and since 1976 they have found that perhaps one-third of all adult Americans describe themselves as "born-again" Christians. This conception, however, comes with at least two problems. The first is that it includes large numbers of people whose ecclesiastical affiliations would normally be considered outside the pale of evangelicalism, notably Roman Catholics and Mormons. The second problem is that it excludes large numbers of people whose basic theological beliefs are very similar to those of most "born-again" Christians, but who would never apply the born-again label to themselves. This is especially true of Protestants from confessional traditions like Lutheranism and Calvinism. The one-third figure may still be useful, however, for the two problem groups noted here may roughly cancel each other out. Unfortunately, pollsters only began asking people if they are born-again after Jimmy Carter was elected president in 1976, so we have no data on how

11. Lars B. Dunberg, President of the International Bible Society, quoted in an advertisement for The Raymond Group, evangelical fund-raising consultants, in Mark Ward, Sr., ed., *National Religious Broadcasters Directory of Religious Media 1995*, 17th ed. (Manassas, VA: National Religious Broadcasters, 1995), p. 27.

12. For this type of definition from social scientists, see John C. Green, James L. Guth, Corwin E. Smidt, and Lyman A. Kellstedt, *Religion and the Culture Wars: Dispatches from the Front* (Lanham, MD: Rowman and Littlefield, 1996), p. 194; from a historian, see David Bebbington, *Evangelicalism in Modern Britain: A History from the 1730s to the 1980s* (1989; Grand Rapids: Baker, 1991), pp. 5-17.

many Americans would have described themselves as born-again back in the late 1940s.[13]

A second way to conceive evangelicalism is to divide American denominations into two groups, evangelical and non-evangelical, based on the denominations' official theological posture. In this sense the denominations classified as "evangelical" are those that have insisted on maintaining non-pluralistic theological environments that are consistent with traditional Protestant beliefs about the authority of the Bible and the doctrine of salvation by grace through faith in Christ. Therefore denominations as diverse as the Assemblies of God, the Association of Vineyard Churches, the Christian Reformed Church, the Church of God in Christ, the Church of the Nazarene, the Churches of Christ, the Independent Fundamentalist Churches of America, Lutheran Church–Missouri Synod, the Mennonite Church, the Seventh-Day Adventist Church, and the Southern Baptist Convention would usually be counted as evangelical. Excluded from this definition would be non-Protestant groups like the Roman Catholic Church and the eastern Orthodox churches, heterodox groups such as the Mormons and Jehovah's Witnesses, and Protestant denominations like the American Baptist Convention and the United Methodist Church that have taken the path of theological pluralism.

The problem with this approach is that some large denominations include substantial numbers of congregations that differ from the "official" orientation. The "evangelical" Southern Baptist Convention, for example, includes many churches and individuals that practice theological pluralism, while the "pluralist" American Baptist Convention includes many churches and individuals that are very traditional in their theology. This means that many of the people who would self-identify as "born-again Christians" attend churches in pluralist denominations, and many people who attend churches in evangelical denominations would never self-identify as "born again."

The advantage of this definition is that denominational statistics can be used to track, in a very rough and approximate way, changes in the fortunes of evangelicalism so conceived. Using these figures, a number of interpreters have argued that the percentage of church members belonging

13. George Gallup, Jr., and Jim Castelli, *The People's Religion: American Faith in the 90's* (New York: Macmillan, 1989), pp. 92-93; George Barna, *The Mind of the Donor* (Glendale, CA: Barna Research Group, 1994), pp. 48-49.

to evangelical denominations has slowly but steadily grown throughout the twentieth century, while the percentage belonging to pluralistic Protestant denominations has declined.[14] It appears that around 1985 evangelical denominations for the first time increased their market share of non-Catholic Christian church members to approximately half, up from perhaps one-third in 1945.[15] During approximately the same period church membership (both Protestant and Catholic) as a percentage of population declined from 75 percent to 68 percent, but most of the loss came in the Catholic sector. Meanwhile, church attendance figures have remained stable.[16] This evidence suggests that the aggregate growth rate of evangelical denominations has been faster than the rate of population growth.

Thirdly, evangelicalism can be conceived as an intentionally transdenominational movement that exhibits a certain pattern of beliefs and behaviors. The theological beliefs are similar to those of evangelical denominations as outlined above, but shorn of denominational particularities (such as mode of baptism) and cultural distinctions (such as ethnic origin). The most prominent behavior is that of developing independent special-purpose "parachurch" organizations that employ an enormous range of strategies to convert people to Christianity, enliven the spiritually dormant, and nurture deeper commitments in the already-persuaded.[17] These

14. Dean M. Kelley, *Why Conservative Churches Are Growing* (San Francisco: Harper and Row, 1972 [rev. ed. 1977]); William R. Hutchison, "Past Imperfect: History and the Prospect for Liberalism," in *Liberal Protestantism: Realities and Possibilities*, ed. Robert S. Michaelsen and Wade Clark Roof (New York: Pilgrim Press, 1986), p. 71; Roger Finke and Rodney Stark, *The Churching of America: Winners and Losers in Our Religious Economy* (New Brunswick, NJ: Rutgers University Press, 1992), pp. 237-75; Dean R. Hoge, Benton Johnson, and Donald A. Luidens, *Vanishing Boundaries: The Religion of Mainline Protestant Baby Boomers* (Louisville: Westminster/John Knox Press, 1994), pp. 175-202; and Joel A. Carpenter, *Revive Us Again: The Reawakening of American Fundamentalism* (New York: Oxford University Press, 1997), pp. 31-32. For the argument (using the same sort of statistics and assumptions) that this trend might be changing, see James Davison Hunter, *Evangelicalism: The Coming Generation* (Chicago: University of Chicago Press, 1987), pp. 203-6, 276n.2.

15. Hutchison, "Past Imperfect," p. 71.

16. Gallup, Jr., and Castelli, *The People's Religion*, pp. 29-31. (Figures on percentage of church members are from 1944 and 1984.) In Gallup, Jr., and Castelli, church membership figures come from self-identification; in Hutchison, "Past Imperfect" (see previous note), figures come from denominational reports.

17. Bebbington, *Evangelicalism in Modern Britain*, pp. 2-17; Carpenter, *Revive Us Again*, pp. 13-32.

parachurch groups all employ people from a wide variety of denominations and promulgate a version of Christianity free of denominational distinctives.

The main problem with this conception is that it excludes substantial numbers of people who would be defined as evangelicals under the first two conceptions. Throughout the record of the twentieth century one can find two kinds of Protestants trying to fend off transdenominational evangelicalism. Protestant pluralists dislike the movement's evangelical theology. Leaders who are theologically evangelical, but whose primary loyalties lie with their own denominational or ethnic tradition (such as Southern Baptists or Dutch Calvinists) dislike the movement's interdenominationalism. Both pluralists and evangelical denominationalists see independent evangelicalism as a threat, undercutting their doctrinal orientation and poaching on their membership. However, several evangelical denominations — the Assemblies of God and the Evangelical Free Church, for example — coexist fairly comfortably with the interdenominational parachurch networks. People connected to the interdenominational movement typically attend local churches affiliated with denominations (both evangelical and non-evangelical), but outside the local church their primary loyalties usually attach to the interdenominational movement and its parachurch organizations. Transdenominational evangelicalism is, in fact, the American form of grass-roots ecumenism. These evangelicals tend to regard denominational particularities as personal preferences that are more or less irrelevant to the task of spreading and nurturing a lively Christian faith.[18]

In the political economy of American religion, denominations are organized like governments. Just as governments are generally exclusive in granting citizenship, denominations are mutually exclusive in their conception of membership. It is quite rare, and not at all encouraged, for any individual or congregation to belong to more than one denomination. In part because governments are mutually exclusive, their internal logic generally pushes them to become centralized providers of a comprehensive range of services for their citizens. Likewise, denominations are usually or-

18. For a parallel discussion, with somewhat different emphases, on various ways to define evangelicalism, see George Marsden, "The Evangelical Denomination," in *Evangelicalism and Modern America,* ed. George Marsden (Grand Rapids: Eerdmans, 1984), pp. vii-xix.

ganized to attempt to provide a wide range of basic religious services to their members, from evangelism programs to education to church management assistance. And finally, just as governments seek basic financial support through compulsory levies on the citizenry, so too denominations have traditionally built their financial structure on a foundation of congregational levies.[19]

The interdenominational parachurch organizations, on the other hand, are organized like businesses. One does not belong to a missionary agency or outreach ministry in the way that one belongs to a church. Just as any citizen of a nation might patronize several businesses, so too any individual member of a church might participate in the activities of, or support financially, several parachurch agencies. The parachurch organizations attract participants and support just as businesses attract customers — by producing and marketing goods and services (in this case, the services are usually particular kinds of ministry activities aimed at particular groups of people). Entrepreneurial personalities — usually laypeople — identify ministry needs, devise programs to meet those needs, and then formulate strategies for publicizing their programs. The object of publicity is to attract support — donations, sales, or workers — that will permit implementation and expansion of the programs. Unlike denominations, but like businesses, parachurch agencies do not attempt to develop a comprehensive range of services from a centrally planned and organized source. Instead each parachurch corporation, in its initial stages, focuses on one very particular task. If it is successful in attracting support for this task, it will often diversify into other areas of ministry, just as successful businesses will often diversify into new markets. The unspoken assumption underlying the parachurch system is that market mechanisms (activated by

19. The generalizations about comprehensive services and congregational levies probably apply more to older denominations than newer ones, more to larger denominations than smaller ones, more to pluralist denominations than evangelical ones, and more to hierarchical denominations than those stressing congregational autonomy. One recent survey of 31 (out of 220) denominations found that 36 percent of respondent denominations levied required assessments upon their congregations, while 56 percent depended on voluntary contributions of congregations. However, most respondents to this survey were small evangelical denominations, which are less likely to make rules requiring financial support. See J. David Schmidt, *Choosing to Live: Financing the Future of Religious Body Headquarters* (Milwaukee: Christian Stewardship Association, 1996), pp. 34, 127. Grassroots commitment to denominations is, however, fading, and as a result denominations are becoming less like governing bodies and more like parachurch service organizations.

an army of potential entrepreneurs who abhor an evangelical vacuum) rather than central planning will provide a sufficiently wide range of religious goods and services to meet everyone's needs.

Financing American Evangelicalism since 1945

All three ways of conceiving evangelicalism are important when thinking about how evangelicalism is financed. Most funds for evangelical denominations and organizations come from individuals and churches, rather than corporations, foundations, or the government. Individuals who participate in the economic life of evangelicalism cover a broad spectrum. They may be members and regular attenders of, or they may have little or no connection to, local churches. The local churches might be part of evangelical denominations, part of pluralist denominations, or completely independent. Local churches from all three categories often serve as conduits of publicity, funds, workers, and participants for parachurch groups. Individuals also establish their own connections, independent of local churches, with parachurch groups; and parachurch groups also function as conduits of information for each other.

In regard to evangelical organizations, it might be helpful to distinguish between three types of financing. *Denominational funding* is built upon a base of local churches that have a common history and are like-minded regarding theology and polity. The local churches typically raise money to fund both their own activities and the denomination's activities, some of which come back to the local churches in the form of services, and some of which are expended in outreach. As for parachurch organizations, there are two main general categories of funding. *Charitable funding* is the collection of funds from one set of individuals, churches, foundations, corporations, or the government in order to provide goods or services to others. Overseas mission agencies are the classic example — American evangelicals donate money to support programs to spread the gospel, plant churches, and provide humanitarian aid in other countries. *Commercial funding* is the collection of funds from the individuals or churches who receive the goods or services. Here a clear example would be the individual who purchases something from a Christian bookstore for his or her own use.[20]

20. A fourth source of funds is not very important at all to the movement as a

In fact, most parachurch organizations raise funds through some combination of charitable and commercial methods, so it is most helpful to imagine a long continuum between the two ideal types. Wycliffe Bible Translators is near the charitable end of the continuum. It raised $89.1 million in contributions for 1996 — 95 percent of its total income — and only $1 million through services it provided for payment by the user. By contrast, evangelical liberal arts colleges are near the commercial end of the continuum. The average evangelical college raises 86 percent of its income through commercial sources — 72 percent through tuition and 14 percent through fees for auxiliary services — and only 12 percent through gift income. Evangelical radio stations vary a great deal, but on average they are somewhere in the middle of the continuum, with their income roughly split between donations and sales (of commercials, program time, and miscellaneous products).[21]

Individuals and Their Finances

In 1970 Americans donated $16 billion to nonprofit organizations of different kinds; by 1992, the figure had climbed to $105 billion. This increase of 556 percent outstripped the increases (over the same period of time) in Gross Domestic Product, personal income, and personal consumption expenditures. More than half of this donated money goes to religious organizations — mostly to local churches and synagogues.[22] One study found that during 1993, some 73 percent of all American households donated money to a nonprofit, with women slightly more likely to do so than men. Of those households that donated, 21 percent gave money only to religious organizations, 33 percent gave money only to other kinds of non-

---

whole, but in individual cases the amounts may be substantial. This is *investment income*, which may include endowments, short-term financial instruments, and sales of appreciated assets.

21. Wycliffe figures are from their annual statement for 1996. Evangelical college figures are from Wesley K. Willmer, ed., *Advancing Christian Higher Education: A Guide to Effective Resource Development* (Washington, DC: Coalition for Christian Colleges and Universities, 1996), p. 2. Radio station figures are from David W. Clark and Paul H. Virts, *Changing Channels: A Guide to Financing Christian Broadcast Ministries* (Milwaukee: Christian Stewardship Association, 1996), pp. 15-16.

22. Barna, *The Mind of the Donor*, p. 1.

profit organizations, and 47 percent supported both religious organizations and other kinds of nonprofits.[23] Another study done about the same time found that evangelicals tend to give a larger-than-average percent of their household income to nonprofit organizations. In fact, 80 percent of all Americans who donated 10 percent or more of their income to nonprofits were found among the 36 percent of Americans who claimed to be born-again Christians.[24]

The documented tendency of evangelicals to give away larger percentages of their income than the average American is reflected in the teachings of prominent evangelical financial advisors. They all insist that Christians have a fundamental obligation to give generously to religious and humanitarian causes. Yet beyond this agreed-upon point, the advice varies wildly. At one end of the spectrum, a good many high-profile independent preachers associated with the Pentecostal or charismatic sectors of evangelicalism — Oral Roberts, Kenneth Copeland, Frederick Price, Ernest Angely — insist that God will reward a generous giver with yet greater financial return in this life.[25] Such teachings are transparently self-serving, for general exhortations to give liberally are soon followed by pleas to give to that preacher's own ministry. But this concept of giving-money-to-get-even-more-money does have a certain appeal, typically to people who would, frankly, like to have more money. Two groups are especially drawn to the prosperity gospel. The first is the poor, who often believe that betting on God's generosity is more likely to pay off than betting on, say, government lottery tickets. The prosperity gospel also appeals to

---

23. Virginia A. Hodgkinson, Murray S. Weitzman, et al., *Giving and Volunteering in the United States: Findings from a National Survey, 1994 Edition* (Washington, DC: Independent Sector, 1994). Figures on total giving, and giving by gender, are on p. 39. Figures on giving by type of recipient organization are calculated from those on p. 35.

24. Barna, *Mind of the Donor*, pp. 49, 56. Barna defined born-again Christians as those who have "made a personal commitment to Jesus Christ that is still important in their lives today and who believe that when they die they will go heaven because they have confessed their sins to God and have accepted Jesus Christ as their savior" (48-49). Figures on donations as a percentage of income are not based solely on self-reporting (which tends to overstate the amount donated), but are corrected by data from the Internal Revenue Service.

25. This teaching goes back to E. W. Kenyon (1867-1948), who fused New Thought philosophy and Keswick "higher-life" holiness ideas into the system of thought that underlies the contemporary prosperity gospel. See Dale H. Simmons, *E. W. Kenyon and the Postbellum Pursuit of Peace, Power, and Plenty* (Lanham, MD: Scarecrow, 1997).

many of the entrepreneurial-minded in the middle classes who are working hard to scramble up the prosperity ladder. These are people who are willing to make higher-risk investments that have the potential for high payoffs. It would be a mistake, however, to assume that either of these groups embrace the prosperity gospel purely for their own gain. Nearly all of them give money also because they want to support the work of Christian organizations.

At the other end of the spectrum are the evangelicals who advocate renunciation of wealth, such as Ron Sider and Jim Wallis. Wallis urges people to make themselves poor and then live with the poor. Sider urges people to simplify their lifestyles and give away increasing percentages of their money as their income exceeds basic living needs.[26] These ideas tend to appeal to middle-class evangelicals who have well-developed sympathies for the poor. The two most typical groups would be idealistic younger evangelicals, who have not yet become dependent upon creature comforts, and a few among the well-educated who are troubled by the difficulty of reconciling middle-class materialism with the teachings of Jesus.

In the middle of the spectrum, and probably having more popular influence than the other two views put together, are the money management teachings of financial planners like Larry Burkett and Ron Blue.[27] Their teachings do not differ in kind from the advice that any sensible contemporary personal financial manager, such as Sylvia Porter, would give. They counsel drawing up a financial plan, avoiding excessive debt, and making safe and prudent investments to achieve financial goals. The theoretical foundation of these books is explicitly Christian, and so they look a bit different from secular advice literature. Burkett, for example, insists in

26. Ronald J. Sider, *Rich Christians in an Age of Hunger: A Biblical Study* (Downers Grove, IL: InterVarsity Press, 1977), pp. 170-88. (Revised and reissued as *Rich Christians in an Age of Hunger: Moving from Affluence to Generosity*, 20th anniversary ed. [Nashville: Word, 1997]). Jim Wallis, *Revive Us Again: A Sojourner's Story* (Nashville: Abingdon, 1983), pp. 185-92.

27. Burkett's breakthrough book was *Your Finances in Changing Times* (Chicago: Moody Press, 1975). After his first book's success he quit his job to found his own non-profit financial advice ministry, Christian Financial Concepts, and other books began flowing off the presses. His first book was later reprinted by the Billy Graham Evangelistic Association with a foreword by Graham. Ron Blue's best-known book is *Master Your Money: A Step-By-Step Plan for Financial Freedom* (Nashville: Thomas Nelson, 1986); the revised editions (1991 and 1997) carry the front-cover imprimatur of Charles R. Swindoll.

strong language that every Christian must surrender ownership of all assets to God. This surrender, however, is entirely mental, for he advocates no physical or legal changes in asset ownership. The only practical differences between the evangelical and secular financial advisers are in the evangelicals' slightly lower tolerance of debt, and in their view that Christians are obligated to tithe (that is, to give 10 percent of their income to religious and charitable causes).

Evangelical Denominations and Their Finances

It would be difficult to come up with a responsible estimate of the total annual income of "evangelical" denominations, but some samples have produced helpful relative data. The financial fortunes of evangelical denominations, as compared to those of "pluralist" denominations, seem consistent with the data on the giving patterns of evangelical individuals. John and Sylvia Ronsvalle's study of giving patterns in eight evangelical denominations and eight pluralist denominations compared average giving levels in 1968 and 1993, with all amounts corrected for inflation. They found that in 1968 the members of evangelical churches each gave to their churches, on average, $608 per year. Meanwhile their pluralist brothers and sisters gave $329 apiece each year. By 1993 the gap had narrowed somewhat, but it was still wide — the average evangelical gave $622; the average pluralist, $433. During this period the membership of the eight evangelical denominations increased by 51 percent. Total giving kept pace, increasing by 54 percent during the same period. By comparison, in the eight pluralist denominations, increased giving per member barely offset steep membership declines. Membership declined 23 percent, while total giving remained stable, increasing by 1 percent.[28]

28. Ronsvalle and Ronsvalle, *The State of Church Giving through 1993*, pp. 29, 31. Figures, in constant 1987 dollars, and are rounded to the nearest dollar. This study also purported to measure giving as a percentage of income, but the income figure used was merely average per capita disposable income for all Americans, not the average income for members of those denominations. Therefore the "percentage of income" figure is not a true figure, nor does it take into account the likelihood that true per capita income figures for members of evangelical denominations would differ both from the figures for members of pluralist denominations and from the national averages. Another limitation of this study is that the figures measure only giving to the local church and the denomi-

Evangelical Parachurch Organizations and Their Finances

The most striking area of evangelical growth has been in its network of parachurch organizations. To give a better idea of the range of these organizations, it is useful to consider them within certain broad categories.

International Concerns/Foreign Missions

In 1953, U.S. and Canadian Protestant mission agencies sent out over 18,000 overseas "career" personnel, less than half of whom were sent by evangelical agencies (independent and denominational). By 1980, North American agencies had over 35,000 overseas "career" personnel, over 90 percent of them sent by evangelical agencies.[29] By 1988, the total number from the U.S. alone had increased to 36,600. In addition to the increase in career personnel, a new phenomenon — that of short-term missionaries — has changed the face of North American overseas ministry activities. By 1988 an additional 11,900 Americans were serving abroad on terms ranging from two to forty-eight months.[30] A second noteworthy phenomenon has been a subtle but discernible shift in the focus of the activities of evangelical overseas ministry groups toward humanitarian activities. In the early 1950s, virtually all emphasis was on evangelization, church planting, and discipleship. However, by 1998 six of the seven largest parachurch mission agencies were World Vision (founded 1950, annual revenues $304 million), Larry Jones International Ministries/Feed the Children (1964, $128 million), MAP International (1954, $85 million), Compassion International (1952, $69 million), Food for the Hungry (1971, $53 million), and Christian Aid Ministries (1981, $43 million). All have been founded since 1945, and all make relief, development, education, and health care their primary focus, with evangelism a secondary concern. Of the seven largest agencies, only Wycliffe Bible Translators (1934, around $100 million) retains a primary focus on religious work, but even at Wycliffe its work in literacy and anthro-

---

nation. However, these same people were also giving money to parachurch organizations, though we have no idea how much, nor the extent of differences in such giving between members of evangelical and pluralist denominations.

29. Robert Coote, "The Uneven Growth of Conservative Evangelical Missions," *International Bulletin of Missionary Research* 6 (July 1982): 120.

30. John A. Siewert and John A. Kenyon, *Mission Handbook*, 15th ed. (Monrovia, CA: MARC, 1993-95), p. 59.

pology have considerably broadened its activities since 1945.[31] In 1992, total U.S. income for all categories of Protestant overseas ministry activities reached more than $2.27 billion. Over half of this (perhaps $1.16 billion) was raised by interdenominational evangelical agencies, and over one-third (perhaps $760 million) was raised by evangelical denominations, meaning that evangelicals raised some $1.92 billion for missions and international concerns. Pluralist denominations and the independent agencies associated with them raised less than one-sixth (perhaps $350 million) of the total.[32]

Domestic Outreach Ministries

Statisticians keep good track of foreign missionary agencies; not so with domestic outreach organizations. A recent survey found 1,025 such organizations, so we know there are at least that many. This study included groups that engage in evangelism, prison ministry, home missions, youth and campus ministries, certain kinds of educational activity, and distribution of Bibles and religious literature.[33] Given that there are at least 30,000 evangelical parachurch groups in all, it is likely that the numbers in this category are much, much higher.

The largest outreach groups are familiar to most evangelicals. Some of these are Campus Crusade for Christ (1953, $241 million), Billy Graham Evangelistic Association (1950, $124 million), Promise Keepers (1990, $117

---

31. Revenue figures are 1996 data from "The Philanthropy 400," *Chronicle of Philanthropy* 10, no. 2 (1997): 1, 32-48; founding dates and primary activities are from Siewert and Kenyon, *Mission Handbook*, pp. 83-244. One large agency for which there are no good figures is Youth With A Mission (YWAM), which is mainly devoted to evangelism (although its single largest division may be Mercy Ships, which is primarily a relief ministry). The agency is so decentralized, not even their own research division knows their aggregate revenues. Based on numbers of personnel and revenue estimates from the 1980s, I estimate that total YWAM revenues might be in the neighborhood of $40 million, but they could be as low as $30 million or as high as $60 million.

32. Figures calculated from Siewert and Kenyon, *Mission Handbook*, pp. 64-67 and 83-244.

33. Tom McCabe, ed., with Bruce Campbell, *Inside Outreach: A Guide to Financing Christian Outreach Ministries* (Milwaukee: CSA, 1996), p. 91. Unfortunately, the response rate was so low, and the internal diversity of the survey group so high, that reliable generalizations from this particular study remain elusive. In fact, some of the groups surveyed might possibly be more accurately categorized as social service ministries.

million), Young Life (1940, $79 million), The Navigators (1933, $77 million), InterVarsity Christian Fellowship (1919, $33 million), Fellowship of Christian Athletes (1954, $26 million), and the International Bible Society (1809, $26 million). Some groups with lesser funding have nevertheless extended their reach deep into most parts of the nation through heavy reliance on volunteer effort. Notable examples are the Bible Study Fellowship (1961, $9 million), Christian Business Men's Committee (1939, $5 million), Full Gospel Businessmen's Fellowship International (1952, $6 million) with 2,700 local chapters, and Aglow International (1967, $3 million) with 3,700 local fellowships.[34]

Communications Media

In 1945, perhaps twenty to thirty of the 936 radio stations in the U.S. were devoted to evangelical programming — approximately one out of every thirty-seven stations. Fifty years later, 1,328 out of 10,024 radio stations were broadcasting all-evangelical formats — one of every eight stations in the country.[35] Christian radio is now the third most popular format in the industry.[36] A recent survey of sixty-two evangelical stations found that they averaged $449,000 in annual income, which suggests that the aggregate annual income of all the stations might total around $600 million. Some 90 percent of these stations, though operating under what the Federal Communications Commission calls "commercial" licenses, are in fact owned by nonprofit corporations as defined by federal tax law. As mentioned above, their source of income is roughly split between gift income

34. Financial figures for Campus Crusade, Billy Graham Evangelistic Association, Navigators, Young Life, and Fellowship of Christian Athletes come from "The Philanthropy 400," pp. 33-40. Figure for Promise Keepers is from Art Moore, "More PK Downsizing," *Christianity Today*, 5 Oct. 1998, p. 20.

35. The number of evangelical stations for 1945 and 1995, respectively: Dennis N. Voskuil, "The Power of the Air: Evangelicals and the Rise of Religious Broadcasting," in *American Evangelicals and the Mass Media*, ed. Quentin Schultze (Grand Rapids: Academic Books/Zondervan, 1990), p. 73; Ward, Sr., ed., *National Religious Broadcasters Directory*, p. 382. Total number of stations for 1945 and 1995, respectively: U.S. Bureau of the Census, *Statistical Abstract of the United States: 1947*, 68th ed. (Washington, DC: U.S. Government Printing Office, 1947), p. 471; U.S. Bureau of the Census, *Statistical Abstract of the United States: 1996*, 116th ed. (Washington, DC: U.S. Government Printing Office, 1996), p. 561.

36. Ward, Sr., ed., *National Religious Broadcasters Directory*, p. 381.

(mainly listener donations) and commercial sources (mainly sale of advertising and program time).[37]

The earliest reliable figures on evangelical television stations are from 1977, when there were but ten full-time stations.[38] These represented only one out of every ninety-seven of the 967 television stations in the country at that time.[39] Less than two decades later, 163 of 1,512 stations were broadcasting evangelical programming full-time — one in nine stations.[40] In addition, there are at least five full-time evangelical cable television channels distributed by satellite all over the country and to many other parts of the world.[41] A recent survey of evangelical broadcasters suggests that aggregate annual revenues for the 163 television stations might run anywhere from $150 million to $300 million. As with the radio stations, the revenue sources are roughly split between charitable gift income and commercial income.[42]

The total number of program producers, television and radio, has likewise increased from 284 in 1975 to its peak of 1,220 in 1991. Since then, considerable consolidation and winnowing of the market has taken place. The advent of satellite distribution and shifts in programming formats away from preaching and local productions cut the number of program producers in half, but the programs of the remaining producers are more widely aired than ever.[43] Most producers of radio and television programming use the electronic media merely as one form of communication, and many are not primarily in the business of media production. James Dobson's Focus on the Family (founded 1977, annual revenues $109 million) is the producer of the two most widely distributed daily radio programs, the second most widely distributed weekly program, and the third, fifth, and tenth most widely distributed syndicated radio "spots" (five minute programs). His most listened-to program, "Focus on the Family," airs

37. Clark and Virts, *Changing Channels,* pp. 2, 3, 15-16.

38. Ward, Sr., ed., *National Religious Broadcasters Directory,* p. 382.

39. U.S. Bureau of the Census, *Statistical Abstract of the United States: 1978,* 99th ed. (Washington, DC: U.S. Government Printing Office, 1978), p. 592.

40. Ward, Sr., ed., *National Religious Broadcasters Directory,* p. 382; U.S. Bureau of the Census, *Statistical Abstract of the United States: 1996,* 116th ed. (Washington, DC: U.S. Government Printing Office, 1996), p. 561.

41. Ward, Sr., ed., *National Religious Broadcasters Directory,* p. 381.

42. Clark and Virts, *Changing Channels,* pp. 2, 3, 15-16. This is based on a sample too small to be reliable (eleven stations), but if these stations are anywhere near the norm, the estimate is at least responsible.

43. Ward, Sr., ed., *National Religious Broadcasters Directory,* p. 382.

daily for a half-hour on some 1,400 stations (which is more than the total number of full-time Christian stations).[44] Yet Dobson's organization engages in many activities besides media programming, including social service functions, political activism, publishing, and education.

Other large evangelical organizations built on a foundation of broadcasting include Pat Robertson's Christian Broadcasting Network (1960, $203 million), Trinity Broadcasting Network (1978, $98 million), Oral Roberts Ministries (1947, $68 million), D. James Kennedy's Coral Ridge Ministries and Church (1960, $40 million), Charles Stanley's In Touch Ministries (1982, $33 million), Radio Bible Class (RBC) Ministries (1938, $24 million), and Charles Swindoll's Insight for Living (1979, $19 million).[45] These are multi-faceted organizations, including periodicals, tape and literature distribution, correspondence courses, counseling services, seminars, political commentary, and schools of various kinds.

Since the mid-1950s, the percentage of U.S. bookstores and mail-order booksellers that specialize in religious books, sound recordings, and other materials has increased only marginally, from 13 percent to 14 percent. Religious bookstores are the second largest category, after general bookstores, which have remained constant at 25 percent of the total. There is, however, evidence to indicate that the percentage of religious bookstores that target primarily an evangelical market has increased tremendously since the 1950s. There are currently somewhat more than 4,000 religious bookstores in the country, and 3,000 — over 80 percent — of these are members of the evangelical Christian Booksellers Association (CBA).[46] An impressionistic perusal of the 1956 list of religious bookstores suggests that at most half of those could have been classified as oriented toward evangelicals.[47] A 1993 survey of the CBA membership found that the average store had sales of $471,000.[48] This suggests that the 4,000 establishments that retail what the CBA calls "Christian products" must today be an industry with sales in the neighborhood of $2 billion.

44. Ward, Sr., ed., *National Religious Broadcasters Directory*, p. 38.

45. Figures for Trinity Broadcasting Network and Oral Roberts Ministries are from "The Philanthropy 400," pp. 33-40.

46. Christian Booksellers Association website, 1998; *American Book Trade Directory 13th Edition* (New York: R. R. Bowker, 1956), p. v; *American Book Trade Directory 41st Edition 1995-96* (New York: R. R. Bowker, 1996), pp. ix-x.

47. *American Book Trade Directory 13th Edition*.

48. Christian Booksellers Association website, www.cbaonline.org/, 1998.

Perhaps $400 to $500 million of that total comes from Christian music recordings and videos. About half of Christian music is sold in Christian bookstores, with the other half being sold in mainstream outlets. Total sales of the gospel music industry in 1998 were $863 million, which amounted to 6.3 percent of the total U.S. recording industry sales of $13.7 billion. Christian music is the sixth best-selling format, after rock and roll, country, rhythm and blues, pop, and rap; it is ahead of classical, movie soundtracks, oldies, jazz, and new age.[49]

Periodical publishing takes on somewhat different contours within evangelicalism than in the rest of American culture. Most large-circulation evangelical magazines are not stand-alone commercial periodicals, but rather vehicles to publicize independent ministries. Examples are *Focus on the Family*, the nation's third-largest circulation religious magazine (2 million), and the Billy Graham Evangelistic Association's *Decision*, the nation's fourth-largest religious magazine (1.8 million). The most widely circulated religious magazine is *Guideposts*, begun by Norman Vincent Peale in 1945, whose circulation of 4.2 million would rank it twelfth among all U.S. periodicals. Guideposts, Inc. belongs to the Evangelical Christian Publishers' Association, but the magazine itself has little identifiably evangelical content. The largest purely commercial evangelical magazine is *Today's Christian Woman*, published by Christianity Today, Inc. With a paid circulation of 400,000, it does not even come close to ranking in the top one hundred U.S. periodicals. Yet it may be that commercial evangelical magazines are artificially restricted in circulation. The economics of contemporary commercial publishing requires substantial income from advertising. Yet the advertising income of evangelical periodicals comes almost entirely from evangelical sources: educational institutions, book publishers, church service industries, and the like. These entities cannot pay the kind of advertising rates that are needed for magazines in the one million circulation category. Therefore, expanding circulation would require the ability to attract non-evangelical advertisers like food, drug, cosmetic, and auto makers. So far, these advertisers have been reluctant to advertise in religious publications. The evangelical public is sufficiently large to push paid circulation of

49. "Gospel Music Achieves Third Year of Consecutive Growth," press release (Jan. 13, 1999), Gospel Music Association website (www.gospelmusic.org). $863 million figure compiled by Recording Industry Association of America, reported in phone conversation with Deanna Grubbs, PR officer for GMA, 29 Mar. 1999. $13.7 billion figure from RIAA website (www.riaa.com).

magazines like *Christian Parenting* (published by Good Family Magazines, 1998 circulation 225,000) well above the one million mark, but if the magazine cannot get Campbell's Soup to place advertisements, circulation will probably remain well below the half-million mark.

Educational Organizations

Since 1959, the number of students in all elementary and secondary schools in the United States has risen from 40.9 million to 48.9 million — an increase of 20 percent. In that same period, the number of students in non-Catholic religious schools (mostly evangelical schools) has risen from an estimated 0.25 million to at least 2.2 million — an increase of 780 percent. And of course, these figures do not include the estimated 1.5 million children — again, mostly evangelicals — who are being schooled at home by their parents.[50] Since 1965 the number of evangelical private schools has risen from less than 1 percent to nearly 14 percent of all schools. Estimates suggest that there are some 85,000 public schools, 15,000 evangelical schools, 8,000 Catholic schools, and perhaps 2,000 non-religious private schools.[51] A recent survey of 606 evangelical schools found that their median annual income/expenditure was $326,000. Most of this (86 percent) comes from tuition, with 2 percent coming from each of the following sources: parents, board members, friends of the school, sponsoring churches, product sales, corporations, and miscellaneous sources.[52] It is

50. "Home Schooling: Student Banned from Tournament," *Christianity Today*, 15 June 1998, p. 11.

51. U.S. Department of Education, National Center for Educational Statistics, *Digest of Education Statistics 1997* (Washington, DC: 1997). Statistics on enrollment by type of school can be found in Table 3, p. 12; and Tables 61 and 62, p. 72. A recent survey of evangelical schools found that median enrollments are 170 students per school, which means that total evangelical-school enrollments may be closer to 2.55 million students. See D. Bruce Lockerbie, *From Candy Sales to Committed Donors: A Guide to Financing Christian Schools* (Milwaukee: Christian Stewardship Association, 1996), p. 134. Statistics on number of schools by type can be found in Table 62, p. 72; and Table 89, p. 96. Estimate of number of evangelical schools is from Lockerbie, who is president of PAIDEIA, Inc. (a firm that consults for Christian schools), in a telephone interview, 26 February 1998.

52. Lockerbie, *From Candy Sales to Committed Donors*, pp. 11, 25, 35. Aggregate income/expenditures calculated by multiplying the median budget times 15,000 schools (see n. 44). This actually produces a low estimate, for the numerical median in a survey of this type will be lower than the numerical mean (which is the proper multiplier).

important to remember that this alternative school system has been built entirely in the last thirty years. Since every parent paying private school tuition is also paying taxes to support public schools, this represents an enormous commitment on the part of a substantial portion of the evangelical population. The growing evangelical support for alternative schooling represents the most significant reconfiguration of American elementary and secondary education since 1884, when Roman Catholic leaders made an official nationwide commitment to erect their own school system.

The largest segment of evangelical education is the network of liberal arts colleges. Ninety-one institutions belong to the evangelical Council for Christian Colleges and Universities (CCCU). These include the major independent schools such as Wheaton College (1860, $73 million), but most of the CCCU schools are attached to several denominational groups that tend to identify with evangelicalism: Wesleyan holiness denominations, Mennonites, Free Churches, Pentecostals, Baptists, Presbyterians, Brethren, Dutch Reformed, and others. The CCCU also includes several schools affiliated with pluralist Protestant denominations, such as the Presbyterian Church USA, American Baptists, Reformed Church in America, and Disciples of Christ. The main common denominator among these schools is that they require faculty members to be professing Christians. In addition to the CCCU schools, there are in North America an approximately equal number of church-related schools that have very similar faculty profiles. These are mainly colleges attached to evangelical denominations that have retained a strong denominational identity — Southern Baptists, Missouri Synod Lutherans, Wisconsin Synod Lutherans, Churches of Christ, and Seventh-Day Adventists. Also in this category are several independent schools, and several historically black colleges that have retained Christian commitments in most areas of campus life.[53] All together these colleges enroll some 300,000 students, or perhaps 2 percent of all students in higher education, and 10 percent of all students at private liberal arts colleges.[54] The total aggregate operating budget of CCCU schools is around $2 billion.[55] Since the CCCU members represent perhaps

53. The list of CCCU schools can be found on the Coalition's website: www.cccu.org. The list of additional evangelical colleges was obtained from the Pew Younger Scholars Program at the University of Notre Dame.

54. Willmer, ed., *Advancing Christian Higher Education*, p. vii.

55. Robert Burkinshaw, "The Funding of Evangelical Higher Education in the United States and Canada in the Postwar Period," p. 285 in this volume.

half of all evangelical colleges, the total aggregate budget for these institutions is likely in the neighborhood of $4 billion. Most of this is raised through commercial sources: 72 percent of these colleges' income is derived from tuition and fees, up from 66 percent ten years earlier.[56]

The other major segment of evangelical higher education are the Bible institutes and seminaries. The largest of these is Moody Bible Institute (1886, $82 million). There are ninety members of the Accrediting Association of Bible Colleges, which in 1996 averaged $3.8 million in expenses each year. This would put their aggregate expenditures at about $342 million per year, serving a total of some 60,000 students. Some 40 percent of their income is commercial (tuition and fees), and some 36 percent is donated. This group, however, represents only a small portion of the number of similar schools throughout North America. Responsible estimates put the number of non-accredited Bible schools between 600 and 1,000. Some of these are quite large; others are little more than church basement operations. Assuming there are perhaps 800 such schools, and assuming they average only half the size of the smaller of the accredited schools, their total annual expenditures might be $400 million, serving a total of 92,000 students. This would mean that the aggregate Bible school expenditures (accredited and unaccredited) may well be around $740 million, serving over 150,000 students.[57]

Finally, there are at least fifty seminaries in North America that can reasonably be regarded as evangelical. One sample of seventeen found that in 1996 the mean annual expenditure of each was $4.5 million, projecting possible total expenditures around $230 million. Some 40 percent of these seminaries' income comes from donations, with perhaps another 40 percent coming from commercial sources (tuition and fees).[58]

56. Willmer, ed., *Advancing Christian Higher Education*, p. 2.

57. All Bible institute financial figures are derived from Accrediting Association of Bible Colleges, "Statistical Report for all AABC Accredited Colleges" Fall 1997, pp. 11-12, 17-18. Enrollment figures are simple headcounts (not full-time equivalents), and are found on p. 1. Estimate of number of unaccredited Bible institutes is from telephone interview with Ralph Enlow, Executive Director, AABC, 28 Sept. 1998.

58. A list of evangelical seminaries has been compiled by the Pew Younger Scholars Program, University of Notre Dame. The sample cites those seminaries that are members of the Evangelical Council for Financial Accountability, and brief financial reports on each of these are given in Evangelical Council for Financial Accountability, *Member Profile Directory January 1998* (Washington, DC: ECFA, 1998).

Social Service Organizations

This is a category of evangelical organizations so large, diverse, and decentralized that it is impossible even to provide a reasonable estimate of either its total size or the total financial resources devoted to its tasks. But a few snapshots will at least begin to give a sense of the scope of evangelical social work.

There are few large evangelical organizations that engage in social service activities on a national basis. The biggest of these, far and away, is the Salvation Army (1865), whose U.S. branch raises over $1 billion every year from private sources and another $1 billion from governmental sources. The Salvation Army raises more money from private sources than any other charity or nonprofit organization in America — more than double the second-place American Red Cross ($480 million). However, several aspects of the Salvation Army make it an anomalous organization. In the first place, it is both a parachurch organization and a denomination, with church buildings and regular Sunday morning church services. Second, despite the fact that it is openly evangelical, it draws extensive support from non-evangelical sources, including governmental agencies.[59] For reasons that are not entirely clear, many Americans apparently think of the Army as a more-or-less secular social service organization. Far behind the Salvationists, the other large national evangelical social service organizations are James Dobson's Focus on the Family (1977, $109 million) and Chuck Colson's Prison Fellowship Ministries (1976, $29 million).[60] Dobson's organization is also anomalous, because it is so difficult to classify. It is probably fair to say that the largest portion of its work might be called "family life education," but its broadcasting foundation and extensive public affairs activity make it a candidate for those categories as well.

Most evangelical social service organizations are local agencies. Maybe half of these are affiliated with a national umbrella organization that may provide different kinds of administrative support, accountability standards, and legal assistance. One group of these evangelical organizations are the 1,500 summer camps and conference centers. Some are owned by denominations, some by groups of churches, and others are

59. "The Philanthropy 400," pp. 1, 32-48. To see how openly evangelical the Salvation Army is, compare its website (www.salvationarmy.org) with that of its now-secularized offspring, the Volunteers of America (www.voa.org).

60. ECFA, *Member Profile Directory,* pp. 160, 337.

free-standing nonprofit organizations. They are all independent of each other, but most are affiliated with Christian Camping International or the American Camping Association. These camps have a median clientele of 3,000 campers per year and a median budget of $200,000 to $400,000, suggesting a total yearly clientele of at least 4.5 million, with an aggregate budget of at least $450 million. Some 83 percent of this comes from camper fees; the rest from donations.[61]

Another subset of the evangelical social service network are the 500 urban "rescue missions," half of which are affiliated with the International Union of Gospel Missions. Besides their traditional activities of feeding and evangelizing the homeless, over half of them now provide clothing, shelter, on-site alcohol and drug rehabilitation, and adult education programs (literacy, tutoring, and job training); over one-fourth also provide children's education programs, professional psychological counseling, recreation programs, counseling and shelter for abused women and children, professional on-site medical care, and prison ministries. There are not many more rescue missions than fifty years ago, but their average size has grown commensurate with their expanded services. In 1946 the average rescue mission budget, in constant 1987 dollars, was around $113,414. Today, they average $1 million each in constant 1987 dollars, and their total aggregate budget may be somewhere in the neighborhood of $625 million.[62]

A more recent social dimension of evangelical service activity is represented by the hundreds of crisis pregnancy centers that have been organized in the past quarter century. Some 450 are affiliated with Care Net, an arm of the Christian Action Council. They serve a clientele of some 225,000, with an average budget of $70,000, total paid staff of 1,000, and 20,000 volunteers. If these are half of all crisis pregnancy centers, the aggregate expenditure for them all may come to some $63 million.[63]

61. Brian Kluth, ed., *Out of the Woods: A Guide to Funding Camp and Conference Ministries* (Milwaukee: Christian Stewardship Association, 1996), pp. 2-3.

62. Figures on the number of rescue missions today, the services they provide, and their aggregate budget are from Ivan Fahs, ed., *From Soup and a Sermon to Mega-Mission: A Guide to Financing Rescue Missions* (Milwaukee: Christian Stewardship Association, 1996), pp. vii, 3, 121. 1946 figures are from W. E. Paul, *Romance of Rescue* (n.p., [1948]), pp. 117, 87. Conversion to constant 1987 dollars is based on the price deflator chart found in Ronsvalle and Ronsvalle, *The State of Church Giving through 1993*, 123.

63. Cecile S. Holmes, "Billboard Campaign Offers Help to Women in Crisis Pregnancies," *Christianity Today*, 28 Apr. 1997, p. 82

Other areas of evangelical social service include adoption programs, alcohol and drug rehabilitation programs (Teen Challenge has some 130 centers nationwide), children's homes, handicapped ministries, senior care organizations, and youth programs. One of the fastest-growing service areas is personal, family, and psychological counseling. Much of the counseling services, though not all, are financed by user fees. One of the newer areas of evangelical involvement is community development, such as the Pittsburgh Project (1985, $0.5 million), a neighborhood-based project that involves 1300 teenagers in volunteer home repair for the poor, elderly, and disabled; an after-school program for urban youth centered on the performing and visual arts; educational tutoring and life skills instruction; and Bible instruction and faith formation.[64]

Public Affairs Organizations

Unlike the other categories of parachurch organizations, there were no evangelical public affairs organizations as such until the 1940s. The first was the National Association of Evangelicals (1941, $1.5 million), which was founded partly to lobby the federal government on behalf of evangelical interests in broadcasting, military chaplaincies, and other matters. In this regard, the NAE remained something of an anomaly in the evangelical world until the advent of the so-called Religious Right in the 1970s. There are a few small evangelical public affairs organizations, such as Ron Sider's Evangelicals for Social Action (1978, $1.2 million), that are not on the conservative end of the political spectrum. Most of them, however — and by far the largest of them — are on the political right.

The national office of the Christian Coalition, founded by Pat Robertson in 1989, spent about $20 million total in 1997. However, the national office has no idea how much money the fifty state affiliates raised. Some, such as Texas and Florida, may be significant in size; many others are probably all-volunteer operations. Dobson's Focus on the Family likes to say that only 4 percent of his organization's activity is concerned with politics, but this is clearly a disingenuously low estimate. With total revenues of $109 million, a generous estimate that one quarter of its activity is devoted to public affairs matters would mean political expenditures of maybe $27 million.[65] D. James

64. ECFA, *Member Profile Directory*, pp. 1-22, 331, 383.
65. This guess, that maybe one-quarter of Focus on the Family's efforts are de-

Kennedy's Coral Ridge Ministries Media (1978, $25 million) is separate from his church organization and schools, so it is probably fair to say that it is predominantly concerned with politics. The other noteworthy evangelical organizations on this front are Gary Bauer's Family Research Council (1981, $14 million), Beverly LaHaye's Concerned Women for America (1979, $11.3 million), Donald Wildmon's American Family Association (1977, $8.9 million), Louis Sheldon's Traditional Values Coalition (1981, $2 million), and Robert Simonds's Citizens for Excellence in Education (1983, $0.6 million).[66]

All told, if we allow another $20 million for the state affiliates of the Christian Coalition, and if we count the NAE and the ESA, and if we assume that the budgets of the organizations mentioned here account for 80 percent of the budgets of evangelical public affairs groups — even then, the total amount that evangelicals spend annually on evangelical political organizations is almost certainly less than $160 million.

What the Numbers Tell Us

Evangelicalism's financial numbers point to several conclusions. First, if spending is the scale, right-wing politics hardly shows up on the map of American evangelicalism. For every dollar evangelicals spend on political organizations, they spend almost $12 on foreign missions and international relief and development; they spend another $13 in evangelical book and music stores; they spend almost $25 on evangelical higher education; and they spend almost $31 on private elementary and secondary schools. The budget of just one organization dedicated to evangelism — Campus Crusade for Christ ($241 million) — is itself far larger than all spending by all evangelical political groups, right and left. Evangelicals spend more on summer camps than on politics, more on urban rescue missions than on

voted to politics, was arrived at in conversation with John C. Green, Dept. of Political Science, University of Akron, phone conversation, 17 Nov. 1998. It may be too high, but it is not likely too low.

66. Figures for the Christian Coalition came from a phone interview with Molly Clatworthy of their media relations office, 17 Nov. 1998; figures for Family Research Council from a phone interview with Kristen Hansen of their media relations office, 18 Nov. 1998; figures for Concerned Women for America, Traditional Values Coalition, and Citizens for Excellence in Education came from the website of People for the American Way (www.pfaw.org).

politics, and more on youth programs than on politics. When we factor in the amounts that evangelicals give to their churches — probably somewhere between $14 billion and $20 billion — there is no doubt that evangelicals devote less than 1 percent of their religious spending to public affairs matters.[67] If we follow the money, it clearly does not lead to politics.[68]

If not to politics, where does the money lead? It will surprise many to learn that in the 1990s, much of evangelicalism's money leads to social involvement. Back in the 1970s and 1980s there was a good deal of talk about the Great Reversal, a term used to describe evangelicalism's turn away from social concerns at the beginning of the twentieth century. The numbers from the 1990s, however, show that the Great Reversal has, apparently, been reversed.[69] Three areas of spending support this conclusion.

Area one: missions and international concerns. These figures reveal a clear shift in the focus of the activities of evangelical overseas ministry groups away from evangelization toward humanitarian activities. In the late 1930s, virtually all emphasis was on evangelization, church planting, and discipleship. However, by 1998 six of the seven largest parachurch mission agencies were World Vision, Feed the Children, MAP International, Compassion International, Food for the Hungry, and Christian Aid Ministries. All describe themselves as evangelical, all were created after 1945,

67. We do not know how much money evangelicals give to their churches. But we do know that in 1991 Americans gave $41.7 billion to their churches (Virginia A. Hodgkinson, Murray S. Weitzman, et al., *From Belief to Commitment: The Community Service Activities and Finances of Religious Congregations in the United States*, 1993 ed. [Washington, DC: Independent Sector, 1992], p. 73). We also know that evangelicals give more than pluralist Protestants, and more than Roman Catholics (Dean R. Hoge et al., *Money Matters: Personal Giving in American Churches* [Louisville: Westminster/John Knox, 1996], p. 13). Therefore, even if 1996 giving remained at about $42 billion (a conservative estimate) and even if evangelicals gave only one-third of that (also a conservative estimate), the total that evangelicals give to their churches would be around $14 billion, which by itself would amount to nearly $90 for every $1 spent on politics. It is probably responsible to estimate evangelical giving to churches at between $14 billion and $20 billion.

68. This conclusion is so counterintuitive that I double-checked it with two scholars who study evangelical political activity, John C. Green of the University of Akron, and Michael Cromartie of the Ethics and Public Policy Center in Washington, DC. Both confirmed that they believe it to be true. Phone conversations of 16 and 17 November 1998.

69. For a recent sociological study that comes to the same conclusion via a very different route, see Mark D. Regnerus and Christian Smith, "Selective Deprivatization among American Religious Traditions: The Reversal of the Great Reversal," *Social Forces* 76 (June 1998): 1347-72.

and all focus on relief, development, education, and health care. Evangelism is a secondary concern. Even more significant is the fact that a few of the above organizations ranked among the nation's seven largest nonprofits dealing with international concerns. This suggests that the average evangelical is likely to be much more concerned about the living condition of non-Americans than is his average non-evangelical counterpart.[70]

Area two: evangelical agencies concerned with domestic human services. These figures suggest that we can see only the tip of the iceberg. Evangelicals clearly prefer local action when it comes to human and social concerns, and their efforts are extraordinarily decentralized. Therefore we need to bracket the large groups like the Salvation Army and Prison Fellowship Ministries, and speculate for a moment about the aggregate size of the small groups. If there are 1,500 summer camps, 900 women's centers, 500 urban rescue missions, and 130 Teen Challenge alcohol and drug treatment centers, how many evangelical day care facilities are there? How many senior centers? How many group homes for the disabled? How many youth programs? How many counseling centers? How many urban development initiatives? Maybe the best example of just how large this phenomenon might be is demonstrated by Crista Ministries of Seattle. Founded in 1948 as a Christian school, it has since expanded into nine additional ministry areas: senior programs, camps and conference centers, broadcasting, counseling, child and family support, urban development, AIDS ministry, job placement for Christian service workers, and international relief and development. Almost all of Crista's activities take place in the Pacific Northwest. Yet despite its regional focus, it is the thirty-first largest parachurch group in America, with a total annual budget of over $52 million.[71] Crista is unusual because it is centralized. And of course it does not even come close to representing most of the evangelical activity in the Puget Sound region. So if a similar range of evangelical social service activity takes place in other urban areas, only in decentralized organizations, the aggregate size of these activities must be enormous.

Area three: evangelical support for non-religious social service activity. The growth of evangelicalism has probably aided the growth of secular

70. See note 31 above.
71. ECFA, *Member Profile Directory,* p. 117.

charitable organizations. Of the 400 philanthropic organizations that raise the most money, only thirty are evangelical organizations. All the large organizations are thriving. How does this square with the fact that perhaps one-third of all Americans are evangelicals? At the very least we can conclude that the rise in the percentage of Americans claiming to be evangelicals has not undercut secular charities. But beyond that limited claim, recent scholarship shows that church members devote great resources to the support of non-religious nonprofit organizations. One set of studies has found that church members are more likely than non-members to support nonprofit groups that engage in human services, youth services, and public and social benefit programs. These same studies show that church members who support such groups give larger average gifts than do non-church members who support such groups.[72] Furthermore, in 1986 churches and synagogues donated $8 billion per year to non-religious charities, as compared to $4.5 billion by foundations and $4.9 billion by corporations.[73] In addition to this $8 billion in donations, the average church spends over 40 percent of its own operating resources on non-religious work, mostly on education, human services, and health and hospital programs.[74]

If we follow the money, it is clear that evangelicals have made but light investments in politics while making deep, heavy, sustained investments in social welfare causes. This suggests that the primary impact of evangelicalism on American culture is to be found outside of politics. If spending is any indication, local churches, international involvement, Bible study groups, radio broadcasts, book publishing, schools, urban homeless centers, counseling programs, drug and alcohol rehabilitation centers, summer camps, and crisis pregnancy centers — not to mention heavier-

72. Virginia A. Hodgkinson, Murray S. Weitzman, and Arthur D. Kirsch, "From Commitment to Action: How Religious Involvement Affects Giving and Volunteering," in *Faith and Philanthropy in America: Exploring the Role of Religion in America's Voluntary Sector*, ed. Robert Wuthnow, Virginia A. Hodgkinson, and Associates (San Francisco: Jossey-Bass, 1990), pp. 93-114.

73. Quoted in Mark Chaves, "The Religious Ethic and the Spirit of Nonprofit Entrepreneurship," in *Private Action and Public Good*, ed. Walter W. Powell and Elisabeth S. Clemens (New Haven: Yale University Press, 1998), p. 48.

74. Hodgkinson, Weitzman, et al., *From Belief to Commitment*, p. 78. I am making the assumption that evangelical congregations do not differ substantially from other congregations in this matter. There is no obvious evidence suggesting major differences. However, this assumption has not, to my knowledge, been tested.

than-average support for secular social service charities — are the places evangelicals are having the most profound influence on their culture.

Within evangelicalism, the major structural change has been the diversification of parachurch organizations as a result of the increased use of electronic media. As recently as 1988 sociologist Robert Wuthnow characterized parachurch corporations as "special-purpose organizations," but that term is growing increasingly obsolete.[75] The largest organizations with high-profile leaders (Bill Bright, Pat Robertson, James Dobson, Chuck Colson) have been extraordinarily successful using multiple media — specialized periodicals and newsletters, radio and television broadcasting, satellite communication, tape distribution, production of entertainment programming, local interest groups, direct mail, and paid advertising — to get their messages out to the evangelical public. In a phenomenon new to evangelicalism, they have used the resulting flood of financial support to diversify their ministry activities. And by diversifying their ministries, they are able to attract a broader spectrum of support. A typical large agency will now have separate ministry divisions that engage in particular kinds of evangelism, humanitarian and social service activity, personal problem counseling, educational activities, research and scholarship, and sometimes public affairs activism. Bright's Campus Crusade for Christ began in 1952 as an outreach to students at UCLA. Now it consists of fifty different ministries targeting university students, university professors, women, urban families, high school students, athletes, non-Christians around the world, married couples, parents, young people struggling with moral relativism, Christians who need training in apologetics, Christians who need training in evangelism, and on and on.

Even though evangelical parachurch organizations are flourishing, it is worth noting that their liveliness is highly dependent upon the legal and political climate that now prevails in the United States. Donors — even corporate donors — receive tax breaks. The organizations themselves are exempt from virtually all taxes. And the organizations receive innumerable small benefits from the government, such as lower postal rates, relatively free access to broadcasting airwaves, and a lax regulatory environment. Americans take these conditions for granted, but they are unique to the United States, and they have a lot to do with the lush growth of private

75. Robert Wuthnow, *The Restructuring of American Religion: Society and Faith since World War II* (Princeton: Princeton University Press, 1988).

charitable, educational, and religious organizations in this country. Slight changes in the regulatory climate — changes that would bring the United States more in line with other Western democracies — could dramatically cut back on the growth of the evangelical parachurch. Restrictions on access to broadcasting airwaves, permission for local governmental units to begin levying taxes, and other small changes could dramatically curtail the ability of parachurch groups to raise and spend money at current levels.

The importance of the legal environment can be illustrated in another way — through the counterexample of evangelical elementary and secondary schools. In this case government policy directly inhibits parachurch growth. In the past thirty years, competing against a state-supported monopoly, evangelicals have begun to build a separate alternative school system that now educates nearly 5 percent of American children. Another 3 percent of children are home schooled, but most of these would attend evangelical schools if the cost were not prohibitive. Yet these figures are tiny when compared to polls that indicate that half of all parents would prefer to send their children to private schools if they could afford to do so. It is therefore reasonable to think that if Americans were allowed to move their educational tax dollars to evangelical schools, those schools would triple in size as quickly as they could add teachers and classrooms. Catholic schools, and other private schools, would also swell, while the public schools would be forced into serious downsizing. But as things stand now, government taxation policies force evangelicals who prefer their own schools to pay for two school systems, thus putting an artificial cap on the growth of evangelical schools.

The generally favorable regulatory and taxation climate that currently prevails depends on the maintenance of good will between nonprofit organizations and the government. Historically, any major scandal in any nonprofit (secular or religious) has resulted in immediate efforts to enact more restrictive regulatory legislation. All nonprofits therefore have a powerful interest in self-regulation, in order to perpetuate the assumption that these organizations are of such high social worth that they deserve special treatment. The same is true of evangelical nonprofits, which is why in the wake of press reports about questionable fund-raising practices, a group of evangelical leaders created the Evangelical Council for Financial Accountability (ECFA) in 1979. The ECFA requires members to adhere to several standards, including regular audits, open finances, and limits on the amounts spent on fund-raising.

Self-regulation through agencies like the ECFA is but one part of a pattern of professionalization that is changing the parachurch organizations. Part of the professionalization process has included adoption of fund-raising strategies used by secular charitable organizations. This has caused a fair amount of soul-searching among evangelical parachurch administrators — though not perhaps so much as some would like to see. Much of fund-raising strategy focuses on technique (for instance, layout and appearance of direct mail letters: Does the printer insert red underlining that pretends to be hand drawn? Does the copywriter place below the signature a carefully thought-out "p.s."?). But immersion in technique often comes to seem like crass manipulation. Some evangelical fund-raisers are blithely unconcerned about this development, but many are more ambivalent. At a recent workshop, one fund-raiser wistfully wished for the day when he could raise sufficient funds simply by telling the story of his organization's accomplishments — no tricks, no gimmicks. But he did not see that day coming any time soon.

Despite the moral ambivalence concerning professionalized fund-raising, it is clear that gimmicks and techniques are not the foundation for evangelicals' generosity. One recent study set out to explore why evangelicals give away more money than do pluralist Protestants and Roman Catholics.[76] In interviews, non-evangelicals talked about their obligations to support their churches in order to keep the bills paid. But evangelicals talked about giving in obedience to God, giving out of love for God, giving as a part of dependence upon God, or giving to meet the needs of others.[77] It may be that evangelical churches have been particularly successful in bringing their members into a sharpened awareness of what God has done

76. Higher evangelical giving levels are documented in Dean R. Hoge and Fenggang Yang, "Determinants of Religious Giving in American Denominations: Data from Two Nationwide Surveys," *Review of Religious Research* 36, no. 2 (Dec. 1994): 123-48; and in Hoge et al., *Money Matters.*

77. Sharon L. Miller, "The Meaning of Religious Giving," in *Financing American Religion*, ed. Mark Chaves and Sharon L. Miller (Walnut Creek, CA: AltaMira Press, 1998), pp. 39-43. It should also be noted here that high giving levels are associated with high levels of personal involvement in church activities, with evangelical theological beliefs, with the importance one places on religion in one's life, and with the desire to live a spiritual life. Evangelicals score higher on all these indices. High giving levels do not correlate with age, income, or level of education. See Dean R. Hoge and Mark A. Noll, "Levels of Contributions and Attitudes toward Money among Evangelicals and Non-Evangelicals in Canada and the U.S.," pp. 351-73 in this volume.

for them through the life and resurrection of Jesus, which in turn translates into greater generosity toward religious and humanitarian causes.

If this is the case, it is surprising in one regard. Recall for a moment the three main lines of financial advice aimed at evangelical individuals — the Oral Roberts prosperity gospel, the Ron Sider/Jim Wallis renunciation of wealth, and the Larry Burkett obligation to pay tithes. All of these lines of advice focus on money itself. None of these lines of advice concentrate on spiritual reasons for giving, such as gratitude to God or compassion for others. None of them focus on the spiritual benefits of giving, such as avoidance of the temptations to sin that accompany wealth. Studies show that evangelicals do have spiritual understandings for why they give, but it is clear they are not getting these from the prominent advice-givers. One wonders, therefore, if evangelicalism is running the risk of forgetting what it knows about why generosity promotes spiritual health.

Evangelicals truly believe that their churches and their favorite parachurch organizations are doing God's work in the world. The good news here is that this has generated enormous creative energy in bringing Christian concerns to bear upon innumerable aspects of contemporary life. In the spirit of Dwight L. Moody, the evangelical entrepreneurs have pioneered new visions and directions for Christian ministry that, though new, are at the same time in line with their constituency's core beliefs.[78] The bad news is that, just as in a business corporation, the growth and survival of the parachurch groups always threaten to become ends in themselves. Any organization that depends on broad popular support inevitably becomes deeply concerned with the image it projects. Concern with image and popular opinion always colors and shapes the biblical and moral criteria by which the evangelical entrepreneurs profess to make decisions.

In the end, evangelical entrepreneurs, and their constituencies, always invest their institutions with a quality of moral goodness. They convince themselves that the successes of the organization are a sign of God's approval, and that any decline of the organization would mean a setback to God's work in the world. So they spend their time and energies building and growing their organizations. Growth requires more money; more money means more ministry. In the worst cases, means and ends become

78. Ralph D. Winter, "Protestant Mission Societies: The American Experience," *Missiology* 7 (1979): 152-57; Nathan O. Hatch, "Evangelicalism as a Democratic Movement," in Marsden, ed., *Evangelicalism and Modern America*, pp. 78-80.

reversed, and entrepreneurs and administrators do ministry in order to grow. In the best cases, more ministry means more people who become newly aware of the great gift God has given them, and who then, in gratitude, reach into their own pockets so that others might also know.

PART II

SPECIFIC STUDIES

CHAPTER 5

Moving Targets:
Evangelicalism and the Transformation
of American Economic Life, 1870-1920

PETER DOBKIN HALL

Brothers, think of what you were when you were called. Not many of you were wise by human standards; not many were influential; not many were of noble birth.

I CORINTHIANS I:26 (NIV)

A glance at the occupational statistics of any country of mixed religious composition brings to light with remarkable frequency a situation that several times provoked discussion in the Catholic press and literature, and in Catholic congresses in Germany, namely the fact that business leaders and owners of capital, as well as the high grades of skilled labour, and even more the higher technically and commercially trained personnel of modern enterprises, are overwhelmingly Protestant. The same thing is shown in the figures of religious affiliation almost wherever capitalism, at the time of its great expansion, has had a free hand to alter the social distribution of the population in accordance with its needs, and to determine its occupational structure. The more freedom it has had, the more clearly is the effect shown.[1]

1. Max Weber, *The Protestant Ethic and the Spirit of Capitalism*, trans. Talcott Par-

These correlations of religious and organizational demography, economic geography, and the stratification of economic and institutional power in Max Weber's observations of *fin de siècle* Germany were paralleled in the United States — not between Catholics and Protestants, but in the distinctions that existed among America's Protestant denominations. In 1900, three quarters of America's publicly held industrial corporations, all of its major financial institutions, every cultural and educational institution of national significance, as well as its largest transportation and communications enterprises, were headquartered in the northeastern United States.[2] Seventy percent of the men who controlled these enterprises professed to be Congregationalists, Presbyterians, Episcopalians, and Unitarians, denominations that commanded the loyalty of fewer than 10 percent of American church members.[3]

Despite the fact that the largest Protestant groups — Baptists and Methodists — generally lived outside the Northeast and stood outside the

---

sons (New York: Charles Scribner's Sons, 1958), p. 35. Thus Weber, in these opening sentences of his classic study of religion and economic life, defines the problem to which the work is addressed.

2. John Moody, *Moody's Analysis of Public Utilities and Industrials, 1914* (New York: Analyses Publishing Company, 1914).

3. The baseline studies of religious affiliation and social stratification include C. Luther Fry, "The Religious Affiliations of American Leaders," *The Scientific Monthly* 36 (1933): 241-49; C. Luther Fry, "The Reported Religious Affiliations of the Various Leaders Listed in Who's Who, 1930-31," in *Yearbook of American Churches 1933 Edition* (New York: Round Table Press, 1933), pp. 311-34; and Frank W. Taussig and C. S. Joslyn, *American Business Leaders: A Study in Social Origins and Social Stratification* (New York: The Macmillan Company, 1932). Later studies include Frances Gregory and Irene Neu, "The American Industrial Elite in the 1870s: Their Social Origins," in *Men in Business: Essays on the Social Role of the Entrepreneur,* ed. William Miller (Cambridge, MA: Harvard University Press, 1952), pp. 193-211; William Miller, "The Business Elite in Business Bureaucracies: Careers of Top Executives in the Early Twentieth Century," in Miller, ed., *Men in Business,* pp. 286-308; William Miller, "The Recruitment of the American Business Elite," in Miller, ed., *Men in Business,* pp. 309-38. Useful recent studies include James Davidson, "Religion Among America's Elite: Persistence and Change in the Protestant Establishment," *Sociology of Religion* 55, no. 4 (1994): 419-40, and Ellen Dubas, "Religious Identity and Ethnicity," *International Journal of Group Tensions* 25, no. 1 (1995): 77-101.

The late E. Digby Baltzell's work on the contrasting contributions of particular religious groups to American leadership is particularly illuminating in its efforts to test Weber's ideas about religion and social stratification in the American setting. See especially his *Puritan Boston and Quaker Philadelphia: Two Protestant Ethics and the Spirit of Class Authority and Leadership* (New York: The Free Press, 1979).

charmed circles of national corporate and institutional power, as late as 1900, they shared with their more privileged brethren a common identity as evangelicals and, on that basis, worked together to engage the challenges offered by an increasingly urban and industrial America.[4] Within a generation, however, this "evangelical united front" would be shattered — and an evangelical identity would become the dividing line between Protestants who embraced the institutions and values of "business civilization" and those who rejected it.

Religion and Economic Culture: History and Theory

Were these powerful associations between economic power and religious affiliation epiphenomena? Did national institutional elites in America embrace liberal Protestantism and reject evangelicalism *because* they were wealthy and powerful? Or did religious beliefs, practices, and ways of organizing activities and structuring relationships lead some groups to gravitate to powerful national institutions and others to reject them? Was the liberal non-evangelical Protestantism that America's leaders embraced by the 1920s emblematic of the secularization that Weber posited as the inevitable accompaniment of the rise of modern economic institutions? Or did religion — albeit in a new and different guise — retain the transformative power that had driven earlier phases of institutional development?

The role of religion in American economic life before the Civil War has been established beyond question.[5] But its influence, once geographically extensive cultural and economic systems were in place, is far more difficult to trace — so much more so that it is obvious why most scholars have been more willing to accept social theorists' grand pronouncements

4. The best sources on religious demography and geography are Edwin Scott Gaustad, *Historical Atlas of Religion in America* (New York: Harper & Row, 1962) and Roger Finke and Rodney Stark, *The Churching of America, 1776-1990* (New Brunswick, NJ: Rutgers University Press, 1992).

5. See Peter Dobkin Hall, *The Organization of American Culture, 1700-1900: Institutions, Elites, and the Origins of American Nationality* (New York: New York University Press, 1982) and Peter Dobkin Hall, "Religion and the Organizational Revolution in the United States," in *Sacred Companies: Organizational Aspects of Religion and Religious Aspects of Organizations*, ed. Nicholas J. Demerath et al. (New York: Oxford University Press, 1998), pp. 99-115.

about secularization as a complement of modernization than to investigate the daunting complexity and ambiguity of the transformative decades between Reconstruction and the Great Depression.

Scholars of religion have long been unhappy with the facile historical assumptions of social scientists, particularly their willingness to lean on theory to explain the movement of religion from the center to the margins of public life rather than investigating the possibility that it remained a persistent influence.[6] But, while the focus of mainstream twentieth-century social and historical scholarship on the rise of the secular state and the political and social movements that brought it into being obscured the role of religion, the seemingly inexplicable fact of religion's resurgence as a powerful social and political force in our own time invites us to reexamine conventional assumptions about the historical role of religion in American life — particularly its economic dimensions.

To investigate the role of religion in American economic life is, inevitably, to investigate the history of evangelicalism, engaging the question of why religious beliefs and practices that were indissolubly identified with the creation of modern economy, polity, and society through the end of the nineteenth century became no less inseparably identified with opposition to modernity in the twentieth.

Locating Evangelicalism in the Nineteenth-Century *Fin-de-Siècle*

Dwight L. Moody's 1878 New Haven revival illustrates the difficulty of addressing this question.[7] The weight of conventional social and historical scholarship would suggest that Yale — which was transforming itself into one of the nation's leading research universities — and the Congregational and Episcopal congregations that dominated the city's religious life, would have turned a cold shoulder to this uneducated, uncredentialed Midwestern shoe salesman turned itinerant revivalist. A cool reception seemed all

6. For a critique of the shortcomings of "grand" social theory, see Thomas Bender, *Community and Social Change in America* (New Brunswick, NJ: Rutgers University Press, 1978).

7. On Moody's New Haven revival, see Barry L. Dastin, "Dwight L. Moody Comes to New Haven," *Journal of the New Haven Colony Historical Society* 23, no. 2 (Spring 1975): 3-57.

the more likely because Moody's visit came in the wake of a bruising battle between wealthy laymen and clergy that had split Yale's faculty between those who favored laicization of governance and modernization of the curriculum and those who clung to the educational standards (set forth in the Yale Report of 1828) that had made Yale the model for evangelical colleges throughout the country.[8]

In fact, Moody was welcomed to the city by a broadly representative committee of clergy chaired by Yale's president, the eminent moral philosopher Noah Porter. His revival was bankrolled by an interdenominational committee composed of New Haven's wealthiest and most prominent businessmen and philanthropists. And the tabernacle where tens of thousands of men and women flocked to worship over a three-month period was erected on the New Haven Green — the central civic space controlled by the city's most exclusive private body, the Proprietors of the Common and Undivided Lands.

Moody's warm reception is all the more puzzling, given the kinds of scholarship being done by some members of Yale's faculty. The critical biblical scholarship that would be anathema to later-day evangelicals was already taking root in the Theological Department. Pioneer political economist (and Episcopal priest) William Graham Sumner had begun teaching immensely popular courses in political economy using the "irreligious" writings of Herbert Spencer (and, at the same time, introducing his students to the unscriptural evolutionary theories of Charles Darwin).[9] Paleontologist Othniel Marsh — discoverer of the brontosaurus — was already deeply engaged in unearthing and displaying the fossil record that undergirded Darwin's challenge to scriptural accounts of creation.

Despite all this, Moody developed a long and close relationship to Yale and to the city. He would send two of his sons to Yale. The muscular Christian student leaders of Dwight Hall — Yale's YMCA and the platform for university social service — would, for a generation, make regular pilgrimages to Moody's home in Northfield, Massachusetts to hone their pi-

---

8. See Peter Dobkin Hall, "'Noah Porter writ large': Reflections on the Modernization of American Education and Its Critics, 1866-1916," *History of Higher Education Annual* 17 (1997).

9. On Sumner's clashes with Porter, see Harris E. Starr, *William Graham Sumner* (New York: Henry Holt and Company, 1925), pp. 345-69. A decade earlier, Sumner also played a prominent role in the efforts of wealthy New Yorkers — under the banner of the "Young Yale" movement — to place Yale under lay control.

ety and make the acquaintance of evangelical leaders from throughout the world. And Leverett L. Camp, the city's wealthiest businessman — and father of legendary Yale football coach Walter Camp — would become the lifelong senior trustee of — and leading donor to — Moody's Northfield Academy.

The careers of the period's Yale graduates also confirm the significance of this unlikely linkage of economic modernity and evangelical religiosity. Clifford Barnes was typical of these young men.[10] Born in 1864 and raised a devout Baptist in western Pennsylvania, Barnes graduated from Yale in 1889. Actively involved in city mission work while an undergraduate, Barnes was one of the many young men who attended conferences at Moody's home in Northfield, where he made the acquaintance of many of the major figures in Anglo-American Protestantism. During this time, he became a protégé of fellow Baptist William Rainey Harper, then a professor of biblical literature in the Divinity School. When Harper was appointed president of the new Rockefeller-funded University of Chicago, Barnes followed his mentor to the Windy City, where he registered as one of its first divinity students. In the course of his studies he met Jane Addams and became a resident of Hull House. His first call was to the nearby Ewing Street Mission where Addams and her partner, Ellen Starr, were members. Exemplifying the inclusive evangelicalism of the period, Barnes's second call was to Christ Chapel Mission, a project sponsored by Chicago's Fourth Presbyterian Church, where he became friends with manufacturer Cyrus McCormick. He combined his parochial ministry with service as a city sanitary inspector, active participant in Hull House's work, instructor in social science at the University of Chicago, and one of the founders of the Chicago Community Trust and the city's interchurch movement — the predecessor of the Church Federation of Chicago. The evangelical Barnes was thus, in every sense, fully identified with individuals and institutions that were the "spearheads for reform."

10. On Clifford Barnes, see Stuart Bruchey, *Faith and Economic Practice: Protestant Businessmen in Chicago, 1900-1920* (New York: Garland Publishing Company, 1989), p. 22. The best source on the religious affiliations and careers of Yale graduates after 1850 are the college "class books," usually published at graduation and twenty and fifty years after graduation. The *Yale Obituary Record*, published by the university between the 1890s and early 1940s, provides detailed biographies of graduates of the college, the graduate school, and the professional schools. For earlier graduates, see Franklin B. Dexter's multi-volume *Yale Annals and Biographies*, which cover Yale College graduates from 1701 to 1815.

Accounts like these call attention to the need to reexamine the familiar contours of the "Age of Reform" that American historians, after a generation of intensive investigation, thought they had well in hand. Because leading postwar historians of American reform like Richard Hofstadter were unabashed in their hostility to religion, they inevitably portrayed it as a negative force — as the refuge of social groups (clergy, small businessmen, "patrician" elites) being pushed to the margins by irresistible modernizing forces.[11] To go back over the same ground from the vantage of our own time — when religion has again become a vital force — one finds a very different "Age of Reform." Astonishingly, wherever one looks, evangelical religion appears — as it did in New Haven in 1879 — to be vital, eminently respectable, and universally embraced by the very institutions and leaders whom the historians of the 1950s and '60s identified as the avatars of the modern and secular.

Rediscovering the vitality of evangelical religion in the Age of Reform makes its retreat from the center of public life in the 1920s all the more puzzling. The historiography of American religious and intellectual life are peculiarly unilluminating: they iterate the iconic events marking evangelicalism's marginalization — the Scopes Trial, the modernist/fundamentalist theological debate — but shed little light on the dynamics of the process.

Economic Culture as a Unifying Concept

Discovering the causes of evangelical marginalization ultimately requires us to repose the kinds of overarching questions that Weber asked about religion, economics, and social stratification — but to do so in ways that combine the conscientious historian's attentiveness to detail, texture, and context with the social scientist's willingness to frame unifying hypotheses about economic culture.

11. Hofstadter's hostility to religion is particularly evident in his studies of American higher education. See Richard Hofstadter and Walter Metzger, *The Development of Academic Freedom in the United States* (New York: Columbia University Press, 1969) and Richard Hofstadter and Wilson Smith, eds., *American Higher Education: A Documentary History* (Chicago: University of Chicago Press, 1961). See also Hofstadter, *The Paranoid Style in American Politics and Other Essays* (New York: Vintage Books, 1964), especially his essay "Free Silver and the Mind of 'Coin' Harvey."

The concept of economic culture (rightly understood) enables us to focus not only on the emergence of large-scale national institutions and the elites who controlled them, but also on their local and regional counterparts. Modern bureaucratic institutions did not simply sweep away the local and traditional "island communities" in which most Americans lived and worked.[12] The emergent national institutions — whether business corporations, religious denominations, professions, political parties, or social movements — were organizationally both centralized *and* segmented: large-scale centralized enterprise required the coordination and instrumental ordering of operating subunits, *not* their elimination. This perspective enables us to assess the extent to which national institutions and modern sensibilities coexisted with economic, political, and social institutions that remained profoundly local and traditional.

The creators of the modern institutional order understood what contemporary social scientists have largely failed to grasp: that the national economy both unified and differentiated the production and distribution of goods and services. The achievement of nationality, as Charles W. Eliot correctly prophesied in 1869, would require both a national capacity to command and coordinate a wide "variety of tools," and "the highest development" of the "peculiar faculties" of particular sectors of economic activity and geographic regions.[13] Thus, in the half century following the Civil War, areas of the South and Midwest became more rather than less wedded to agricultural production; the development of manufacturing and extractive industries in the Northeast and upper Midwest became more rather than less intense; the administrative, finance, and communications centers in the eastern metropolitan centers became more rather than less concentrated. And, despite this overall specialization, localities continued to sustain diverse communities of economic, political, and social actors.

Although fueled and accelerated by the Civil War, the forces of economic concentration and segmentation to which Eliot referred had been shaped by the religious beliefs of antebellum Americans. As Weber correctly noted, Protestantism is a peculiarly dynamic body of beliefs because

12. See Bender, *Community and Social Change in America*.
13. Charles W. Eliot, "Inaugural Address as President of Harvard University, October 19, 1869," in *Educational Reform: Essays and Addresses* (New York: The Century Company, 1898).

it requires its adherents to act on their convictions in the world — to transform economic, political, and social institutions as part of a thoroughgoing process of Christianization of every aspect of life. This transformative drive has powerful economic implications: the occupation becomes a calling; the economic enterprise becomes both an arena and an instrument for the enactment of religious beliefs; and the settings in which individuals and enterprises pursue their callings become the landscapes upon which God's intentions become manifest.

Because of its transformative power, Protestantism is also peculiarly unstable. Because its emphasis on the spiritual sovereignty of the individual is in tension with responsibility to an omnipotent deity, it not only drives believers to challenge constituted political, social, and economic authority, but also drives them into schism from established religious bodies. From the early eighteenth century on, sects formed and hived off from establishments — a process that accelerated after the Revolution, when the federal and state constitutions gave legal sanction to freedom of worship. Because it was inevitably tied to worldly interests, sectarianism fueled economic and political differentiation in the antebellum era. But because sectarianism for the most part took place within a broad domain of agreement over theological fundamentals, however, its divisive tendencies did not preclude episodic cooperation and collaboration between religious groups that at other times were equally likely to be locked in battle with one another.

The deeper institutional dynamics of American religious and economic life suggest that the divergence of liberal and evangelical Protestantism in the twentieth century is only an episode in a broader and more complex evolutionary process involving successive realignments of the interrelationships of religion and economic, political, and social power.

Religious Demography and the Geography of Economic Life in Antebellum America

In the first half of the nineteenth century, a broad alliance of self-identified evangelical religious groups succeeded in "rechurching" Americans and, in the process of doing so, made the voluntary association the mechanism of choice for defining and pursuing collective purposes "of a thousand kinds" — ranging from commercial and manufacturing companies through "religious, moral, serious, futile, general or restricted, enormous or diminutive" bodies.[14]

But even as early as 1800, voluntary associations meant different things to different people — and these differences had significant religious overtones. The South led the nation with its outspoken assertions of the right of citizens to worship freely and its opposition to religious establishment. In doing so, it vigorously defended the right of believers to establish and contribute to congregations. But there were distinct limits to this policy. Having confiscated the glebe lands and charitable funds controlled by the established Anglicans, states like Virginia were not about to empower any religious body to accumulate property and power. Thomas Jefferson's nephew, Virginia jurist Henry St. George Tucker, summarized the attitudes of most southerners in an opinion he handed down in 1832. "No man at all acquainted with the course of legislation in Virginia, can doubt for a moment, the decided hostility of the legislative power to religious incorporations," Tucker declared. "Its jealousy of the possible interference of religious establishments in matters of government, if they were permitted to accumulate large possessions, as the church has been prone to do elsewhere, is doubtless at the bottom of this feeling. The legislature knows . . . that wealth is power."[15]

The South's hostility to religious establishments, to charitable trusts, and to corporate enterprise was rooted as much in Thomas Jefferson's agrarianism as in the theology and polity of the Baptists and Methodists who dominated the religious life of the region. With their stress on religious voluntarism and churches as gathered bodies, they naturally opposed mechanisms that might diminish the spiritual sovereignty and responsibility of individual believers.

In contrast, New England — where the Congregational Church remained established through the first quarter of the nineteenth century — was notable for its liberal attitudes towards corporations. Viewed as instruments for maintaining and extending the power of the Congregationalist/ Federalist "Standing Order," the legislatures of Connecticut and Massachusetts issued charters to religiously and politically orthodox leaders in

14. Alexis de Tocqueville, *Democracy in America,* trans. Henry Reeve (New York: Alfred A. Knopf, 1945), vol. 2, p. 114.
15. Opinion in Gallego's Executors v. Attorney General et al., 3 *Leigh's Reports* (1832), pp. 450-91.

the expectation that, by combining ecclesiastical and commercial power, they might hold back the rising tides of popular dissent.

By 1800, the institutional consequences of these sectional differences were already evident. New England led the nation in corporate establishments, with 200 of the new nation's 332 corporations, boasting 16.3 chartered corporations for every 100,000 inhabitants — as opposed to 4.6 per hundred thousand in the Middle Atlantic and 2.9 in the southern states.[16] This naturally had an enormous impact on economic and cultural development: by 1850, New England, despite its lack of natural advantages, had become the manufacturing and banking center of the country — and its colleges, libraries, hospitals, and charitable institutions set the pace for the rest of the country.

As Protestants, most Americans shared the New Englanders' appreciation for the importance of education, charity, and commerce. However, by limiting the scope, scale, and influence of private enterprise and favoring public institutions, they placed significant obstacles in the way of efforts to provide these services, since governmental action necessarily required political consensus that was invariably difficult to achieve.[17] Because of this, state institutions like the University of Virginia, as well as the dozens of private academies, seminaries, and colleges founded in the years before the Civil War, would remain not only poor — relative to institutions like Harvard and Yale — but locally oriented.[18]

In his argument defending Dartmouth's charter against the Jeffersonians who sought to transform the college into a state institution in 1819, Daniel Webster predicted the consequences of making corporations sub-

16. Joseph S. Davis, *Essays in the Earlier History of American Corporations* (Cambridge, MA: Harvard University Press, 1918).

17. This is what political scientist James Douglas calls a "categorical constraint," which in this case means the limits on the ability of democratic governments to provide services that can only be used by small numbers of citizens. On this, see James Douglas, "Political Theories of Nonprofit Organization," in *The Nonprofit Sector: A Research Handbook,* ed. W. W. Powell (New Haven: Yale University Press, 1987), pp. 45-48. See also Burton Weisbrod, "Toward a Theory of the Voluntary Non-Profit Sector in a Three-Sector Economy," in *Altruism, Morality, and Economic Theory,* ed. Edmund S. Phelps (New York: Russell Sage Foundation, 1975) and *The Voluntary Nonprofit Sector: An Economic Analysis* (Lexington, MA: D. C. Heath, 1977).

18. See Colin B. Burke, *American Collegiate Populations* (New York: New York University Press, 1982).

ject to the popular will. "The case before the Court is not of ordinary importance, nor of every day occurrence," Webster declared.

> It affects not this college only, but every college, and all the literary institutions of the country. They have flourished, hitherto, and have become in a high degree respectable and useful to the community. They have all a common principle of existence, the inviolability of their charters. It will be a dangerous, a most dangerous experiment, to hold these institutions subject to the rise and fall of popular parties, and the fluctuations of political opinions. If the franchise may be at any time taken away, or impaired, the property also may be taken away, or its use perverted. Benefactors will have no certainty of effecting the object of their bounty; and learned men will be deterred from devoting themselves to the service of such institutions, from the precarious title of their offices. Colleges and halls will be deserted by all better spirits, and become a theatre for the contention of politics. Party and faction will be cherished in the places consecrated to piety and learning. These consequences are neither remote nor possible only. They are certain and immediate.[19]

Webster's argument was as much legal as religious and political. To defend the inviolability of corporate charters in this period was — as Webster's auditors knew well — to defend the power of religious groups like the Congregationalists to expand their influence in places where their numbers were insufficient to provide them with electoral power.

Connections between civil privatism and religious demography were causal, not correlative: in an era when religion shaped political preferences and churches were actively partisan, religious bodies took positions on issues of incorporation and elaborated theological views that explicitly tied questions of moral agency to particular organizational forms.[20] Moreover,

---

19. Dartmouth College v. Woodward, 4 *Wheaton* 518; 4 L. Ed. 629 (1819).

20. On antebellum views of the theological implications of organizational forms, see Lyman Beecher, *Autobiography*, ed. Barbara Cross (Cambridge, MA: Harvard University Press, 1961); William Ellery Channing's 1829 essay, "Associations," in *Channing's Works* (Boston: Unitarian Association, 1900); Leonard Bacon, *The Christian Doctrine of Stewardship with Respect to Property* (New Haven: Leonard Whiting, 1832) and "Responsibility in the Management of Societies," *The New Englander* 1 (1847): 21-41; Francis Wayland, *The Limitations of Human Responsibility* (New York: D. Appleton & Company, 1838). For an interpretation of these views, see Peter Dobkin Hall, "Religion and the Origin of Voluntary Associations," PONPO Working Paper #213 (New Haven: Program on Non-Profit Organizations, Yale University, 1994).

before the 1830s, the preference for using voluntary associations appears to have been carried westward by the New England Diaspora: everywhere New Englanders settled, they not only became the leading proponents of associational activity, but also — largely through the use of these associations — became the economic and social leaders of communities in which they settled outside New England.[21]

In places that drew their populations from both North and South, the positions people took regarding corporations and other legal instruments that promoted the privatization of power (especially the capacity to establish charitable trusts) tended to be closely tied both to religion and place of birth. In Ohio, for example, a coalition of northern Congregationalists and Presbyterians fought fierce and protracted legislative and judicial battles with Methodist and Baptist southerners over the powers of corporations.[22] Even in New England, where private corporate enterprise was most fully advanced and accepted, opposition to civil privatism — most notable in the famous Dartmouth College case — was closely tied to the politics of religious dissent, with the Baptists, Methodists, and, occasionally, the Episcopalians aligned against the Congregationalist-Presbyterian establishment.

21. In *Democracy in America,* de Tocqueville noted that, in 1830, "thirty-six members of Congress were born in the little state of Connecticut," whose population "constitutes only one forty-third part of that of the United States, thus furnished one eighth of the whole body of representatives. The state of Connecticut of itself . . . sends only five delegates to Congress; and the thirty-one others sit for the new western states," vol. 1, p. 294. On the economic preeminence of migrant New Englanders, see Lee Soltow, *Men and Wealth in the United States, 1850-1870* (New Haven: Yale University Press, 1975). Mary P. Ryan's *The Cradle of the Middle Class: The Family in Oneida County, New York, 1790-1860* (New York: Cambridge University Press, 1981) provides a superbly detailed account of the interconnections of religion, economic life, and social activities among migrant Yankees.

22. Peter Dobkin Hall, "The Spirit of the Ordinance of 1787: Organizational Values, Voluntary Associations, and Higher Education in Ohio, 1803-1830," in *". . . Schools and the Means of Education Shall Be Forever Encouraged": A History of Education in the Old Northwest, 1787-1880,* ed. Paul Mattingly and Edward Stevens, Jr. (Athens: Ohio University Libraries, 1987), pp. 97-114; Peter Dobkin Hall, "Cultures of Trusteeship in the United States," in Peter Dobkin Hall, *Inventing the Nonprofit Sector and Other Essays on Philanthropy, Voluntarism, and Nonprofit Organizations* (Baltimore: Johns Hopkins University Press, 1992), pp. 135-206.

Nationalism and Localism

Religious factors continued to shape institutional life as a national economy and culture began to emerge on the eve of the Civil War. But the shared commitment to national redemption that had promoted cooperation among evangelical Protestants during the first quarter of the century dissipated in the face of theological and political differences that, to a significant extent, paralleled the divergent trajectories of economic development.

Theology shaped organizational preferences and investments of money and time. Particularly important in this regard were the modifications of Calvinism wrought by the "New Divinity" clergy built on Jonathan Edwards's synthesis of theology and psychological and political ideas. Although continuing to operate within the providential framework of Calvinism, Edwards and his followers came to distinguish the activity of conversion — which involved leading people to believe and to surrender themselves to God — from sanctification — which continued to depend entirely on God's inscrutable will. This distinction enlarged and clarified the role of clergy and church in what had been treated as secular affairs, as literacy, charity, and even the social and political order itself came to be viewed as domains with significantly spiritual dimensions.

By the early nineteenth century, theologians like Yale's Timothy Dwight — Edwards's grandson and the "pope" of New England Congregationalism — were actively expanding the implications of this perspective, coupling aggressive political engagement with industrious institution building, arguing that "whatever is to be done, except the work of sanctification, which man cannot do, is to be done by man as the instrument of his Maker. Man is to plant, and water; and then, and then only, is warranted either to hope, or to pray, that God will give the increase."[23] Though some of their contemporaries took issue with what they regarded as the New Haven Theology's embrace of an activist perfectionism that verged perilously on Arminianism, this did not deter Dwight and his protégés from planting and watering — schools, colleges, seminaries, and other voluntary institutions everywhere they settled.

This impulse was given added impetus, after the 1840s, by Dwight's

23. Timothy Dwight, *Travels in New England and New York* (New Haven, 1822), vol. 4, p. 407.

protégé, Lyman Beecher. "The thing required for the civil and religious prosperity of the West," he declared, "is universal education, and moral culture, by institutions commensurate to that result — the all-pervading influence of schools, and colleges, and seminaries, and pastors, and churches." But, he warned

> large masses of unenlightened mind lie in almost every portion of this nation. . . . a million of voters without intelligence, or conscience, or patriotism, or property, and driven on by demagogues to forbid recoil and push us over, in a moment all may be lost. . . . This danger from uneducated mind is augmenting daily by the rapid influx of foreign immigrants, unacquainted with our institutions, unaccustomed to self-government, inaccessible to education, and easily accessible to prepossession, and inveterate credulity, and intrigue, and easily embodied and wielded by sinister design. What is to be done to educate the millions which in twenty years Europe will pour out upon us?[24]

Although the efforts of Beecher and other northern evangelical institution-builders produced impressive public and private commitments to education in areas where their co-religionists had settled in significant numbers — in the northeast and the upper tier of the Old Northwest — their endeavors had little impact on the South. Despite Jefferson's pleas to the Virginia legislature to establish a common school system, the state rejected his plans — and other southern states followed suit, not only resisting the creation of public schools, but placing major legal obstacles in the way of private educational and eleemosynary initiatives of every kind.

As noted, the South — and the southerners who migrated westward — did not completely reject voluntary associations, however. Their deep commitment to religious freedom gave broad rights to religious groups. But it strictly limited the ability of religious and other corporate bodies to accumulate property, to hold funds in trust, and to receive charitable bequests. Nor did the South turn its back on education — although it distinctly favored public over private institutions. While virtually every southern state could boast a state university by 1860, none had been founded in New England. (Indeed, the Morrill Act funds, which gave such impetus to the establishment of state institutions west of the Mississippi, were initially granted to private institutions in New England.)

24. Beecher, "A Plea for the West" (1835), in *Autobiography*.

Divergent Institutional Impacts of Evangelicalism

By 1880, divergent religious and institutional orientations had produced pronounced differences in educational opportunity that had significant economic implications. In the North, the ratio of schools to population averaged 1:235, public education expenditures per capita averaged $2.50, the ratio of public and private libraries to population averaged 1:11,849, and the proportion of illiterates in the population (despite the influx of foreign immigrants!) averaged 4.5 percent. In the South, the ratio of schools to population averaged 1:319, public education expenditures per capita averaged $.49, the ratio of public and private libraries to population averaged 1:53,516, and the proportion of illiterates in the population ranged between 29 and 44 percent.[25] While the problem of illiteracy in the South was due in part to the large number of unschooled freedmen, between a quarter and a third of illiterates in the region were white.

Obviously, young men growing up in the South, which was still overwhelmingly rural and agricultural, and sustained only the most primitive kind of cultural and educational infrastructure, lived in a far more constricted universe of occupational and economic opportunities than their counterparts in the Northeast and Midwest. Not only were emergent national enterprises more likely to be headquartered in the North, the colleges — all of them tied to northern denominations — that served as the major arenas for training and recruiting the executives and administrators of national endeavors were located there.

This was not to any significant extent a by-product of the war. Southern colleges and universities — the largest of them state-run — never aspired to serve national constituencies, in contrast to the northern colleges — all of them private and most of them tied to evangelical denominations — which almost invariably saw themselves as serving the nation as a whole, not just their states.[26] While Thomas Jefferson's "Report of the

25. Education and literacy statistics come from U.S. Department of the Interior, Census Office, *Compendium of the Tenth Census (June 1, 1880).* (Washington, DC: Government Printing Office, 1883). Statistics on libraries come from U.S. Department of the Interior, Bureau of Education, *Public Libraries in the United States of America — Their History, Condition, and Management. Special Report* (Washington, DC: Government Printing Office, 1876).

26. For an excellent overview of the relative contributions of colleges and universities to leadership in occupations and professions, see George W. Pierson, *The Education of*

Commissioners for the University of Virginia," in defining the purposes of the institution, wrote of its intention to "give every citizen the information he needs for the transaction of his own business . . . and [to] understand his duties to his neighbors and country," it was quite clear — in a document that contained not a single reference to the nation — that the citizens the university intended to educate were citizens of Virginia.[27] It is equally clear that when the Yale Report of 1828, the paradigmatic statement that would define the form and content of northern evangelical higher education for most of the nineteenth century, spoke of the importance of "thorough education" to "our republican form of government" and of the "active, enterprising character of our population" — concluding with the question "when even our mountains, and rivers and lakes, are upon a scale which seems to denote, that we are destined to be a great and mighty nation, shall our literature be feeble, and scanty, and superficial?" — it was concerned with producing educated citizens who would serve the nation, not just a state or region.[28]

Although some wealthy southerners attended northern colleges (among such notables Princetonian James Madison, Yalie John C. Calhoun, and Harvardian "Rooney" Lee, son of Robert E. Lee), by 1855 the southern presence — which at Yale had stood above 10 percent for the previous fifty years — dropped to nearly nothing. Even Princeton, which has always borne a reputation as an institution favored by "southern gentlemen," never recruited more than 5 percent of its students from the South until after World War II.[29] Southern higher education, public and private, reinforced the localism of predominant religious beliefs, serving to focus the energies and aspirations of political and economic leaders on their own communities rather than in broader civic and national directions.

But if the South was paradigmatic in its localism — a localism that would be powerfully intensified by slavery and war — it is also evident that it was not alone in its parochialism, which was often shared by the small

---

American Leaders: Comparative Contributions of U.S. Colleges and Universities (New York: Frederick A. Praeger, 1969).

27. Thomas Jefferson, "Report of the Commissioners of the University of Virginia" (1818), in *Public and Private Papers* (New York: Vintage Books, 1990), pp. 131-47.

28. "Original Papers in Relation to a Course of Liberal Education [The Yale Report of 1828]," *The American Journal of Science and Arts* XV (January 1829).

29. See George W. Pierson, *A Yale Book of Numbers: Historical Statistics of the College and University, 1701-1976* (New Haven: Yale University Press, 1983), pp. 65-81.

denominationally tied institutions of the Midwest. When Miami University president Robert Hamilton Bishop spoke in 1824 of his institution educating "lords of the soil" who would be "at once farmers and scholars," he was surely thinking of the benefits it would bring the locality rather than the nation.[30]

By the mid-nineteenth century, a bifurcation of the nation's cultural infrastructure — and with it the orientations of its economic and political leadership — was already evident. A handful of colleges — all of them located in the Northeast and closely identified to varying degrees with "liberal" Calvinist theological views — had begun self-consciously preparing their graduates for national leadership. And spread throughout the country were scores of institutions committed to building healthy, learned, and virtuous populations in their immediate environs. Attending the latter did not preclude embracing the perspectives and methods of the nationalists — nor was college education a requisite for eventual national leadership. Nonetheless, it seems clear that certain kinds of educational experiences greatly increased the likelihood of participation in national enterprises, while others were more likely to direct graduates into local and regional arenas.

The transformation of economic life in the decades following the Civil War, particularly the emergence of large-scale national enterprises, was neither inevitable nor irresistible. While it is unquestionably true that wartime imperatives compelled consolidation of the railroad and telegraph industries, it is equally true that neither the incentive of greater efficiencies and profitability nor the compulsion of federal legislation were sufficient in themselves to sustain these national outcomes. Like the military effort itself, the national economy required cadres of individuals who not only possessed technical skills and administrative competencies, but the values and training that would enable them to work together in large-scale, geographically extensive enterprises.

Early nineteenth-century America was not a place where individuals with these skills, competencies, values, and training were easily found. The individualistic, competitive, mobile, and unstable features of the American economy and polity coexisted uneasily with the efforts of conservative religious and political leaders to promote civic, corporate, and collectivist values needed by large-scale trans-local enterprises. Even though the ante-

---

30. Robert Hamilton Bishop, "Inaugural Address" in *Oxford Addresses* (Hanover, 1835), pp. 20-21.

bellum evangelicals had succeeded in rechurching their countrymen, the multiplication of sects and increasing geographic and occupational mobility made it easier for Americans to shrug off inherited religious preferences for more membership-congenial congregations — making the imposition of social discipline and transmission of values increasingly difficult.

The Bureaucratic Vision, Religion, and the Origins of National Institutions

Reflecting on the Civil War, which had not only affirmed political nationality, but — in their own eyes at least — vindicated the claims of the wealthy, learned, and respectable to national leadership, Harvard's young patrician president, Charles W. Eliot, would in 1869 decry the fact that Americans

> do not apply to mental activities the principle of division of labor; we have but a halting faith in special training for high professional employments. . . . The civilization of a people can be inferred from the variety of its tools. . . . As tools multiply, each is more ingeniously adapted to its own exclusive purpose. So with the men that make the State. For the individual, concentration, and the highest development of his own peculiar faculty, is the only prudence. But for the State, it is variety, not uniformity, of the intellectual product, which is needful.[31]

This soaring vision of enterprises that "divide and subordinate responsibilities," each "ingeniously adapted to its own exclusive purpose" but united by commitments to common purposes, was a clarion call to fulfilling the national purposes in ways that went beyond the political and governmental. The "wilderness" Americans were fighting, as Eliot had declared at the beginning of the essay that persuaded Harvard's elders to select him as the university's youngest president, was not merely physical, but moral. Working out the "awful problem of self-government" would require not only that Americans be "trained and armed," but also that they be ready to deploy the principle that "makes the modern army a possibility in government bureaus, in manufactories, . . . in all great companies" — and in higher education itself.[32]

31. Eliot, "Inaugural Address."
32. Charles W. Eliot, "The New Education," *Atlantic* 23 (1869): 203.

Eliot's nationalist and corporatist vision was widely shared in the circles of Boston, New York, and Philadelphia business leaders who were committed to building national enterprises. And their willingness to do so was as deeply religious as it was intensely patriotic. Eliot's contemporary and fellow Unitarian, Henry Varnum Poor, had found his calling as a pioneer business journalist and statistician in his "buoyant, optimistic belief in man's progress and perfection."[33] Brother-in-law of Unitarian theologian Frederick Henry Hedge and intimate of Ralph Waldo Emerson, the Channings, Theodore Parker, and George Ripley, Poor shared their belief that

> God had given man a mind as the means for his perfection. Man's mind was stronger than man-made institutions and could alter these institutions which had brought sin and evil into the work. Yet the mind, in order to progress toward perfection, must be carefully trained and disciplined both intellectually and morally. . . . To Henry Poor, the coming of the industrial and transportation revolutions was, in fact, a magnificent verification of his basic concepts.

By creatively applying their minds to the labor-saving machine, men were making strides here towards the physical perfection that was the first and necessary step to intellectual and spiritual perfection. Of all the new technical instruments that were furthering the progress of mankind, the railroad was having the most profound effect. By lowering the cost of transportation and making possible widespread commercial agriculture and large-scale industry, the railroad was making food, clothing, and the other necessities of life plentiful to all classes of people. By breaking down the barriers of place and time, by permitting the interchange of ideas and beliefs as well as goods, the railroad was allaying petty regional antagonisms and narrow provincialism. In time it would even bring an end to the more traditional national boundaries and usher in the millennium of universal peace and prosperity.[34]

As the university was for Eliot the essential instrument for "training and arming" the American people to fight "the wilderness, physical and moral," so for Henry Varnum Poor, "the efficient construction and opera-

33. Alfred Chandler, "Henry Varnum Poor: Philosopher of Management," in Miller, ed., *Men in Business*, pp. 254-85.
34. Chandler, "Henry Varnum Poor," p. 256.

tion of the American railroad system was even more a moral than an economic necessity."[35]

Looking at the struggles of the 1860s and '70s retrospectively from the vantage point of the late twentieth century, it would appear that the commitment to evangelicalism that had been the common property of all reformed Protestant bodies before the Civil War was being abandoned by the theological liberals who embraced critical biblical scholarship, perfectionist philosophies, social Darwinism, increasingly bureaucratized "scientific" approaches to charity, and continuing efforts both to celebrate nationalism and to construct national religious, charitable, and reform organizations.

But things looked very different from the standpoint of those living through the sweeping institutional transformations of the post–Civil War decades. For the men and women of the Gilded Age, locating evangelicalism in the institutional and denominational landscape would have been far less easy. Although some institutions and denominations — like Unitarianism and the constellation of interlocked cultural and economic enterprises anchored in and around Boston — had clearly and unquestionably left evangelicalism far behind in their quest for the reform of national public life, virtually all other Protestant groups retained strong commitments to evangelical beliefs and methods, despite the growing presence of modernist and forthrightly anti-evangelical ideas in their midst.

Locating evangelicalism requires more than attention to denominational taxonomies because these were part of more inclusive and increasingly more elaborate interdependencies between the religious culture, the economy, and locational and affiliative communities — all of which were in an ongoing process of transformation. As this paper has tried to suggest, institutional decision making was never governed solely by economic considerations: just as economic rationality is inevitably bounded by the values of decision makers and the ways in which values and values-mediated affiliations framed access to key financial, social, and political resources, so the institutional considerations governing decisions about religious, cultural, and charitable entities were inevitably framed by linkages to economic and political stakeholders. As organizations and the arenas in which they operated became more extensive and complex, the location of individuals embracing certain beliefs and practices became more difficult to ascertain.

35. Chandler, "Henry Varnum Poor," p. 256.

National economic, political, social, and cultural institutions did not simply supplant local and regional ones. Because their emergence was both gradual and selective, even in industries where the efficiency and effectiveness of large-scale organizations was demonstrable, older systems and relationships persisted. And even by the end of the century, when economic superiority of large-scale organizations of every kind seemed unquestionable, they almost invariably coexisted with more traditional forms of enterprise operating in local and regional settings. Analogously, the intrusions of modernism and the retreats of evangelicalism transpired so gradually and selectively that at times the two coexisted within the same institutions and frameworks of belief.

Most national institutions — whether economic enterprises, religious bodies, professional societies, fraternal/sororal associations, or groups promoting social or political reform (like the Sanitary Commission, the freedmen's aid societies, and the charity organization movement) — varied considerably in the extent to which they were administratively centralized. Most were franchise form or federated entities that delegated significant — if variable — autonomy to regional and local subunits. In some instances authority flowed upward from subunits to the national organization; in others authority moved downward; most had mixed polities in which subunits were autonomous in some areas but not in others. In secular entities, as in religious bodies, organizational structure and process were shaped not only by the nature of the organization's activity, but also by its mission.

National economic enterprises were similarly mixed. As Alfred D. Chandler notes, large-scale integrated enterprises tended to be clustered in industries that used "capital-intensive, energy-consuming, continuous or large-batch production technology to produce for mass markets."[36] They "failed to thrive in industries where the processes of production used labor-intensive methods which required little heat, energy, or complex machinery" or where "existing middlemen had little difficulty in distributing and selling the product."[37]

Although technology and the material circumstances of specific industries shaped the scale and scope of firms, so too did the vision and val-

36. Alfred D. Chandler, *The Visible Hand: The Managerial Revolution in American Business* (Cambridge, MA: Harvard University Press, 1977), p. 347.

37. Chandler, *The Visible Hand*, p. 347.

ues of the entrepreneurs who created them. Even in industries that adopted large-scale administrative structures, there were significant variations in integration and centralization. In railroad management, for example, the Erie Railroad — organized by retired military officer Daniel McCallum — favored a highly centralized administrative model. The Pennsylvania Railroad — organized by civil engineer J. Edgar Thompson — favored a decentralized structure that granted significant authority to divisional executives. Although the markets for sewing machines and agricultural implements were similar in many respects — requiring highly personalized interactions between sellers and purchasers — manufacturers like Singer Sewing Machine and McCormick Harvester organized their distribution networks along very different lines: Singer favored a system of salaried employees working within a rigidly centralized structure that enabled top managers to better coordinate production and marketing; McCormick preferred a loose network of franchised dealers who, its top managers believed, were better positioned to "supply specialized services of demonstration, installation, after-sales service and repair, and consumer credit" than salaried operatives working within a rigidly bureaucratized structure.[38] Although Standard Oil is generally regarded as a model of monopolistic centralization, its administrative structure was remarkably loose: the subsidiary companies that belonged to the Trust — most of them concerned with marketing petroleum products in particular localities — operated with a high degree of autonomy (although key strategic decisions involving the Trust as a whole were made at the top).[39] General Electric, on the other hand — in part because of the role of investment bankers in creating the firm — embraced the centralized, integrated, functionally departmentalized structure that had been perfected by the railroads.

The role of religion in shaping these preferences is a topic that very much needs to be investigated. It has been established that the national sales organization set up by financier Jay Cooke to create a mass market for government bonds during the Civil War was modeled on the evangelical bodies with which he had been involved as a youth.[40] R. Richard Wohl

---

38. Chandler, *The Visible Hand*, p. 420.

39. Chandler, *The Visible Hand*, p. 420.

40. Ellis P. Oberholzer, *Jay Cooke — Financier* (New York, 1907); Henrietta Larson, *Jay Cooke: Private Banker* (Cambridge, MA: Harvard University Press, 1939).

makes a persuasive case for the influence of religion on the entrepreneurial activities of Congregationalist Henry Noble Day, who left the ministry for a successful career as a railroad promoter in Ohio.[41] The Unitarian influence on the economic ideas of financial journalist Henry Varnum Poor and management reformer Frederick W. Taylor is well documented.[42] It seems likely that John D. Rockefeller's experiences with loosely coupled Baptist bodies served as a model for management of the Standard Oil Trust which, rather than being tightly integrated, granted subsidiaries considerable autonomy and coordinated their activities through committees.[43] In contrast, J. P. Morgan's preference for top-down coordinated enterprises seems peculiarly reflective of his devout Episcopalianism!

Along with various forms of administrative centralization, large-scale enterprises also became astonishingly concentrated geographically. Regardless of the nature of their products or how far-flung their production facilities and distribution networks, nearly all (75 percent) of the publicly held industrial firms listed in the 1914 edition of Moody's Analyses of Investments were located in five Northeastern states — New York, New Jersey, Connecticut, Massachusetts, and Pennsylvania. Of these, 60 percent listed their headquarters as being in New York City, 20 percent in Philadelphia, and 7 percent in Boston. These firms included agricultural products companies like the American Cotton Oil, American Snuff, American Sugar Refining, American Tobacco companies, most of whose subsidiaries and sources of supply were in the South, and the American Linseed and the Corn Products Refining companies, most of whose subsidiaries were located in the Midwest. Moody's listed only six major industrial firms as being headquartered in the South.[44]

This extraordinary geographical concentration of corporate head-

41. R. Richard Wohl, "Henry Noble Day: A Study in Good Works, 1808-1890," in Miller, ed., *Men in Business*, pp. 153-92.

42. Chandler, "Henry Varnum Poor"; Robert Kanigal, *The One Best Way: Frederick Winslow Taylor and the Enigma of Efficiency* (New York: Viking Press, 1998).

43. On management structure in the Standard Oil Trust, see Chandler, *Visible Hand*, p. 417. On Rockefeller's religiosity and how it influenced his business methods, see Ron Chernow, *Titan: The Life of John D. Rockefeller, Sr.* (New York: Random House, 1998). On his peculiarly non-directive manner of bringing up his son, John D. Rockefeller, Jr., see Peter Dobkin Hall, "The Empty Tomb: The Making of Dynastic Identity," in *Lives in Trust: The Fortunes of Dynastic Families in Late Twentieth Century America*, ed. George E. Marcus and Peter Dobkin Hall (Boulder: Westview Press, 1992).

44. Moody, *Moody's Analysis of Public Utilities and Industrials, 1914*.

quarters meant, in effect, that graduates of Northeastern schools — particularly those from which top corporate executives had graduated or to which they had made major contributions — were relatively advantaged in terms of hiring and promotion. And because these schools, until the early years of the twentieth century, continued to reflect the religious proclivities of their founders to a greater (Yale and Princeton) or lesser (Harvard) degree, religion remained an important element both in the recruitment of the national corporate elite and in the composition of the governing boards of the institutions they supported. All of these universities ardently embraced nationalism and viewed themselves as producers of national leaders.

On occasion, corporate leaders from more conservative traditions made major philanthropic bequests outside of the Northeast. James B. Duke (founder of American Tobacco) and Cornelius Vanderbilt (New York Central Railroad) gave major gifts to sectarian institutions in the South — Duke to Methodist Trinity College in North Carolina and Vanderbilt to Methodist Central Tennessee University in Nashville. Baptist John D. Rockefeller (Standard Oil) gave millions to the University of Chicago and other national Baptist charities. But their sectarian intentions had little national impact. Neither Duke nor Vanderbilt would be anything more than institutions of local consequence until after World War II. Rockefeller's hope that the University of Chicago would become a powerful and distinctively Baptist force in American higher education was subverted by the predominantly nonsectarian/liberal religiosity of its faculty and his own unwillingness to continue subsidizing the university's development after the retirement of William Rainey Harper.[45]

The aggregate impact of philanthropic giving by men associated with particular religious persuasions and financial interests tended to provide the greatest benefit to institutions like Yale, Harvard, and Princeton, which had firm commitments to national institutionalist values. Because the New York Central's long-time chief executive, Chauncey DePew, was a Yale alumnus, giving by the Vanderbilts and by top executives of the railroad tended to go to New Haven. The fact that key associates of John D. Rockefeller — Stephen Harkness, John W. Sterling, and Oliver and Harry Payne — were Yale alumni assured that Congregationalist Yale would reap where Baptist Rockefeller had sown.

45. Chernow, *Titan,* pp. 495-96.

The linkages of the emerging national corporate elite to self-pro-
claimed national cultural institutions had the effect over time of weighting
economic and occupational opportunities not only in favor of the graduates of institutions that embraced the values of big business, but to those
who identified with religious bodies that shared those values. Certain
firms came to be known for their preference for hiring the graduates of
certain institutions: the New York Central and the United States Trust
Company, for example, were considered to be Yale firms; the Morgan
Bank, the Chicago, Burlington, and Quincy Railroad, on the other hand,
were known to favor Harvard graduates. Whether these hiring preferences
carried with them weightings in favor of particular religious groups is unknown, though it has been established that by 1900 — a time when Baptists
and Methodists vastly outnumbered Congregationalists, Presbyterians,
Episcopalians, and Unitarians nationally — nearly 70 percent of the top executives of major national firms were members of "liberal" Protestant denominations and more than 60 percent had been born in New England or
the Middle Atlantic states.[46] By the 1920s, the top levels of corporate management had become so homogenized in terms of executives' origins that
scholars of economic life began to worry that the business "class" was in
danger of becoming a business "caste."[47]

Although providing privileged entree to national business leadership,
the majority of graduates of Ivy League institutions returned to the
smaller towns and cities from which they had come.[48] Like the alumni who
had settled in the South and West and served as crucial links in the national
evangelical network in the antebellum decades, the businessmen, doctors,
lawyers, engineers, ministers, and educators who graduated from Yale,
Princeton, and Harvard in the late nineteenth and early twentieth centuries — now linked by active alumni organizations and publications, graduates clubs, and regular reunions — played key roles in connecting localities
to national centers. Graduates of institutions like Yale, with its strong tradition of evangelical institutionalism, were especially active organizationally; they were more than twice as likely as Harvard alumni to serve on
corporate boards and were commonly members of local chapters of na-

46. Miller, "The Business Elite," and "The Recruitment of the American Business
Elite."

47. Taussig and Joslyn, *American Business Leaders*, pp. 233-70.

48. See Pierson, *A Yale Book of Numbers*, pp. 453-64.

tional professional associations and fraternal orders, as well as being active in their religious congregations.[49]

Economic Culture and "Business Civilization"

But it would be a great mistake to suppose either that national institutions had overwhelmed local and regional ones or that the continuing vitality of local and regional economies was a mere by-product of national systems of production and exchange. Markets for most products — except for heavy industrial goods like locomotives and electrical generating equipment — continued to be local, and the enterprises that bought and sold these goods continued to be locally owned. Moreover, the manufacturing, processing, and extractive activities of national firms were not only located wherever human and natural resources and the transportation infrastructure required them to be, but usually operated as components of local and regional economies. Thus, for example, though the American Steel and Wire Company might be a part of the mighty United States Steel Corporation, it was only one of many components of the diversified industrial economy of a city like Allentown, Pennsylvania. As a part of US Steel, it drew on the executive talent and economies of scale associated with units of a large integrated national enterprise; at the same time, it employed and provided opportunities for advancement for bright young Allentonians — graduates of local schools like Muhlenburg, Lehigh, and LaFayette. Economic nationality thus had a dual impact, simultaneously strengthening both national and local economic and institutional communities.

The presence of national firms in localities helped to shape their political cultures. In the wake of the Populist revolt of the 1890s — whose platform, in proposing public control of the railroads, communications, and banking industries, had posed a very direct threat to national corporate interests — national corporate leaders turned their attention from economic to social and political concerns. While a few, like Pennsylvania coal baron George F. Baer, would continue to insist that "the rights and interests of the laboring man" would "be protected and cared for — not by the labor agitators, but by the Christian men to whom God in His infinite wisdom" had "given control of the property interests of this country,"

49. See Hall, "Cultures of Trusteeship," p. 319.

most were willing to endorse the more moderate positions of industrialist and Republican party leader Marcus Alonzo Hanna, who — proclaiming "any employer who won't meet his men half-way is a damned fool" — endeavored to create forums like the National Civic Federation, a national organization with local chapters, for the adjudication of industrial disputes.[50] The Civic Federation movement gave expression to the deeper convictions of leaders like Andrew Carnegie, whose 1889 essay, "Wealth," had argued that the "men of affairs" who had created the great industrial enterprises held their fortunes and their positions as trustees, not as mere proprietors.

The American business class did not abandon evangelicalism because it had become secularized (indeed, the fact that, of all the occupational groups listed in *Who's Who,* business leaders were the most likely to include religious affiliation in their biographies, suggests that their religious attachments remained strong).[51] Nor did the groups that continued to identify themselves as evangelical by 1930 (despite their criticism of aspects of the emerging consumer culture) become opposed to business as such. Rather, the particular economic, social, and political circumstances of evangelical faith communities and local and national business elites after the turn of the century altered their understandings of values — of asceticism, frugality, plain living, and ceaselessly productive activities grounded in beliefs in Protestant exclusivism, scriptural inerrancy, and the spiritual sovereignty of the individual — understandings once broadly embraced across the continuum of reformed Protestantisms. These circumstances — products of the aggregated interactions of religious beliefs and practices, organizational elaboration, population and religious demographics, and the intensified division of labor and productive activity — threatened on the one hand to disrupt the civic solidarity that underlay the

50. On Hanna, see Herbert Croly, *Marcus Alonzo Hanna: His Life and His Work* (New York: The Macmillan Company, 1919). It is no coincidence that Hanna's biographer was both a protégé of Charles Eliot's and the leading theoretician of the progressive movement — for, despite his popular image, he was one of the real pillars of business progressivism.

51. Luther Fry makes this observation in "Religious Affiliations," p. 243. Affirming the importance of religious affiliation to businessmen, the Lynds write that membership in "religious groups is generally taken for granted, particularly among the business class, and a newcomer is commonly greeted with the question, 'What church do you go to?'" Robert Lynd and Helen Lynd, *Middletown: A Study in American Culture* (New York: Harcourt, Brace & Company, 1929), p. 315.

economic prosperity and political order of the triumphant "business civilization" of the 1920s while, on the other, endangering the moral community that those on the periphery of the national economy had come to embrace as a means of adapting to the new economic and political order.

Maintaining the new American economic and social order had come to require practices and lifestyles inimical to an evangelical ethos. Faced with a climactic conflict between labor and capital — which had burst into widespread episodic violence in the years between 1877 and 1919 — national economics had implemented and promoted what amounted to a tradeoff of traditional equality of condition (obviously no longer possible under an industrial society based on large-scale enterprises) for new kinds of equality of opportunity. Based not only on a vast expansion of access to education, but also on management policies that, on the one hand, increased workers' wages to enable them to purchase the goods they produced and, on the other, adopted innovative production techniques that lowered the price of manufactured goods, the new economic order, by the 1920s, led business and government to stimulate consumer purchasing in order to stabilize the economy.[52]

The elements of the condition/equality tradeoff are present in the series of essays written by Andrew Carnegie between 1886 and 1889, in which he applied a Social Darwinist analysis of the "labor struggle" to discuss the growth of large-scale enterprises as outcomes of the "struggle for survival" in competitive economies and the "survival of the fittest" economic enterprises.[53] To this he added, in his essay "Wealth," an argument about the responsibility of the "men of affairs" who created these enter-

52. U.S. Department of the Interior, Office of Education, *Report of the Commissioner of Education* (Washington, DC: Government Printing Office, 1879). On the public policies of business in this period, see David Noble, *America by Design: Science, Technology, and the Rise of Corporate Capitalism* (New York: Oxford University Press, 1977); Martin Sklar, *The Corporate Reconstruction of American Capitalism, 1890-1916* (New York: Cambridge University Press, 1988); Louis Galambos and Joseph Pratt, *The Rise of the Corporate Commonwealth: United States Business and Public Policy in the Twentieth Century* (New York: Basic Books, 1988). See also Stuart Ewen, *Captains of Consciousness: Advertising and the Social Roots of the Consumer Culture* (New York: McGraw-Hill, 1976). On the social thought of turn-of-the-century business leaders, see Morrell Heald, *The Social Responsibilities of Business: Company and Community, 1900-1960* (Cleveland: Case Western Reserve University Press, 1969).

53. Andrew Carnegie, "An Employer's View of the Labor Question," *Forum* 1 (1886): 114-25 and "Results of the Labor Struggle," *Forum* 1 (1886): 538-51.

prises to strategically invest their wealth in institutions and activities that would "place within the reach of the aspiring the ladders upon which they might rise."[54] The underlying argument of the essay was that the long-term survival of the economic system required: 1) that "men of affairs" proactively work to prevent the growth of the kinds of "clogged layers" of inherited wealth and privilege that were strangling England's economy; and 2) its continuing vitality — and stability — could only be assured by institutions that sorted men according to their abilities and assured that the "aspiring" could rise to positions of responsibility.

Quaker millionaire turned public servant Herbert Hoover's 1922 best-seller, *American Individualism*, represented the most complete formulation of the line of economic thought that began with Carnegie nearly 40 years earlier.[55] The difference between the pre- and postwar iterations of these ideas lay in the mechanisms through which they were implemented. Industrialists like Carnegie and Frederick W. Taylor assumed that economic equity — and the consumer empowerment that accompanied it — would result from increased earnings. Social engineers like Hoover and his contemporaries, on the other hand, framed economic empowerment as a matter of purchasing power — which could be substantially increased through consumer credit and through advertising methods that, in their view, constituted a form of consumer education.[56] Enabling people to buy things they didn't need with money they didn't have — and the impact of these economic practices on the stability of domestic life, gender roles, and sexual morality — brought the new order into conflict with the evangelicals' deep-seated asceticism.

Under these circumstances, causal links between religious and eco-

54. Andrew Carnegie, "Wealth," *North American Review* 148 (1889): 653-64.

55. Herbert Hoover, *American Individualism* (New York: Doubleday, Doran & Co., 1922).

56. Mark H. Rose's *Cities of Light and Heat: Domesticating Gas and Electricity in Urban America* (University Park: Pennsylvania State University Press, 1995) provides a uniquely detailed account of the activities of utility companies as investors in consumer education through public school programs. See also Janet Hutchison's important dissertation, "American Housing, Gender, and the Better Homes Movement, 1922-1935" (Ph.D. diss., University of Delaware, 1990), which provides a fine account of Hoover-era programs of consumer education. For overviews of these policies, see Ellis Hawley, "Herbert Hoover, the Commerce Secretariat, and the Vision of an 'Associative State,'" in *Men and Organizations: The American Economy in the Twentieth Century*, ed. Edwin Perkins (New York: G. P. Putnam's Sons, 1977), pp. 120-48.

nomic forces appear to be multidirectional. Even as late as the 1920s, it seems evident that all economic actors were, as people of professed faith, also religious actors, while all religious actors were, as participants in the economy, also economic actors. What mattered, as Weber suggests, is how the workings of the economy had, over time, produced geographically and socially segmented constellations of interests — which, as they became more differentiated from one another, carried increasing potential for conflict with one another. In spite of an increasing divergence of their social and economic situations and interests, the Protestants who identified themselves as evangelicals could sustain a broad ethical consensus — much as most Americans could, until the 1840s, and agree to disagree over slavery. But, much as the effort to maintain the balance of power between free and slave states eventually faltered as it became increasingly difficult to accommodate their interests through compromise, the "big tent" of post–Civil War evangelicalism was torn asunder by religious quarrels that masked more profound differences in economic and political interests and values.

The efforts of business leaders like Marcus Alonzo Hanna and Andrew Carnegie helped to rekindle civic values appropriate to the economic and political conditions of the new century. Not only did they stimulate a remarkable outpouring of philanthropic giving — much of it locally focused (including Carnegie's gifts of libraries and church organs) — they also helped inspire new kinds of civic organizations that mirrored the structures of national business enterprises, particularly national service clubs like Rotary, Kiwanis, Lions, and others. Despite the scorn of the literati, these organizations brought together local business and professional leaders for commendable purposes.[57]

By convening local businessmen and professionals, the service clubs helped define their collective identities and responsibilities as community leaders and, in so doing, created arenas for articulating the collective interests of communities. As such, they helped to domesticate and constrain the powerful forces of national economic life — the railroads, utility holding companies, the national communications network, and the metropoli-

57. On the service clubs, see Jeffrey Charles, *Service Clubs in American Society: Rotary, Kiwanis, and Lions* (Urbana, IL: University of Illinois Press, 1993). See also Charles Marden, *Rotary and Its Brothers: An Analysis and Interpretation of the Men's Service Club* (Princeton: Princeton University Press, 1935), and Lynd and Lynd, *Middletown*.

tan financial interests — whose decisions were seldom made with reference to the welfare of the localities in which they operated. Though inevitably "pro-business," in the increasingly differentiated economy of the twentieth century, this could mean a variety of things. Certainly, the clubs functioned as more than rubber stamps for powerful outside interests: through tax, planning, and zoning decisions, as well as through control of the resources of local banks and capital markets, local leaders controlled powerful instruments for influencing higher-level decisions about plant location and the nature and extent of corporate commitment to the welfare capitalist programs which, before the New Deal, constituted the "safety net" for America's dependent and disabled. At the same time, by throwing their prestige and their resources behind such public initiatives as modernizing the educational infrastructure and private initiatives like the Community Chest and community foundations, the service clubs helped determine the success or failure of these charitable enterprises.

The importance of the business-led reorganization of civic life cannot be underestimated. It unquestionably inspired the "New Era" programs of Herbert Hoover — the millionaire businessman turned public servant who served as director of international food relief under President Wilson and as Secretary of Commerce under Harding and Coolidge, and was elected President in 1928. Hoover's civic vision made abundant reference to the spiritual underpinnings of the new order, based on what he called "the higher purposes of individualism" that he saw emerging in the United States after World War I. "Our social and economic system cannot march toward better days unless it is inspired by things of the spirit," he declared in his best-selling 1922 book, *American Individualism*.

> It is here that the higher purposes of individualism must find their sustenance. Men do not live by bread alone. Nor is individualism merely a stimulus to production and the road to liberty; it alone admits the universal divine inspiration of every human soul.[58]

Echoing his Quaker skepticism about institutions, Hoover continued, "the divine spark does not lie in agreements, in organizations, in institutions, in masses or in groups. Spirituality with its faith, its hope, its charity, can be increased, by each individual's own effort. And in proportion as each individual increases his own store of spirituality, in that proportion increases

58. Hoover, *American Individualism*, p. 27.

the idealism of democracy."[59] For Hoover, organizations were not the source of spirituality, but their most powerful expression. "The vast multiplication of voluntary organizations for altruistic purposes," he wrote, are

> proof of the ferment of spirituality, service, and mutual responsibility. These associations for advancement of public welfare, improvement, morals, charity, public opinion, health, the clubs and societies for recreation and intellectual advancement, represent something moving at a far greater depth than "joining." They represent the widespread aspiration for mutual advancement, self-expression, and neighborly helpfulness.[60]

Hoover's spiritualized rhetoric pays tribute to the importance of evangelical religion in creating the progressive movement, as well as to its continuing involvement in progressive causes — the social gospel, interchurch cooperation, and international missionary work — through the end of the First World War. But the national political and economic crisis that followed the war's end brought nascent conflicts to the surface. A wave of labor strife involving general strikes and walkouts in key industries, combined with government crackdowns on political activists and a revival of nativism, pulled clergy and religious groups in different directions. Religious groups identified with national academic and denominational institutions shared a liberal pluralist vision that led them to support the efforts of workers and immigrants to claim a place in American life and to oppose the repressive actions of government agencies. Those who identified with more locally anchored religious bodies and economic constituencies — many of them evangelicals — tended to favor government efforts to regulate personal and political behavior. Political conflicts over prohibition, the rights of labor, First Amendment issues, and race opened up and were sharpened by the revival of the Ku Klux Klan — which, working through a sophisticated national organization, recruited millions of urban native-born working- and lower-middle-class American Protestants and rapidly became a powerful political force throughout the country. These political differences masked deeper divergences in lifestyle and religious orientation within communities. The Lynds' study of "Middletown" (Muncie, Indiana) suggests that, by 1925, there was a "tightening of denominational lines," as competition for the

59. Hoover, *American Individualism*, p. 27.
60. Hoover, *American Individualism*, pp. 28-29.

loyalties of citizens intensified between churches, the public schools, and such secular civic groups as the service clubs and fraternal and sororal bodies. The "liberal" churches, to which the business and professional classes tended to belong, responded by starting youth groups, athletic teams, and other "extra-religious activities" — and by identifying themselves with the civic agenda of the business community. The more conservative churches, which drew their members from the lower-middle and working classes, became more exclusive, placing support of denominational obligations ahead of local causes. Despite this, the Lynds found that despite efforts to "stir up the spiritual life" of some churches by inviting revivalists to "galvanize fading differences into new life," Middletown's "preoccupation with the daily necessities of life and with such new emotional outlets as the automobile, together with the pressure for civic solidarity, tends soon to dull such acute doctrinal self-consciousness."[61] As economic and social cleavages replaced sectarian divisions, religious differences tended to be associated with increasingly divergent styles of consumption, community participation, education levels, and cultural allegiances rather than theological loyalties.

There was nothing new about the linkage of religion and lifestyle. The novelty lay in the material, social, and institutional consequences of the breakup of the evangelical "united front." Until the 1920s, business had promoted values consonant with the evangelical ethos, stressing the virtues of frugality, self-denial, and living within one's means. But as post–World War I business leaders — haunted by the specter of the Russian Revolution — sought to stimulate the economy by encouraging consumers to buy things they didn't need with money that they didn't have, they were, in effect, challenging these traditional values and the ways of life that went with them. If the fashion shift from corsets and long petticoats to brassieres, knickers, knee-length dresses, low shoes, and silk stockings, was (as the Lynds noted) "greeted as a violation of morals and good taste," shifts in long-established patterns of housework were even more disturbing,[62] as women of the upper classes gave up making their families' clothing and increasingly left the tasks of cooking and cleaning to servants and labor-saving devices. Distress at the passing of the "old rule-of-thumb, mother-to-daughter method of passing down

61. Lynd and Lynd, *Middletown*, pp. 333-34.
62. Lynd and Lynd, *Middletown*, p. 160.

the traditional domestic economy" in favor of the foodways and cooking methods taught in high school home economics classes and touted in mass-circulation magazines came not from differences in food preferences, but from deeper concerns about social morality and traditional values.[63]

If the consumer culture threatened to unsettle traditional gender roles, it also destabilized parent-child relationships. Between 1870 and 1930, schools and schooling changed dramatically.[64] The proliferation of kindergartens enabled schools to enroll children at younger ages, while increasing numbers of high schools enabled children to stay in school until late adolescence. Moreover, the purposes of schooling broadened beyond merely imparting literacy and numeracy to include activities that can only be described as social engineering. Not only were students taught civic values, citizenship skills, and hygiene, but generous investments by utility companies, appliance manufacturers, and brand-name food producers underwrote an elaborate home economics curriculum that taught the young how and what to consume. Added to this by the 1920s were educational testing and a diversified curriculum, which steered youngsters into general, commercial, academic, and industrial tracks. The lessons of the classroom were reinforced by the growth of an elaborate "extracurriculum" of clubs, teams, and social events designed to regulate students' leisure and recreational activities, while imparting what professional educators regarded as appropriate values. Helped along by compulsory school attendance laws and the regulation of child labor, school enrollments increased impressively: in 1870, only 2 percent of American seventeen-year-olds were still attending school; by 1930, this had increased to nearly 30 percent.[65] Although the number of young people graduating from high school remained relatively low until after World War II, by 1930 more than 90 per-

63. Lynd and Lynd, *Middletown*, pp. 71, 157.

64. For the most comprehensive overview of the changing role of schools — and the linkages of educational changes to public policy — see President's Commission on Recent Social Trends, *Recent Social Trends in the United States* (New York: McGraw-Hill Book Co., 1933). The Lynds provide a finely textured account of the scope and impact of these changes in *Middletown*, pp. 181-224. For a detailed look at school curricula in the 1920s, see *The Work of the Public Schools — Rochester, New York* (Rochester: Board of Education, 1928).

65. U.S. Department of Commerce, Bureau of the Census, *Historical Statistics of the United States* (Washington, DC: Department of Commerce, 1975), p. 379.

cent of all children between the ages of five and seventeen were enrolled in school.[66]

Inevitably, such a massive institutional intervention in child rearing had noticeable impacts on children's social and occupational choices. The Lynds noted the growth of a distinctive school-centered "youth culture" in Middletown that was closely tied to the new business-controlled civic institutions. At the same time, both curriculum and extra-curriculum directed children to educational and vocational opportunities that lay beyond Middletown and the traditional occupations and lifestyles of their parents.[67] This posed particular challenges to those who looked to Scripture and tradition as sources of family authority.

The relationship of religious affiliation to changing patterns of civic life is suggested by W. Lloyd Warner and Paul Lunt's study of Newburyport, Massachusetts, in the 1930s. Warner and Lunt not only found significant connections between congregations and their members' patterns of organizational participation; they also took particular note of the differences between Yankee City's liberal (Congregationalist, Unitarian, and Episcopalian) and conservative (Baptist and Methodist) Protestant congregations, and how these affected the overall associational architecture of the community.[68]

The liberal Protestants were notable not only for the extensiveness of their associational ties, but also for their willingness to sponsor secular or ecumenical groups like the YMCA, Boy Scouts, and Campfire Girls — organizations that served the whole community rather than their own members.[69] Yankee City's liberal Protestant congregations tended to give rise to "primary associations around which satellite associations are clustered."[70] These primary associations, in turn, gave rise to and "ultimately control[led] the behavior and policies of the secondary associations" to which they were linked.[71] Overall, the liberal Protestant churches had 238 satellite connections to a wide variety of associations including the YMCA, Scouts, athletic associations, hobby groups, and fraternal and sororal orga-

66. Lynd and Lynd, *Middletown*, pp. 181-82.

67. Lynd and Lynd, *Middletown*, p. 51.

68. W. Lloyd Warner and Paul Lunt, *The Social Life of a Modern Community* (New Haven: Yale University Press, 1941), p. 324.

69. Warner and Lunt, *The Social Life of a Modern Community*, p. 328.

70. Warner and Lunt, *The Social Life of a Modern Community*, p. 310.

71. Warner and Lunt, *The Social Life of a Modern Community*, p. 311.

nizations.[72] Notably, associations anchored in the liberal congregations were far more likely to include Catholics, Jews, and members of other Protestant groups than those anchored in conservative congregations: 174 or nearly 40 percent of the city's associations — most of them connected to liberal Protestant congregations — had Catholic and Jewish members. Associations of this type included the Yankee City Women's Club, the Yankee City Country Club, the Rotary, the Chamber of Commerce, and the Boy Scout troops.[73]

In contrast, Yankee City's conservative Protestant congregations (Methodists and Baptists) displayed in proportion to the size of their memberships the fewest formal (interorganizational) and informal (membership) ties to other associations in the community. On the formal level, they were not sponsors of youth and athletic groups or ecumenical bodies like the YMCA or the Interdenominational Council. On the membership level, their members were the least likely of all of Yankee City's residents to be members of voluntary associations.

These differences in organizational orientation have proved to be remarkably persistent. Recent studies of religious affiliation and civic engagement show significant differences between religious conservatives and religious liberals in type and intensity of civic engagement. In their charitable giving, religious conservatives and evangelicals show them far more likely to give to their own congregations and to causes identified with their own faith communities than for broader civic purposes.[74] Liberal Protestants are far more likely to sit on the boards of secular institutions than conservatives, even in communities (like Atlanta and Los Angeles) where they are distinctly in the minority.[75] On the other hand, boards dominated by liberal Protestants are far more likely to be religiously heterogeneous

72. Warner and Lunt, *The Social Life of a Modern Community*, p. 322.

73. Warner and Lunt, *The Social Life of a Modern Community*, pp. 346, 348.

74. On denominational difference in giving, see John and Sylvia Ronsvalle, *The State of Church Giving through 1995* (Champaign, IL: Empty Tomb, 1997); Dean R. Hoge et al., *Money Matters: Personal Giving in American Churches* (Louisville: Westminster/John Knox Press, 1996); Mark Chaves and Sharon Miller, eds., *The Financing of American Religion* (Walnut Creek, CA: AltaMira Press, 1998). For an insightful interpretation of fundamentalist giving, see Laurence Iannacone, "Why Strict Churches Are Strong," in Demerath et al., eds., *Sacred Companies*, pp. 269-91.

75. David Swartz, "Secularization, Religion, and Isomorphism: A Study of Large Nonprofit Hospital Trustees," in Demerath et al., eds., *Sacred Companies*, pp. 323-39.

than those controlled by Catholics or conservative Protestants — which seldom include members of other faiths. The geography of charitable tax-exempt nonprofit organizations tends to reflect religious demography: regions with the largest liberal Protestant presence contain a far greater density of nonprofits than those dominated by conservative Protestants.[76] Taken together, these findings suggest that the relationships between religiosity and associational life that Warner and Lunt found in Newburyport in the 1930s were characteristic of national patterns.

Conclusion

Although traumatic events like the Scopes trial, the misdeeds of revivalists (real, like Aimee Semple McPherson, or imagined, like Elmer Gantry), and theological battles between fundamentalists and modernists undoubtedly catalyzed the break-up of evangelicalism, they were merely symptomatic of the deeper economic and institutional forces that were driving Protestants into definably conservative and liberal camps. Religious divisions and accompanying differences in wealth and organizational preferences cut across the nation and divided communities.

The contemporary resurgence of evangelical religion as a political and economic force, while pointing to the possibility that theological conservatism may not doom evangelicals to marginality (as Weber seemed to suggest that Catholicism did in Germany), does not answer the question of whether evangelicalism, because of its deep-seated discomfort with the materialism and pragmatism of modern life, can ever effectively institutionalize itself.

The experience of immigrant groups in the United States suggests interesting parallels with the situation of evangelicals. Like many immigrant groups, evangelicals after 1930 created parallel institutional structures — schools, colleges, seminaries, charities, and hospitals — that provided services and professional and economic opportunities for their co-religionists. The political mobilization of conservative Christians after 1960 led to the establishment of institutions — foundations, advocacy

---

76. William G. Bowen, Thomas I. Nygren, Sarah E. Turner, and Elizabeth A. Duffy, *The Charitable Nonprofits: An Analysis of Institutional Dynamics and Characteristics* (San Francisco: Jossey-Bass Publishers, 1994).

groups, think tanks — that sought to reach a broader public.[77] At this point, evangelicals — like the immigrants before them — encountered the core dilemma of assimilation: the fact that power and influence in a pluralistic society require individuals to sacrifice their core identities and to embrace the values and styles of dominant elites.

Whether evangelicals will be willing to make such sacrifices remains to be seen — as does the more interesting question of whether evangelicalism contains within itself as-yet unrealized ways of operating in the highly institutionalized setting of modern economic and political life without diluting its fundamental tenets. Just as Weber predicted that the religious imperatives that had created and then been imprisoned by the modern economic order might eventually escape its "iron cage," it is not impossible to envision a potent combination of religious fervor and worldliness fully capable of remaking the world as we know it. (The willingness of conservative Protestants to overlook doctrinal differences in order to form political alliances with Catholics and Jews who share their view on such issues as charitable choice and reproductive rights suggests that evangelicals may yet find a way to build coalitions without sacrificing their principles.)

As noted, the history of evangelicalism has featured both inclusive and exclusive phases. The former phases, in which every form of organizational and political innovation and capacity for alliance-building flourished, as it did from the 1790s through the 1840s and from the 1870s through the 1920s, alternated with periods of intolerance, rigidity, and exclusivity. This fact highlights an important difference between the linkages of religious affiliation and power that Weber found in Germany and those of the United States. Although Old World Catholics and Protestants might learn to co-exist, they could never fully overcome their differences. In the United States, on the other hand, the evangelical identity has, over time, proved to be remarkably elastic, enabling distinctions based on creed, class, politics, and geography to wax and wane in significance.

77. The best account of the political mobilization of Christian conservatives/conservative Christians is in Geoffrey Hodgson, *The World Turned Right Side Up: A History of the Conservative Ascendancy in America* (Boston: Houghton Mifflin, 1996).

CHAPTER 6

"Let Christian Women
Set the Example in Their Own Gifts":
The "Business" of Protestant Women's Organizations

SUSAN M. YOHN

*As he looked up, Jesus saw the rich putting their gifts into the temple
treasury. He also saw a poor widow put in two very small copper
coins. "I tell you the truth," he said, "this poor widow has put in more
than all the others."*

LUKE 21:1-3 (NIV)

L ooking back over forty years of women's missionary activity, Helen
Barrett Montgomery, longtime president of the Woman's American
Baptist Foreign Mission Society,[1] noted with great satisfaction that the mil-

---

1. Montgomery also served as the president of the National Federation of
Women's Boards of Foreign Missions, as well as President of the Northern Baptist Convention.

I would like to thank the members of the Women and Twentieth-Century Protestantism Project, under the direction of Virginia Brereton and Margaret Bendroth, for their support and comments on early drafts of this article. I am also grateful to the Louisville Institute for the Study of Protestantism and American Culture for supporting the research on which this article is based.

lions of Protestant women who had donated their pennies to this effort had "astonished the world with their success." What had started in 1861 with one mission society supporting one woman in the field, by 1909 had grown into an enterprise composed of 44 societies supporting 4,710 unmarried women in the field. Collections for the effort had risen from a modest $2000 in 1861 to four million dollars in 1909. The women's mission enterprise had built colleges, orphanages, asylums, training schools, and industrial plants and had created organizations "from which they could reach from headquarters to the remotest auxiliary, with appeal and information."[2]

The literature discussing the various denominational organizations that comprised the Protestant women's mission movement has focused attention on the ways in which women used mission work as the means to extend their influence into the public arena and into matters not simply religious, but also social and political.[3] With the mission movement as a base, women pursued work and politics that put them squarely in the midst of debates concerning various social and political policies. In the process they called into question popularly held ideas that limited or confined women to a domestic role. What has been largely overlooked, however, has been the role played by these organizations in the economic history of American women. Barred from many kinds of economic activity, either by law or by custom, women in the nineteenth century turned their attentions instead to the "business" of social reform. They did this at a time of economic transition, when American businesses were growing ever larger and more complex, and when there was increasing emphasis on rationalization, efficiency, and scientific method. Cognizant of these developments, women adapted the language and methods of the business sector to build

2. Helen Barrett Montgomery, *Western Women in Eastern Lands* (New York: Macmillan, 1911), pp. 38, 243-44.

3. See, for example, R. Pierce Beaver, *American Protestant Women in World Mission: A History of the First Feminist Movement in North America* (Grand Rapids: Eerdmans, 1968); John P. McDowell, *The Social Gospel in the South: The Woman's Home Mission Movement in the Methodist Episcopal Church, South, 1886-1939* (Baton Rouge: Louisiana State University Press, 1982); Peggy Pascoe, *Relations of Rescue: The Search for Female Moral Authority in the American West, 1874-1939* (New York: Oxford University Press, 1990); Patricia Hill, *The World Their Household: The American Woman's Foreign Missionary Movement and Cultural Transformation, 1870-1920* (Ann Arbor: University of Michigan Press, 1985); Susan M. Yohn, *A Contest of Faiths: Missionary Women and Pluralism in the American Southwest* (Ithaca, NY: Cornell University Press, 1995).

innovative and vibrant organizations that raised millions of dollars to provide much needed social services. They marshaled what were the limited resources of their female members, whom they also thought of as "investors," in the process promoting strategies of philanthropy that insured a steady flow of income. Protestant women active in the mission enterprise generated social capital and engaged in social entrepreneurship; they built institutions that increased the nation's capacity to respond to its needs. They cared for the needy, worked to foster good will, and generally reminded people that they were members of an interdependent community. The end result was a network of organizations built largely with money raised by Protestant women that provided a variety of services, with, as Helen Montgomery pointed out, international scope and appeal.

This essay examines the "business" of women's missions, focusing on the strategies and methods leaders used to generate the donations that supported their efforts and fueled the growth and expansion of the enterprise. This associational experience, which historians and sociologists — Max Weber among them — have identified as an important springboard to greater economic success for men, proved more limited for women. So successful were women in raising money and expanding their enterprise that they became targets for "takeover" by the men in their respective churches who ran parallel organizations. In a period of business merger and consolidation, missions organizations were not exempt from pressures to do the same. Beginning in the early twentieth century, men in Protestant churches sought to gain control of the mission enterprise by merging and consolidating parallel male and female organizations. This female missionary enterprise, carefully nurtured by women, became the object of contest between men and women. As men sought to convince women of the importance of merger, they raised a host of questions about the efficacy of a separate women's enterprise, not the least of which called into question women's motivations in building their organizations and their ability to administer the funds they raised.

At the heart of this struggle was an inability by both men and women to acknowledge that in creating these organizations women wielded a degree of economic power they had never before imagined. Women gained invaluable economic experience but could not think of the funds they raised as profits, nor did the nature of their enterprise — social service — allow them to. When they spoke about their accomplishments, they did not highlight their business acumen or sensibility but focused instead on social gains. This enterprise served principle before people; it served God, and in the case of African-American women, God and race. Where women gave way to male demands to consolidate their efforts, they lost control over the enterprise they had created. For example, in the mainline Presbyterian and Baptist churches women gave way to men in positions of leadership. Where they did not, as in the case of Nannie Helen Burroughs of the National Baptist Convention, they fought an ongoing battle against charges, intended to undermine their work, that they were personally profiting from their church association. Mission activism opened new political and social arenas to Protestant women, but the ethic underlying the work — self-denial and self-sacrifice — limited both its economic and political impact. Here women were allowed to embrace the business practices and philosophies of their day — to test their entrepreneurial skills. The reaction to their success, however, shows the limits (or that era's "glass ceiling") these women encountered as they pursued this social entrepreneurship.

Women's mission organizations were built on the small donations of millions of women. With relatively few large donations, leaders came to stress a high rate of participation among their members rather than the amount they gave. They were also concerned to develop strategies to insure that women gave on a regular basis. Tithing, or systematic or proportionate giving, was encouraged even if it meant that a woman was giving only a few cents a week, or a dollar a month. What may have appeared "inefficient" to those who sought to rationalize giving in the late nineteenth century was in fact highly effective in tapping women's limited resources. The mission leaders insisted that every woman could and should participate no matter how small her donation; Christian stewardship was not just the province of men. The secret, as one observer noted, was "plodding perseverance . . . not waiting for great windfalls, bequests, the gifts of millionaires, but picking up the pennies and trudging on."[4] The goal was to instill in women patterns of regular giving — an idea that later efforts like the Community Chest and United Way would come to depend upon.

For Protestant women there was a dual message in the appeals made by mission organizations. Women were encouraged to participate, to develop an ethic of stewardship — to contribute in a regular, systematic, and rational fashion whether by tithing or proportionate giving — but they

---

4. Mrs. J. Fowler Willing, "I Can Plod," *Heathen Woman's Friend* 25 (Feb. 1894): 226.

were never to forget that they were God's messengers and that their donations were an act of self-sacrifice and selflessness. What profits were generated were measured in the numbers of people converted or the lives helped. One's contribution yielded no tangible return, except the emotional and spiritual satisfaction of having participated in a good cause.

Typical of the earliest fund-raising appeals made by the Presbyterian Woman's Board of Home Missions (PCWBHM) was that made by president Mary James who, as she addressed the annual convention in 1877, intoned "let us pray for money." In her efforts to raise money for mission purposes, James railed against the "rust of hoarded wealth," warning that the nation's wealth would be a "curse if spent upon ourselves while souls are perishing without knowledge." Recognizing that most women did not "hold the purse," James encouraged her followers to exert their influence on those who did. Equating donations to the Board to "offerings," she called on the supporters of the enterprise to tithe the first tenth of their income.[5]

As James's comments suggest, the PCWBHM was engaged in a constant fight against what it called "spasmodic" giving.[6] As it expanded its activities, hiring additional women and opening new missions, the Board found it had to inculcate an ethic of stewardship among supporters. With many different charities competing for women's limited funds, the Board championed a system whereby women divided up their monies, allocating them to a variety of causes. This was a strategy uniformly pursued by all the groups across denominations. Women were encouraged to begin their training in stewardship by keeping a "mite" box in their kitchen, depositing whatever extra pennies and nickels they could save. The next step was to pledge a certain amount, either on a monthly or annual basis. The organizations broke down, by month, what the money might be used for. In the Woman's Home Missionary Society of the Methodist Episcopal Church (WHMSMEC), September was "dues paying" month, November was "Thank-offering," May was "mite" month, and April and October were for "student aid."[7]

Within such giving schemes, however, regularity was stressed over

5. "Address of the President," *Home Mission Monthly* (July 1887): 198-99.

6. The reference to "spasmodic" giving comes in "A True Story; or, Aunt Margaret's Experience," *Home Mission Monthly* (Oct. 1890): 268.

7. Report of the Corresponding Secretary, Delia Lathrop Williams, 28th Annual Report, Woman's Home Missionary Society of the MEC, October 1909, p. 5.

amount. Indeed, all donations were applauded, no matter what size. The Boards were acutely aware that many contributors were dependent on husbands who gave their wives little, if any, allowance. The so-called "third class passenger," the small donor, was celebrated as the one who "gets out and pushes." When times are difficult, noted one observer, "it is the third class passengers that we want not only in this, but in every department of mission work, for there is many an upgrade which calls for vigorous pushing, if we would keep things moving."[8] Women were encouraged to save their pennies, to hoard small amounts to be offered up monthly in a mission society meeting. The excuse of an "empty purse" or a lack of money was not accepted. Testimonials were published that told of poor and widowed women who gave what little they had, and then encouraged others to give more. In one such account, readers were introduced to a miner's wife who, over the objections of her husband, endeavored to save her pennies:

> Tempted often by strenuous times to give it up, but persevering and repeatedly testifying to its blessing, she not infrequently lays upon the collection plate of the class a dollar, and sometimes brings the teacher two dollars, with the words, "Give it [to] someone who needs it more than I do."

To shame wealthier members who hesitated to contribute, the author added, the poor woman "always has her church envelope . . . ready for the annual collection for the Boards, and it contains more than many members of prominence subscribe." By way of conclusion, readers were admonished: "We shall never know how much we can give till we try the systematic way."[9]

Mission organizations were acutely aware that women's limited economic resources circumscribed the scope of mission work. They championed "allowances" for wives, suggesting that every married woman should have one. One correspondent wrote in favor of allowances saying that "it causes embarrassment to listen to stirring appeals and to make no response by a contribution, and it is still more humiliating to say that one has no money to call her own, and her husband disapproves."[10] The benefits of allowances would come not just to the mission enterprise; a wife with an

8. *Home Mission Monthly* (July 1897): 201.

9. May D. Strong, "Systematic and Proportionate Giving," *Home Mission Monthly* (Sept. 1908): 265-66.

10. "The Problem of the Empty Purse," *Home Mission Monthly* (Mar. 1906): 112.

allowance would be encouraged to "budget," in the long run saving her family money as well.

Mission leaders argued that the impact of these small donations, added up, would be to reinvigorate Protestantism. By using a variety of plans from a voluntary pledge system, envelope system, systematic gleaning, to the free-will gift, Presbyterian women, for example, "would pool their money to make their impact felt."[11] The PCWBHM warned against thinking of oneself as autonomous; instead one should think of her contribution in combination with others. "If $18 a year seems little for one to give let us look at it in this way," wrote the Treasurer. "Suppose fifty women in our church can each give that amount." Such donations would not be "despised" by the church.[12] The Methodists employed the metaphor of the quilt to describe the process involved in this enterprise. Pennies multiplied into dollars as "she hath done what she could." An "indispensable factor in any gathering of woman's product," they reported, was that "heritage from our grandmothers — a quilt" that "bears 1200 names, and each name is worth, in ready currency, ten cents — an easy calculation making the quilt thus transformed into a roll of profit, if not of honor."[13]

By collecting money in this fashion the women's mission societies experienced continual growth. While technically subordinate to the male mission boards and subject to their final authority, the women's societies designated the funds they raised to support schools and community centers employing women missionaries. Within the Presbyterian Church, for example, women would not be allowed to serve as elders until the late 1920s and they would not be ordained as ministers until the early 1950s, but nevertheless, as fund-raisers they came to wield considerable economic influence within the church decades earlier. So much so that the male hierarchy moved to consolidate all the mission boards of the church in the early 1920s, hoping the women would maintain high levels of giving even though there was no longer an autonomous women's organization. What the women who ran the Board expected was that regularized contributions would sustain the growth of the organization, would serve as the "vertebrate system" of the organization's treasury.

11. "Best Plans for Giving," *Home Mission Monthly* (Sept. 1900): 257.
12. "The Treasury," *Home Mission Monthly* (Mar. 1902): 106-7.
13. Fourteenth Annual Report of the Woman's Foreign Missionary Society of the MEC, 1883, p. 62.

Katharine Bennett, who took over as president of the PCWBHM after Mary James, was guided by a more corporate model of management. As the Board employed more missionaries and new fields of work were added, the organization grew more complex and bureaucratic. Located in New York City, the Woman's Board's purpose was twofold. First, it set policy and provided support to women missionaries in the field. Second, it promoted philanthropy among the women who stayed at home. One goal of the organization was to bring together women from different regions to exchange information and resources in a common cause. As the leader of an organization that was national in scope, private (though in the public service), with a centralized authority, and focused largely on one product — in this case the development of a national culture — it is perhaps no wonder that Bennett took to comparing this organization with that of other major corporations of the day.[14]

In this spirit, Bennett moved the Board to institute more businesslike procedures. Whereas James had likened contributions to "offerings" — reiterating the evangelical nature of the project — Bennett used more secular language. Probably influenced by the growing emphasis on "scientific philanthropy," she saw her role as president of the Board to institute "planned growth." Even as the Board was critical of the social dislocation caused by corporate capitalism, Bennett likened her organization to the powerful railroad industry. Gone was an emphasis on teas, fairs, and luncheons (the staples among women fund-raisers in the mid-nineteenth century and referred to in 1890 as the "lazy way" of giving),[15] to be replaced with the much heralded "business methods." The PCWBHM took every opportunity to impress upon its supporters that this was a "business operation." This "business of benevolence," reminded the Board, involved women in both financial and legal matters beyond their domestic role. Because the treasury often found itself without funds to cover operating expenses (while it waited for contributions to come in), it borrowed money from banks to tide it over, involving it in the dealings of the national bank-

14. See Alfred D. Chandler, *The Visible Hand: The Managerial Revolution in American Business* (Cambridge, MA: Belknap Press, 1977) for a discussion of the corporate model of this period.

15. See "Seven Ways of Giving," *Heathen Woman's Friend* 22 (Sept. 1890): 63. The "lazy way" was number three on this list. The list included, in the following order: The careless way, the impulsive way, the lazy way, the self-denying way, the systematic way, the equal way, and the heroic way.

ing community. The women who ran this organization did not hesitate to tell their supporters that they were well informed as to the ups and downs of financial markets.[16] Leaders were very careful, however, to temper the rhetoric of business with reminders of the spiritual motives underlying the enterprise. The secretary of Home Affairs of the Woman's Missionary Society of the Methodist Episcopal Church, South (WMSMEC, South) warned her followers in 1893 that there was a danger to the spirit of the enterprise in "pushing forward business methods." She cautioned that "while the work must be based upon solid business principles, it should never be prosecuted with unsanctified hearts, unconsecrated hands." The mission society should not let its success be a "snare," she advised, tempting them to expand "beyond our financial strength," and take on debt.[17]

These appeals for money had the effect of making women more conscious about how much — or how little — financial control they exercised within both their families and their churches. When mission organizations found the amount a woman could contribute depended on how much she was able to hoard out of the money her husband had given her for household expenses, leaders pushed for wives to be given an allowance, one part of which would go towards donations of her own determination. Indeed, mission literature was replete with stories of women who, emboldened by their desire to more actively participate in mission fund-raising efforts, had gone home to their husbands and demanded allowances. In one story the main character related that her husband "never seemed to understand that a woman needed a little money of her very own." She described herself as "proud-spirited," so "the question of finance at our house was like an electric battery, and neither of us knew how to manage it." When she finally did bring herself to broach the topic with her husband, it was not in a "proud-spirited" manner however. She "went home as *meek* as you please, and told John all about it." They "talked" the issue through and she then "had" her allowance every month.[18] The very act of raising money for mis-

16. See "Treasury Notes," *Home Mission Monthly* (July 1908): 219; Mary Bennett, "The Art of Giving," *Home Mission Monthly* 23 (Mar. 1909): 113-14; Mary Torrance, "The Hungry Gap," *Women and Missions* 3 (Jan. 1927): 376.

17. "Report of the Secretary of Home Affairs," 15th Annual Report of the Woman's Missionary Society of the MEC, South, 1892-93, p. 81.

18. Mrs. O. W. Scott, "A Reminiscence Meeting," *Heathen Woman's Friend* 25 (Mar. 1894): 258.

sions changed the way women thought about money; their "need" for money was legitimated and their credibility established.

Or so thought the women active in the mission movement. Their male counterparts, however, spoke of the women's efforts with both disdain and envy. The leadership of the women's organizations presented a heroic face but this masked a deeper gendered debate about the role of the church in the production of social capital. Church men and women were in agreement about the need for evangelization, for expanding mission activities. Both groups celebrated the successes women had in generating millions of dollars for the mission cause. What they could not agree about was who would control those dollars and the activities they funded. While most correspondence between the men and women engaged in these struggles was cordial (they were, after all, trying to be "Christian"), the antagonism is best represented in a letter from one Rev. R. B. Dunmire to G. Pitt Beers, the executive secretary of the American Baptist Home Mission Society (ABHMS) concerning the proposed merger between the male-controlled ABHMS and the Woman's American Baptist Home Mission Society (WABHMS) in 1941. Dunmire wanted to know the inside scoop on the merger. He was perfectly willing to allow women to raise monies for mission societies, saying "let the women go to it and raise *all* the money if they can beat the men." But about administration, there he drew the line, writing "two bosses on the same job? It is a bit hard for a missionary or anyone else to serve two Masters." He spoke, he said, from his experience in Alaska, where he had worked with women missionaries who were managed and financed by the New England Ladies from Boston, but "who could not *even hold their own.*" "I think kindly," he wrote sarcastically, "of those Boston ladies giving of time, effort and money, meaning so well, and yet pouring most of it as 'Mark Twain' said, just down a 'rat hole.'"[19]

Historians of philanthropy have described the latter part of the nineteenth century as a period in which charities came under increasing pressure to put their activities on a more "businesslike basis." The Civil War proved a

---

19. Rev. R. B. Dunmire to G. Pitt Beers, 5/8/1941 [Beers, G. Pitt, #52-22], American Baptist Archives Center (ABAC), Valley Forge, PA. For a more focused discussion of Protestant men's fears of the church becoming feminized and their attempts to reassert masculine dominance, see Gail Bederman, "'The Women Have Had Charge of the Church Work Long Enough': The Men and Religion Forward Movement of 1911-1912 and the Masculinization of Middle-Class Protestantism," *American Quarterly* 41 (Sept. 1989): 432-65.

tremendous impetus both for the proliferation of new organizations and for formal giving, which continued to increase as opportunities for giving grew. Some have suggested, moreover, that most of these fund-raising efforts were decidedly inefficient, uncoordinated, and unbusinesslike. Robert Bremner notes, for example, that the fund-raising efforts of benevolent groups were in a "chaotic condition," with "duplication or overlapping of effort, rivalry for public favor, [and] competition for funds."[20] It took the massive fund-raising efforts of World War I and the rise of the Community Chest movement, he argues, to bring some order and a sense of professionalism to fund-raising as an activity. Perhaps in part as a response to this seeming "chaos," this period also saw the rise of "scientific philanthropy," out of which came the large general-purpose foundation that set criteria against which the effectiveness of charity and social service organizations were judged.[21]

Not insulated from these developments, church organizations found themselves being influenced by the wider movement as they engaged in debates about the purpose of philanthropy and voluntarism. As organizations that occupied a central position in debates about social service and in the delivery of social services, and as the recipients of millions of dollars of contributions from American men, women, and children, they were not unaware of nor unaffected by discussions about making philanthropy more effective. The leaders of the women's mission enterprise, women like the Baptists Helen Barrett Montgomery and Nannie Helen Burroughs, and the Presbyterian Katharine Bennett, for instance, were acutely aware of the need to bring some order to their efforts. Their attempts to bring order to and systematize fund-raising indicates their commitment to making their organizations more efficient and instilling discipline in their supporters.

Furthermore, a survey of the administrative records of the mainline Protestant (primarily Baptist, Methodist, and Presbyterian) women's mission organizations indicates the extent to which the women who founded and ran these groups viewed their efforts as an education in entrepreneurship. They believed themselves to be in the "business" of promoting social and moral reform, and they took their lessons on how to run these organizations from their male colleagues. They wanted very much to run their

20. Robert Bremner, *American Philanthropy* (Chicago: The University of Chicago Press, 1960), pp. 123-24.
21. Thomas H. Jeavons, *When the Bottom Line Is Faithfulness: Management of Christian Service Organizations* (Indianapolis: Indiana University Press, 1994), p. 16.

organizations in a "business-like" fashion. Presbyterian women were thankful to their male mentors who served on the Board of Home Missions, acknowledging that the PCWBHM was "comparatively a small undertaking and simple in management, but it was before the days when there were many organized efforts by women and few women had business experience." As they grew more successful, their dependence lessened and their relationship to the men's Board evolved into something much more akin to one between client and attorney.[22] What women learned in these early years was the art of running a business. They familiarized themselves with the legal niceties of incorporation, they expanded their control over their own finances (the extent to which they did so varied from denomination to denomination), taking over the collection and disbursement of receipts, the administration of bequests and annuities, and worrying about how much money they had to borrow against future receipts to meet their debts. They exhibited a proficiency for investment and money management, from exhorting their membership on the virtue of buying annuities to explaining the complications of international currency exchange. At the high point of the mission enterprise, the female leadership oversaw financial portfolios worth millions.

Proud of their achievements, Katharine Bennett, president of the PCWBHM, compared her organization to the railroad companies of the day, noting that "it is as if a railroad were all surveyed, graded, track laid, stations built, trains running, business flourishing, credit sound."[23] Not only was this an expanding enterprise, but an efficient one. The leadership liked to point out that they operated with low overhead, thanks to the dedication of a largely volunteer staff. "It would, no doubt, surprise many business men to know," wrote one supporter of the Woman's Foreign Missionary Society of the Methodist Church (WFMSMC), "that there is an organization with a total membership of over three hundred fifty thousand people, carrying on activities in all parts of the world, with a yearly turnover of approximately one and a third million dollars, with as low an overhead as this Society has."[24]

22. See "An Appreciation," RG 305, Box 1, File 20, History of Incorporation, Presbyterian Historical Society (PHS), Philadelphia.

23. Katharine Bennett, "Annual Address of the President," *Home Mission Monthly* (July 1911): 200.

24. Ruth M. Wilson, "Membership and the Modern Woman," *Woman's Missionary Friend* 71 (Feb. 1938): 43.

The rapid growth of these Protestant women's organizations and their ability to attract members and volunteers and to show consistent economic growth was envied by the men who dominated parallel church groups. The organization and proliferation of women's mission groups had been allowed, even encouraged, in the late nineteenth century by male leaders as a way to raise extra monies to support activities not readily funded by the already established, and male-dominated, mission boards. Women's fund-raising activities were clearly defined as "extra," as being above and beyond those ordinarily undertaken. In the constitution of the WFMSMC, for example, it stipulated that "funds of the Society shall not be raised by collection or subscriptions taken during any church services or in any promiscuous public meeting, but shall be raised by securing members . . . and by such other methods as will not interfere with the ordinary collections or contributions for the treasury of the missionary society of the Methodist Episcopal Church."[25] Women soon discovered that these funds were the wedge by which to expand their own participation in mission activities and earmarked the money they raised to specifically support female missionaries. By all measures they were tremendously successful. Their revenues increased annually, as did the scope of the activities they undertook. Most importantly, women were increasingly distinguishing themselves as the financial backbone of the church. Not only did they give to women's mission organizations, but they also played a crucial role in supporting local parish activities. In the Episcopal Church, for example, the Woman's Auxiliary began in 1875 by raising one-third of the amount raised by parishes for the support of missions. Thirty years later their fund-raising efforts yielded $100,000 more than parish contributions.[26]

Early in the twentieth century, moves were made to consolidate the women's groups, to integrate, to merge, to unify them (the wording changes depending on the denomination, as well as the decade) with the respective denominational men's groups. Many of the women involved in these groups perceived these moves as attempts to usurp the power

25. Quoted in Patricia Hill, "Heathen Women's Friends: The Role of the Methodist Episcopal Women in the Women's Foreign Mission Movement, 1869-1915," *Methodist History* 19 (Mar. 1981): 147.

26. In 1875 the Woman's Auxiliary raised $75,524 to the $226,472 raised in parishes. By 1905 those figures were Woman's Auxiliary $452,835 to $346,800 for the parishes. See Mary S. Donovan, "Women as Foreign Missionaries in the Episcopal Church, 1830-1920," *Anglican and Episcopal History* 61/62 (Jan. 1992): 21.

women had gained by their work. Others feared that consolidation would lead to fewer opportunities for women within church administration. Yet others argued that integrating the parallel efforts of men and women would dampen the enthusiasm of the female constituency that had generously supported the movement's work. Exchanging letters with WFMSMC president Evelyn Nicholson, William Shaw, corresponding secretary for the Board of Foreign Missions, went out of his way to "remind" Nicholson of his personal commitment to the women's work. His sister had been a missionary; his mother and his wife were active members of women's mission societies. As a pastor, he himself had given twenty "Thank Offering Addresses" for the Woman's Foreign Missionary Society. He was proposing, he wrote, a United Board of Missions, so as to enlarge the scope of women's work, not reduce it. His intention was to secure a wider base of support for the "General World Service program," for which women did not feel a responsibility. He described men as feeling "overburdened" and expressed frustration that the woman's missionary group had not created "an interest and sense of responsibility in the entire membership for the total missionary task." While it is not completely clear what Shaw meant by women feeling a lack of "responsibility," however, the implication is that the women's societies were not sharing their resources nor encouraging members to give to other more general missionary causes. Shaw proposed that a united Board would also allow women to be brought into the "councils of general missionary work."[27]

Evelyn Nicholson was not so easily flattered. "I know that you desire to be cooperative," she wrote Shaw, "and to see the largest possible number of individuals, men and women, so related to this missionary enterprise as to be able and glad to make their contribution freely. I know the attitude of the women in this section of the country. They have given themselves without stint or limitation to the work for which they feel responsible. They desire to continue working according to their own plans and under their own administration." Certainly women would expect to be given the opportunity for "autonomy, initiative and administration" should the Boards be united, contended Nicholson, but she was skeptical that women would be given equal representation in a united governing

27. William Shaw to Evelyn Nicholson, 9 February 1939, Admin. Vol. 3, Folder: 1109-1-1:21, General Commission on Archives and History, The United Methodist Church (UMCA), Drew University, NJ.

council. Furthermore she doubted whether this matter could be satisfactorily addressed at a "United Conference" as "the women will have inadequate representation because of their lesser numbers and because of their reluctance to take the floor."[28] While it is difficult to pinpoint just what kind of impact these discussions about unification had on the larger population of women who worked for and supported missions, it is the case that in this same period there was a decline among women in their support for mission efforts. This was precisely Evelyn Nicholson's fear. In an especially biting letter to Shaw on the subject of unification, she apologized for appearing "contentious." "Above all things," she said, "I do want to have right attitudes and to stand for what is most likely to enlist the service and loyalty of the women of the church. Too many secular channels and other activities and interests are luring them away as it is."[29]

The move toward merger or unification, however, was as much welcomed by women as it was feared. Evelyn Nicholson insisted, for example, that she wanted to have the "right attitudes." By the twentieth century what the records indicate is that the administrators and executives of the women's mission enterprise were very much concerned to get the most for their money. They too believed that merging men's and women's groups could lead to greater efficiency, allow for a greater range of services to be offered, and make better use of mission resources — all of which would strengthen the church. They wanted to centralize both mission services and administration — and here they were echoing the corporate ethos of their day, that bigger was better. However, at the same time, female administrators feared for their jobs and were concerned that women's power and influence would be diminished.

This concern seemed to be true across denominations throughout this era. The first effort at consolidation in the MEC, South, came with proposals that the multiple women's boards within denominations merge. This was generally a proposal made by male leaders and was seen as the first step towards merger of all disparate mission organizations to be administered by one body — again, for the most part, a male-dominated Board of Missions. At the 1906 General Conference a union with women's

28. Evelyn Nicholson to William Shaw, 6 January 1939, Admin. Vol. 3, Folder 1109-1-1:21, UMCA.
29. Evelyn Nicholson to William Shaw, 6 September 1938, Admin. Vol. 3, Folder 1109-1-1:20, UMCA.

societies was proposed without first consulting the women involved. Unable to speak at the conference, the women chose not to argue against a closer relation but instead to seek equal representation on the general board that was to oversee the work. "So foreign was the idea of equal representation to the time-honored policy of Methodism," reported one female observer of the proceedings, "that the formal announcement of the bill met with a good-humored ripple of laughter."[30] The men of the MEC, South ultimately succeeded in merging mission Boards. The women maintained some financial autonomy but were not equally represented on the governing board. It is no wonder, then, that when William Shaw pointed as a model to the example of the MEC, South, Evelyn Nicholson grew suspicious and defensive. Merger might, on the one hand, enhance evangelization efforts, but what benefits women working in mission societies gained were not clear. When considering whether or not to merge in the early 1950s, the Woman's American Baptist Foreign Mission Society pointed to the history of other Protestant women's groups and noted that similar developments earlier in the century had left women in other denominations like the Presbyterians and Congregationalists with little power. From the Congregationalists in the mid-1930s came the comment, "There is a feeling that we have lost in this merger."[31]

Women's concerns seem to have been justified. Where integration did take place, women's divisions remained, although under a male-dominated administration. Additionally, women sat on executive boards (or boards of directors), though they were generally guaranteed only a minority (often no more than a third) of seats. When women raised concerns about what was to happen to female leadership in the process of integration, it was generally too late. Such was the case of Margaret Wenger, the Executive Secretary of the Woman's American Baptist Home Mission Society, for example, who, as plans for the merger with the male-dominated mission society were almost complete, protested that "probably it is time to ask what the title means in relation to other staff. Am I some kind of Executive in more than name only?"[32] From the Congregationalists came the

30. Quoted by McDowell, *The Social Gospel in the South,* p. 127.

31. Memo, "Data Regarding the Merger of Congregational Foreign Boards," and "Data Regarding the Merger of the Foreign Board of the Presbyterian Church in the U.S.A.," File — AB/WABFMS Merger, 1933-35, ABAC, Valley Forge, PA.

32. Jewel Asbury, "Integration of the Woman's American Baptist Home Mission Society and the American Baptist Home Mission Society from a Feminist Perspective,"

comment, "some of the best women workers are not at their best working with men, and vice versa." Added as a note was the information that the Woman's Home Secretary of the American Board (Congregational Church) had resigned, saying "I have come to feel, because of difficulties inherent in the organizational machinery as well as for personal reasons, that I can no longer render the most effective service in an official capacity."[33]

The merger process varied across denominations. In every case, women approached the new relationship with some trepidation. The Presbyterians cautioned the Baptists, "Be sure if you unite that all matters which you want to guard are written in the plan of union."[34] Among Presbyterians, plans for merger generated a flurry of letters, most expressing concern that women's interests be safeguarded. "Why should the women of the church who are loyal faithful supporters of our Woman's Work have this taken from our hands, and given to management of men who can't begin to do it well?" asked one supporter in a letter to the Presbyterian Woman's Board of Home Missions protesting the merger and reorganization of Mission Boards. "I note that fifteen women are to be placed on the Foreign Missions Board but learn nothing of the fate of Mrs. Bennett, Miss Dawson, yourself and others [directors of the Woman's Board of Home Missions] — who have showed such efficiency, devotion and enthusiasm in the Christianizing of America. What is to become of the Synodical and Presbyterial Machinery of the Women's Societies? No men can match the unselfish unpaid work of these organizations."[35] They feared, and rightly so, that their successes, apart from those in fund-raising, would go unappreciated and that women administrators would be relegated to lesser roles. Reflecting back in 1969 on what had been the gradual incorporation of the Woman's Auxiliary of the Episcopal Church into the National Council, Avis Harvey remembered that women active in the Aux-

---

(copy at the ABAC, Valley Forge, PA), p. 19. See also letter from Margaret Wenger to a Miss Hazzard, 23 January 1954. In it she spells out her dissatisfaction at finding herself stripped of many of her duties. File name, "Integration 1945-54, Committee Reports Background," pp. 35-37, ABAC.

33. "Synopsis of Information from Two Women's Boards Which Have Merged," p. 1. File — AB/WABFMS Merger, 1933-35, ABAC, Valley Forge, PA.

34. "Synopsis of Information," p. 2.

35. Katherine Williams to the Board of Directors of the Woman's Board of Home Missions, 11 June 1922, RG 305, Box 1, File 37, PHS, Philadelphia, PA.

iliary had initially thought integration a "good thing." "We believed that it [integration] would give greater representation to the women in all aspects of the church's work. We thought we were doing something good," she commented. What they did not realize, Harvey concluded, was that it would "mean less women's work throughout the church and in the mission field."[36]

However positive the gains women made through the mission enterprise — establishing independent mission boards, proving their abilities in administrating and fund-raising for a growing organization, and on a more personal level, learning to be philanthropists — this was also a movement that promoted an ethic of self-denial. The very same woman who was finally able to confront her husband and request an allowance also related that she would "always believe that there has been something miraculous about our funds [meaning mission funds]."[37] Whatever benefits women realized, either as individuals or as a class, were to be subordinated to the needs of the church, and ultimately to the word of God. It was this ethic that led women in positions of administrative power, for instance, to reserve comment about fears for their own jobs when mergers were discussed. If merger or unification meant a stronger church, women felt compelled to support the initiative. They wanted, after all, to be seen as having the "right attitudes." The church could never be more than only a training ground for economic independence, a place where women could be educated about how to run a successful institution. Women who wanted to realize a different kind of economic power or independence, who looked to run an organization that was truly autonomous, or who desired a business partnership that was more egalitarian had to look beyond mainstream Protestant denominations or to the secular world. For many, this very likely proved a frustrating experience; the church had given women access but then limited what they could accomplish — a model other businesses were to follow in the twentieth century. This seems to have been especially true for white Anglo-Protestant women, who generally developed a contradictory relationship to capitalism during this period.

36. Quoted by Ian T. Douglas, "A Lost Voice: Women's Participation in the Foreign Mission Work of the Episcopal Church, 1920-1970," *Anglican and Episcopal History* 61 (1992): 54.

37. Scott, "A Reminiscence Meeting," p. 258.

The Anglo-Protestant wives, sisters, and daughters of the emerging entrepreneurial and managerial class were the beneficiaries of the wealth generated by corporate capitalism during this era. Yet, they were building organizations that were exposing and attempting to redress the worst abuses of that same system. Their mission societies were an attempt to bridge class differences, to put to good use the wealth of the period, and in some small way, to redistribute that wealth. They celebrated self-denial; what they recommended as the "heroic way" was to "limit our own expenditures to a certain sum, giving away all the rest of our income."[38] This was a model of economic behavior suited for a housewife of privilege and means. Celebrated were women like Helen Barrett Montgomery. She and her husband, a successful and wealthy businessman, were regarded "as exemplary trustees of personal resources." Montgomery was remembered as "careful" with her money and as one who "avoided all display and extravagance."[39] What is not so clear, however, was how this ethic benefited poor widows, or the struggling "business women" (salaried employees or proprietors of small businesses) — women who could not count on a husband, or some other male relative, to support them.

Married to affluent businessmen, Katharine Bennett and Helen Barrett Montgomery had no financial worries.[40] That they were so determined to "grow" their organizations was a testament to their religious zeal as well as entrepreneurial acumen for which there was no other suitable outlet. Men like Rev. Dunmire might belittle women's efforts as "pouring money down a 'rat hole,'" but his charges did not reflect personally on any of the leaders of the women's mainline denominational groups; and women like Bennett and Montgomery, insulated by their privileged class position, could easily deflect such accusations as the words of a bitter man. For the mission leader whose economic position was more precarious, charges that she had acted in a selfish manner or for personal gain could be devastating. Such was the case with Nannie Helen Burroughs, who had built the National Training School for Women and Girls under the auspices

38. "Seven Ways of Giving," p. 63.

39. Helen Barrett Montgomery, *From Campus to World Citizenship* (New York: Fleming H. Revell Co., 1940), p. 240.

40. Helen Montgomery's husband, William, was a businessman whose venture, the North East Electric Company, became the Rochester Products Division of General Motors Corporation. Katherine Bennett's husband, Fred, listed his occupation as a manufacturer. In 1915 he was an officer in the William L. Burrell Company of New Jersey.

of the Woman's Convention Auxiliary to the National Baptist Convention (hereafter referred to as the Woman's Convention or as the WC). For decades she battled charges that she had abused her relationship with the Woman's Convention to build the Training School, an institution that brought her a certain prominence and a degree of personal profit (for which she was castigated by critics but which was the primary source of her personal income).

The example of the African-American Woman's Convention illustrates just how broad and inclusive was the Protestant women's mission enterprise but also suggests how the gendered struggles found in the mainline Protestant denominations took on an added dimension when issues of race and class intervened. This Woman's Convention faced many of the same problems its white counterparts did: male ministers who resented the money women were able to raise and who tried on numerous occasions to reign in their autonomy. Like their white counterparts, the leaders of the Woman's Convention also employed a variety of strategies to educate women about the importance of systematic giving. They too relied on the monies raised in small amounts from a great number of women.

What set the Woman's Convention apart from its white counterparts was its celebration of successful businesswomen. Female entrepreneurs such as Madame C. J. Walker (manufacturer of hair products) and Maggie Lena Walker (president of the St. Luke Penny Savings Bank) were invited to address the annual meetings of the WC. Maggie Walker was consulted by the organization for financial advice. These women served as models for others to follow. They embodied the primary goal of the WC, the uplift of the race. They understood that this organization was a means by which they could achieve social mobility. As Anna Cooper stated, "When and where I enter . . . then and there the whole Negro race enters with me." Their emphasis on uplift and self-determination for the race tempered their concern with self-denial.[41]

African-American women may have celebrated the entrepreneurial successes of individual members, but like their white counterparts their successes were seen through gendered lenses. They too juggled a desire to build

41. My discussion of the Woman's Convention Auxiliary to the National Baptist Convention is drawn largely from Evelyn Higginbotham's *Righteous Discontent: The Women's Movement in the Black Baptist Church, 1880-1920* (Cambridge, MA: Harvard University Press, 1993).

successful institutions, and to achieve a certain measure of recognition, with an ethic that judged these desires in a woman as suspect. The personal papers of Nannie Helen Burroughs chronicle a decades-long struggle with the National Baptist Convention leaders over control of the National Training School for Women and Girls. Because these papers relate both to her professional and private lives (indeed, she did not make a distinction between the two) they allow historians to sketch a much fuller picture of the conflicts and dilemmas faced by a woman mission leader who was both a servant of God and church and an entrepreneur.[42] Burroughs was an enormously competent businesswoman who ran her National Training School on a shoestring, traveling throughout the country to raise funds for its support.[43] She also owned several properties and had investments on the side.[44] What kind of living these afforded her remains unclear. She lived, it seems from her correspondence, hand to mouth, yet she managed to maintain the School through years of adversity and near bankruptcy.

Burroughs first proposed the National Training School and was elected the Corresponding Secretary of the Woman's Convention in 1900. The school was officially incorporated in 1907, and Burroughs and two others acquired property in Washington, D.C., for an institution that she envisioned would provide young black women "first class training for missionary, Sunday School and Church work." In addition, the school would also provide lessons in "household arts, such as cooking, sewing, housekeeping, nursing and . . . horticulture."[45] As incorporated, the Institute was

42. Unable to locate personal papers or correspondence of Katharine Bennett or Helen Barrett Montgomery, I have relied primarily on the institutional records found in the archives of the mainline Baptist and Presbyterian denominations.

43. For biographical sketches that focus primarily on her politics, feminism, or offer a more general overview of her life see Higginbotham, *Righteous Discontent;* Casper LeRoy Jordan, "Nannie Helen Burroughs," in *Notable Black American Women,* ed. Jessie Carney Smith (Detroit: Gale Research, Inc., 1992), pp. 137-40; Evelyn Brooks Higginbotham, "Burroughs, Nannie Helen," in *Black Women in America: An Historical Encyclopedia,* ed. Darlene Clark Hine (Brooklyn, NY: Carlson Publishing, Inc., 1993), pp. 201-5.

44. For a full picture of Burroughs's financial dealings, see the Administrative and Financial File, 1900-63, of the Nannie Helen Burroughs Papers (NHBP), in the Manuscript Division of the Library of Congress (MDLC). This file contains papers dealing with her personal financial affairs and the financial records of the National Training School for Women and Girls as well as the Woman's Convention Auxiliary to the National Baptist Convention.

45. Minutes of the Corresponding Secretary's Report for the Executive Commit-

the property of trustees who served under the auspices of the Woman's Convention. The project began with a $500 donation from Mrs. Maggie L. Walker. Walker, whose bank in Richmond was one of the most successful African-American enterprises at the turn of the century, intended her donation to inspire the contributions of many other, poorer, black women.[46] By 1922 the Woman's Convention's Annual Report was showing that the school was valued at over $80,000. Of the monies collected by the WC the majority were earmarked for the National Training School. Burroughs's project: to build a "great national institution for our girls . . . at the Nation's Capital, a great Christian University for women — a university that will be as sacred to the Negro race as Holyoke or Vassar or Wellesley is to the Anglo-Saxon race."[47]

The School was to be Burroughs's life project, but by 1917, she was confronting charges by the male-dominated National Baptist Convention (as well as women within the Woman's Convention who opposed her) that the school was hers for personal gain and profit.[48] Her refusal to support a revision in the School's charter so that it would fall wholly under the control of the Convention further fueled the attacks. In 1938, after years of controversy, the National Baptist Convention moved to disassociate itself from the Institute. Although Burroughs remained a Corresponding Secretary of the Woman's Convention, she was largely exiled by both the male and female leaders of the National Baptist Convention and Woman's Convention and her school received no funding from the WC. However, she remained popular with the rank and file. They continued to send letters of support throughout this long battle, and in 1948 she was made President

---

tee, Woman's Convention, 1904, p. 346. Container 310, File 2, Controversy, NHBP, MDLC.

46. Circular of Information for the 17th Annual Session of the National Training School for Women and Girls, 1925-26, p. 9. Container 310, Miscellany — National Trade and Professional School Brochures and Catalog, NHBP, MDLC.

47. "You Can't Have My Baby She Cries: Nannie Burroughs Gets Militant," *Black Dispatch*, Oklahoma City, OK, 12 Jan. 1928, p. 2. Container 46, File: Speeches and Writings, NHBP, MDLC.

48. About these charges one supporter observed as to the motivations of the leaders of the National Baptist Convention that in 1907 when the Training School was worth only $7,000 the Convention had cared nothing about it. Not until 1917 when the School was worth over $200,000 did the Convention look to intervene. See undated and anonymous article in Container 310, File 4, Controversy, NHBP, MDLC.

of the Woman's Convention and the Institute re-affiliated with the National Baptist Convention.

Burroughs was especially incensed at the attempts by men in the National Baptist Convention to take over women's efforts. It rankled her that the Woman's Convention had no autonomy and that the charter of the National Baptist Convention denied women the right to manage and control their own institutions. The Convention, she argued, was a "man's organization." While she did not challenge this as illegitimate, she did note that "Negro Baptist women should have a parallel national organization just as distinct and powerful." If the men would not grant the Woman's Convention autonomy, then the Training School would remain a "woman's institution . . . conceived, developed, managed, owned and controlled by Negro Christian women." As for charges that she had somehow personally profited from the School, she wholeheartedly denied a personal interest, writing that "there was never any thought of personal ownership or personal glory."[49]

Burroughs went to great lengths to defend herself against attacks that she was somehow abusing her connections to the National Baptist Convention. "Nothing but love for the advancement of Negro women and girls has actuated me," she wrote. "I have no selfish motive." She reiterated her loyalty to the church, saying:

> I think more of the National Baptist Convention that [sic] Dr. Williams can ever think of it, because I have worked harder and longer and have made more sacrifices to build it up than he has. I have scrubbed floors, edited papers, washed windows, written books, produced supplies and literature of all kinds, directed and instructed women, developed leaders, sold my little substance to help the Cause, pled the Cause of Missions. I have stook [sic] by the Secretaries of the Boards, worked for the Convention for seventy-five dollars a month — practically nothing — and I'll be blessed if I'll let Dr. Williams run me out of a Convention for which I have worked like a galley slave, not for pay and honor but for the Cause.[50]

49. See Container 46, file: "Statement made by Miss Burroughs at the Close of Her Annual Report to Woman's Convention, at St. Louis," September 1938, NHBP, MDLC.
50. See Container 310, File 4: Controversy, "Eight Allegations of Dr. L. K. Williams, Not Founded in Fact," p. 8, NHPB, MDLC.

Over a period of four decades, Burroughs reiterated time and again that her motives were "pure," that she did not seek personal profit. One supporter, writing to Burroughs in 1924, noted that she did not understand why the "brother's board" wanted to change the Charter, but added "that is the way with most all things, the beginner has the work and all the trouble and after getting things in running order the looker on comes in and wants the job of bossing."[51] Unlike many of her white counterparts, Burroughs was not going to give way. She chose to be cut off first.

Perhaps her ability to withstand the pressures exerted by the National Baptist Convention was a function of a forceful and strong personality (one supporter called her "our Moses"),[52] but Burroughs's personal papers show a woman as adept at raising money and doing business as she was dedicated to the Cause.[53] While a major asset to the Woman's Convention, the Training School survived on a prayer and a promise and lots of hard work and constant effort on Burroughs's part. Burroughs invested substantial money in the project. She was granted a salary as its executive but it seems not to have been paid in full or very regularly. Her financial records reveal that she struggled to keep the school going, collecting rent from properties she owned to pay a raft of unending bills. Bills were rarely paid on time or in full. By 1930 she was struggling to keep up payments on the school's mortgage and negotiating with the mortgage holder, Columbia Building Association, for more time to pay. She assured John Harrell, the president, that she had been "working earnestly to get the money to put our loan in satisfactory condition."[54] To repay these debts she spent many months on the road, fund-raising.

Burroughs had many different business faces. She could be tough

51. Mollie Nugent Williams to Burroughs, 22 February 1924. Container 310, File 1, "Controversy over Status of National Training School," NHBP, MDLC.

52. Fannie Carter Cobb to Burroughs, 29 November 1932. Container 5, General Correspondence, Carter, Fannie Cobb, 1930-57, NHBP, MDLC.

53. Apparently after she became president of the Woman's Convention in 1948, she set about to reorganize the fiscal operation of the Auxiliary. One of the things she did was to institute a plan whereby members were authorized to raise funds for specific categories of activities — one of the things that had gotten her into trouble with the Auxiliary and Convention earlier. See "Scope and Content Note," Finder's guide to the Papers of Nannie Helen Burroughs, p. 5.

54. Burroughs to John Harrell, 23 October 1930; Harrell to Burroughs, 6 November 1930; Burroughs to Harrell, 7 November 1930. Administrative and Financial Records, Container 56, File: Correspondence, October-December 1930, NHBP, MDLC.

and unforgiving; she once ordered the agent who managed her properties to evict tenants for nonpayment.[55] She could also dissemble, appearing apologetic, as she did with Harrell. She could also make herself out
to be pitiable if the occasion called for it. At the height of the Depression
when one of her creditors wrote asking that she send him her payments
on a more regular basis as he had just lost a substantial amount of his
own in a bank failure, she responded that she could not because she had
"been sick and afflicted and am still poor and needy." She added that she
was making a "heroic effort to keep my word and to keep the most important things going."[56] Though she never gained any real measure of
wealth (perhaps not even comfort), Burroughs proved flexible and persistent in her efforts to maintain the Training School. She would argue that
this reflected her commitment to the Cause, but the point should also be
made that the Cause in this case defined her life, not just spiritually but
also practically and materially. If she gave up the Training School to the
National Baptist Convention, she also gave up power — including what
little bit of economic power she wielded. Perhaps it was not coincidental
— indeed, even a show of her support — that when Helen Barrett Montgomery died in 1934 she left a legacy of $1,107 to Burroughs's Training
School, even though she must have known about the controversy in
which Burroughs was embroiled.[57]

Max Weber suggested that in the United States, religious associations
were the "vehicles of social ascent into the circle of the entrepreneurial
middle class."[58] Religious affiliation and expression of faith served as a
guarantee of a man's creditworthiness, argued Weber:

> Admission to the congregation is recognized as an absolute guarantee of
> the moral qualities of a gentleman, especially those qualities required in
> business matters. Baptism secures to the individual the deposits of the

55. Burroughs to Arthur Carr, 6 February 1931. Administrative and Financial Records, Container 56, File: Correspondence, January-May 1931, NHBP, MDLC.
56. Burroughs to Charles Cole, 30 November 1933. Administration and Financial
Records, Container 56, File: Correspondence, 1933, NHBP, MDLC.
57. See Administrative and Financial Records, Container 114, File: National Trade
and Professional School Legacies, NHBP, MDLC.
58. Max Weber, "The Protestant Sects and the Spirit of Capitalism," in *From Max
Weber: Essays in Sociology,* ed. H. H. Gerth and C. Wright Mills (New York: Oxford University Press, 1958), p. 308.

whole region and unlimited credit without any competition. He is a "made man."[59]

Working within and through Protestant churches offered women a kind of moral guarantee as well. Their affiliation secured their reputation and the small donations of the women who joined their organizations. But a gendered reading of church history suggests that Weber's understanding of the results of this process must be qualified. My intention in this essay has not been to celebrate the capitalist and corporate ethos that mission women embraced when they built these organizations, nor to lament their exclusion from the larger marketplace and their relegation to the production of social capital. It is more important to understand the limitations of the economic experience and vision of these women whose work was integral to the creation of the modern welfare state. They recognized and were critical of what they believed to be the excesses of corporate capitalism, but they did not, by and large, challenge the underlying economic ideas of their day.[60] Indeed, they hoped to make their own organizations more dynamic and powerful by embracing as their model the corporate structures of their day. They may have succeeded in their religious mission, but as individuals and collectively as women they were simultaneously limited by the popular belief that entrepreneurial success was best left to men. The result: In most cases mission women lost control over the institutions they had created. Ironically, it seems that black women (members of communities trying to build economic foundations after the Civil

---

59. Weber, "The Protestant Sects and the Spirit of Capitalism," p. 305.

60. In his recent book, *Poor Richard's Principle: Recovering the American Dream through the Moral Dimension of Work, Business, and Money* (Princeton: Princeton University Press, 1996), pp. 202-4, Robert Wuthnow suggests that this may be an ongoing problem facing voluntary or charitable organizations in the United States which try to balance the need to raise money for their activities with a mission to shape the social "values" of the larger society. He argues that the donations given to charitable organizations are an "ambiguous commodity." We prefer to think of them as "gifts" and these organizations as untainted by money and the market place. Reluctant to discuss the issue head-on, contemporary voluntary associations do much as their predecessors did when they embraced the popular corporate models of the day and end up justifying their programs "much as a business would, in terms of cost-benefit analysis." Wuthnow argues that this is unfortunate, for the result is that "much of the public views these as service organizations, functioning mainly to perform some unprofitable social function, rather than recognizing their potential to instruct the public in how better to think about values."

War) best fit the model Weber envisioned, though not — as the example of Burroughs suggests — without generating controversy within those communities. For many other women — especially white women — who so desired, the church and church work did not provide the experience or the network by which they would enter the "entrepreneurial" middle class. They were not to grow "rich" in the fashion envisioned by Weber; the "profits" they generated were not to be monetary ones but rather social. In the developing economic order, these women were the producers of "social capital," a category of economic activity that would continue to be undervalued and overshadowed. And as the struggle between the men and women who are the subjects of this essay suggests, even in the arena of social capital, women's power and authority were challenged.

CHAPTER 7

No Solicitation:
The China Inland Mission and Money

ALVYN AUSTIN

And he sent them out to preach the kingdom of God and to heal the
sick. He told them: "Take nothing for the journey — no staff, no bag,
no bread, no money, no extra tunic."

LUKE 9:2-3 (NIV)

In 1888 Hudson Taylor came to America. A tiny man with few oratorical
skills and dressed in a Chinese gown, he was the most famous missionary of his day, a friend of D. L. Moody, A. T. Pierson, and A. J. Gordon.
Thirty-three years earlier, he had founded the China Inland Mission (now
the Overseas Missionary Fellowship), which had by the late 1880s grown to
over three hundred missionaries in fourteen provinces of China — and all
of it run on faith. At a time when religious organizations were becoming
corporations with armies of fund-raisers and battalions of accountants,
the CIM seemed a return to apostolic Christianity, the instructions Jesus
gave to the disciples in Matthew 10:

> Heal the sick, cleanse the lepers, raise the dead, cast out devils; freely
> you have received, freely give. Provide neither gold, nor silver, nor brass
> in your purses, nor scrip for your journey, neither two coats, neither
> shoes, nor yet staves: for the workman is worthy of his meat.

The CIM represented a new idea in evangelical economics, the faith mission, whose principles could be summed up in one simple motto: the Lord will provide.

To one schooled in the genteel mores of English denominational and class structure, America must have seemed like the land of milk and honey. Taylor's rule of "no solicitation," never asking for money, was tested at his first stop, Northfield, Massachusetts, where he helped incorporate the Student Volunteer Movement (1888). When Moody, a giant of a man, tried to take up a collection, Taylor publicly corrected him. Moody stared at him like "a new species of being" and told the ushers, "Go on. Take up the collection. I'll get it to him in some way."[1] The wife of evangelist Reginald Radcliffe, one of Taylor's traveling companions, exclaimed with a touch of envy, "There are big hearts and heavy purses in America, but like the old country, men are bound by preconceived notions."

At his next stop, the prophetic conference in Niagara-on-the-Lake, Ontario, Taylor spoke "as a little child might speak, as a prophet might speak, as one who sees a vision of a needy land and a dying people might speak. And when, after an hour, he finished, there was a great sigh from the listening throng, followed by a silence which was profound." After he left, the meeting broke into "organized pandemonium" as people became "intoxicated with the joy of giving," pledging enough to support eight "North American workers" in China for a year. This would have amounted to $2,000, since Taylor's secretary translated the British £50 into $250 U.S. (This was far too low, as it did not include travel or outfits. The figure was widely repeated and got the CIM into hot water with other, more generous missions.)

When Taylor heard about the money, he was deeply disturbed. The

---

1. The story of Hudson Taylor's 1888 visit has been told many times. The main sources, described below, are Dr. and Mrs. Howard Taylor, *"By Faith": Henry W. Frost and the China Inland Mission* (Philadelphia etc.: CIM, 1938), pp. 76-104; and Frost's typescript memoirs on which it was based, *The Days That Are Past* (copies in CIM/OMF Archives in Toronto, and Archives of the Billy Graham Center [ABGC], collection 215) [cited as Frost, *Memoirs*]. Alvyn Austin, *Saving China: Canadian Missionaries in the Middle Kingdom 1888-1959* (Toronto: University of Toronto Press, 1986), describes the effect on Canadian foreign missions.

This incident is from Frost, *Memoirs*, pp. 198-99. It gets bowdlerized in *"By Faith,"* p. 93, with the opposite moral: "You are the first man I ever met who refused a good collection," Moody said, with tears in his eyes, and "no offering was taken, and the great meeting closed with prayer."

next morning, after a night of prayer, he abruptly canceled his travel plans, announced the formation of the North American CIM, and issued an appeal for workers:

> To have missionaries and no money would be no trouble to me, for the Lord is bound to take care of his own. . . . But to have money and no missionaries is very serious indeed. And I do not think it will be kind of you dear friends in America to put this burden upon us, and not to send from among yourselves to use the money. We have the dollars, but where are the people?[2]

In response to Taylor's plea, the CIM was besieged by applications, over sixty in three months, and raised over $3,000 in additional funds. Three months later, in September 1888, he sailed from Vancouver with fourteen young recruits, twelve Canadians and two Americans.

Taylor's visit was like a comet, sparking in all directions, and he visited often over the next dozen years, using the Canadian Pacific railway and steamships as a shortcut between England and China. Once established in Toronto, the CIM and its faith principles spread through the interconnected circles that centered around Moody: the Niagara prophetic movement, Keswick, the YMCA, the Bible school movement, and A. B. Simpson's Christian & Missionary Alliance, permeating the growing proto-fundamentalist and proto-pentecostal movements. The CIM became the model for dozens of faith missions that adopted its policy of no solicitation. These included large and important missions like the Africa Inland Mission (1895), founded by A. T. Pierson as a copy of Grattan Guinness's Congo missions; the Kansas Sudan Mission; the International Missionary Alliance; the Sudan Interior Mission (1898), founded by Roland V. Bingham in Toronto; and on down to the tiny Hephzibah China Mission in Utah. By the 1930s, the CIM was "the favorite mission of Fundamentalists."

It was a potent idea, then as now: to lay one's all on the altar, to surrender self, and to step out on the promises. It touched a deep well of "anti-mammonism" and self-sacrifice among evangelicals, the ideal of holy poverty for the gospel's sake. It was also implicitly an anti-capitalist critique, that one man could stand apart from the modern money system and create a communal "family" that shared things in common. D. E. Hoste,

2. Dr. and Mrs. Howard Taylor, *Hudson Taylor and the China Inland Mission*, vol. 2, *Growth of a Work of God* (London: CIM, 1918), p. 449.

Taylor's successor, would tell probationers to throw their pretty home things (tablecloths, pictures) in the muddy Yangtze lest they become "idols" of Westernization.[3]

Americans like to write things down in black and white. Once the CIM introduced the model, its promoters created a theology of faith and money, which could be boiled down to five simple "principles," published in almost every issue of *China's Millions,* the CIM's monthly magazine:

1. The Mission does not go into debt.
2. It guarantees no income, but ministers to workers as funds sent in will allow.
3. All members are expected to depend on God alone for temporal supplies.
4. No collection or personal solicitation of money is allowed.
5. Duly qualified workers are accepted irrespective of nationality and without restriction as to denomination.[4]

It is significant that four of the five principles have to do with money: no debt, no income, no salary, no solicitation. In fact, since the 1890s, money has been the defining principle of "faith" missions. On a mundane level, faith finances offered a critique of conventional mission methods: the CIM claimed to support a missionary for half or less than the salaries of denominational missions, somewhere between $250 and $500 compared with $750 to $1,000. This led to charges of "inefficiency," that code word of modernism thrown back on itself, which implied that educated missionaries were not successful because they were isolated from "the people" inside compounds of capitalism. In spiritual terms, money was the external marker of inner grace: "I use the term 'faith missions' as but imperfectly describing a class of noble evangelical enterprises," wrote A. J. Gordon, one of the movement's tireless promoters.[5] Faith principles implied "a better brand of Christian or at least one which connotes greater

3. In 1998 Promise Keepers, the evangelical men's movement, announced that it was adopting faith principles and would rely on God to provide the salaries of its employees. Its aggressive publicity ("means"), though, would have shocked poor Hudson Taylor.

4. *China's Millions* 33, no. 1 (Jan. 1925): 2. Beginning in 1917, *CM* included three of the five indicated principles. After 1925, the five principles listed were consistently included on the inside cover of the magazine.

5. Adoniram Judson Gordon, *The Holy Spirit in Missions* (London, 1893), p. 63.

faith and trust in God," echoed Harold Lindsell sixty years later.[6] As Henry Frost, North American Director of the CIM, mythologized the early years in Toronto, "We lived from hand to mouth, but it was God's hand and our mouth. . . . Our episodes of scarcity were intended to be new revealings of God's love and power, if only we could be attentive to the inner meaning of things."[7]

A. T. Pierson, in *Forward Movements of the Last Half Century*, took the inner meaning of money one step farther, making a distinction between the "pure faith" of George Müller and Hudson Taylor, who never begged for money, and the "modified faith" of Moody. (Actually Taylor and the CIM, as we shall see, more properly belong in the modified category.) Moody, Pierson argued, would write hundreds of letters to rich and famous patrons whenever he needed money. However, when he died, there was no one to carry on, and a financial crisis ensued. By contrast, Pierson pointed out, Müller never solicited funds, making his requests known to God alone. After his death the workers continued to pray, and God supplied food for two thousand children.[8]

And yet, examining the China Inland Mission from the perspective of money upsets the apple cart: as Taylor's experience at Niagara showed, when money leads, faith follows. When money comes in, God is blessing the work. If money fails, has God withdrawn His blessing? or is it because Satan controls the banks? This paper traces the financial underpinnings of faith missions in England, starting in the 1830s, and the CIM's first forty years — 1888 to 1929 — in North America. One is reminded of Jackson Lears, who suggested that modernism was so pervasive that even antimodernism itself streamlined people and institutions into modernism.[9] By the 1920s the CIM was rich beyond Taylor's wildest dreams: in 1929, the year of the Crash, it raised $500,000 in North America alone, and a similar amount (in pounds sterling) in Britain. It was telegraphing vast amounts of money around the world — using international banks, depen-

6. H. Lindsell, "Faith Missions since 1938," in *Frontiers of Christian World Mission since 1938*, ed. W. C. Harr (New York, 1962), pp. 193-94.

7. Frost, *Memoirs*, p. 397.

8. Arthur Tappan Pierson, *Forward Movements of the Last Half Century* (London and New York: Funk and Wagnalls Co., 1900), pp. 93-99, devotes several pages to a discussion of degrees of financial piety.

9. See T. J. Jackson Lears, *No Place of Grace: Antimodernism and the Transformation of American Culture, 1880-1920* (New York: Pantheon Books, 1981).

dent on the fluctuations of silver — from Kansas to Sweden to Toronto to Philadelphia to Brisbane to Shanghai to the farthest reaches of inland China. What happened when an organization that preached a gospel of poverty came into "a wealthy place," a wealthy American place?

Divine Bookkeeping

First a word about sources. The old CIM was surrounded by an aura of secrecy which A. J. Broomhall, in the recent authoritative seven-volume biography of Hudson Taylor, described as a "conspiracy of silence" and a "cocoon of silence" impossible for outsiders to penetrate.[10] Within the mission, "family secrets" permeated every level: by the 1890s the rank and file in China were in open rebellion, London was not on speaking terms with Shanghai, Toronto would not reveal its finances to London, Australia was in debt, and Hudson Taylor was threatening to resign and take the work with him. The silence extended to the mission's archives, where Taylor decreed that "nothing detrimental to the mission be written and any documents which might prove an embarrassment in later years were to be destroyed." After Dr. and Mrs. Howard Taylor wrote the official histories, the archives were purged so that little material remains, in the CIM archives or elsewhere, "which does not merely substantiate what they wrote."[11] The biggest secret was money. True to its word, one can read through years and years of *China's Millions* and find no reference to money, except in the vaguest terms. In England the CIM adopted George Müller's system of divine bookkeeping: each donor must be thanked publicly, and each donation acknowledged in print. He would issue numbered receipts, which he published in numerical order so the "identity of the donor remained hidden while every gift could be publicly acknowledged."[12] This system satisfied the auditors and maintained the fiction that all gifts came from God, that the people were merely God's visible hand. Hudson Taylor considered the identity of the donors "sacredly private," and except for a

---

10. A. J. Broomhall, *Hudson Taylor and China's Open Century* (Sevenoaks, UK: Hodder & Stoughton, and OMF, 1981-1989) [cited as *HTCOC*]. Quotes are from vol. 6, *Assault on the Nine*, p. 60, and vol. 7, *It Is Not Death to Die!*, p. 134.

11. Moira Jane McKay, "Faith and Facts in the History of the China Inland Mission 1832-1905" (M.Litt. Dissertation, University of Aberdeen, 1981), p. 63.

12. McKay, "Faith and Facts," p. 206.

few individuals, no record of donors has survived.[13] Nevertheless, Moira McKay, whose thesis examined the finances of the early CIM, claims, "There is no indication that money was ever received and not receipted."[14]

When the CIM was starting in North America, its annual reports seemed calculated to confuse. The annual "Abstract of China Accounts," which listed money received in Shanghai, tabulated the money from Britain in pounds sterling translated into silver taels. North America and Australia were lumped together and listed only in taels.[15] The finances, wrote Henry Frost, "are not mere figures. They represent the gifts of little children; they represent also, the gifts of those who are wealthy, and such as have learned the true meaning of stewardship, their gifts meaning as much in human sacrifice as the gifts of those who are poor. Hence, these figures mean flesh and blood, mean devotion, mean the constraint of the Spirit of God, and as such, they lead us once more to give God thanks."[16]

The CIM combined a reticence about money with a mass publicity machine. In addition to *China's Millions*, whose North American circulation reached 4,000 copies,[17] "almost 300 titles were published by CIM authors" between 1865 and 1952, with an additional 259 by 1984. These books, actively marketed, brought in considerable income. Foremost among these were the classic hagiographies written by Dr. and Mrs. Howard Taylor: he was Hudson Taylor's son, while she, the real author, Geraldine Guinness, was daughter of that other evangelical empire builder, Grattan Guinness. Her biographies of Hudson Taylor sold hundreds of thousands and have never been out of print; they are still required reading in many American Bible schools.[18] The one-volume condensation, aptly named *Hudson Taylor's Spiritual Secret*, was described as "a spiritual

13. Broomhall, *HTCOC,* vol. 6, p. 61.

14. McKay, "Faith and Facts," p. 63.

15. For example, *China's Millions,* August 1892, lists three pages of accounts from London, which raised £27,000. Of this, £16,000 (74,000 taels) were remitted to China. "Donations in China and Receipts from America and Australia" amounted to 37,000 taels, itemized in 200 receipts (in taels).

16. *China's Millions* (Feb. 1902): 28. Note: all references after 1893 are to the North American (NA) edition.

17. Subscription List in Minutes of combined Toronto and Philadelphia Councils, 26 June 1919, in ABGC #215, file 3/49.

18. Daniel W. Bacon, *From Faith to Faith: The Influence of Hudson Taylor on the Faith Missions Movement* (Philadelphia: OMF Books, 1984), pp. 137-38, cites a survey of thirty-four Bible schools of which thirty-two required or recommended the Taylor biographies.

classic to be placed on the same shelf as *Pilgrim's Progress*. It has a timeless, intrinsic quality."[19]

In addition to the financial statements, there are two sources for the CIM in North America: Mrs. Taylor's biography of Henry Frost, North American Director from 1888 to 1932, *"By Faith": Henry W. Frost and the China Inland Mission;* and Frost's surprisingly candid autobiographical memoirs on which it was based. These allow the historian to see how she created the mythology, snipping and splicing, deciding what was suitable for public consumption. From the perspective of money, a peculiar pattern emerges in *"By Faith."* When Frost is young, money is seldom mentioned except that his wealthy father gave him a stipend while he worked in a Bowery mission. Once he espouses faith principles, he resolves never to go into debt, even to the fraction of a penny. As long as the CIM is poor, money is a constant topic; when it becomes rich, the subject evaporates. Frost's memoirs reveal a darker side. Far from the carefree attitude towards money that Mrs. Taylor would suggest, Frost was deeply, intensely, prayerfully obsessed with it.

Compelled to Rely on God

Although the Christian church has always had movements that equated poverty with saintliness, modern faith missions can be traced back to August Franke and the Moravians of Halle in Germany. In England, the trumpet call came in 1824, when Edward Irving, a radical Presbyterian who was urging his fashionable London congregation to speak in tongues, called for a new strategy of missions, of "roving figures" who called themselves "revivalists" or "evangelists." These men, and a few women — for this was a period when "female ranting" was still common along the sectarian fringe — took their enthusiasm out of the churches and into the marketplaces, factories, and theaters. Unlike conventional societies, which were "embodiments of worldly expediency," Irving sent them forth "destitute of all visible sustenance, and of all human support." They should be "compelled" to rely on God alone, he said. "Why should they need the bureaucratic organization of a missionary society?"[20]

19. J. C. Pollock, *Hudson Taylor and Maria: Pioneers in China* (New York: McGraw-Hill and OMF, 1962), p. 10.
20. David Bebbington, *Evangelicalism in Modern Britain: A History from the 1730s to the 1980s* (London: Unwin Hyman, 1989; reprinted Grand Rapids: Baker, 1992), pp. 76-77.

The exemplar was the Plymouth Brethren George Müller (1805-98), an abstemious Prussian of the old school who is often called the father (or grandfather) of faith missions. Müller turned the principle of not asking for money into a high art. In 1834-35, he founded two institutions in Bristol: a Bible school cum mission society known as the Scriptural Knowledge Institution for Home and Abroad, which funneled tens of thousands of pounds to Brethren missions throughout the British Empire and practically funded the CIM; and an orphanage (still in operation), which grew into the largest social service agency in the west of England. All this was run by faith: no public appeals, not even a mite box (like the Society for Waifs and Strays) at the back of the room. "There was a supernatural ease with which Müller discovered the secret that God's people will give sacrificially to God's work," wrote his biographer.[21]

Müller's own testimony, *A Narrative of Some of the Lord's Dealings with George Müller: Written by Himself,* published in 1850 with annual updates running to a million words, was an important influence on the faith missions movement. It is surely one of the strangest textbooks ever written on fiduciary economics. On the first page he announced that his father, an excise collector "who educated his children on worldly principles, gave us much money, considering our age; not in order that we might spend it, but as he said, to accustom us to possess money without spending it." This led the boy into many sins: wasting money, falsified accounts, hiding money, playing cards, and stealing, until he was sent to the cathedral school. Once he adopted faith principles, the rest of the book — six hundred densely printed pages — is an itemization of every gift he ever received:

> January 4, 1836 . . . one dish, three plates, two basons [sic], two cups and saucers, and two knives and forks. . . . All this money, and all these articles have been given . . . without my asking any individual for any thing; moreover, almost all has been sent from individuals concerning whom I had naturally no reason to expect any thing, and some of whom I never saw.[22]

And so on, day after agonizing day, year in and year out, from 1830 to 1898.

21. Roger Steer, *George Müller: Delighted in God* (London: Hodder & Stoughton, 1975), p. 56.
22. George Müller, *A Narrative of Some of the Lord's Dealings with George Müller: Written by Himself,* 4th ed. (London: J. Nisbet, 1850), pp. 1, 164-65.

By the 1860s there was a network of urban evangelists who more or less espoused faith principles. Some lived on stipends, like Lord Radstock who preached to the Czar of Russia. Others became entrepreneurs, constructing evangelical empires within the expanding British Empire: the Baptist Charles Haddon Spurgeon had no compunction about asking for money when he built the Metropolitan Tabernacle, the largest church in London. By the 1870s, 300,000 copies of his weekly sermons were mailed throughout the world. In the Church of England, Canon William Pennefather (1816-73) brought people together and taught them to "expect things." A man of simple faith, he "simply asked his Heavenly Father for whatever was needed for this or that project according to his Father's will, and who found these childlike requests granted." His project was called Mildmay Park, which opened in 1864 and quickly became a regional organizing center, with a 1,500-seat church, a deaconess home, a hospital, a nursing and missionary training school, and a 2,500-seat conference hall that had an air of "severe respectability, reminding one of a Friends' or Moravian Meeting House."[23] It was such small "unnoticed religious movements," reminisced secretary of the Church Missionary Society, Eugene Stock, in 1899, that contributed "whatever of life and power the Evangelical wing of the Church possesses today."[24]

In 1865-66, six years after the revival that had swept many working-class converts into the churches, three organizations were founded on faith principles — the Salvation Army, Dr. Barnardo's orphanages, the China Inland Mission — and a few years later, Grattan Guinness's East London Missionary Training Institute. Each was the vision of one man, an autocrat with great charisma from the educated middle class who was called to the poorest of the poor — the factory girls, the street arabs and navvies of the urban underclass — a man who took his wife and family to live among them in the warrens of "darkest London." In financial terms, their problem was how to move money from the West End to the East End. All four grew into international octopuses: Barnardo's and its allied institutions sent over 80,000 orphans to Canada and Australia, in parties of one and

---

23. *China's Millions* UK (July 1888): 77.

24. Eugene V. Stock, *The History of the Church Missionary Society: Its Environment, Its Men and Its Work*, vol. 3 (London: CMS, 1899), p. 20. See also Bebbington, *Evangelicalism in Modern Britain*, pp. 159-64.

two hundred;[25] the East London Institute trained 1,500 missionaries for foreign service, most under the burgeoning faith missions in China and Africa;[26] and by 1900 the China Inland Mission supported 800 missionaries in China.

Hudson Taylor and His Special Agency

Hudson Taylor (1832-1905) was a fourth-generation Methodist from Barnsley, a grimy industrial town in Yorkshire, whose father was a chemist with "one of the best shops in town." He grew up with a typical Nonconformist fear of debt. His father was scrupulous with money, calculating interest tables to "four or five places of decimals." Generous to the poor, he was "tight-fisted" with his family, saving to pay each debt the day it fell due. "If I let it stand over a week," he would say, "I defraud my creditor of interest . . . if only a fractional sum." Here we can see Hudson Taylor's faith principles in embryo, exactly reversed, though, in the definition of "work" and "earning" and "saving."[27]

Taylor first went to China under a Brethren organization, the Chinese Evangelization Society, in 1853, when he was twenty-one. For years he had been dreaming of living deep in the interior, "far away from all human aid, there to depend on God alone for protection, supplies and help of every kind. . . . I thought to myself, when I get out to China I shall have no claim on anyone for anything; my only claim will be on God."[28] The term was disastrous, culminating in Taylor's resignation in 1857. What could he do? Stuck in Shanghai he was "an odd sparrow," "a mystic absorbed in religious dreams" who "forever looked poor." Sometimes he was forced to

25. For Taylor's influence on Barnardo, and Barnardo's deviation from faith principles, see Gillian Wagner, *Barnardo* (London: Eyre & Spottiswoode, 1979). The figures are from Kenneth Bagnell, *The Little Immigrants: The Orphans Who Came to Canada* (Toronto: Macmillan of Canada, 1980).

26. Christof Sauer, "The Importance of Henry Grattan Guinness for the Opening of the Sudan-belt to Protestant Missions: His vision and the resulting attempts and missionary organizations," paper presented at North Atlantic Missiology Research Forum, Fuller Theological Seminary, Pasadena, 18 March 1998. See also Michelle Guinness, *The Guinness Legend* (London: Hodder & Stoughton, 1989).

27. Broomhall, *HTCOC*, vol. 1, p. 287; Dr. and Mrs. Howard Taylor, *Hudson Taylor and the CIM*, vol. 1, *The Growth of a Soul* (London: CIM, 1911), p. 32.

28. Pollock, *Hudson Taylor and Maria*, p. 20.

borrow from his servant or pawn a bar of soap — his last bar! — until in unexpected ways, by prayer alone, God reminded a friend at home and a check came in the mail. But, one senior missionary recalled, "when the vocation found him, it made him a new man, with iron will and untiring energy."[29]

When he established the China Inland Mission in 1865, Hudson Taylor called it a "special agency" for less qualified, spirit-filled lay workers, men and women. The foreign field was "so extensive," he wrote, "and the need of laborers of every class so great, that 'the eye cannot say to the hand, I have no need of thee'; nor yet again the head to the feet, 'I have no need of you.' Therefore persons of moderate ability and limited attainments are not precluded from engaging in the work."[30] Thus Taylor opened the door of foreign missionary work to working-class "yeoman types," artisans and blacksmiths, bookkeepers and milliners, who would have been rejected by conventional missions, which insisted on educated clergy or medical doctors. They were also used to living near the poverty line.

Taylor's mistrust of armchair committees led to a conundrum: some sort of home committee was necessary, if only to collect donations and forward them to Shanghai. He left the "entire administration" in the "sole charge" of a pious tycoon named William T. Berger (1812-99), who is credited as "co-founder" of the CIM. During the critical year 1865-66, it was Berger who paid for three thousand copies of *China: Its Spiritual Need and Claims,* contributed several hundred pounds for passages and outfits, and two hundred pounds for a printing press. Taylor left no instructions, except that Berger should look "prayerfully to God for guidance, [and] to act without unnecessary delay in every matter as it arose." Nevertheless, Berger was responsible for "receiving and remitting funds, rendering accounts, editing the Occasional Paper, and corresponding with supporters — often curious or excited by the news from China."[31]

It was a fine line between facts and appeals, as Berger found in the first Occasional Paper, when he announced:

29. Ralph Covell, *W. A. P. Martin: Pioneer of Progress in China* (Washington, DC: Christian University Press, 1978), p. 21. See also Broomhall, *HTCOC,* vol. 3, *If I Had a Thousand Lives,* p. 65.

30. Marshall Broomhall, *The Jubilee Story of the China Inland Mission* (Philadelphia: CIM, 1915), p. 30.

31. Broomhall, *HTCOC,* vol. 4, *Survivors' Pact,* p. 70, and appendix, "William Berger and Mission Funds," pp. 420-22.

To meet the expense of the outfits and passage of so large a party, funds (in addition to what is needed for current expenses) to the amount of from £1500 to £2000 according to the number going, will be required.[32]

Again, in No. 4, Berger "ventured on to thin ice" when he described poor Stephan Barchet,

> suffering so frequently from fever and ague, through sleeping on the ground floor, it has been thought advisable by friends in Ningpo, to build him a two-storied house; the upper part to be used as a dwelling, and the lower as a place for preaching, etc. The cost will be about £200. Friends desiring fellowship in the above, may send their contributions.[33]

Nothing this blatant would have appeared in the later CIM publication, when "no solicitation" became a "conspiracy of silence." Berger's system was simple: he was "confident that the Lord would supply all needed funds — through themselves if necessary. But he wanted and expected to see them come in from the wide circle of sympathizers in many different congregations."[34] In 1865-66 the CIM collected over £4,000, of which £2,000 paid for outfits and passages of twenty-one adults and four children. Over the next year a further £3,000 was received. At first contributions came in large amounts ("by no means inconsequential") from a small group who gave sums between £10 to £700. Half the individual donors (631) gave less than one pound; 88 were "large donations" of £10 or more. As the CIM's constituency grew, the significance of the large donations declined, and more than 85 percent of contributions came in small sums from many people.[35]

In 1875 Hudson Taylor appointed Benjamin Broomhall, his brother-in-law, as London director. Dapper, even worldly, "B.B." was a YMCA success story, Taylor's childhood friend who owned a well-regarded tailor shop in Bond Street. He made the CIM respectable, an ally of Keswick and the YMCA. Broomhall became the backbone of the anti-slavery and anti-opium movements, and would continually stride into the House of Lords to present yet another petition against opium traffic. Even Broomhall contradicted Taylor's rules against solicitation. In *The Children's Treasury*, for

---

32. Broomhall, *HTCOC*, vol. 4, p. 129. This would have amounted to $7,500 to $10,000 U.S.

33. Broomhall, *HTCOC*, vol. 4, p. 420.

34. Broomhall, *HTCOC*, vol. 4, p. 348.

35. McKay, "Faith and Facts," p. 211.

example, he wrote of a "devoted Christian missionary" [i.e., Taylor] who had "organized a most interesting Mission which is doing a great deal of good . . . and if some of my little readers will pray earnestly for him, and for the poor heathen among whom he labours, and at the same time send him some money to help teach the Chinese boys and girls to love Jesus, I am sure it will encourage and cheer his heart, and be most pleasing to our Lord Jesus." This prompted one response:

> Dear Sir,
>   I want to help the boys and girls of China to love Jesus, as it says in The Children's Treasury for 1876. I have just been reading about it. If you have not died since then, I want you to let me know, and I will send you a little money I have saved.
>   Your affectionate, Gracie.[36]

This letter, so innocent and so rare, shows the depth of the CIM's secrecy, which prompted one supporter to recount the rumor that CIM missionaries were "reduced to such depths of poverty that they are induced to give up the work and take up with secular pursuits . . . and that even their children are sometimes so destitute that the heathen take pity on them. . . . For this cause I have not continued my support of your mission." There was some truth in her charges, Taylor admitted somewhat ingenuously, but "No one has been hindered in work by lack of funds; no one has ever suffered in health from this cause; no one has ever left the Mission on this ground, or has remained dissatisfied on this score, to my knowledge."[37]

Despite (or because of) its published receipts, there were always questions. One persistent rumor was that Hudson Taylor himself, who was supposedly on the same stipend as everyone else, had substantial personal reserves, gifts that were given for his personal use. In addition, there were the royalties from his books, which sold in the hundreds of thousands. He ploughed some personal money back into the CIM: when Berger died in 1899, Taylor donated his legacy as down payment for a new mission home in Toronto. In any other religious organization, these lapses from "pure faith" would seem like peccadilloes; in the CIM they became magnified into charges of hypocrisy.

36. McKay, "Faith and Facts," p. 221.
37. McKay, "Faith and Facts," p. 221; see also *HTCOC*, vol. 6, pp. 41-42.

God's Hand

When Taylor left Toronto in 1888, he left Henry Frost (1858-1945) no instructions on how to select candidates or raise funds, save a cheery "the Lord will help you." This statement, Frost commented, was "distressingly simple, characteristic of the man, but not exactly practical in its application." Thus, with no guidance or oversight from the Old Country, Frost had to reinvent the CIM's "Principles and Practice" in a new land. "It became clear to us," he wrote, "that we could not look to the [China Inland] Mission in England for advice in the developing of our North American work. This was not because our English friends were lacking in wisdom, but because their experience had been insular while our need was continental."[38]

Henry Frost typified one pattern of American faith leaders. He was a patrician, related to Benjamin Franklin; his wife Abbie Ellinwood (whose uncle was secretary of Presbyterian foreign missions) was a descendant of Priscilla and John Alden of the *Mayflower*. He had a peripatetic childhood, moving to eighteen cities, before he graduated from Princeton College as an engineer. Later he moved to Attica, New York, where he married and bought mills and gas plants. When he first heard of faith principles through reading the story of the Cambridge Seven in 1885, he determined to adopt them wholeheartedly: up until that time he had never shaved himself, and after firing the manservant, he considering shaving a lesson in faith. He was "much exercised about the matter of indebtedness," and in searching the scriptures found two texts that became his watchwords: "Provide things honest in the sight of all men" and "Owe no man anything."[39]

These were fine general rules, but what was their application in America's Gilded Age, when debt was becoming a way of life for many individuals and organizations? Frost formulated certain rules: "a 'debt' is not a debt if one has assets to cover it; second, that a debt is only a debt when one owes for something for which he finds it impossible to pay; and third, that a debt of this latter kind is wholly and forever forbidden by the Word of God, whether in the individual or collective life." Thus, he wrote fifty years later, he never, "except in one or two cases of unintentional miscalculation," owed a debt.[40]

38. Broomhall, *HTCOC*, vol. 6, pp. 41-42.
39. Frost, *Memoirs*, pp. 217, 522.
40. Frost, *Memoirs*, pp. 178-80.

The CIM's first years in Toronto were hand-to-mouth, as Frost built two networks. One, which was local, consisted of churches and council members who sustained the mission through hard times. A second, and much more far-flung constituency, reached every part of the United States. All applicants, whether they lived next door or arrived penniless from Iowa, lived in the Toronto home. This was a time of "testing" — not "training" in biblical exposition or missionary methods — practical lessons on how to live without money. More than once a dozen candidates and Frost's six children sat down to the table without a scrap of food in the house; always, providentially, someone would appear at the door with a brace of partridges, a hamper of groceries, or a ton of coal, whatever was needed to survive the next day or week. These stories, repeated endlessly when the CIM became rich, reinforced the notion that it was always a poor faith organization.

Since Frost was creating faith principles not only for himself and the CIM, but a larger world of evangelicals, it is instructive to examine the issues he faced at the nexus of faith, money, and modern banking. The first lesson was how to accept money gracefully, the little ritual of deference, hesitation, and sincerity, thanking the donor while acknowledging that the gift came from God's hand.

The next was how to pray for money. It was not enough to pray in the abstract, though, as Frost discovered when he had "a season of prayer" with no result except "the mystery of a silent heaven." In "a flash of heavenly light," he calculated the mission needed $600 for expenses, placed the bills on the seat in front of him, and prayed for exactly that amount; the next day he received a check for $600, with instructions to "use it as He may lead." "We were emboldened to be more specific in our requests," Frost wrote.[41] A few days later, he and a council member prayed for a "full five thousand dollars" to send six young women to China. "It was one of those Spirit-filled petitions that go like an arrow to their mark. Humble, yet confident; reverent, yet bold, it laid hold upon the promises of God and made them, for the time being, blank cheques, to be filled up according to the need." The $5,000 came in within three months.[42]

41. Frost, *Memoirs*, pp. 285-86. Taylor, *"By Faith,"* pp. 128-30, quotes a different passage, not in Frost's *Memoirs*, and adds a heavenly voice asking, "Just what is it, young man, that you want? Be specific."

42. Frost, *Memoirs*, pp. 288-92; Taylor, *"By Faith,"* pp. 146-50.

In 1893 Frost launched the CIM on a "new beginning" with a North American edition of *China's Millions* to highlight "our part of the work." He also aligned the CIM with the burgeoning Bible school movement, particularly Moody Bible Institute and T. C. Horton's Northwestern Bible College in St. Paul. In 1894, the CIM was instrumental in founding Toronto Bible College (now Tyndale College and Seminary), though under the financial sponsorship of Elmore Harris, an independently wealthy Baptist minister (from the Massey-Harris farm implement family). The CIM and TBC always had a special relationship, since the candidates in the mission home, most of whom had no theological training, attended classes there in remedial Bible reading and missionary medicine.[43] God's blank checks did not work at the bank, though, when it came to leases and mortgages. When the CIM moved out of its cramped downtown building into a seventeen-room house, at $52.50 a month, three members of the council had to sign the lease, since the mission "could not sign rental leases or deal in other futurities."[44] By 1899 this house was too small and Frost had his eye on a larger one three blocks away, which was for sale at $15,000. Hudson Taylor contributed Berger's legacy of £1,000, which translated into $4,816. The owner reduced the price by $2,000, which left a mortgage for $8,000. Again, three council members acted as trustees, supposedly the first such legal document in the city. Within a week another $4,000 came in, much of it from council members.

Then the unexpected happened. Hudson Taylor suggested putting a notice in *China's Millions* to let "our friends know of our need and giving them opportunity to minister to us." Frost was shocked to learn that Taylor had done this before, but since "truth and the prosperity of the work were at stake," he wrote a "frank" letter to Taylor, four single-spaced pages, which outlined the strict policy he had followed. A mortgage was not a "debt," he wrote, because the unpaid amount was protected by the value of the land; nevertheless, considering the number of local religious institutions who were over their heads in debt, it was better not to compromise the mission's testimony by taking a mortgage. As to solicitation, Frost warned, "a single note in *China's Millions*" would "disappoint many Chris-

---

43. Alvyn Austin, "Hotbeds of Missions: The China Inland Mission and Toronto Bible College," *Distant Seeds, American Harvest: The Missionary Impulse in United States History,* forthcoming.

44. Frost, *Memoirs,* pp. 388-91.

tians, that it would even unsettle the faith of some in a prayer-answering God." Frost did not learn what effect his letter had on Taylor, for the latter answered courteously and never brought the subject up again. (Frost dubbed the new house "Solomon's Temple" because the main room had a ceiling decorated in gold.)[45] There was another, particularly American, problem that vexed the international CIM at this time, the question of "special support." At first it had appealed to donors who wanted a personal connection with one missionary, but eventually the guaranteed salaries meant "certain of our missionaries were provided for in full by individual donors, while others were dependent upon the general fund." In other words, some lived on a fixed income ("and that salary on a gold basis, which is not the basis of the Mission in China"), while everyone else was on "a different footing," with a fluctuating salary dependent on income. This was a mistake, "a hindrance to spiritual blessing," and after years of discussion, the CIM abolished special support in 1899, stipulating that private donors could contribute a missionary's salary, but it was put into the general fund to be ministered to all alike.

Since the North American *Millions* had not yet adopted the policy of publishing numbered receipts, there is no way of tabulating how money came in except the annual "income received in North America." From $3,400 in its first year (1888), the income rose steadily if not spectacularly to $50,000 in 1901, when the North American headquarters moved to Philadelphia. To understand the blips and dips in detail one must overlay several templates: Hudson Taylor's visits (1889, 1894); the new beginning of 1893-94; the financial depression of 1888-92 and boom of 1893; and news from China, such as the sudden increase in contributions after the Boxer Rebellion of 1900.[46]

By 1901 the CIM was in an anomalous situation. Frost and J. S.

45. Frost, *Memoirs*, pp. 575-86, recounts this incident at length, including Frost's entire letter. Needless to say, Taylor, *"By Faith,"* pp. 238-42, mentions the landlord's surprise but neither Taylor's suggestion nor Frost's reaction.

46. To put the CIM figures in perspective: in 1901 when the CIM raised $49,798, this was more than the Canadian Methodist church spent on all its overseas missions ($45,511, of which $12,203 went for China); the Canadian Presbyterians collected $167,652, of which $19,000 went to China. In other words, the CIM raised over 60 percent of all Canadian missions to China, even though most of the money came from the United States. See John Foster, "The Imperialism of Righteousness: Canadian Protestant Missions and the Chinese Revolution, 1925-1928" (Ph.D. diss., York University, 1977), pp. 555, 557.

Helmer, the treasurer, "were Americans, but we were living on British soil. *China's Millions,* our monthly paper, was printed in Toronto, but its chief circulation was in the States. . . . And, most interestingly, our greatest opportunity for witnessing to the needs of China was in the States, but almost all of our speakers were from Great Britain."[47] Always the expatriate, for twelve years Frost had been hoping for a "movement of the clouds, this time toward the States."[48] When he was given a mansion in Norristown, a suburb of Philadelphia, he moved so quickly it made everyone's heads spin. He did not even have time to confer with the Toronto council, merely announcing "my intention of transferring our family residence and beginning the work of the Mission at the new center." Toronto felt "abandoned," believing Frost had built the work around himself and thought it would collapse if he left.[49]

Heavy Purses

In 1901, while Frost was in China in the wake of the Boxer horror, a "new friend" of Dr. and Mrs. Howard Taylor offered to buy a house if the CIM would transfer its headquarters to Philadelphia. The Taylors traveled in the haute monde of evangelicalism, making a tour of American colleges at the invitation of John R. Mott and the Student Volunteer Movement. By the time Frost returned, the matter had been settled. Horace Coleman, the new friend, a bachelor businessman of few words, one fine fall day took Frost for a walk up De Kalb Street. He pointed to a large house, and said, "You can have it if you want." At a second house: "You can have it if you want." And a third, on the crest of a hill "where the houses and grounds were more inviting" — a veritable Delectable Field — he asked Frost to look out of the corner of his eye. Frost was "deeply moved . . . too grateful to speak." The next day Coleman donated the house as North American headquarters of the China Inland Mission.

I need not emphasize the similarity with Christ's temptation in the wilderness; nor, out of the corner of my eye, notice the eternal Canadian complaint about big American money. Be that as it may, Coleman, who be-

---

47. Frost, *Memoirs,* p. 523.
48. Frost, *Memoirs,* p. 570.
49. Frost, *Memoirs,* pp. 37-38.

came a council member and generous donor for thirty-five years, had succeeded in buying his way into the CIM. Two years later, when the house was too small, Coleman repurchased it from the mission, which set him back $25,000, while the CIM moved to a larger house in Germantown, given by Miss Charlesanna Huston, another "new-found friend." "We were finding out that divine leadings were sometimes very strange, but that they always went from good to better and from better to best. Mr. Coleman had his way."[50]

According to *"By Faith,"* the Philadelphia years were "rich in a new way, as regards the experience of Mr. and Mrs. Frost themselves — rich in trial, working patience and leading to fresh discoveries of the grace of God. Not that they had been without trial in the early days of the work in Canada; but this was different."[51] Frost's own memoirs continue to be quite revelatory on the subject of money. Reverting to his natural class, he was coming into "intimate contact with a number of well-to-do persons." The "by-product of [his] financial experiences" was a new appreciation for rich philanthropists. They deserve our pity, he wrote: "I say it deliberately, that the lives of such persons, often, are hardly worth living. They are written to, they are called upon, they are supplicated, they are pestered, they are hounded, all for a few paltry dollars. . . ."[52] The CIM was different, fresh, apostolic. Miss Huston, a middle-aged Quaker whose father had been a doctor, was reduced to snooping around the mission home, which she had paid for, to "spy out the land, discover some new need and then supply it . . . and a day or two afterwards, a van would drive up . . . [with] a new rug for the living room or new pieces of furniture for some bedroom."[53]

One more rich young man should be mentioned: William Borden, the milk company heir, whose life was told by Mrs. Howard Taylor in *Borden of Yale.* He was one of the golden boys of the years before the Great War, "prepossessing [in] appearance, with a strong and attractive face and a well developed and athletic body. He was besides, rugged of character, consecrated of spirit, generous of disposition and lofty of aim and purpose — a unique man." In 1909 at the age of twenty-two, he joined the CIM

50. Frost, *Memoirs,* pp. 634-36. *"By Faith,"* pp. 259-62, tones down the questions and removes the Taylors from the story. It mentions Coleman by name and thereafter refers to him as "the giver."

51. Taylor, *"By Faith,"* p. 293.

52. Frost, *Memoirs,* p. 733.

53. Frost, *Memoirs,* p. 753.

council as its youngest member. When he applied for China, though, he was turned down until two years later; at the council meeting, he had to withdraw while the others reviewed his application. He died tragically on the way to China in 1913, in Cairo; in his will he left over a million dollars to charities, including $250,000 to the CIM.[54]

From such experiences Frost reformulated his theology of money. His first lesson was how to deal with "tainted money." Yet another "unknown friend," a pseudonymously named Mr. Gray, sent checks totaling $3,000, followed by regular $500 gifts over several years. Rumors reached the mission that, "while a godly man in some particulars," he was depriving his wife and children of "the average comforts and necessities of life; and that his wife was not in sympathy with him." After much prayer, Frost returned the last check with a letter lecturing Mr. Gray on his duty, "otherwise we should be, unwittingly, a cause of estrangement between you and your family, of stumblings to Christians at large, and of reproach upon the precious name of Christ." Mr. Gray did not reply.[55]

A lesson of a different sort "had a considerable effect upon the financial policy of the Mission in North America, and also, some effect upon the policy of the Mission at large": how to deal with banks and investments, the mundane financial institutions that dominated modern economics. Another "unknown friend" left a legacy of $50,000 on the condition that the principal be invested and the CIM use the interest. "We did not desire, in our work of faith, to have sinking funds, whether small or large, and shrank from beginning a practice which might diminish our need of trust and exercise of prayer." In the end Frost accepted the bequest, because it was better than giving the money to "an irreligious State" and besides, Miss Benson had not "given us the principal but had simply made us trustees." Half the money was invested in Toronto, half in Philadelphia. Nevertheless, Frost concluded years later "that endowments are not constant with the principles of the China Inland Mission. It is our hope, therefore . . . that those who will money to the Mission will allow it the privilege of using the principal as well as any interest."[56] This was not a hard and fast rule, for the mission continued to receive legacies ($17,000 in 1925) and be-

54. Frost, *Memoirs,* pp. 737, 773. See also Mrs. Howard Taylor, *Borden of Yale* (Philadelphia etc.: CIM, 1926), pp. 176-78: he also gave $100,000 each to the National Bible Institute, MBI, and the Moody Church.

55. Frost, *Memoirs,* pp. 665-67, gives the text of the letter to Mr. Gray.

56. Frost, *Memoirs,* pp. 731-33.

quests, and interest from investments brought in $7,000 a year, a not inconsiderable sum.

Opening the Books

The financial abstracts confirm that Philadelphia was "rich in another way." From $50,000 in 1901, the last year in Toronto, the CIM's income climbed slowly to $90,000 in 1915, the first year of the Great War, when it doubled with the Borden legacy (1916-17) to $175,000. Surprisingly, rather than dropping, it leveled and picked up in the postwar boom. This pattern was repeated in the 1920s, when it doubled to $340,000 in 1926, spiked at $500,000 in 1929, then dropped in half in 1930, the Depression. Here are the figures:

Toronto HQ	1888-1901	$385,788	(13 years)
Philadelphia HQ	1902-1914	799,393	(13 years)
	1915-1928	2,772,612	(13 years)
	1929	502,017	
	1930-1937	1,922,894	(8 years)
Total	1888-1937	$6,382,704	(50 years)[57]

In September 1907, for the first time, the North American *China's Millions* printed a list of receipts, long a feature of the English CIM. The lists appeared sporadically until 1914, when they were published monthly, and ended abruptly in 1943, when possibly such information — how much (and how?) money was shipped to China — would be considered wartime secrets. In other words, we can track every cent the North American CIM received from 1914 to 1943, excluding personal sums forwarded through CIM channels. Until the 1930s the accounts were broken down into income received in Philadelphia and in Toronto, giving a window onto national differences. Although the donors' identities are not known, the donations itemized by size and place reveal interesting patterns.

The early accounts from 1906-14 have one peculiar feature: each acknowledges a gift for $1,000. From the fragmentary evidence, we cannot

<hr/>

57. Taylor, *"By Faith,"* pp. 292-93.

know whether $1,000 was common or unusual: or did the donors pressure the mission to acknowledge their gifts in print?

The number of individual donations is staggering. By 1914 Philadelphia received 800 donations (average 67/month), and Toronto somewhat higher, 950 (average 80). Yet total income in Philadelphia was higher: $36,000 against $25,000 from Toronto. The superiority of Philadelphia was not complete, though, for occasionally Toronto's monthly sum was higher. Gifts in Toronto tended to cluster around the low end: gifts of $20 or less made up almost 80 percent of all donations, with only eight of $500 or more. Philadelphia counted only 65 percent of $20 or less, and 15 individual gifts of $500 or more. These large gifts, 2.5 percent, gave almost half (48 percent) of all income.

By January 1921 gifts in Philadelphia skyrocketed to 400 a month, and to 450 in Toronto. This was the height of the North China famine, when churches across North America were raising millions of dollars for famine relief. It coincided with the postwar revival within the churches, and affluence in society in general. The CIM had collected and distributed famine relief for fifty years, both under its own auspices and together with cooperative agencies, and its efforts in 1921 brought it to a new prominence in America. In January alone, the two offices received over 400 contributions, including one of $8,500 and four of $1,000 or more, totaling almost $30,000. By this time, though, famine relief was becoming a contentious issue among evangelicals, as the liberals and conservatives were girding for religious war. During the 1920s the CIM in China gradually withdrew from large-scale ecumenical social movements, concentrating on its core message of front-line evangelism. By the end of 1921 the famine had passed, and although famine gifts continued sporadically as news from China occurred, the CIM (NA) did not organize special fund-raising again until the Second World War.

Before giving a detailed analysis of the four crucial years from 1928-31, a few words may be said about cliometrics, and what can be gleaned from analysis of the numbers themselves. First, the pattern of many small gifts and a few large ones was remarkably consistent. Second, virtually every donation came as an even amount, confirming that they came by check, through the mail. It took less thought to write a check for $5 than for $5.01. The most common amount — one in every four or five gifts, in 1906 as in 1943 — was a $5 bill, then $10, then $1; but there were more $50s, and often more $100s, than $20s. The donations in uneven amounts were probably the result of some previous transaction, such as the 8 cents forwarded from children's mite boxes, or a premium that came due. The most intriguing record is a donation of $416.66 that arrived about the tenth of each month from 1913 to 1931, totaling nearly ninety thousand dollars.

The period from 1928 to 1931 was one crucial moment in mission history. By 1929 the religious turmoil in Canada and the States had subsided, sides had been chosen, and the CIM came out on top. It had cut its few remaining ties to the mainline churches, and became the strong right arm of overseas Fundamentalism. Momentous events were happening in China, too. In 1927 the civil war forced the evacuation of all missionaries from the interior. Many mainline missionaries, as many as half of some missions, did not return, and the 1930s was a time of retrenchment and devolution. With so many missionaries in Shanghai, the CIM had an unprecedented opportunity, its first internal exchange of ideas and methods since the Boxers. In 1929 it announced an appeal for "The Two Hundred" new recruits in the next two years. By the last day of 1931, 203 young missionaries had sailed from Britain, Canada, the United States, Sweden, and elsewhere. Significantly, almost half, 97 men and women, were from North America. The Two Hundred proved to be a pivotal event in worldwide missions, leading to the ascendancy of evangelical faith missions after the Second World War.[58]

Against this background — the stock market crash, class, American religion, and overseas turmoil — the bare statistics of the CIM, then, can reveal in microcosm the financial underpinnings of one of the great inspirational moments of the twentieth century. Henry Frost gives a snapshot of the euphoria behind the scenes. Philadelphia treasurer Roger Whittlesey, a native of Cleveland who had served two terms as business manager in China, was "having a good time." He would break "forth into unconcealed praise, marveling at what he saw, in letters and otherwise, of the goodness of the Lord," and announce,

Miss Huston has been in this afternoon and left her cheque for $1000!! Isn't it just grand! A similar amount is in today from Mr. Smith of Chi-

58. Joel A. Carpenter, "Propagating the Faith Once Delivered: The Fundamentalist Missionary Enterprise 1920-1945," in *Earthen Vessels: American Evangelicals and Foreign Missions 1880-1980*, ed. Joel A. Carpenter and Wilbert R. Shenk (Grand Rapids: Eerdmans, 1990), discusses the MBI/Wheaton College connection with the Two Hundred.

cago. And Mrs. Wyman asks if we can sell a bond for $1000. Of course, I was able to say, Yes. Praise God!

A few months later Mrs. Eldridge Torrey gave $5,000 in memory of her husband. This confirmed, Frost concluded, that "God liked to be the Provider, with Mr. Whittlesey as His Treasurer."[59]

Rather than tabulating each year individually, the appendix gives an average for 1928-29, the fat years, and 1930-31, the lean years. This disguises minor currents, such as the monthly fluctuations: many gifts at Christmas and New Year's, a slump in February and in the summer, picking up after Labor Day. In addition, 1929 and '30 were famine years in China, when the CIM (NA) collected $11,000 a year for famile relief; by contrast, only $2,000 per year was collected during 1928 and 1931. The donations were listed in three categories: General, Special Purposes, and Famine. Special funds were not the same as the old "special support," which merely channeled stipends through the CIM, but they were earmarked for certain projects such as the "Home Special Account, for taxes on Philadelphia Home" ($583). Special funds tended to come in larger amounts, $10 to $100, indicating the donors were close friends of the mission, rather than more casual contributors to the general funds.

The old CIM pattern of many small gifts (especially $5s and $10s) and a few large ones is still evident. What is new is the total eclipse of Toronto: in 1914 the two offices were more or less at par; by 1928 Toronto brought in only 12 percent of the total income. The supremacy of Philadelphia was due to several factors. First was an increase in gifts, a comfortable 200 donations a month, which shows a broad national constituency. Although three-quarters were for less than $20, the main increase came from a small number of very large gifts, $1,000 or more. These gifts, less than 2 percent of the total, sometimes made up 80 percent of the monthly income, or half the annual income. These large donations skew the average size of the gifts: if they are included, the average gift in the United States is $89; if they are left out, the average drops to $40.

One donation stands out, the explanation for the dramatic increase in 1929. In 1924 Charlesanna Huston died, very publicly, Frost recalled, in a room "overflowing" with bishops and clergymen. She had been an "absolutely unique" person within the inner circle, and one suspects that many

59. Frost, *Memoirs*, p. 835.

of the $1,000 gifts over the years had come from her hands. Starting in December 1924 and continuing through February 1929, the mission received bequests from her estate, between $5,000 and $50,000 a month. The residual was settled for $246,275.88 in March 1929. Altogether, Miss Huston gave over $700,000 through her will.[60]

Meanwhile Toronto limped along like a poor cousin. Actually, it was bringing in a respectable $50,000 a year, about the same as 1901. There were a few $1,000 gifts — two or three a year — and a few for $500. Toronto did have more bequests, a modest $200 or $500, which indicates an aging constituency. Overall, however, the average donation in Toronto was less than $30. The Depression hit hard: not only did the number of individual donations drop, so did the amount, with many gifts for less than $5. Reading between the lines, one can see that the CIM in Toronto, which had always relied on a broad alliance of evangelicals, had lost support among the mainline, and was still groping toward a reconfigured fundamentalist network. The impression one gets is a working-class constituency who gave small amounts — the widow's mite — coupled with a middle-class core who gave medium-sized gifts of $50 to $100.

By contrast, the Depression hardly seemed to touch Philadelphia. There might have been some drop in the middle range, but that was more than offset by very large gifts: in 1931, it received twenty-two gifts of $4,000 and more. Actually, if one removes these large donations, Philadelphia was not bringing in all that much more a month than Toronto, somewhere in the range of $70,000 or $80,000 a year.

There is one final aspect that I have not mentioned. As the income spiraled, the number of new missionaries dropped by half. Henry Frost tabulated them by decade:

Decade	Women	Men	Total
1888-1897	71	52	123
1898-1907	46	18	64
1908-1917	30	22	52
1918-1927	94	37	131
	241	129	370[61]

60. Frost, *Memoirs*, pp. 859-66, gives the full six-page text of Frost's eulogy. Taylor, *"By Faith,"* p. 331, mentions her passing but not her bequest. Miss Huston gave three times Borden's bequest, yet she is written out of the official history.

61. Frost, *Memoirs*, pp. 730, 828, 891.

There were many reasons for the lack of recruits, not the least of which was the quandary between capital advance and maintenance expenses. Considering the longevity of CIMers, at any given time the North American CIM was supporting two or three hundred Americans in China and dozens on furlough at home. The selection process, with its obligatory times of testing and prayer, was more lengthy and expensive. So, home expenses rose in higher proportion. The CIM had always prided itself that compared to conventional missions, it was a well-run charity that supported a large number of missionaries on a shoestring budget. In 1929, of $500,000 raised, less than $400,000 (77 percent) went to China, either in the general funds or special purposes. The rest was spent at home: $33,000 for homes in six cities; outfits and passages ($15,000); a furlough and "annuity fund for support of missionaries permanently detained at home"; and office expenses, including $5,000 for "attorney's fees" and postage, etc.

God so manifestly blessed the CIM, it began to feel it could see God's invisible hand behind the world economy. During the First World War, the exchange rate between American dollars and Chinese taels soared, which "cruelly cut the value of our money in half as it went to China." After the war, at the height of the 1921 famine, the rate dropped, which *China's Millions* described as "one of God's mercies; an answer to prayer and an encouragement in a time of great difficulty in mission work and great want in China." This theme was picked up in *"By Faith,"* with a graph that showed the correlation, as income in America rose in proportion to the declining exchange rate.

Epilogue

One would have thought that during the Depression the troubles of poor old China would have seemed like an oriental nightmare. At a time when money was tight and mainline missions were scaling back, why were ordinary people in America so eager to give money to save China's millions? It would be like pouring money into a bottomless pit. And yet, moving people to give through prayer alone brought staggering amounts of money into the China Inland Mission, the Sudan Interior Mission, the Africa Inland Mission, and the myriad special-purpose faith missions that sprang up in the 1930s like mushrooms after a spring rain. If the world economy fails, the Lord will still provide.

In this paper I have shown how one or two rich people can change the direction and policy, even the theology, of faith missions. Just as William Borden's legacy fueled the CIM's expansion after the First World War, Charlesanna Huston's bequest paid for The Two Hundred in 1929-31. Thus she helped pave the way for the Americanization of the faith mission movement in the 1930s.

By the 1950s strict faith principles were going out of fashion among evangelicals, as Michael Hamilton shows in his chapter in this book. Nowadays, faith missions actively and often aggressively beg for money, even staid old organizations like the Sudan Interior Mission (now the Scripture International Mission) and the Africa Inland Mission. The China Inland Mission changed its name after the exodus from China to the Overseas Missionary Fellowship, but not its principle of no solicitation. Now, almost alone among evangelical organizations, the OMF does not ask for money. Its policy is to "supply financial information commensurate with interest, while recognizing that communication with supporters and potential supporters is very important." In other words, the books are open but the mission waits until it is asked for details. Financial reports are sent to members (i.e., missionaries) once or twice a year. When I asked Gerald Dykema, financial officer in Toronto, which other organizations still practiced such stringent principles, he could only think of the Worldwide Evangelization Crusade in Hamilton, Ontario, and the World Mission Prayer League, an American Lutheran mission copied from the CIM.[62]

I came along at the tail end of the China Inland Mission, a child in the reluctant exodus of 1950. Looking back, I was a junior member of a vast international family, a tribe that traveled the world, sent its children to the "best school east of Suez," and lived in a world without money. There was a supernatural ease with which we boarded a plane in Hong Kong without a ticket, landed in London, lived in the mission home for three months, and then set sail for Toronto. The best thing was that we never needed money; the worst was that we never had any.

---

62. Gerald Dykema, CIM Toronto Financial Officer, Mississauga, interview by author, 6 July 1999. The quotation marks are his, indicating a technical statement.

CHAPTER 8

Unpaid Debts: Metaphors and Millennialism
in Southern Sectarian Movements

TED OWNBY

But Zacchaeus stood up and said to the Lord, "Look, Lord! Here and now I give half of my possessions to the poor, and if I have cheated anyone out of anything, I will pay back four times the amount." Jesus said to him, "Today salvation has come to this house, because this man, too, is a son of Abraham."

LUKE 19:8-9 (NIV)

The sectarian Protestant movements that formed in the American South in the early twentieth century would seem to have had great potential for experimental and perhaps even radical understandings of the economy. Drawing their strength from people who were self-consciously plain and in many cases relatively poor, coming from the same part of the country where the populist movement began, and making dramatic theological and congregational innovations within the goal of restoring the principles of the early Christian church, new church groups in the South might seem to have been poised to join their religious experimentation to critiques of the economic system. But did they?[1]

1. The author acknowledges the help of Daniel Glenn Woods, who kindly shared his sources and knowledge of early southern Pentecostalism, and also thanks Beth Schweiger, Margaret Bendroth, and Larry Eskridge for their help with this paper.

235

This essay compares the economic perspectives Pentecostal groups[2] and the Churches of Christ developed in the American South in the early twentieth century. Both groups were new, the Pentecostals drawing new members from a number of established evangelical groups and building on some new holiness congregations that began in the late 1800s, the Churches of Christ rejecting the Disciples of Christ to the point that they appeared in the religious census as a new group in 1906. Both groups made some dramatic new departures. The Churches of Christ toyed with rejection of government, both ecclesiastical and civil, and Pentecostals brought to American Protestantism an intensified hunger for experience that went beyond individual conversion. Although the old argument that Pentecostals were "the disinherited" is no longer commonplace, and the most recent scholar of the Church of Christ questions the notion that they arose as the redneck cousins of the big-city Disciples of Christ, it remains true enough that both defied conventional opinions, styles, and priorities they associated with establishment churches and the wealth that supported them.[3] Did these very different sectarian groups

2. This essay studies two of the larger, almost exclusively white Pentecostal groups in the South, the Church of God, with its headquarters in Cleveland, Tennessee, and the Pentecostal Holiness Church, with its headquarters in Franklin Springs, Georgia.

3. The clearest early version of this argument was the *Vision of the Disinherited: The Making of American Pentecostalism*, by Robert Mapes Anderson (New York: Oxford University Press, 1979). Mickey Crews tends to follow the class argument, and its church-sect model, in his book *The Church of God: A Social History* (Knoxville: University of Tennessee Press, 1990). Among the scholars to question that interpretation are Edward Ayers, *The Promise of the New South: Life after Reconstruction* (New York: Oxford University Press, 1992); Daniel Glenn Woods, "Living in the Presence of God: Enthusiasm, Authority, and Negotiation in the Practice of Pentecostal Holiness" (Ph.D. diss., University of Mississippi, 1997); Grant Wacker, "The Holy Spirit and the Spirit of the Age in American Protestantism, 1880-1910," *Journal of American History* 72 (1985): 45-62; Grant Wacker, "Playing for Keeps: The Primitivist Impulse in Early Pentecostalism," in *The American Quest for the Primitive Church*, ed. Richard T. Hughes (Urbana: University of Illinois Press, 1988), pp. 196-219. By arguing that Pentecostalism lay in a distinctive Appalachian tradition of revivalism and local church independence, Deborah Vansau McCauley also diverges from Anderson's interpretation in *Appalachian Mountain Religion: A History* (Urbana: University of Illinois Press, 1995). The argument that the Churches of Christ split lies in the tradition of lower-class groups splitting from wealthier, more respectable groups is clearest in David Edwin Harrell, Jr., *The Social Sources of Division in the Disciples of Christ, 1865-1900: A Social History of the Disciples of Christ*, vol. 2 (Atlanta: Publishing Systems, 1973); Harrell, "Christian Primitivism and Modernization in the Stone Camp-

use their anti-authoritarian experimentation as a basis for rethinking economic questions?

The most persistent scholarly argument about southern evangelicals' economic perspective is that they didn't have one. Samuel S. Hill first asked why the religion of most white southerners did not inspire them to work for social justice more often. According to Hill, essential elements of their religion should have led white evangelicals in the South to fight against slavery, racism, poverty, and inequality, but they did not, primarily for theological reasons. For southern evangelicals, he argued, the conversion experience was such a central reality that nothing else really mattered. Hill reasoned that evangelicals in the South saw the status of the individual as a "basically ontological" proposition — one was either converted or not converted. Therefore, questions of how people related to each other were not significant. Hill argued that southern evangelicalism, far from being conservative in its essence, had egalitarian and even revolutionary potential. Instead, much of its conservatism was almost incidental. Any idea that challenged the status quo in economics or race or class relations as part of a religious mission failed the ultimate test of what really mattered. Thus, by not challenging power relations, evangelicalism in the South proved to have conservative consequences.[4]

It should be no surprise that few members of Pentecostal churches and Churches of Christ developed a fully articulated economic theory. For both groups, concerns about specific religious objectives limited the attention they showed to economic issues. Both condemned materialism. But evangelicals tend to criticize materialism the way that people complain

---

bell Movement," in Richard T. Hughes, ed., *The Primitive Church in the Modern World* (Urbana: University of Illinois Press, 1995); Harrell, "The Southern Origins of the Churches of Christ," *Journal of Southern History* 7 (Aug. 1964): 261-77; Harrell, "The Evolution of Plain-Folk Religion in the South, 1835-1920," in *Varieties of Southern Religious Experience,* ed. Samuel S. Hill, Jr. (Baton Rouge: Louisiana State University Press, 1988). Rejecting the class argument, or at least its centrality in the Church of Christ/Disciples of Christ schism, is Richard T. Hughes, *Reviving the Ancient Faith: The Story of Churches of Christ in America* (Grand Rapids: Eerdmans, 1996).

4. The clearest examples of Samuel Hill's argument appear in Hill, *Southern Churches in Crisis* (New York: Holt, Rinehart, and Winston, 1967); Hill, with Edgar T. Thompson, Anne Firor Scott, Charles Hudson, and Edwin Gaustad, *Religion in the Solid South* (Nashville: Abingdon Press, 1972); "Introduction," in *Religion in the Southern States,* ed. Hill (Macon: Mercer University Press, 1983); Hill, *The South and the North in American Religion* (Athens, GA: University of Georgia Press, 1980).

about the weather — without plans to do anything about it. Instead of asking whether we should consider early Pentecostals and Churches of Christ to have been liberals, radicals, or conservatives, we should analyze where and how economic thinking fit into their religious ideas and innovations. On what subjects did they raise economic issues? And why did they raise those issues?

Southern Pentecostals talked a great deal about debt. Joseph Hillery King, an important figure in the early Pentecostal Holiness Church, used debt as a dramatic metaphor that illustrated humanity's condition in salvation history. "The condition of humanity is one of complete insolvency." For creation and for the life of Jesus, "Payment is demanded, satisfaction must be given, and the day arrives for it to be done. We are insolvent, utterly bankrupt, and have nothing to pay."[5] In this metaphor, one hears both the sense of human hopelessness outside the grace of God and the farmer's traditional lament about the dangers of debt. A powerful metaphor, the fear of debt was also a living reality in Pentecostals' understanding of their place in the world. Its significance was apparent in a list of questions the Church of God–Cleveland, Tennessee asked those who wanted to become preachers. Two of the ten were "Have you any unpaid debts?" and "If so, do you see your way out?"[6]

The goal of freedom from debt had deep roots in the history of rural southerners. Debt seemed, in different metaphors, to enslave them, to rape them, to unman them, to humble them. It threatened to deprive them of their cherished independence, forcing them to work for someone else, whether the creditor himself or a cash-paying employer.[7] Pentecostals stressed the biblical basis for avoiding debt. Church of God leader A. J. Tomlinson once wrote in his diary that he was praying about his debts.

5. Joseph Hillery King, *Christ — God's Love Gift: Selected Writings of Joseph Hillery King*, vol. 1, ed. B. E. Underwood (Franklin Springs, GA: Advocate Press, 1969), pp. 80-81.

6. The Church of God General Assembly, "Teachings," *The Evening Light and Church of God Evangel*, 15 Aug. 1910, p. 3.

7. Among the best works to analyze white southerners' beliefs about debt are Steven Hahn, *The Roots of Southern Populism: Yeoman Farmers and the Transformation of the Georgia Upcountry, 1850-1890* (New York: Oxford University Press, 1983); Lacy Ford, *The Origins of Southern Radicalism: The South Carolina Upcountry, 1800-1860* (New York: Oxford University Press, 1988); T. H. Breen, *Tobacco Culture: The Mentality of the Planters on the Eve of Revolution* (Princeton: Princeton University Press, 1985); Bradley G. Bond, *Political Culture in the Nineteenth-Century South* (Baton Rouge: Louisiana State University Press, 1995).

"Father will have to come to our rescue, or I will fail to keep the demand, 'Owe no man anything.' God, help us right now, right now, for Jesus' sake."[8] This biblical foundation reinforced the traditions of southern farm life, making the concept of debt-free independence an essential part of the mindset of rural or once-rural southerners who made up the great majority of the early Pentecostal movement.

Sanctification was a theological concept closely connected to debt-free independence. An elaboration on the Wesleyan doctrine of perfectionism, sanctification constituted a crucial second step beyond conversion.[9] For most of the people hoping to take it, sanctification was a new step that was vital but somewhat mysterious. Was sanctification a deep love of God that led to a sensitive and lively conscience that produced a life of sinless behavior? Was it an intense feeling of the presence of God that negated temptations to sin? Do you work at it? How do you get it? How do you know you have it?

In the Pentecostals' trinity of conversion, sanctification, and Holy Ghost baptism, the idea of sanctification played a central role in their thinking about individual economic behavior. One economic interpretation of the meaning of sanctification was especially clear in their desire to make restitution for past acts of economic dishonesty. The actual theology behind restitution was not always clear, but its importance was undeniable. On a list of twenty-five basic teachings published by the Church of God in 1910, restitution made the list just above the second coming of Jesus.[10]

The restitution narrative was a favorite confessional story for Pentecostals who testified about the reality of God's presence in their lives. A man named M. A. Screws, for example, wrote from Macon, Georgia, to the *Pentecostal Holiness Advocate* in 1928 to confess an old sin and to celebrate the power of "a living God that is able to take the burdens away." Screws was praying when "a turning plow came up before me that I bought 18 years ago." He had bought the plow on credit for about six dollars and never paid his debt. After seeing a vision of the plow in prayer, he wrote the company to ask what he owed. The company charged him ten dollars for the price of the plow, plus interest, and promised to contribute

8. A. J. Tomlinson, *Diary of A. J. Tomlinson* (New York: The Church of God, 1949), p. 57.

9. See Vinson Synan, *The Holiness-Pentecostal Movement in the United States* (Grand Rapids: Eerdmans, 1971).

10. The Church of God General Assembly, "Teachings," p. 3.

the money to charity. Most intriguing was the fact that for his testimony in the *Advocate,* Screws included letters from the Gantt Manufacturing Company to verify that he had made restitution.[11]

Joe Campbell, a Pentecostal Holiness preacher, recalled the desire to correct past sins as an immediate consequence of his conversion experience. "When I became a born-again Christian, I was immediately prompted by God's Spirit to make amends where such could be done by going back to persons whom I may have wronged or offended or in any way defrauded. . . . Real salvation will make a fellow pay an old grocery bill, and return goods that may have been stolen." Campbell listed the ways he made restitution. He remembered putting slugs into telephones to get free calls, went to the telephone company, and wrote them a check. He told long stories about jumping freight cars, and he wrote a check to the railroad company. As a teenager, he had taken payments for newspaper subscriptions he did not actually solicit, so he went to the newspaper office, gave his testimony, and left a check. He even recalled hunting down the descendent of a shopkeeper who had given him an extra dollar in change to make restitution and to give his testimony.[12]

Campbell stressed, "We don't do these things to *get* saved,"[13] but he did not take the next step and discuss sanctification. To him, making restitution was a consequence of salvation, of trying to be sinless, and a significant part of witnessing to the unsaved.

Similar stories abound of paying for cakes of soap individuals had stolen eight years earlier, or restoring fifty cents an individual had long ago received as extra change.[14] Claudius Roberts, the mother of Oral Roberts, told the story of her husband Ellis, who wanted to follow her in having a conversion experience. Using the same language as M. A. Screws, she said, "Looming up before him was the memory of a wrong he had done," for which he believed he had to first make restitution before he could be converted. Twelve years earlier, Ellis Roberts had killed a hog running free on his land and hidden the deed from the hog's owner. Almost immediately

11. M. A. Screws, Letter to the Editor, *Pentecostal Holiness Advocate,* 19 July 1928, p. 13.

12. Joe E. Campbell, *'Pappy' Just Passing Through* (Raleigh, NC: World Outlook Publications, 1975), pp. 30-37, quote p. 30.

13. Campbell, *'Pappy,'* p. 38.

14. Mattie E. Perry, *Christ and Answered Prayer* (Nashville: Benson Printing Company, 1939), p. 38.

after Ellis Roberts asked if he could make restitution, he not only had his conversion experience, he began his career as a preacher.[15]

Restitution narratives reveal that sanctification, no matter how widespread a goal among Pentecostals, was a particularly unclear concept. As part of a growing new movement, Pentecostals were giving it meaning. The connections among the narratives seem especially revealing. Killing a neighbor's hog violated traditional practices of the open range — practices no longer common in the law but still part of people's understandings of how society should work. Monumentalizing the paying of small debts recalled the traditional goal of independent farm life. Fearing even tiny acts of economic dishonesty recalled face-to-face communities in which personal status and the ability to make future economic deals depended on an individual's reputation for honesty.

Insecurities about the meaning of sanctification help explain the well-known Pentecostal penchant for strict codes of personal morality. Grant Wacker describes as "ethical primitivism" Pentecostals' early efforts to strip themselves of everything not explicitly encouraged in the primitive Christian church.[16] The long list of activities Pentecostals either prohibited or discussed prohibiting has a wide range of historical and cultural associations: tobacco, alcohol, coffee, chewing gum, soft drinks, motion pictures, sport coats, neckties, open-toed shoes, good china, gold, silver, and diamond rings, bracelets, earrings, lockets, short hair among women, changes in women's fashion, and many more.

Some Pentecostal groups forbade some of these items and practices and not others; some were merely topics for debate. But in the debates, Pentecostals were trying to figure out what it meant to live a sanctified life. Worries about things like china, jewelry, and perhaps neckties were part of long-standing evangelical rejection of the badges of elitism. Concerns about stimulants showed a special worry about anything that threatened to override an individuals' will — one could not be completely open to the will of God if one were controlled by physical addictions. The prohibition against tobacco seems especially striking (and not a case of old-fashioned people rejecting new-fangled sinfulness). Many nineteenth-century Americans simply considered tobacco a necessity. Church records stated specifically that addic-

15. E. M. and Claudius Roberts, *Our Ministry and Our Son Oral* (Tulsa, OK: Oral Roberts, 1960), pp. 20-25, quote p. 20.

16. Wacker, "Playing for Keeps," pp. 207-9; Crews, *Church of God*, pp. 38-68.

tion itself was central to the criticism of tobacco users. One church excluded a member who "acknowledged she used snuff and could not quit its use."[17] This rejection of anything that promised to control the will also helps to explain the prohibition against joining labor unions or lodges.

The prohibitions against motion pictures and changing fashions embodied the evangelical fear of both the sensualism of mass culture and the constant change of consumer culture. The modern consumer expects and even demands that things change. At its logical extreme, the consumer state of mind says today should always be better than yesterday and that tomorrow should be even better, with more and different goods and opportunities for shopping.[18] For southern Pentecostals, rejecting the consumer ideal was not simply "ethical primitivism"; it also embodied a rejection of a vision of constant change and the addictive or nearly addictive allure of a culture centered around shopping. Church of God preacher Sam C. Perry, for example, wrote a treatise on self-denial that concluded with a rejection of selfish desire. "A great victory has been gained indeed when he so gives up that he has no preference in any thing, but just desires the Lord's truth."[19]

Not insignificantly, avoiding all of these things — traditional luxury goods, stimulants, and modern consumer goods — helped keep people out of debt. And, always, debt threatened a single-minded love of God and pursuit of sanctification. Again, it is important to stress that Pentecostals did not have a moral system worked out for all church members to follow. But in their worries about what was acceptable and unacceptable, one can see a once-rural people trying to understand the meaning of sanctification.

Among Pentecostal leaders, two offered specific, well-developed critiques of the twentieth-century economy. G. F. Taylor, a leader in the Pentecostal Holiness Church and editor of the church's newspaper *The Advocate,* worked out his economic ideas in two books, *The Second Coming of Jesus* (1916) and *The Rainbow* (1924), and in an inspired series of 1932 edito-

17. North Cleveland (TN) Church of God Membership and Conference Minutes, October 6, 1913, Box 97, Hal Bernard Dixon Jr. Pentecostal Research Center, William G. Squires Library, Lee College, Cleveland, TN. The North Cleveland Church disciplined over twenty-five members for tobacco use in the 1910s.

18. See Colin Campbell, *The Romantic Ethic and the Spirit of Modern Consumerism* (Oxford: Basil Blackwell, 1987).

19. Sam C. Perry, "Self-Denial, a Chief Characteristic in the Lives of All Three Followers of Jesus," *Church of God Evangel,* 22 Jan. 1916, p. 2.

rials. Flavius J. Lee preached in the home congregation of the Church of God in Cleveland, Tennessee and became the second general overseer of that group. He developed his understanding of the millennium in *Lectures on Revelation* and a volume called *Book of Prophecy: Questions and Answers on the Entire Book of Revelation* (1923). Both emphasized the fifth chapter of James, especially the verse, "Ye have laid up your treasure in the last days," and spelled out both what was wrong with the current economy and how it signified the coming end of the world. G. F. Taylor was an especially appealing character, a premillennialist scholar who tried to prove through history, economics, and biblical interpretation that the end was coming soon. Far too much end-of-time thinking, Taylor said, was wildly general, but careful research and clear thinking showed that the early twentieth century was the time, and economic change provided the proof.

According to Taylor and Lee, the organizations laying up their treasures were large international corporations. Private companies and individual ownership had been the rule for business until late in the 1800s, but as Taylor wrote, "Now men are heaping their moneys together forming trusts, combines, etc." Lee agreed, condemning "those who have hoarded their money until it has rusted or cankered."[20] Taylor continued with a narrow interpretation of the same chapter of the book of James: "'Behold the hire of the laborers who have reaped down your fields, which is of you kept back by fraud, crieth.' Today in many places the hire of the laborers is kept back for two weeks." Again, Taylor connected millennial thinking to an economic critique. Since organized economic interests profited from holding back the wages of workers, they were not simply exploiting the masses, they were bringing on the end. Employers in America were hoarding "millions of dollars every week, and this great amount falls into the coffers of the rich. This was never done before these days." Since this was a new realization of James's depiction of the end, Taylor wrote, "we may conclude that we are in the last days."[21]

G. F. Taylor put considerable energy into the millennial implications of economic centralization. In one long passage, he developed an elaborate conspiracy theory. A single power, he wrote,

20. F. J. Lee, *Lectures on Revelation* (Cleveland, TN: Church of God Publishing House, n.d.), p. 23.

21. G. F. Taylor, *The Second Coming of Jesus* (Franklin Springs, GA: The Publishing House, Pentecostal Holiness Church, 1950, [1916]), pp. 23-24.

monopolizes nearly all legislation, governs the conferences of kings, dictates international treaties, cuts ship canals, builds railways, employs thousands of engineers, subsidizes the press, tells us of the markets of the world yesterday that we may know what to do today, has her organizations in every town and city, interlinked with each other, and coming every day into closer and closer combination, so that no great government on earth can any longer move or act against her will, or without her concurrence or consent. It is a power that is entwining itself like a serpent about religious organizations. . . .

He asked dramatically, "What is this power? . . . It is COMMERCE." This centralization of economic organizations paralleled the political centralization he saw in peace conferences and international financial developments to the point that a small group of people had become "the money powers." "Let things go on as they are now going, and in a short time a few moneyed men will own the whole world."[22] Lee stressed that the conspiracy involved a relatively small group of men. "While this is not just one man or two or even a dozen, but as all can see it is the combines, trusts, etc., that are formed to hold down the poor of this earth, until at the end of time of culmination none shall be allowed to buy and sell that do not line up with them."[23] Taylor predicted that soon, those men would form one "grand commercial centre" where the money powers would gather to dominate the world. "To this power every government under the sun will have to submit."[24]

All evangelicals denounce worldliness, but Lee and Taylor did so in especially purposeful ways. In tortured interpretations of Zechariah 5, they read the prophetic vision about a woman appearing in the midst of an ephah (an Old Testament measure) as a sign of "the church sitting down in the lap of commerce, being embraced by the world, and ruled by its powers. . . ." From the prophecy, Taylor jumped to the present to describe "a great world system now at work that is calculated to capture everything that does not belong to the true church."[25]

22. Taylor, *Second Coming*, pp. 104-5.
23. Lee, *Lectures on Revelation*, pp. 23-24.
24. Taylor, *Second Coming*, pp. 104-5.
25. G. F. Taylor, *The Rainbow* (Franklin Springs, GA: Advocate, 1924), p. 49. On the ephah, see also F. J. Lee, ed., *Book of Prophecy: Questions and Answers on the Entire Book of Revelation* (Cleveland, TN: Church of God Publishing House, 1923), p. 141.

Late in the summer of 1932, during the national election campaign that sought to address the best way to deal with the Depression, Taylor filled out his ideas with the information he believed proved the end was near. In the United States, the Federal Reserve System had centralized the process by which creditors collected money and, most importantly, kept it in their hands. By providing security for the banking system, the federal government allowed creditors to lend the same money to numerous debtors. Taylor considered this an especially vivid example of James's prophecy of the wealthy profiting by keeping money back. In Taylor's language, "In this way the treasures of the rich are increased by multitude ratio." He continued by citing statistics that in 1930, American farmers paid almost exactly as much money in interest as they made from their crops. He interpreted that as another example of how bad things had become — not merely a sign of poverty but of the oppression of working people by wealth concentrated in the hands of creditors.[26]

There was good credit and bad credit. Bad credit was inescapable and added to the wealth of the money powers. Taylor blamed the Depression on the "few families" who were hoarding gold for themselves and using credit to force everyone else to pay them never-ending interest. Taylor admired the barter system he found in several examples in the Bible, but he saw no possibility to return to it. "The money is locked up, and those who have it locked up will not turn it loose to the extent of bringing general benefit, and so there we are. That is why there is now so much suffering for the necessities of life amid a world of plenty."[27]

Good credit lay in Old Testament descriptions of the promised land. Every fifty years in Israel, land that had been rented reverted to the families of its original owners. Debt and credit, therefore, were helpful as long as they stayed within a community setting that recognized customary rights of families. Israelites were not supposed to borrow from outsiders, and no families ultimately lost their land. As Taylor concluded, "Such was, in part at least, God's financial plan."[28] It is hard not to notice that his picture of credit relations in Canaan had some similarities to the portrait historians have drawn of tight-knit communities in the nine-

26. G. F. Taylor, "Panics and Signs," *Pentecostal Holiness Advocate*, 1 Sept. 1932, p. 8.
27. G. F. Taylor, "Panics," *Pentecostal Holiness Advocate*, 4 Aug. 1932, p. 8.
28. G. F. Taylor, "The Canaanian Plan," *Pentecostal Holiness Advocate*, 11 Aug. 1932, p. 8.

teenth-century South in which small loans from family and friends helped households keep their independence within a group setting.[29] Almost certainly, Taylor and Lee remembered good credit as part of face-to-face relationships they could imagine in both their own pasts and in the Old Testament, but they believed credit had become part of an impersonal international system.

The most revealing aspect of Taylor's analysis of the Depression was his conclusion. With considerable concern about the federal reserve system, world finance, credit relations, and coinage ratios, he did not sound like the stereotypical evangelical Samuel Hill described as being so interested in conversion that nothing else really mattered. Much of Taylor and Lee's language lay in the populist tradition that drew on Biblical images to condemn moneylenders, feared the possibility of becoming hewers of wood and drawers of water, and drew economic issues as stark moral dichotomies of right and wrong.[30] But the Pentecostal leaders had no interests in the populists' solutions, or in any man-made remedies. Taylor brought his series of articles on the Depression to a conclusion full of economic and political befuddlement but confident in the assurance of the coming millennium. He wrote briefly in populist language about currency policies, ending with the statement, "Many think the remedy for the present situation is the free coinage of silver." He denounced concentrated wealth in language so similar to labor radicals that he felt he should point out he was not a communist. The closest thing he offered to an economic solution to the Depression was advice "for the rich to turn the land back to the poor, and make it possible for them to go back to the farm."[31]

Taylor's final paragraph was the most important. We were not going back to the farm, and we were not returning to the credit relations prescribed for the Israelites. No voting or political changes or economic reforms mattered, and there was little point in spending time and energy on them. No economic system could bring "permanent relief. The entire world system, including the monetary system, is rapidly preparing for the anti-Christ."[32] The entire system of worldwide commerce, dominated by a

29. See Hahn, *Roots of Southern Populism*.

30. On the Populists and religious imagery, see Bruce Palmer, *"Man Over Money": The Southern Populist Critique of American Capitalism* (Chapel Hill, NC: University of North Carolina Press, 1980).

31. Taylor, "Panics and Signs," p. 9.

32. Taylor, "Panics and Signs," p. 9.

few financiers, was "the seventh head of the anti-Christ."[33] One powerful and deceptive individual would arise and claim to have solutions for all human problems. "He will form a world-wide federation" dedicated to economic and political reform. When the lies and ultimate strategies of this deceiver became apparent, Jesus would return. There was nothing people could do to fight the anti-Christ. "All efforts to put it down are fruitless."[34]

He did not call for Christians to reform the economic system. In a statement solidly in the apolitical tradition Samuel Hill described, Taylor concluded, "The only thing we can do is to seek to save individuals from its power."[35] The significant addition for Pentecostals was that conversion was not all that mattered. Sanctification, the baptism of the Holy Ghost, and the belief in the coming end of the world all had meanings far outside issues of politics and economic policy.

Compared to the Pentecostal groups, the Churches of Christ had fewer unique perspectives on economic issues. The Churches of Christ were a largely southern denomination that split from the Disciples of Christ around the turn of the century in one of the countless movements by churches whose members believed the larger group had become too comfortable and staid to practice the true doctrine of the first Christians. Compared to the Disciples, Churches of Christ tended to consist of relatively poor people, especially after they had formed their own churches and sometimes had to start from scratch with buildings and finances.[36] However, by contrast with the Pentecostals, they do not seem especially poor or rural or isolated.

Churches of Christ had one defining theological feature. Within the context of American evangelicalism, the Churches of Christ stand out for their rationalist plan for achieving salvation. As historian Paul Conkin writes in *American Originals,* "The plan often seems formulaic and can become very legalistic. In a virtual litany Churches of Christ still ask people to hear, believe, repent, confess, and accept baptism for the remission of sins. The baptism is most distinctive, but unique is the reasonable, practical, staged steps that precede it."[37] Individuals learned how to achieve con-

33. Taylor, *Second Coming,* p. 105.
34. Taylor, *The Rainbow,* p. 102.
35. Taylor, *The Rainbow,* p. 102.
36. See Harrell, *Social Sources of Division in the Disciples of Christ,* vol. 2.
37. Paul K. Conkin, *American Originals: Homemade Varieties of Christianity* (Chapel Hill, NC: University of North Carolina Press, 1997), pp. 40-41.

version through a step-by-step process they learned through careful reading of the Bible. As David Lipscomb, for years the leading figure in the southern wing of the Disciples of Christ and then the Churches of Christ, said, "The Bible is science, is knowledge, classified by God."[38] One learned how to become a Christian and to live the Christian life. As a Texas preacher recalled with particular clarity, "I can remember very well how I was converted to Christ. It was not by some irresistible operation of the Spirit, but it was by the Spirit through the word that God had selected, the medium that God had selected, the medium that took years to be brought about."[39]

As individuals, Church of Christ members studied the Bible. As a group, their leaders debated the meanings of the Bible. What seems most intriguing about their economic thinking is that in spelling out those meanings, some Church of Christ preachers used economic metaphors. To illustrate how people could understand the intricacies of the Christian plan of salvation and the biblical program for Christian life, they often turned to the intricacies of economic life. R. H. Boll, the editor of the leading Church of Christ publication in the early twentieth century, used thoroughly capitalist language in describing God's plan to expand the body of Christians. "God wants results: interest, increase, and profit. The talents he grants to his servants must be laid out to usury. They must trade with their pounds and make other pounds."[40] Here borrowing, investing, and profit — things Pentecostals respectively loathed, feared, and worried about — served simply as metaphors for Christian usefulness and church growth. A. B. Lipscomb likewise described a well-funded church as "a joint stock company of which Jesus Christ is the Head."[41]

Another Church of Christ leader, N. B. Hardeman, used a telling metaphor during a series of sermons in Nashville's Ryman Auditorium in 1922. In the sermon "Theory and Practice," he urged strict attention to the theory behind whatever one was pursuing. "It is not only true of our religion and our Christianity, but it is true of every occupation and every endeavor of life. If a man be a farmer, first of all, he needs to learn the theory

38. Hughes, *Reviving the Ancient Faith*, p. 120.

39. E. M. Borden, *Jacob's Ladder*, ed. G. H. P. Showalter (Austin, TX: Firm Foundation Publishing House, 1914), p. 211.

40. R. H. Boll, "God's Business Ways," *Gospel Advocate*, 20 Oct. 1910, p. 1153.

41. A. B. Lipscomb, ed., *Christian Treasures: An Exposition of Vital Themes by Earnest and Forceful Writers*, vol. 2 (Nashville: McQuiddy Printing, 1916), p. 5.

of agriculture. He needs to understand the elements that go into the make-up of the fertility of the soil."[42] Here was a clear distinction between Pentecostal and Church of Christ figures of speech. When Pentecostal leaders talked about farming, they held up personal ideals with roots in household independence; when Church of Christ ministers discussed farming, they taught lessons illustrated by scientific agriculture.

A third Church of Christ figure, Deep South preacher Marshall Keeble, went into detail about financial practices to show how the necessity of careful bookkeeping paralleled the necessity for careful Bible-reading. To prove a point he summarized with his sermon title, "The Power of the Written Word," stressing the need for contracts, deeds, and receipts. One needed a written contract to buy a house and then a deed to guarantee it. When one paid a debt, one should always get a receipt. "Above everything, keep your receipts. If you are going to heaven and appear before Jesus Christ at the final consummation of all things and at the judgment seat of Christ where all nations must appear and you haven't got a receipt written by Jesus Christ, signed with His blood, you will have to check off with your debt unpaid."[43] For Keeble, debt was not a metaphor for humanity's ultimate weakness and reliance on God. It was an understandable condition that one paid with great care and study. Ultimately, Keeble used these metaphors simply to show that individuals needed to learn the rules and live by them.

Such metaphors may be the most revealing statements Church of Christ figures made about economic matters. The fact that one must look to metaphors to find such statements suggests that they simply did not write very much about economic issues. These metaphors in no way challenged the practice of credit, investment, and scientific agriculture. Keeble, Hardeman, and Boll used these metaphors to build on the assumptions and understandings common among their listeners to prove other points — points they considered far more important.

Compared to Pentecostal publications, the Church of Christ's literature was relatively free of discussions about the economic side of personal morality. As David Edwin Harrell, Jr., has shown, the southern wing of the

42. N. B. Hardeman, *Hardeman's Tabernacle Sermons*, vol. 1 (Nashville: McQuiddy Printing, 1922), p. 276.
43. Marshall Keeble, *Biography and Sermons*, ed. B. C. Goodpasture (Nashville: Gospel Advocate, 1959, [1931]), p. 26.

Disciples of Christ, especially their leader David Lipscomb, showed considerable sympathies for populists and union leaders and sometimes criticized corporations for acting in ways individual Christians should never act.[44] For reasons that are not clear, however, the publications of the Churches of Christ were less strident on economic and political questions. In fact, publications such as the *Gospel Advocate,* for which Lipscomb served as either editor or contributor for most of his life, almost always stayed silent on public issues. A few Church of Christ figures believed in perfectionism, but not many; the intense debates about clothing, jewelry, gum, and stimulants that were so important to Pentecostals were simply not present. And there was a premillennialist wing among Church of Christ preachers, but their number and influence were declining in the early twentieth century and they did not interpret signs to try to understand the coming end of the world.[45] In fact, one finds little discussion about the directions of the national or world economy.

Compared to the Pentecostals, some Church of Christ figures made surprisingly positive statements about the future of the world. Richard Hughes has detailed disputes among Church of Christ leaders about the desirability of different definitions of progress. Those who believed they were the reconstituted version of the original Christian church thought they could move forward with optimism about expanding their vision of Christianity. Others were not so sure.[46] As a point of comparison, the Pentecostals had no debates about progress. G. F. Taylor spoke for many in making the point that premillennialists like himself "appreciate the telegraph, the telephone, the automobile, the airship, and all other modern inventions for good, but they do not say these things are bringing the world to Christ, nor helping in any way to bring the Millennium. To them the world seems to be drifting away from God, and getting worse all the time."[47] In contrast, David Lipscomb could sound positively upbeat in describing material and economic progress. In his book *Salvation From Sin,* he

44. Harrell, *Social Sources,* vol. 2, pp. 33-47, 133-34.

45. On the limited premillennialist movement in the Churches of Christ, see Hughes, *Reviving the Ancient Faith;* Robert E. Hooper, *A Distinct People: A History of the Churches of Christ in the Twentieth Century* (West Monroe, LA: Howard Publishing Co., 1993).

46. Hughes, *Reviving the Ancient Faith.*

47. Taylor, *The Rainbow,* pp. 48-49.

compared parts of the world without the Bible to what he called "the state of civilization" where people knew and tried the follow the Bible.

> When we make this comparison, we find that the Bible has made better hogs, sheep, cattle, horses, clothes, houses, grains, fruits, vegetables, and all bodily comforts and conveniences for man; it has lifted man up and quickened his energies and activities and trained his mind, and, in doing this, has improved all the animals and conditions dependent upon him; it has built every steam engine, steamboat, railroad, and every improved and high order of mechanical and manufacturing work in the world.[48]

For Lipscomb, all of these things — railroads, steam engines, bodily comforts and conveniences — were signs of God's approval of people who followed the plan for Christianity.

Church of Christ preachers were also far more likely than Pentecostals to make conciliatory remarks about wealthy people. Their discussions and their worries about economic issues sound familiar in the southern evangelical context. Sometimes they feared the consequences of wealth, and sometimes they reassured people that most features of wealth were not so bad as long as they kept more important Christian principles in mind. The most striking comparison with the Pentecostals is the frequency with which they discussed wealth; in the early twentieth century, there were probably not enough wealthy southern Pentecostals to need reassurance. Church of Christ preachers knew someone was listening to a sermon entitled "Money as a Blessing," in which David Lipscomb assured people that wealth could bring either "curses or blessings" depending on how they used it.[49]

Occasionally, Church of Christ preachers spelled out ways in which Christian messages with potentially radical meanings were in fact not radical at all. A Kentucky preacher explained why contemporary Christians did not continue the economic practices of some of the first Christians who sold what they owned and lived communally. He assured readers that many of those early Christians traveled long distances to join the church of Jesus' day and that they could only have survived financially by selling their belongings. It was a matter of expediency and not Christian principle, and

48. David Lipscomb, *Salvation from Sin*, ed. J. W. Shepherd (Nashville: Gospel Advocate, 1950), p. 12.
49. David Lipscomb, "Money as a Blessing," *Gospel Advocate*, 11 Nov. 1909, p. 1420.

the preacher did not recommend it.[50] N. B. Hardeman warned against stinginess and covetousness but immediately made clear, "Now, from that I would not have you draw the conclusion that I am against a man's making money. Exactly the reverse. I wish to-day, if it were not perhaps vain, that every child of God on earth had an abundance of this world's goods."[51]

If one asks Samuel Hill's old question — Did the religion of white evangelicals in the American South lead them to critique and try to reform the existing economic order? — the student of these two sectarian movements should return to Samuel Hill's old answer: No. Some Pentecostals like G. F. Taylor built elaborate critiques of the American economy, but they said reform was ultimately insignificant compared to sanctification, Holy Ghost baptism, and the second coming of Jesus. Many figures in the Churches of Christ condemned greed and selfishness, but they were certainly not economic reformers. As Hill argued, the salvation of the individual was far more important than any economic issues.

If, however, one asks a different question, one can see how economic issues related to the specific theological perspectives of the two groups. Early Pentecostals, most of them from the rural South, interpreted the relatively new doctrine of sanctification through the lens of old ideals of debt-free independence. Pentecostals' vision of the apocalyptic meanings of commercial centralization make more sense in light of the belief that economic changes were making the true Christian life harder and harder to live. By comparison, the Churches of Christ fit Hill's paradigm far more easily. Their distinguishing feature, the rational understanding of the biblical plan for salvation, led them to use metaphors — sometimes extremely conservative metaphors — about learning the rules and living by them.

For both groups, economics was not a matter of ultimate importance. For members of the Churches of Christ, issues of wealth and poverty, justice and injustice, paled before the rationalist plan for salvation. Church of Christ preachers warned people not to let wealth and its pursuit get in the way of higher callings, reminded church members to tithe, and moved on to subjects they found more important. Pentecostals made impassioned critiques about worldwide commerce, but they had no plan or

---

50. I. A. Douthitt, *Apostolic Sermons*, vol. 1 (Sedalia, KY: I. A. Douthitt, 1937), pp. 55-56.

51. N. B. Hardeman, *Hardeman's Tabernacle Sermons*, vol. 2 (Nashville: McQuiddy Printing, 1923), p. 124.

desire to put their critiques into action. Their practical, day-to-day response was to reject anything, whether wealth, labor unions, or tobacco, that might control their will and thus interfere with the possibility of conversion and sanctification.

Compared to the Pentecostal Holiness Church and the Church of God, the Churches of Christ in their early years seem much more comfortable with twentieth-century economic developments. Compared to the Pentecostals, their condemnations of worldliness had fewer implications for everyday life, nor were they rooted in old images of farm life, nor were they as far reaching in their ideas about the future. However, on issues of church finances — of getting money and spending it — the Churches of Christ seem far more rooted in the nineteenth century. In the raising of money, the Church of God was much more "worldly" in its drive for a centralized financial structure.

One of the most important developments of the early twentieth century was the organizational revolution, characterized by the bureaucratization and professionalization of most aspects of American life. This so-called revolution centralized lines of authority and finance to make things work as efficiently as possible, with trained experts in charge.[52] The Churches of Christ resisted the organizational revolution. Rather than forming organizations to collect money or to rationalize its spending, they operated on a decidedly congregational basis.

Churches of Christ held firm to the idea that no distant authority should tell them what to do. Institutions, they believed, always tended to operate in the interests of their own survival and growth. David Lipscomb based his rejection of government on the idea that powerful institutions were likely to develop their own sources of authority, instead of relying on the Bible, and to work for their own good, instead of concentrating on converting people to Christianity.[53]

The straightforward description of the financial workings in a Church of Christ in Lewisburg, Tennessee, makes clear the localistic, congregational nature of getting money and spending it. C. M. Pullias described how one Monday morning a month, the elders met along with all

52. On the organizational revolution, see Robert Wiebe, *The Search for Order, 1877-1920* (New York: Hill and Wang, 1967).

53. The clearest statement of his beliefs about congregational autonomy appear in David Lipscomb, *Civil Government: Its Origin, Mission, and Destiny: And the Christian's Relation to It* (Wesson, MS: M. Lynwood Smith, 1984, [1866]).

male church members who wanted to attend, and decided how to spend their money. "The collections and distributions are at the proper time announced to the whole church in its worshiping capacity. No suppers, bazaars, or anything of the kind, nor assessment plan — only the Lord's day contributions."[54] The records of a small church in Giles County, Tennessee show this local focus. The thirty members of the Lynnville Church of Christ took in $372.23 in 1902, and paid the total amount to the regular preacher, a revival meeting preacher, and a cleaning man, as well as to cover the cost of coal, oil, insurance on the building, and a subscription to the *Gospel Advocate*. No money left the church to support distant institutions of any kind, to contribute to missionary work, or to support anything that did not involve the thirty members, their families, and the work of the local congregation.[55]

The obvious question was how congregations could spread the gospel with such a decentralized church structure. Many Churches of Christ rejected missionary work and missionary societies, while others gave missionary work only token approval. What they rejected were organized, bureaucratized efforts to collect money and train and send out missionaries. For those Churches of Christ who supported such efforts at all, missionary work generally meant helping start new churches down the road, or among friends. One Tennessee preacher happily noted in the 1910s that growing numbers of rural churches were supporting what he called missionary work by giving money to a preacher "while he holds meetings in the schoolhouses around them."[56]

Members of one of the larger Church of Christ congregations, the Twelfth Avenue Church of Christ in Nashville, received frequent requests from small groups of fellow believers to help them fund a church building or a revival meeting in the 1910s and 1920s. Usually they sent money, occasionally they did not, but they always made their decisions on a church-by-church basis, without institutionalizing a way to collect or send out money. Church leaders often asked for reports about how well revivals were going to reassure them that their money was helping

54. C. M. Pullias, "How to Meet the Current Expenses," in A. B. Lipscomb, ed., *Christian Treasures*, vol. 2, p. 123.

55. Lynnville (TN) Church of Christ Record Book and Cancelled Checks, 1902, Special Collection, Beaman Library, David Lipscomb University, Nashville, TN.

56. F. B. Srygley, "Just Plain Country Folks," in A. B. Lipscomb, ed., *Christian Treasures*, vol. 2, p. 134.

to convert new Christians. The church had special nights in 1911 and 1912 to raise money for foreign missions, but they stopped the practice, apparently deciding its aid should be concentrated on more local concerns. When the Twelfth Avenue congregation discussed "our mission work" in 1916, it was referring to an effort to start a new church on Nashville's Twenty-Third Avenue — eleven blocks away.[57] Not until the period after World War II did a broader conception of missionary work become common among the Churches of Christ.[58]

The Church of God–Cleveland differed dramatically from the Churches of Christ in its centralization of church finances and its vigorous approach to missionary work. Early in the history of the Church of God, some leaders called for an organized system of raising and spending money. In this centralized, bureaucratic approach to finances, the Church of God took part in the organizational revolution far more aggressively than the Churches of Christ. In this sense, they seem in one significant way far more "worldly."

The most aggressive centralizer among southern Pentecostals was A. J. Tomlinson. The first general overseer of the Church of God, Tomlinson early in the church's history called for local congregations to send money to a national organization, which would support preachers and missionary workers. What Tomlinson called "The Money System" was a detailed plan connecting the contributions of every church member to a national organization that would support world missions. Every church member, according to the system, should pay a tithe to his or her local church. The treasurer of each church should send a tenth of that money to a state organization, which in turn should send a tenth of its total receipts to a central Church of God organization. The central organization had the responsibility to spread church efforts into new parts of the world.[59]

Tomlinson campaigned aggressively for centralization and the world-wide successes it could bring. In his first address to the annual assembly that brought together Church of God leaders in 1911, he suggested forming a fund to pay all preachers. A year later, just seven years after the form-

57. 12th Avenue Church of Christ Minute Books, 1911-1920, Special Collection, Beaman Library, David Lipscomb University.

58. Hughes, *Reviving the Ancient Faith*, pp. 138-39, 233-35.

59. On "The Money System," A. J. Tomlinson, *The Last Great Conflict* (New York: Garland Press, 1985, orig. pub. 1913), pp. 163-83.

ing of the first Church of God congregation, he proclaimed that the church's "voice is echoing around the world. It is not too much to say that every state in the Union will hear the voice of this Assembly. Canada, South America, Europe, Asia, and Africa and many of the islands of the sea will hear the sound that goes forth from the platform of this auditorium."[60]

In *The Last Great Conflict* (1913), Tomlinson connected his system for financial centralization to his broader theology. Confident in his belief in the coming millennium, Tomlinson wrote to inspire immediate missionary action throughout the world. He stressed the immediacy of the need to sacrifice time, energy, family, and money to convert as many people as possible. "Money that has been hoarded up must be put into use. This is the time for the last message to go forth and it must go. Some who cannot go must send. It is no time to leave legacies and estates for children yet unborn. Everything must be put into the one great effort to take the gospel to all the world." Tomlinson stressed that centralized efforts to collect and spend money were crucial to that effort. If Christians understood the degree and immediacy of their responsibilities, he emphasized, "there would be a rattling of coins and passing of checks as has never been known in the business world!"[61] Tomlinson's language recalls the language G. F. Taylor and Flavius Lee used to describe the economic aspects of the coming millennium. They associated "hoarding up" money with the growing power of commerce. Thus, Christians needed to spend as much as possible to support missionaries. Just as activities never before known in the business world could signify the coming of the end, so Christians had to match and exceed that activity in doing battle with the anti-Christ.

The first congregation in what became the new denomination, the North Cleveland Church of God, organized in 1905. That church was supporting missionaries to other southern states by 1910, and in 1915 it started a special fund for foreign missionaries. By 1917, the still small denomination was sending missionaries to the Bahamas, Jamaica, Canada, South America, India, and China; in 1921, it sent a team of ten missionaries to the Bahamas. By the late 1910s, Church of God congregations from through-

---

60. A. J. Tomlinson, "Third Annual Address," Eighth Annual Assembly, Jan. 7-12, 1913, Cleveland, TN, in A. J. Tomlinson, *Historical Annual Addresses*, compiled by Perry E. Gillum (Cleveland, TN: The White Wing Publishing House & Press, 1970), p. 20.

61. Tomlinson, *The Last Great Conflict*, pp. 29, 30.

out the South were sending small donations to the national headquarters to use for foreign missions.[62]

The financial records of Bridge Ford Church of God in Hazelhurst, Georgia in 1931 dramatize the simultaneous rural traditionalism and world-conquering centralization of the early Church of God. In the depths of the Depression, members of the small congregation had very little cash. The church recorded the monthly contributions of eleven members,[63] most of whom gave between two and five dollars for the entire year. Two features stand out about the church's finances. All eleven members paid at least part of their contributions in produce — eggs, chickens, milk, corn, potatoes. For example, every month Georgia Brantley gave milk and eggs worth between 40 cents and $1.50. The other striking feature of church finance is that the congregation sent small, regular amounts to the national headquarters, the Georgia State overseer, and to a special fund for foreign missions. During 1931 the church sent a total of $4.65 to help support mission work.[64]

This was egg money for world missions. Such contributions represent an extreme example of a Pentecostal imperative. Not all southern Pentecostals supported a Tomlinson-like money system. Troubled by those he believed wanted "no form or system — no government — no control,"[65] he battled for years before the system was fully implemented in 1920 and lost his place in the church shortly thereafter.[66] However, the emphasis on world missions and the complexity of the money system dramatize the ways Pentecostals put to work their beliefs about the millennium.

Studying these sectarian groups from the early twentieth-century South seems especially productive because they do not fit into neat sect-to-church models. It is accurate enough to begin with an image of evangelical

62. North Cleveland Church of God, Membership and Conference Minutes, 1910-1919, Box 97; Foreign and Home Mission Ledgers, 1917-1927, Boxes 83-84, all in Hal Bernard Dixon Jr. Pentecostal Research Center, Lee College.

63. Twelve other members gave money, but records do not list the monthly or total amounts.

64. Bridge Ford Church of God Order Book, 1931, Box 250, Hal Bernard Dixon Jr. Pentecostal Research Center, Lee College.

65. Tomlinson, *The Last Great Conflict*, p. 31. See also his repeated criticisms of his opponents in his *Historical Annual Addresses*.

66. On Tomlinson and the controversies in the Church of God over the money system, see Crews, *Church of God*, pp. 23-30.

sects as practicing world-denying asceticism. But these two groups complicate that model by going in different directions at the same time. Their distinctive theological commitments — sanctification and premillennialism among the Pentecostals, rationalism and congregational autonomy among the Churches of Christ — helped define how each group addressed economic questions, and in fact, which economic questions they chose to ask. The southern Pentecostal groups looked back to the nineteenth century for the background of their critique of the twentieth-century economy. They believed that society was in moral decline, and they tried to remain separate from it. At the same time, they enthusiastically embraced economic and bureaucratic centralization as the best way to support missionary programs that put into action their beliefs about the coming millennium. Thus, they grew more worldly and less sect-like in their financial and bureaucratic practices at the same time they intensified their rejection of forms of "worldliness" that interfered with sanctification. On the other hand, Churches of Christ were relatively "worldly" in their perspective on the twentieth-century economy. Wealth was worrisome, but its pursuit could teach useful religious lessons about following clear rules for a higher purpose. However, in upholding traditions of rigid congregational autonomy, they rejected a world that expected more bureaucratization, more centralized authority, and more interconnectedness.

CHAPTER 9

Fundamentalist Institutions and the Rise of Evangelical Protestantism, 1929-1942

JOEL A. CARPENTER

Then I said to them, "You see the trouble we are in: Jerusalem lies in ruins, and its gates have been burned with fire. Come, let us rebuild the wall of Jerusalem, and we will no longer be in disgrace."

NEHEMIAH 2:17 (NIV)

In April of 1952 an article in *Christian Life* magazine proclaimed Chicago "the evangelical capital of the U.S.A."[1] To back this claim, editor Russell Hitt cited a host of evangelical agencies in greater Chicago: mission boards, denominational offices, colleges, Bible institutes, seminaries, publishing concerns (including *Christian Life* itself), and youth organizations. In total, the author mentioned over one hundred different agencies such as Youth For Christ International, the Slavic Gospel Association, Scripture Press, and the Swedish Covenant Hospital.[2] At first glance, the article ap-

1. Russell T. Hitt, "Capital of Evangelicalism," *Christian Life* 5 (Apr. 1952): 16.
2. Hitt, "Capital of Evangelicalism," pp. 16-18, 46-48. *Christian Life* itself was an interesting symbol of a growing evangelical wing of Protestantism. *Christian Life* was

This chapter is a revision of an article that originally appeared in *Church History* 49, no. 11 (Mar. 1980): 62-75; reprinted with permission.

pears to present a confusing list of unrelated organizations, but closer inspection reveals a coherent pattern. The agencies in the Chicago area represented the swiftly growing evangelical movement that observers have labeled the third force of American Christianity.[3] Most institutions listed did not belong to the older, more prestigious denominations. The mission boards, such as Wycliffe Bible Translators, the Worldwide Evangelization Crusade, and the International Hebrew Christian Alliance, were independents. The denominational headquarters, including those of the Conservative Baptist Association, the Evangelical Mission Covenant Church, the North American Baptist General Conference, and the General Association of Regular Baptist Churches, represented fundamentalists and other evangelicals. The schools — the Moody Bible Institute, North Park College, Trinity Seminary and Bible College, Wheaton College, the Mennonite Biblical Seminary, the Salvation Army Training College, and Emmaus Bible Institute — came from the same source.[4]

Whether or not Chicago was the capital of evangelicalism is not as important as the image the article revealed. Chicago was a regional evangelical stronghold in the 1950s when the evangelicals were leading a revival of popular religious interest. This revival developed largely from the institutional base that evangelicals had established in the previous decades. The fundamentalists were especially prominent in the postwar evangelical revival, a fact that might seem surprising to anyone who supposed the movement had been crushed twenty years earlier. Fundamentalism was not a defeated party in denominational politics, but a popular religious movement that in the 1930s developed a separate existence from the older denominations as it strengthened its own institutions. By the 1950s, this building phase had paid off, and Billy Graham, a fundamentalist favorite son, became the symbol of evangelicalism's new prominence.

As a complex aggregate movement, evangelical Protestantism in the

---

formed in 1948 by enterprising young evangelical publishers who wanted a market for a breezy, "Christian" version of *Life* magazine. *Christian Life* 1 (July 1948): 3.

3. "The Third Force in Christendom," *Life*, 9 June 1958, pp. 113-21; and Henry P. Van Dusen, "The Third Force's Lesson for Others," *Life*, 9 June 1958, pp. 122, 125. See also William G. McLoughlin, "Is There a Third Force in Christendom?" *Daedalus* 96 (Winter 1967): 43-68; Winthrop S. Hudson, *American Protestantism* (Chicago: University of Chicago Press, 1961), pp. 153-76.

4. Hitt, "Capital of Evangelicalism," pp. 16-18, 46-48.

twentieth century demands closer attention. Earlier studies of the 1930s and early 1940s in particular yielded little understanding of its development. The prevailing opinion among historians was that Protestantism suffered a depression during at least the first half of the 1930s, a depression relieved only when neo-orthodox theology renewed the vision and vitality of the old-line denominations.[5] Evangelical Protestants fit into this scheme only tangentially. Sydney Ahlstrom noted that "something like a revival took place" among the holiness, fundamentalist, and Pentecostal churches; and William McLoughlin credited evangelicals with keeping alive the tradition of revivalism during the depression. Other historians, however, viewed the activity of this third force as a symptom of Protestantism's depressed condition rather than a sign of grassroots vitality.[6] The institutional growth in the 1930s of the most vocal and visible evangelicals, the fundamentalists, challenges the widespread notion that popular Protestantism experienced a major decline during that decade. What really transpired was the beginning of a shift of the Protestant mainstream from the older denominations toward the evangelicals.

Looking back, it is clear to see that the older "mainline" denominations did experience what Robert T. Handy called a "religious depression," beginning in the middle of the 1920s until the late 1930s, when their fortunes revived somewhat. For example, membership in the northern Presbyterian and the Protestant Episcopal denominations declined 5.0 and 6.7 percent respectively between 1926 and 1936. The foreign missionary enterprise lost momentum as budgets tightened and many missionaries returned home at mid-career for lack of funds.[7] Social programs also suffered from the loss of contributions as the churches had to cut off the lower end of their priority

---

5. Martin E. Marty, *Righteous Empire: The Protestant Experience in America* (New York: Dial Press, 1970), pp. 233-43; Robert T. Handy, *A Christian America: Protestant Hopes and Historical Realities* (New York: Oxford University Press, 1971), pp. 217-19. See also Paul A. Carter, *The Decline and Revival of the Social Gospel* (Ithaca, NY: Cornell University Press, 1954).

6. Sydney F. Ahlstrom, *A Religious History of the American People* (New Haven: Yale University Press, 1972), p. 920; William G. McLoughlin, *Modern Revivalism: Charles Grandison Finney to Billy Graham* (New York: Ronald Press Co., 1959), pp. 462-68; Handy, *A Christian America*, p. 203; Marty, *Righteous Empire*, p. 237.

7. Robert T. Handy, "The American Religious Depression, 1925-1935," *Church History* 29 (Mar. 1960): 4-5; percentages computed from membership statistics in U.S. Department of Commerce, Bureau of the Census, *Religious Bodies, 1936*, 2 vols., vol. 2: *Denominations* (Washington, DC, 1941), pp. 1386, 1478.

lists.[8] At the onset of the Great Depression of the 1930s, many Christians wondered if a revival would descend, bringing with it the return of prosperity. But Samuel C. Kincheloe reported to the Social Science Research Council in 1937 that "the trend over the past thirty years" had been "away from emotional revival services" and that the Depression did "not seem to have produced much variation in this major trend."[9] When Robert and Helen Lynd revisited "Middletown" in 1935, they saw little evidence of a religious awakening. "If the number of revivals is any index of religious interest in the Depression," they concluded, "there has been a marked recession."[10] McLoughlin and Ahlstrom recognized, however, that the slight overall growth in Protestant membership in the 1930s stemmed largely from what the Lynds had called "working-class churches."[11]

In singular contrast to the plight of the major denominations, fundamentalists and other evangelicals prospered. During the 1920s, fundamentalists had grown more vocal and apparently more numerous, but the leaders had been publicly defeated in denominational battles, and had made themselves look foolish in the anti-evolution crusade.[12] Adverse publicity from public controversy had discredited fundamentalists and established the Menckenesque image that has dogged them ever since.[13] Yet these defeats by no means destroyed the movement. Fundamentalism cannot be understood by studying only its role in headline-making conflicts. Rather, we must examine the growing network of institutions upon which fundamentalists increasingly relied as they became alienated from the old-line denominations.

One of the most important focal points of fundamentalist activity in

8. Handy, "The American Religious Depression," pp. 5-9.

9. Samuel C. Kincheloe, *Research Memorandum on Religion in the Depression, Social Science Research Council* #17 (New York, 1937), p. 93. See also "Why No Revival?" *The Christian Century,* 18 Sept. 1935, pp. 1168-70; "Billy Sunday, the Last of His Line," *The Christian Century,* 20 Nov. 1935, p. 1476.

10. Robert S. and Helen M. Lynd, *Middletown in Transition* (New York: Harcourt, Brace, and Co., 1937), p. 303.

11. Ahlstrom, *A Religious History of the American People,* p. 920; McLoughlin, *Modern Revivalism,* p. 464.

12. Norman F. Furniss, *The Fundamentalist Controversy, 1918-1931* (New Haven: Yale University Press, 1954), pp. 103-76; Stewart G. Cole, *The History of Fundamentalism* (New York: R. R. Smith, Inc., 1931), pp. 65-225; Sandeen, *The Roots of Fundamentalism,* pp. 250-64.

13. Furniss, *The Fundamentalist Controversy,* pp. 76-100; Cole, *The History of Fundamentalism,* pp. 259-80.

the thirties was the Bible institute, a relatively new type of institutional structure. The two pioneers of Bible institute education were A. B. Simpson, founder of the Christian and Missionary Alliance, who in 1882 established the Missionary Training Institute in New York City, and Dwight L. Moody, who founded in 1886 what became the Moody Bible Institute of Chicago.[14] The idea of a teaching center for lay Christian workers caught on quickly, and other schools sprang up across the country. By 1930 the fundamentalist weekly *Sunday School Times* endorsed over fifty Bible schools, most of which were in major cities.[15]

The Bible institutes became the major coordinating agencies of the movement by the 1930s, as popular fundamentalist alienation toward the old-line denominations reached new heights. True, most fundamentalists had not left the older denominations, but after the controversies over evolutionary theory and theological liberalism in the 1920s, they were more aware than before of the intellectual attitudes engendered by church-related colleges and seminaries. While the nondenominational Bible institutes had been founded to train lay and paraministerial workers such as Sunday school superintendents and foreign missionaries, now they faced demands for educating pastors and for other services that denominations formerly provided.[16]

Since the Bible institutes had already branched out into activities not directly connected with in-residence instruction, they were well equipped to meet such demands. Some of the schools had extension departments, such as those of the Philadelphia School of the Bible, or the Moody Bible Institute of Chicago. These agencies organized week-long summer and other shorter Bible conferences, supplied staff evangelists for revival meetings, and provided churches with guest preachers.[17] Many schools ran publishing and/or

---

14. S. A. Witmer, *The Bible College Story: Education With Dimension* (Manhasset, NY: Channel Press, 1962), pp. 34-37.

15. "Bible Schools That Are True to the Faith," *Sunday School Times,* 1 Feb. 1930, p. 63 (hereafter cited as *SST*).

16. Ernest R. Sandeen suggests this development, pointing out in *The Roots of Fundamentalism* (pp. 241-43) that the scope of Bible institute activity was such that the schools functioned as denominational surrogates.

17. Renald E. Showers, "A History of Philadelphia College of Bible," (M.Th. Thesis, Dallas Theological Seminary, 1962), pp. 69, 81, 86; *Brief Facts About the Moody Bible Institute of Chicago* (Chicago, 1928); *Moody Bible Institute Bulletin* 12 (Nov. 1932): 14; 16 (Nov. 1936): 15.

distributing ventures, including the Bible Institute of Los Angeles' BIOLA Bookroom, Approved Books of the Philadelphia School of the Bible (PSOB), and the mammoth Bible Institute Colportage Association at Moody.[18] In addition many magazines provided their schools with publicity and the readers with fundamentalist literature and opinion: *The Moody Monthly, The King's Business* of BIOLA, *Serving and Waiting* of PSOB, Northwestern (Minneapolis) Bible and Missionary Training School's *The Pilot,* and Denver Bible Institute's *Grace and Truth.*[19] As centers of religious enterprise, the Bible institutes soon saw the potential impact of radio broadcasting, both as a religious service opportunity and a way to increase their constituency. BIOLA led the way with its own station, KJS, in 1922. Moody installed WMBI three years later, and, although they did not own stations during the 1930s, Providence (R.I.) Bible Institute, Columbia Bible College in South Carolina, and Denver Bible Institute all sponsored radio programs.[20]

With so many services to provide to fundamentalist individuals and small Bible classes and congregations, the Bible schools became regional and national coordinating centers for the movement. Moody Bible Institute (MBI) became the national giant of institutional fundamentalism. The MBI Extension Department held weekend Bible conferences in nearly 500 churches during 1936, more than doubling its exposure of six years earlier. By 1942, WMBI was releasing transcribed programs to 187 different stations, and the radio staff had visited nearly 300 different churches since the station's inception, returning to many churches several times. The Institute had over 15,000 contributors in 1937 and about the same number enrolled in Correspondence School, while the *Moody Monthly* showed a net increase of 13,000 subscribers over the decade, totalling 40,000 by 1940.[21]

18. "Institute Items," *The King's Business* 3 (Nov. 1912): 295-96; Showers, "Philadelphia College," pp. 69, 89; *A Brief Story of the Bible Institute Colportage Association of Chicago: Forty-five Years of Printed Page Ministry* (Chicago, 1939).

19. "Interdenominational Christian Magazines," *SST,* 7 Feb. 1931, p. 72.

20. Daniel P. Fuller, *Give the Winds a Mighty Voice: The Story of Charles E. Fuller* (Waco, TX: Word, 1972), pp. 75-77; "WMBI," *Moody Monthly* 30 (Jan. 1930): 270; "Radio Station WMBI," *Moody Monthly* 31 (May 1931): 480; "The Sunday School Times Radio Directory," *SST,* 30 May 1931, p. 313. Hereafter, *Moody Monthly* is cited as *MM.*

21. *Moody Bible Institute Bulletin* 12 (Nov. 1932): 14; 16 (Nov. 1936): 15; "Miracles and Melodies," *MM* 42 (Apr. 1942): 487. Figures on radio staff itineraries compiled from *Annual Report of the Radio Department of the Moody Bible Institute of Chicago* for the years 1929-1941; "President's Report," *Moody Bible Institute Bulletin* 17 (Oct. 1937): 3; typescript table taken from file six, "Enrollment," The Moodyana Collection, Moody Bible Institute; "And

Other schools could not match MBI in scale but carried strong regional influence. By the mid-1930s, for instance, Gordon College of Theology and Missions had supplied 100 pastors in greater Boston, and 48 out of the total 96 Baptist pastors in New Hampshire. At one time in the 1930s, every Baptist pastor in Boston proper was either a Gordon alumnus, professor, or trustee.[22] In Minnesota, William Bell Riley, the Pastor of Minneapolis First Baptist Church, held virtually a fundamentalist bishopric by virtue of the 75 pastors statewide who had attended his Northwestern Bible and Missionary Training School.[23] BIOLA had 180 alumni Christian workers in California by 1939.[24] Considering all the activity Bible institutes engaged in, the influence they wielded through direct contact and alumni, and the support they received, it is no wonder that one confused reader of the *Moody Monthly* asked, "Why don't you publish something on the other denominations once in a while?"[25]

Fundamentalists who desired a Christian liberal arts education for their children in the 1930s sought it for the most part outside the movement proper. The fundamentalists themselves operated only a few such schools, notably Wheaton College near Chicago and Bob Jones College (then located in Cleveland, Tennessee), while Gordon College of Missions and Theology in Boston was developing an arts and sciences division. Advertisements in fundamentalist periodicals show, however, that colleges sponsored by other evangelicals, including Taylor University in Upland, Indiana and Grove City College in Pennsylvania, attracted students from fundamentalist congregations.[26] These evangelical colleges prospered during the thirties. A survey of evangelical higher education in 1948 found that the total enrollment of seventy such schools in the United States doubled between 1929 and 1940.[27]

Now for 50,000," *MM* 41 (Sept. 1940): 4; *N. W. Ayer and Son's Dictionary of Newspapers and Periodicals,* 65th anniversary edition (Philadelphia, 1933).

22. Nathan R. Wood, *A School of Christ* (Boston: Gordon College of Theology and Missions, 1953), pp. 165-66.

23. "The Sweep of Northwestern Schools," *The Pilot* 17 (Jan. 1937): 108.

24. "BIOLA's Workers in the Homelands," *The King's Business* 30 (July 1939): 268-70.

25. "A Magazine for All," *MM* 40 (Feb. 1942): 249.

26. Several such colleges were advertised in *MM* issues from September 1930 to August 1931.

27. Harry J. Albus, "Christian Education Today," *Christian Life* 1 (Sept. 1948): 26, 46; quoted in Louis Gasper, *The Fundamentalist Movement* (The Hague, 1963), p. 104.

Wheaton College, founded in 1857, provides perhaps the most striking example of the rapid growth of fundamentalist higher education. J. Oliver Buswell, Wheaton's president from 1926-1940, labored to improve its enrollment and academic standing. During his administration the college won a high accreditation rating, and for three years Wheaton led all liberal arts colleges in growth nationwide. By 1941 Wheaton's enrollment of 1100, up from about 400 in 1926, led all liberal arts colleges in Illinois.[28] The school had become the "Harvard of the Bible Belt," a producer of such evangelical leaders as theologian Carl F. H. Henry and Billy Graham.[29]

As millions of Americans motored each summer to popular resorts, a growing number of summer Bible conferences competed with tourist camps and resort hotels for the patronage of vacationing fundamentalists,[30] including such places as the Boardwalk Bible Conference in Atlantic City, the Montrose Summer Gatherings in the Pennsylvania hills, Winona Lake in Indiana, Redfeather Lakes in the Colorado Rockies, and Mount Hermon, California,[31] Bible conferences offered a unique vacation: a blend of resort-style recreation, the old-fashioned camp meeting, and biblical teaching from leading fundamentalist pulpiteers.[32] Enrollees might hear Harry A. Ironside of Chicago's Moody Memorial Church, Paul Rood of BIOLA, or Martin R. DeHaan of the "Radio Bible Class." The conferences offered different programs so that one could choose among sessions featuring missions, young people, the pastorate, Bible study, "Victorious Living," prophecy, sacred music, business men,

28. "The World Is Wondering About Wheaton," *Baptist Bulletin* 3 (Mar. 1938): 14; "Wheaton College, 'For Christ and His Kingdom,'" *Baptist Bulletin* 1 (Nov. 1935): 5, 11-12; "Dr. Buswell to Be President of the National Bible Institute," *SST*, 24 May 1941, p. 434; "Wheaton Annuities," *SST*, 4 Sept. 1937, p. 61; "Wheaton College," *Watchman-Examiner*, 16 Oct. 1941, p. 1067. The survey of higher education in the Oct. 11, 1936 issue of *The New York Times*, section 2, p. 5, confirms the claims for that year.

29. "Wheaton College, Harvard of the Bible Belt," *Change* 6 (Mar. 1974): 17-20; McLoughlin, *Modern Revivalism*, p. 486; Carl F. H. Henry, "Twenty Years a Baptist," *Foundations* 1 (1958): 46-47.

30. Dixon Wecter reported that as many as thirty-five million Americans went on vacation trips each summer in the thirties. Wecter, *The Age of the Great Depression, 1924-1941* (New York: Macmillan, 1948), p. 225.

31. "Forthcoming Conferences," *MM* 35 (Aug. 1935): 589.

32. "Shall I Go to a Summer Bible Conference?" *SST*, 18 May 1935, p. 337; C. H. Heaton, "The Winona Lake Bible Conference," *Watchman-Examiner*, 4 Sept. 1941, p. 826.

business women, or Sunday school.[33] The lists of forthcoming conferences published each summer by the *Moody Monthly* grew steadily larger
during the thirties, from twenty-seven sites and eighty-eight conference
sessions in 1930, to over two hundred sessions at more than fifty different
locations in 1941.[34]

A report in the Baptist *Watchman-Examiner* of the Bible Conference
at Winona Lake, Indiana in 1941 portrays the character of such meetings.
Each summer the whole Winona Lake community became a religious resort, with thousands of fundamentalists renting cottages and streaming to
the conference grounds. The meetings that capped off the 1941 summer
schedule at Winona Lake attracted more than 2,000 enrollees, including
some 400 ministers. They were joined by perhaps 2,000 more daily visitors.
Participants listened to as many as six sermons a day out of the thirteen to
fourteen total sessions scheduled between seven in the morning and ten in
the evening. The men on the platform included several fundamentalist ce-
lebrities: William Bell Riley of First Baptist Church, Minneapolis; Harold T. Commons, executive director of the Association of Baptists for the
Evangelization of the Orient; and evangelists J. C. Massee, Ralph E. Neighbor, and J. Hoffman Cohn. The master of ceremonies was Billy Sunday's
former partner Homer Rodeheaver, "the leading song director of America."[35] The sense of brotherhood at the conference was apparently without
denominational bounds; a Methodist Bishop, a Baptist evangelist, a Presbyterian professor, a Lutheran pastor, a Christian layman, and a Rescue Mission superintendent could stand on the same platform and preach the common tenets of the Christian faith, while multitudes of believers wept and
rejoiced together as if some glorious news had burst upon their ears for the
first time.[36]

Such events were a powerful force for cementing the bonds of commitment within the movement. In 1937 the *Sunday School Times* reported a
poll taken at a small Bible college showing that all but fifteen of the 150
students had attended a summer conference. Sixty-five first accepted
Christ or made a recommitment to the Christian life there, and sixty-two

33. "Forthcoming Conferences," *MM* 34 (July 1934): 528; "Forthcoming Conferences," *MM* 35 (Aug. 1935): 589.

34. "Forthcoming conferences," *MM* 30 (June 1930): 517; "Forthcoming Conferences," *MM* 41 (June 1941): 614.

35. Heaton, "Winona Lake Bible Conference," p. 826.

36. Heaton, "Winona Lake Bible Conference," p. 826.

claimed that they were in Bible college because of a summer conference. According to the editor, the Bible conference had become "one of the most powerful factors in the spiritual life of the church."[37]

In the 1930s the rapidly rising commercial radio industry provided the fundamentalists with a new medium through which to send out their "old gospel" to the rest of the nation. The number of radio sets had doubled between 1930 and 1935 to over eighteen million. By 1938 a *Fortune* survey named radio listening the first preference for leisure-time entertainment in America. Fundamentalist preachers quickly took to the airwaves. A casual, reader-contributed directory in the January 23, 1932 *Sunday School Times* lists over four hundred evangelical programs on eighty different stations nationwide.[38]

Interest in religious broadcasting was not limited to the fundamentalist movement. For a time they and other evangelicals feared restrictive network policies would force them off the airwaves. The Federal Council of Churches, the United Synagogues of America, and the National Catholic Welfare Conference cooperated with the Columbia Broadcasting System and the National Broadcasting Corporation to produce nonsectarian programs on free network time. The CBS "Church of the Air" featured such prominent preachers as Harry Emerson Fosdick, Bishop Fulton J. Sheen, and Rabbi Stephen S. Wise. This venture reflected the intention of CBS and NBC to limit religious broadcasting to a few hours a week and to "representative" national religious bodies.[39] Father Charles E. Couglin's controversial radio blasts over the CBS network had led that network to adopt a policy that would ensure bland, "safe" religious programming.[40] This change directly affected the evangelical broadcasters, especially the fundamentalists, many of whom had paid for network time. These preachers were often controversial or sectarian in tone and received no place in ecumenical broadcasting schemes. Yet the fundamentalists and friends

37. "Why Attend a Summer Conference?" *SST*, 15 May 1937, p. 348.

38. Herman S. Hettinger, "Broadcasting in the United States" and Spencer J. Miller, "Radio and Religion," *Annals of the American Academy of Political and Social Sciences* 177 (Jan. 1935): 6, 140; "Fortune Survey: Radio Favorites," *Fortune* (Jan. 1939): 88; "A Directory of Evangelical Radio Broadcasts," *SST*, 23 Jan. 1932, pp. 44-45.

39. Miller, "Radio and Religion," pp. 136-39; Fuller, *Give the Winds a Mighty Voice*, p. 101-3.

40. "Directory of Evangelical Radio Broadcasts," p. 44; "Another Year of Miracle Gospel Broadcast," *SST*, 21 Oct. 1939, pp. 720-22.

were by no means driven from the air. The religious programs were too attractive a market for commercial stations to turn down, and hundreds of local stations sold them time, as did the new Mutual Broadcasting System until 1944.[41] Indeed, it became clear by the late thirties that paid programs drew the greater share of popular support. Charles E. Fuller's weekly "Old-Fashioned Revival Hour" became the most popular religious program in the country.[42]

The "Old-Fashioned Revival Hour" climbed rapidly to national prominence. From modest beginnings in 1925, Charles E. Fuller, fundamentalist pastor of Calvary Church in the Los Angeles suburb of Placentia, expanded the work in its early years to include three weekday broadcasts, two Sunday broadcasts from Calvary Church, and a Sunday broadcast sponsored by BIOLA over the CBS Pacific Coast network. Fuller left his church for full-time radio ministry in 1933 and soon was heard each Sunday on the Mutual Network. Six years later the "Old-Fashioned Revival Hour" was broadcast weekly coast to coast and overseas to an estimated fifteen to twenty million listeners. Fuller's coverage consisted of 152 stations in 1939 and 456 three years later, the largest single release of any prime-time radio broadcast in America.[43]

As a whole, fundamentalist forays into national broadcasting were immensely successful. Other programs captured regional and national audiences, most notably Martin R. DeHaan's "Radio Bible Class," Philadelphia Presbyterian Donald Gray Barnhouse's "Bible Study Hour," and the "miracles and Melodies" series transcribed by Moody Bible Institute's studio. Programs with smaller coverage supplemented them to fill the airwaves with the old-time gospel. More than any other medium, radio kept revivalistic religion before the American public.[44]

41. Fuller, *Give the Winds a Mighty Voice*, pp. 151-57.
42. "Another Year of Miracle Gospel Broadcast," p. 720; Fuller, *Give the Winds a Mighty Voice*, pp. 113-22.
43. Untitled listing of radio programs, *SST*, 12 Apr. 1931, p. 184; "*The Sunday School Times* Radio Directory," *SST*, 30 May 1931, p. 313; Charles E. Fuller File, Baptist Ministers and Missionaries Benefit Board Registry, the Samuel Colgate Library of the American Baptist Historical Society, Rochester, New York; Gasper, *The Fundamentalist Movement*, p. 77; "Another Year of Miracle Gospel Broadcast," p. 720; Fuller, *Give the Winds a Mighty Voice*, p. 140.
44. Gasper, *The Fundamentalist Movement*, pp. 19-20, 76-78; George W. Dollar, *A History of Fundamentalism in America* (Greenville, SC: Bob Jones University Press, 1973), pp. 255-57; "Hear WMBI Favorites on Your Station," *MM* 41 (Sept. 1940): 31.

Of all the activities pursued by both fundamentalists and major Protestant denominations during the 1930s, their foreign missionary work portrayed most starkly their contrasting fortunes. The great missionary enterprise of the Protestant churches had entered the twentieth century with unbounded hope and zeal; but liberal disillusion with evangelism, inflation, and constituents' dislike of liberal programs depleted the denominational mission budgets and stifled enthusiastic young volunteers. For instance, the Northern Baptist Convention (NBC) experienced an extremely heavy decline in its mission program. Its staff dwindled from 845 in 1930 to 508 in 1940. The year 1936 was particularly disastrous, as NBC contributions for missions totaled $2.26 million, down 45 percent from 1920. That year no new missionaries went out, and many in the field came home for lack of money.[45]

Fundamentalists wanted missionaries who preached the old gospel of individual repentance and redemption. They recoiled from the denominational boards because of alleged theological liberalism, social gospel programs, and high overhead costs.[46] But fundamentalist interest in missions did not flag. Fundamentalists supported independent "faith" missions that were not denominationally connected and did not solicit funds directly. They also founded new denominational agencies. While the Laymen's Foreign Missions Inquiry reported in 1932 that evangelism in missions was passé, the fundamentalist-backed missions grew stronger, better financed, more evangelistically aggressive, and more successful in recruiting volunteers than ever before.[47] The China Inland Mission (CIM), a giant among the independents, experienced the greatest growth of its history during the thirties. Even though China was then involved in conflict with Japan and suffering internal strife, CIM sent out 629 new missionaries in

45. Curtis Lee Laws, "Shall Baptists Go Out of Business?" *Watchman-Examiner*, 2 Jan. 1936, p. 13; "The Tragedy of the Northern Baptist Convention," *Watchman-Examiner*, 11 June 1936, p. 699; "The Tragedy of It All," *Baptist Bulletin* 6 (July 1940): 1; *Annual of the Northern Baptist Convention, 1937* (Philadelphia, 1937), p. 28.

46. A classic fundamentalist exposé of the missions situation is in Robert T. Ketcham, *Facts for Baptists to Face* (Rochester, NY: Interstate Evangelistic Assoc., 1936), pp. 5-15. Lewis A. Brown, "A Missionary Speaks Plainly," *Watchman-Examiner*, 18 Mar. 1937, p. 300, and Carey S. Thomas, "Is Non-Cooperation Justifiable?" *Watchman-Examiner*, 18 Feb. 1937, pp. 179-81, are lamentations of the nonsupport of conservatives.

47. Handy, *A Christian America*, pp. 190-96. William E. Hocking, ed., *Rethinking Missions* (New York, 1932), is the major report of the findings of the Laymen's Foreign Missions Inquiry.

1930-1936, for a total force of almost 1,400.[48] CIM was but one of a growing group of independent fundamentalist missions. Each year, the *Sunday School Times* published a list of fundamentalist mission agencies, which showed forty-nine in 1931 and seventy-six by 1941. These missions ranged in size from the tiny Layyah Barakat (Syria) Home for Orphan Girls to the Sudan Interior Mission, which received $250,000 in 1937 and doubled its army of missionaries during the decade.[49]

These missions worked in close association with Bible institutes, which trained missionaries, housed mission offices, and helped raise funds. From the Moody Bible Institute alone came over 550 new missionaries from 1930 to 1941, while BIOLA housed both the Orinoco River Mission and the United Aborigines Mission offices.[50] Evangelical fervor for missions generated by the Student Volunteer Movement had not died but rather had changed its institutional base. As a traditional indicator of religious vitality, missionary activity demonstrated the vigor of fundamentalism no less than the movement's other enterprises.

In these four areas of fundamentalist activity — education, summer Bible conferences, radio broadcasting, and foreign missions — the evidence shows a growing, dynamic movement. Other activities thrived also: publishing houses such as Fleming H. Revell, Loizeaux Brothers, and Moody Press; and seminaries, notably Evangelical Theological College in Dallas and Westminster Theological Seminary of Philadelphia. Even this brief survey, however, demonstrates that the fundamentalist movement did not decline during the thirties. Rather, there was a shift of emphasis within the movement. Fundamentalist efforts to cleanse the denominations of liberal trends had seemed to fail. Rather than persisting along the 1920s lines of conflict, fundamentalists during the 1930s were developing

48. Robert Hall Glover, "What Is a Faith Mission?" *Missionary Review of the World* 58 (Sept. 1935): 409-11; "Suggestions for Your Christmas Giving," *SST,* 26 Dec. 1931, p. 737; Ernest Gordon, "A Survey of Religious Life and Thought," *SST,* 24 June 1939, p. 430; Robert Hall Glover, "Decrease in Missions Giving — Its Real Cause and Cure," *Revelation* 7 (June 1937): 241

49. "Suggestions for Your Christmas Giving," *SST,* 26 Dec. 1931, p. 737; "A New Missionary Board for the Old Faith," *SST,* 5 May 1934, p. 287; "The Presbyterian Controversy," *MM* 35 (May 1935): 411; "Suggestions for Your Christmas Giving," *SST,* 6 Dec. 1941, pp. 1010-11; Gordon, "A Survey of Religious Life and Thought," p. 430.

50. President's yearly reports, *MBI Bulletin* 12 (Nov. 1932): 5; 13 (Apr. 1933): 3; 14 (Nov. 1934): 4; 16 (Nov. 1936): 6; 17 (Feb. 1938): 3; 18 (Feb. 1939): 3; 19 (Feb. 1940): 8; 20 (Feb. 1941): 6; 21 (Feb. 1942): 5; *The Appeal of the Century* (Chicago, ca. 1937), p. 5.

their own institutional base from which to carry on their major purpose: the proclamation of the evangelical gospel.

Was there an "American Religious Depression" among Protestants during the 1930s? Not among fundamentalists and apparently not among other evangelicals either. Fundamentalist activities mentioned here had parallels. The other evangelical groups grew during the 1930s, some very rapidly indeed. The Assemblies of God increased fully fourfold, from 47,950 members in 1926 to 198,834 in 1940. The Church of the Nazarene more than doubled its membership from 63,558 to 165,532. The Southern Baptists gained almost 1.5 million members over the same period to total 4,949,174, while the Christian Reformed Church counted 121,755 members in 1940, an increase of 25 percent.[51] Old-line Protestantism may have been depressed, but popular evangelicalism flourished.

Did the evangelicals provide the impetus for the post–World War II revivals? The fundamentalist community played a leading role. Billy Graham's crusades and other agents of revivalism such as Youth For Christ were not merely throwbacks to the Billy Sunday era. They were the postwar descendants of a continuing revival tradition preserved and transformed by the fundamentalist movement. For instance, Youth For Christ held its first nationwide convention at the Winona Lake Conference in the summer of 1944. Its first president, Torrey Johnson, was a Wheaton College graduate. Of course, Graham was a Wheaton graduate also. His evangelistic team included George Beverly Shea, a former soloist at WMBI, and song leader Cliff Barrows, a Bob Jones College graduate.[52] Revivalism had not died during the depression. Rather, the fundamentalist movement nurtured that tradition, introduced innovations, and produced a new generation of revivalists.

Once again, as had happened so many times in the past, part of Christianity had taken the form of a vigorous popular movement. Fundamentalists surged out of the bonds of older denominational structures to create flexible, dynamic institutions, such as independent mission agencies, radio programs, and Bible schools. Despite or perhaps in part because of opposition, the movement grew. According to anthropologists Luther P.

51. United States Department of Commerce, Bureau of the Census, *Denominations;* Benson Y. Landis, ed., *Yearbook of American Churches, 1941* (New York: Federal Council of Churches, 1941); compare Ahlstrom, *A Religious History of the American People,* p. 920.

52. McLoughlin, *Modern Revivalism,* pp. 480-87.

Gerlach and Virginia H. Hine, movements arise to implement changes, to pursue goals that people think the established order is unsuccessful in attaining. Thus, a movement often grows in opposition to the established order from which it came. Because movements are decentralized and based on popular support, they are virtually irrepressible.[53] So it has been with fundamentalism. This widely dispersed network of conservative evangelicals became increasingly at odds with the old-line Protestant establishment. Defeats in the denominational conflicts of the 1920s forced fundamentalists to strengthen their own institutional structures outside the old-line denominations. They responded creatively to the trends in contemporary popular culture and made a lasting place for themselves in American Protestantism. Fundamentalists and other evangelicals prospered — the outlines of a changed Protestant order had begun to emerge.

53. Luther P. Gerlach and Virginia H. Hine, *People, Power, Change: Movements of Social Transformation* (Indianapolis: Bobbs-Merrill, 1970), pp. xvi-xix.

CHAPTER 10

The Funding of Evangelical Higher Education in the United States and Canada in the Postwar Period

ROBERT BURKINSHAW

Study to shew thyself approved unto God, a workman that needeth not to be ashamed, rightly dividing the word of truth.

2 TIMOTHY 2:15 (KJV)

A comparative look at the funding of American and Canadian evangelical institutions of higher education in the past half-century is instructive for understanding why the United States provides an environment more conducive to the establishment and funding of evangelical higher education, especially liberal arts colleges and universities, than does Canada. An exploration of the United States' situation reveals three areas in which the United States is unique and which largely explains the relative advantage American evangelical higher education has traditionally enjoyed: (1) the high regard for liberal arts college education; (2) the relative advantages and consequent strength of the voluntary sector, and (3) the relative strength of American evangelicals.

A glance at the number of institutions and their enrollment amply displays the contrast between the American and the Canadian situation. Nearly one-quarter million students in the United States enroll in eighty-eight member institutions of the Coalition of Christian Colleges and Universities (CCCU) and in thirty-six Southern Baptist schools not belonging to the CCCU.[1] By contrast, the comparable figure in Canada — under 3,000 in three CCCU institutions — amounts to only about 1 percent of the American total. Moreover, several of the U.S. institutions enjoy relative financial security in terms of gift and endowment income whereas the Canadian schools are relatively new, heavily indebted, and possess very little endowment.

Even though Canada has proven to be a more fertile ground for Bible colleges, most of those are not financially strong. The near collapse of Ontario Bible College and Seminary in the mid-1990s (since renamed Tyndale Seminary and College), one of the older, more established evangelical schools in the nation, provided graphic illustration of this insecurity. A number of schools closed in the 1990s due to declining enrollments and even venerable Bible schools such as Prairie Bible Institute experienced financial exigencies throughout much of the 1980s and 1990s.

The funding of private higher education generally involves three primary sources of income: tuition and fees, donations, and endowment income. Compared to many other types of evangelical organizations in which donations comprise the bulk of the budget, donations play a proportionately much less significant role in meeting the expenses of institutions of higher education. What Michael Hamilton terms "commercial funding," the raising of funds from services rendered, especially in the form of tuition and other fees, is by far the most important source of educational funding in the private sector.[2] Between the late 1980s and mid-1990s, tuition alone accounted for between two-thirds and nearly three-quarters of the revenue of CCCU institutions.[3] Thus, the ability to recruit sufficient numbers of students able to pay tuition and fees sufficiently high to meet most of the expenses is the single most important factor in the financial

1. "CCCU at a Glance," *The 1998 National Forum on Christian Higher Education* (Washington, DC: CCCU, 1998); "Enrollment Up at Baptist Colleges for Sixteenth Year," *The Southern Baptist Educator* 62, no. 4 (Summer, 1998): 1-2. In addition, an unknown number of students are enrolled in U.S. evangelical institutions not part of either the CCCU or the Southern Baptist Convention.

2. Michael S. Hamilton, "More Money, More Ministry: The Financing of American Evangelicalism Since 1945," pp. 104-38 in this volume.

3. Wesley K. Willmer, "Christian Higher Education Advancement in Overview," in *Advancing Christian Higher Education,* ed. Wesley K. Willmer (Washington, DC: CCCU, 1996), Table 1-12, p. 10.

health of most such colleges and universities. Certainly not all evangelical colleges in the United States have proven successful in this regard, and some have been forced to close their doors. However, it is clear that a number of factors in the United States have historically favored evangelical institutions in the race to attract tuition-paying students.

Relative Value Placed on Liberal Arts Education

A far higher proportion of Americans than Canadians support higher education because the American public has historically viewed post-secondary education in fundamentally different ways than has the Canadian public. Martin Trow baldly states the American view: "Americans have an almost religious belief in the desirability and efficacy of post-secondary education for almost everybody; no other nation in the world makes that commitment or holds that belief."[4] In 1836 Lyman Beecher based his justification for establishing a multiplicity of colleges on political and economic liberalism. "Colleges and schools . . . break up and diffuse among the people that monopoly of knowledge and mental power which despotic governments accumulate for purposes of arbitrary rule, and bring to the children of the humblest families of the nation a full and fair opportunity. . . . giving thus to the nation the select talents and powers of her entire population."[5] Similarly, many Americans adopted a view in which post-secondary education was seen as nearly a right that would prompt both national development and individual social advancement.

Evangelical enthusiasm, fueled by the Second Great Awakening and frequently manifesting itself in denominational ambition, often proved a major factor in fostering a massive wave of college establishment in the nineteenth century, most notably in the Midwest. In the aftermath of that awakening, the populist Methodists and Baptists shed some of their suspicion of college education and surpassed Congregationalists and Presbyterians in the number of colleges established.[6] In ad-

4. Martin Trow, "American Higher Education: 'Exceptional' or just Different," in Byron E. Shafer, ed., *Is America Different? A New Look at American Exceptionalism* (Oxford: Clarendon Press, 1991), p. 139.

5. Cited in Frederick Rudoloph, *The American College and University: A History* (New York: Alfred A. Knopf, 1962), p. 63.

6. Rudoloph, *The American College and University: A History*, p. 55. See also Na-

dition, localism contributed to the phenomenon as many small towns eagerly sought colleges, not only as means of advancement for local sons and, sometimes, daughters, but also as a means to advance the prestige and economy of the town.

Absalom Peters, a supporter of the college movement, noted in 1851 that "Our country is to be a land of colleges," and soon the statistics bore out his claim. By 1868 Illinois had twenty-one colleges; a year later, Iowa had thirteen.[7] By the 1870s, a period in which England with its 23 million people supported only four universities, the state of Ohio with its 3 million people boasted thirty-seven colleges. In a statement that has since been interpreted in various ways, the man who would later become the president of the University of Michigan highlighted how commonplace colleges had become in the United States: "We have cheapened education so as to place it within the reach of everyone."[8]

In stark contrast, Canada, like Great Britain and Europe, held to an elitist outlook that viewed higher education as the preserve of a relative few. Some denominational colleges were founded in the nineteenth century, but very few in comparison with the prodigious number just south of the border. In relatively populous and increasingly prosperous Ontario, for example, a significant hotbed of Methodist revivalism, Canadian Methodists struggled to maintain one small college they founded in 1841, compared to American Methodists who established thirty colleges in nineteen states between 1830 and 1860.[9]

Even in the twentieth century, when public financing increasingly became the norm, Canadian universities remained few in number and, to a large degree, a preserve of the elite. Many argued that Canada's more stratified society, in which the upper ranks of society were more closed than in the U.S., did not need a large number of institutions of higher education.[10] For example, for several decades into the twentieth century, the

---

than O. Hatch, *The Democratization of American Christianity* (New Haven & London: Yale University Press, 1989), pp. 193-209; William C. Ringenberg, "The Old-Time College, 1800-1865," in *Making Higher Education Christian: The History and Mission of Evangelical Colleges in America*, ed. Joel A. Carpenter and Kenneth W. Shipps (Grand Rapids: Christian University Press, 1987), pp. 77-97.

7. Rudolph, *The American College and University: A History*, pp. 47-48 and 55.

8. Rudolph, *The American College and University: A History*, p. 63.

9. Hatch, *The Democratization*, p. 205.

10. Seymour Martin Lipset notes, for example, that as late as the mid-1970s far

rapidly growing province of British Columbia had no degree-granting institution. In fact, opposition to a proposed provincial university was voiced in the provincial legislature by socialists who believed it "would turn out fops not men, and would serve only the top 10 per cent of the population." Similar opposition was voiced by the Trades and Labour Council, which labeled a university as a "class institution."[11] As was the case in Great Britain and Europe, a massive expansion of public universities did not take place in Canada until the 1960s.

Meanwhile, the pattern in the U.S. became self-reinforcing. The very number of institutions established, combined with the widespread acceptance of market forces in various spheres of endeavor, including education, created a situation in which colleges competed for students, an almost unimaginable scenario in Canada before the 1990s. Instead, in Canada as in Europe, the reverse situation, in which students competed for relatively scarce spaces, was the norm. But in the U.S., in order to ensure survival, colleges needed to actively work to create loyalty among students and alumni to ensure their survival. Martin Trow argues that the competitive situation in the U.S. had some beneficial effects, especially for private institutions:

> American colleges and universities compete actively for students, for financial support, and for prestige. And these kinds of competition make them responsive to a wide range of trends and forces in American life, some of them economic and demographic, others intellectual. As a result, American higher education exhibits an enormously dynamic character, both as a system and in its component institutions. We see this in many ways, among them the ability of many private American colleges to survive in circumstances that many observers have predicted would lead to their closure.[12]

Not surprisingly, rates of participation bear out the differing views of higher education. In 1985, even after several decades of a massive expan-

more top Canadian executives were from upper-class origins (61 percent) than in the U.S. (36 percent). *Continental Divide: The Values and Institutions of the United States and Canada* (New York & London: Routledge, 1990), pp. 162-63.

11. R. Cole Harris, "Locating the University of British Columbia" *BC Studies* 32 (Winter 1976-77): 122.

12. Trow, "American Higher Education," p. 167.

sion of Canadian universities, only 14.5 percent of 18 to 24-year-olds in Canada were enrolled in college or university, two-thirds the American rate of 22 percent.[13] A 1997 cross-border survey in adjacent areas of British Columbia and Washington state revealed that 62 percent of the U.S. families expected their high school age children to attend college; only 43 percent of the Canadian families had similar expectations. In order to meet those expectations, more U.S. families were saving for their child's higher education than were their counterparts across the border.[14]

American participation rates are also very high when compared to other developed nations. At 5.14 percent of the total population in the mid-1980s, university and polytechnic enrollment in the U.S. was far higher than that in most other western nations. Rates elsewhere ranged from one-third to just over one-half the American rate. The United Kingdom's was the lowest at 1.79 percent, Japan's next at 2 percent, West Germany's at 2.54 percent, and the Netherlands, 2.7 percent.[15] Canada's rate, at just over 3 percent, was still closer to the average of the other nations than to the high U.S. figures.[16]

A related and contributing factor to the lower rates of post-secondary participation lies in the different role that secondary education plays in Canada. The upper levels of high school have traditionally been quite rigorous academically, and graduation generally was not expected of the majority of students. Indeed, completion of high school has been much less common in Canada than in the U.S. throughout the past half-century. Until World War II, high schools were not geographically or intellectually accessible to all Canadians, and only about 15 percent of students graduated. That proportion did not rise to 25 percent until several years after the war and did not reach 50 percent until 1960.[17] As late as the mid-1970s, more than a third of Canadians completed less than twelve years of school and,

13. Lipset, *Continental Divide*, p. 160.

14. CV Marketing Research, "Trinity Western University: Educational Needs Canadian Study," Abbotsford, BC, March 1997.

15. James Beckford, "Great Britain: Voluntarism and Sectional Interests," in *Between States and Markets: The Voluntary Sector in Comparative Perspective*, ed. Robert Wuthnow (Princeton: Princeton University Press, 1991), p. 33.

16. Extrapolated from Statistics Canada figures.

17. G. Ronald Neufeld and Allen Steven, *Stay in School Initiatives: A Summary of Research on School Dropouts and Implications for Special Education* (Kingston, ON: The Canadian Council for Exceptional Children, 1992), p. 2.

because of high entry standards, a relatively small proportion of the 64.5 percent who graduated were eligible for college or university. In contrast, proportionately 2.5 times that number in the United States both completed high school and were eligible for entrance to college.[18]

One consequence of the elitist environment and relative lack of high school completion and eligibility for college is that Canadians have more often tended to seek post-secondary "training" rather than liberal arts education. This was also true among evangelicals who sought inexpensive, practical Bible school training, which did not usually require high school graduation for admittance, at least until the 1960s and 1970s.[19] In Western Canada, in particular, where high schools were not widespread until the 1940s but where western Canadian evangelicals felt a great need for home and foreign mission workers, the world's proportionately strongest concentration of Bible schools developed.[20] While in the U.S. an increasingly large majority of the students in evangelical higher educational institutions enrolled in liberal arts colleges, as late as the mid-1990s enrollment in the practically oriented Bible colleges in Canada stood at about 7,000 — triple the enrollment in evangelical liberal arts colleges and universities.[21]

Perception of Private vs. Public institutions

Not only is there greater general demand for college and university education in the United States than in Canada, the private sector is a substantial and highly regarded component of the college scene. This must be seen as one very important manifestation of the overarching importance of the voluntary sector in the United States. Robert Wuthnow observes that "What is

18. Richard A. Wanner, "Educational Inequality: Trends in Twentieth-Century Canada and the United States," *Comparative Social Research* 9 (1986): 53-55. Richard A. Wanner, cited in Lipset, *Continental Divide*, p. 15.

19. See Virginia Brereton, *Training God's Army: The American Bible School, 1880-1940* (Bloomington: Indiana University Press, 1990). It is interesting to note that suspicions among Western Canadian Baptists of the Baptist Union's liberal arts college, Brandon College, in Manitoba, during the 1920s were not only due to concerns over more liberal theology but also because it was not as effective as Bible schools in training 'workers' needed for Home Missions in Western Canada.

20. Henry H. Budd, "The Financial Future of Canadian Bible Colleges" (Ph.D. diss., University of Oregon, 1980).

21. *Faith Today,* Jan./Feb. 1992, pp. 32-49.

perhaps as distinctive about the United States as the actual services provided by the voluntary sector is the *ideology* that surrounds voluntarism in American society. . . . we believe strongly that voluntarism is the best way of doing things. We cherish the traditions and values it stands for. . . . we view it as an alternative to the other main sectors of our society."[22]

The U.S. appears to be unique in the western world in that privately controlled and funded liberal arts colleges and universities comprise a very significant, and widely accepted, component of the higher education scene. Indeed, Americans very often view private institutions as providing credible, quality education in contrast to massive public institutions which are sometimes seen as compromising quality. Americans often take for granted that many of the most prestigious institutions in the nation, including Princeton, Harvard, Yale, and Stanford are, and should be, privately controlled and funded. Further, a considerable measure of recognition and respectability is provided for the hundreds of less well-known colleges by regional accreditation bodies. In 1976 President Gerald Ford underscored the great respect accorded private colleges when he proclaimed on a visit to Wheaton College that the institution ". . . is a fine example of privately supported institutions that have made America great."[23]

American private liberal arts colleges and universities enroll 21 percent of the total post-secondary enrollment in the U.S. (2,933,000 of 13,673,000) and private colleges outnumber public institutions by a narrow margin (1,656 to 1,563 in 1991). In terms of expenditures the role of private colleges is even more significant than the enrollment figures would indicate. In 1991 private institutions controlled one-third of the total spent for higher education in the nation, $53 billion of the total of $155 billion.[24]

In Canada, the opposite is generally true. No long-established university is privately controlled and funded. For more than a century the trend has been towards government funding and control of higher education. The process of secularizing church-related colleges, which almost always in-

22. Robert Wuthnow, "Tocqueville's Question Reconsidered," in Wuthnow, ed., *Between States and Markets,* p. 300.

23. Cited in Paul M. Bechtel, *Wheaton College: A Heritage Remembered, 1860-1984* (Wheaton: Harold Shaw, 1984), p. 323. Obviously, such visits by presidents and presidential candidates also signify the importance attached to the evangelical vote and also Wheaton's perceived central role in U.S. evangelicalism.

24. Council for Aid to Education, *Voluntary Support of Education,* 1991, vol. 1 (New York: Council for Aid to Education, Washington, 1991).

volved either becoming a public institution or moving under the educational jurisdiction of a public institution, began late in the nineteenth century, made great headway by the 1920s, and was virtually complete by the 1950s and 1960s.[25] Some colleges that affiliated with provincial universities remained privately controlled but, in exchange for public funding, surrendered much of their autonomy and degree-granting authority.[26] That historical process in Canada has been accompanied by the widespread growth of the assumption that higher education is primarily and fundamentally a responsibility of the provincial governments. Legitimacy and credibility in the realm of higher education, according to this assumption, comes from being a public institution, or at least through affiliation with one. Private degree-granting institutions thus must continuously seek to reassure the public and, especially prospective students and their parents eyeing substantially higher tuition, that they indeed can offer legitimate and credible degrees.

In recent decades, attempts to establish and gain recognition for new private liberal arts colleges similar to those in the U.S. frequently engendered suspicion within the general public and opposition from public institutions and bodies with jurisdictional control. Adding to the difficulty, no accreditation body similar to the regional accrediting bodies in the United States exists in Canada to lend recognition and respectability to newly established private institutions. Instead, institutions seeking legitimacy must undertake the slow and difficult processes of gaining provincial government charters granting the right to award degrees and being admitted into membership in the Association of Universities and Colleges of Canada (AUCC). A virtual government monopoly of higher education in most provinces combined with a considerable suspicion of institutions applying religious tests in the selection and retention of faculty have made it extraordinarily difficult for Canadian evangelical liberal arts institutions to gain a provincial charter and membership in the AUCC.

The relative advantages enjoyed by private institutions in the United States are also shared to a considerable degree by confessionally based

25. D. C. Masters, *Protestant Church Colleges in Canada* (Toronto: University of Toronto Press, 1966), and "Educating for the Kingdom? Church Related Colleges in English-Speaking Canada," Conference proceedings, St. Jerome's College and Conrad Grebel College, Waterloo, Ontario, 1990.

26. The variety of models is treated by John G. Stackhouse in "Respectfully Submitted for American Consideration: Canadian Options in Christian Higher Education," *Faculty Dialogue* 17 (Spring 1992): 52-71.

schools, including evangelical ones. In addition to the large numbers of evangelical students and the numbers of evangelical faculty that may be found in a range of public and private institutions in the United States, explicitly evangelical colleges form a reasonably substantial component of the private sector. The Coalition of Christian Colleges and Universities (CCCU), an evangelical organization, lists eighty-eight institutions in the United States with approximately 158,000 students. Thirteen liberal arts colleges for the Southern Baptist Convention (SBC) belong to the CCCU, but another thirty-six SBC institutions, enrolling 82,000 students, do not belong to the CCCU and are not included in its figures. Thus, a total of 240,000 students, or a little under 10 percent of the 2,933,000 enrolled in private U.S. colleges, are in evangelical institutions aligned with either the CCCU or the SBC.[27] The number of evangelical students and colleges is pushed even higher when it is noted that an additional number of Pentecostal, Church of Christ, and Seventh Day Adventist institutions are not aligned with the CCCU.

The evangelical institutions are, however, generally not as wealthy as many of their private counterparts. Operating budgets of the CCCU schools amounted to $2 billion in the 1997-98 academic year. Assuming they spent a similar amount proportionately, the non-CCCU member SBC schools budgets would amount to approximately $1 billion. The resultant total of $3 billion amounts to only about 6 percent of the total expenditures of all private colleges in the U.S.[28]

It could be argued that, given the large number of evangelical believers in the United States, these figures are not particularly impressive. Indeed, some analysts have stressed the fragility and vulnerability of many of the evangelical colleges in terms of enrollment and finances.[29] However, a cross-border comparison makes them appear far more impressive. In Canada, fewer than 3,000 students enroll in private, autonomous, degree-granting evangelical liberal arts colleges that belong to the AUCC, with only several thousand more enrolled in semi-autonomous schools.[30]

27. "CCCU at a Glance," "Enrollment Up at Baptist Colleges for Sixteenth Year," pp. 1-2.

28. Calculated from "CCCU at a Glance," "Enrollment Up at Baptist Colleges for Sixteenth Year," and Council for Aid to Education, *Voluntary Support of Education,* 1991.

29. For example, see Melissa Morris-Olson, *Survival Strategies for Christian Colleges and Universities* (Washington, DC: Coalition of Christian Colleges and Universities, 1996), pp. 5-8.

30. "Weighing 124 Options," *Faith Today,* Jan./Feb. 1992, pp. 34-49.

The comparatively significant presence of evangelical institutions of higher education in the United States owes much to the general factors already outlined; the larger role of liberal arts education in American society and the wider acceptance of voluntaristic principals in higher education. However, several other factors have augmented those wider forces and assisted in creating an environment that allowed for their growth and survival.

Confessionally based institutions of a variety of persuasions have been accommodated in the United States by means such as the "Limitations Clause" found in the "Statement of Principles on Academic Freedom and Tenure" adopted by the Association of American University Professors and the Association of American Colleges. Adopted in 1940, this clause represented a compromise solution to tensions perceived to exist between the principle of Academic Freedom and accountability to a religious community. It accomplished this by allowing termination over religious issues that were made clear at the time academic appointments were made.[31] In contrast, north of the border, the AUCC only very reluctantly and after much debate over the issue of academic freedom, accepted into membership in the 1980s and 1990s several confessionally based conservative Protestant institutions. Even then, some faculty members and administrators in public universities continued the battle against institutions committed to a religious stance and fought to prevent the AUCC's adoption of a statement on academic freedom similar to the American "Limitations Clause."[32]

In addition, their private status and religious orientation have not prevented American evangelical colleges from receiving many significant public privileges and powers such as the training of teachers for public school districts. For example, Fresno Pacific University, a very new and relatively small liberal arts college owned by the Mennonite Brethren, successfully made the transition from its status as a Bible institute to that of a liberal arts college, largely as a result of gaining accreditation for a profes-

31. See George M. Marsden, "The Ambiguities of Academic Freedom," *Church History* 62 (June 1993): 221-36.
32. See Tom Sinclair-Faulkner, "We weren't sure they want Academic Freedom . . . ," paper presented to the Canadian Society for the Study of Religion, Calgary, June 1994, and "*Quid Athenae Hierosolymis:* The new relationship between evangelical Protestant churches and the university system," paper presented to the Canadian Society for the Study of Religion, St. Catherines, Ontario, 1996.

sional development program for teachers in 1970. That program and a subsequent graduate program in education and a professional development program for practicing teachers made Fresno Pacific the leading institution for the training of teachers in California's populous Central Valley, preparing more teachers than does the large nearby state university.[33]

Again in contrast, until June 1998, Canada's largest province, Ontario, denied even the granting of arts and science degrees by private institutions. Until that date public institutions held a total monopoly of arts and science degree-granting privileges. Thus, despite offering a solid, reputable liberal arts program for nearly two decades, the Christian Reformed-related Redeemer College near Hamilton was restricted to offering a Bachelor of Christian Studies. Somewhat similarly, concerns over the biblically oriented standards of behavior required by Trinity Western University caused the British Columbia College of Teachers in 1996 to disregard the recommendations of its own credentials committee and deny certification of the university's professional program for the training of teachers.

Federal Government Financial Aid Policies

In both nations, federal financial aid for higher education became a significant factor beginning in the 1960s, serving as a major contributor to the growth of university and college enrollments. However, the nature of that aid has significantly affected the shape of higher education. In the U.S., the majority of federal aid has been geared primarily towards individual students who are able to apply it toward costs at the institution of their choice, public or private. Indeed, by the late 1960s such funds from federal sources amounted to approximately 20 percent of the current income of private colleges and universities in the U.S., even higher, by several percentage points, than that received by public institutions.[34] Further, according to a study by Stephen Monsma, religiously based colleges reported that a slightly higher proportion of their budgets came from public sources than

33. Arthur Wiebe, former president, Fresno Pacific College (now University), interview by author, Fresno, California, 20 May 1997.

34. Chester E. Finn, Jr., *Scholars, Dollars, and Bureaucrats* (Washington, DC: The Brookings Institute, 1978), p. 15.

was the case with their secular, private counterparts. Even more surprising to some observers, conservative Protestant colleges reported somewhat higher proportions of public funding than did their mainline Protestant and Catholic counterparts.[35] While the receipt of government funds has proved problematic and controversial on occasion,[36] the vast majority (81 percent) of the evangelical schools responding to Monsma's survey reported no government pressures or disputes whatsoever as a result of receiving them. In fact, the largest number of reported problems had nothing to do with student aid funds but rather with funds provided as loans for building construction.[37] The net effect of the federal financial aid policy is to provide many more U.S. students with the ability to pay the much higher tuition rates for private colleges than would otherwise be the case. Because much of the aid is need-based and because tuition costs are factored into calculations of levels of need, private colleges benefit proportionately more than do public institutions.

In Canada, however, most federal funds to support higher education do not go directly to students but are transferred to provincial governments which, in turn, provide grants to public institutions.[38] The net effect of this type of federal aid has been to keep Canadian public university tuition rates relatively low. Because a small proportion of the aid is directed to the student, private institutions find it difficult to charge students the high tuition rates necessary for them to survive.

The U.S. federal government granted students a total of just over $6.7 billion in 1989-90, a figure nearly thirty times greater than the $.25 billion granted by the Canadian federal government in the same year.[39] Overall, the Canadian federal government was proportionately much more sup-

35. Stephen V. Monsma, *When Sacred & Secular Mix: Religious Nonprofit Organizations and Public Money* (Lanham, MD: Rowman & Littlefield, 1996), pp. 69-73.

36. For example, see George Roche, *The Fall of the Ivory Tower: Government Funding, Corruption, and the Bankrupting of American Higher Education* (Washington, DC: Regnery, 1994).

37. Roche, *The Fall of the Ivory Tower,* pp. 81-87.

38. In some provinces, private colleges affiliated with public universities receive some of the public funds and in Alberta, several semi-autonomous private colleges receive government funds for operating expenses. The King's University College, for example, reported in 1997 that it received 23 percent of its budget from government sources.

39. Jaimie P. Merisotis, ed., *The Changing Dimensions of Student Aid,* New Directions for Higher Education, No. 74 (Summer 1991), Table 1, p. 7; Statistics Canada, *Financial Statistics of Education, 1989-90,* Table 17.

portive of higher education, but the vast majority of the funds were transferred to provincial governments ($2.2 billion) for the support of public institutions of higher education, rather than to individual students.[40] Only in 1998 did the federal government announce a significant new student aid program, the Millennium Fund, which was to bear greater similarities to U.S. federal aid programs in that it was designed to provide significant aid to lower-income students. Very significantly, students enrolled in AUCC-member private liberal arts institutions were recipients of the first payments, issued early in 2000.

Charitable Giving and Higher Education

While "commercial" income, in the form of tuition and other fees, is the most important source of income for higher education, significant donation income almost always has proven necessary for survival and growth. In this regard, once again, the situation of American evangelical colleges appears to be favored by factors prevalent in the larger society as well as by the size of the evangelical constituency.

Seymour Lipset notes regarding the United States, "the country's people, the most antistatist in the developed world, continue to be the most generous on a personal basis." Over the past four decades American charitable donations have averaged approximately 2 percent of personal income; the 1987 total of $94 billion amounted to 2.09 percent of GNP. In Canada, charitable donations have been declining in constant dollars and by the late 1980s amounted to only 0.8 percent of personal income. Canadian evangelicals appear to be more generous than other Canadians, reporting that they gave 6.2 percent, on average, of their income to churches and other religious organizations. However, they still lagged behind their American evangelical counterparts, who reported giving 7.2 percent of their income to similar causes.[41] Just as significant, Canadian Protestants in the higher income brackets reported that they donated somewhat lower proportions of their income than did those in the lower brackets, while

40. Statistics Canada, *Financial Statistics of Education, 1989-90*, Table 5.
41. Dean R. Hoge and Mark A. Noll, "Levels of Contributions and Attitudes Toward Money Among Evangelicals and Non-Evangelicals in Canada the United States," Table 6, p. 365 in this volume.

American Protestants in the higher brackets reported a slightly higher proportion of income donated.[42]

In the United States, higher education ranked second after churches and other explicitly religious enterprises, and ahead of health and welfare agencies, as a major beneficiary of Americans' charitable largesse. Significantly, although they gave the largest sums to their churches, Americans identified educational institutions as having the greatest need of financial donations.[43] They donated $11.2 billion to colleges and universities in 1993, up from $8.2 billion five years previously. Private institutions received nearly two-thirds of the total donated.[44] Voluntary support totaled approximately 12 percent of annual institutional expenditures in 1990-91.[45] Evangelical institutions relied upon donations to a somewhat greater degree, at least in the 1980s. In 1987, an average of 17 percent of CCCU member institutional budgets were met by donation; by 1994 that figure had fallen to 12 percent.[46]

However, charitable giving to higher education in Canada only began to become a significant issue in the 1990s, as institutions responded to government downsizing. Typically, Canadians pay income tax at rates significantly higher than those in the United States and thus feel that they have already "contributed" to higher education and consequently are less moved by appeals for voluntary contributions.[47]

The corporate sector is far more active in charitable giving in the U.S. than in Canada. Donations of all types as a proportion of pre-tax income rose from double that in Canada in the 1970s to three times by the mid-1980s. By 1993, American corporate support of higher education had risen to $2.5 billion and represented 21 percent of total donations received. Measured in constant dollars, corporate support nearly tripled between the

42. Hoge and Noll, "Levels of Contributions," Table 8, p. 369.

43. George Barna, The Mind of the Donor (Glendale, CA: Barna Research Group, 1994), pp. 52-53.

44. Council for Aid to Education, Voluntary Support of Education, 1993: National Trends (New York: Council for Aid to Education; Washington, 1993).

45. Council for Aid to Education, Voluntary Support of Education, 1991, vol. 1.

46. Willmer, "Christian Higher Education Advancement in Overview," Table 1-12, p. 10.

47. Income tax rates vary between provinces, but the highest rates of between 40 and 50 percent begin at income levels of about $60,000; highest rates in the United States begin at approximately $200,000.

early 1960s and the early 1990s.[48] While some corporate donors do not make a practice of supporting evangelical colleges because they view them as too "sectarian," many corporate donors accept the validity of religiously based private colleges and contribute to a range of colleges, including confessionally based institutions.

In the state of Iowa, for example, thirty private colleges and universities, many religiously affiliated, have organized a successful fund-raising consortium that mounts one unified, statewide campaign to the state's corporate community. The proceeds are distributed proportionately among the member institutions, regardless of religious orientation. Similar consortiums, operating what are sometimes known as "independent college funds," exist in many states.[49]

A further type of business support arises from the "college town" phenomenon so frequently found in the United States due to the pattern of nineteenth-century college establishment. The small-town colleges often develop patterns of very close, mutually supportive relationships with the town's business community. Recognizing the college's contribution to the economic, social, cultural, and athletic life of the town, its business people, regardless of their own religious orientation, frequently can be counted on to support the college financially.[50]

More significant as donors, however, are alumni. American colleges, many with a relatively long history and a tradition of inculcating loyalty among students, have been unusually successful in creating supportive alumni. By the 1980s alumni had become the single most significant source of donations for U.S. higher education in general, providing 27 percent of all donations received. For private liberal arts institutions the proportion from alumni rises to 43 percent, over five times the proportion from corporations and nearly three times that from foundations.[51] Among CCCU in-

---

48. Task Force on Funding Higher Education, *From Patrons to Partners, Corporate Support for Universities* (Montreal: Corporate Higher Education Forum, 1987).

49. Gerry Ebbers, interview by author, Langley, British Columbia, 7 May 1997. Mr. Ebbers served as Director of Development for Dordt College, Sioux Centre, Iowa, from 1992 to 1996. Ron Kuehl, interview by author, Langley, British Columbia, 16 May 1997. Mr. Kuehl served as Director of Development at Tabor College, Hillsboro, Kansas, from 1982 to 1991.

50. Ebbers, interview, 7 May 1997; Kuehl, interview, 16 May 1997.

51. Council for Aid to Education, *Voluntary Support of Education; National Trends*, 1993.

stitutions, many of them more recently founded, alumni play a somewhat less significant role. In 1989, CCCU alumni support stood at 16 percent of donations, behind "other individuals" (21 percent) and "churches" (20 percent).[52] The alumni proportion appears to be growing, however, as increasing numbers of evangelical colleges reach the stage of development at which they have large numbers of financially secure alumni. For example, Wheaton College, in 1996-97, received $7,090,000 from 8,900 (38 percent) of its 29,000 "Alumni of record," representing 35 percent of the just over $20,000,000 received in donations for the year.[53]

In contrast, alumni play a relatively small role in supporting Canadian evangelical liberal arts colleges, largely because they have such a short history that few alumni have entered their peak earning years or have even paid off their student loans. Older Bible colleges have a larger number of alumni but their average donations are relatively small because the strong ministry orientation of those schools resulted in fewer of their graduates going into business or the more lucrative professions.

A further hurdle, however, is the very different view of financing higher education. A recent Canadian study on funding universities graphically highlights the different role alumni are expected to play in Canada, compared with the United States. "In the United States, many colleges derive a substantial share of their income from the contributions of successful alumni. In Canada, voluntary contributions are not nearly as important. Instead, we have a system in which alumni contributions are compulsory — they are collected through the tax system."[54]

Other U.S. government policies also encourage charitable support of the voluntary sector. Tax regulations have long favored planned giving from estates to charitable organizations because significant donations are able to nearly eliminate high estate taxes. Canadian tax laws did not begin to encourage large estate gifts to charity until 1997.

All these factors cause many directors of development in Canadian institutions to cast wistful looks across the border. Larry Willard, vice president for advancement at Tyndale College and Seminary (formerly Ontario

52. Adam J. Morris, "Development through the Eyes of Faith," in Willmer, ed., *Advancing Christian Higher Education*, Table 3-13, p. 68.
53. *Wheaton* 1, no. 1 (Winter 1998): 9-11.
54. Robert Allen, "University education: A good money-back guarantee," *Vancouver Sun*, 27 Oct. 1998; Robert Allen, *Paid in Full: Who Pays for University Education?* (Canadian Centre for Policy Alternatives, 1998), p. 22.

Bible College and Theological Seminary), a venerable institution only recently rescued from the brink of bankruptcy, voiced the concern of many in a similar position when he declared "Americans understand the necessity of Christian institutions being properly sponsored, so that a college doesn't have to go clawing and begging for funds."[55]

Further compounding the differences that favor American evangelical colleges are raw demographic factors. As a proportion of total population American evangelicals outnumber Canadian evangelicals by between two and three times, depending on what definition is used.[56] Because Canada's total population is only one-tenth that of the U.S., the evangelical population thus is a tiny fraction (between 3 and 5 percent) of its American counterpart. Consequently, the critical mass necessary to support a costly enterprise such as a liberal arts college, in terms of students and donations, is often missing.

In addition, those who have worked in college development departments on both sides of the border frequently refer to the lack of "old money" among Canadian evangelicals compared to that found in the U.S. Because a relatively very high proportion of the late nineteenth- and early twentieth-century Canadian evangelical constituency — including the wealthier families — came to identify with the liberal mainline of Protestantism, large sectors of late twentieth-century evangelicalism tends to lack established wealth. A very high percentage of Canadian evangelicals, especially in Western Canada, are recent immigrants from Europe (Mennonite or Reformed) or Asia. The development office of one of western Canada's larger institutions noted that all five of its top five donors were recent immigrants who had made their fortunes since the 1970s, and the largest since the mid-1980s.[57]

55. Cited in "Larger colleges pursue U.S. endowment model," *Christian Week*, Fall '98 Higher Education Supplement, 20 Oct. 1998, p. 7. Interestingly, no directors of development interviewed at Canadian institutions needed to be prodded to discuss differences between Canada and the United States. All quickly made observations similar to that made by Willard.

56. Mark A. Noll, "Religion in Canada and the United States," *Crux* 34 (Dec. 1998): 13-25, reporting on a 1996 cross-border poll by the Angus Reid Group.

57. Kuehl, interview, 16 May 1997.

ROBERT BURKINSHAW

Professionalism in Fund-raising

Under the leadership of L. E. Maxwell, Prairie Bible Institute (PBI), founded in 1922 and the largest evangelical institution in Canada for many decades, adopted an approach to fund-raising quite atypical of institutions of higher education. An organization passionately dedicated to training missionaries, it functioned much like a "faith" mission organization itself and adopted as its financial motto Hudson Taylor's saying "God's work, done in God's way, will never lack."[58] Until 1992 its faculty and staff were not paid a regular salary but instead received free housing and other services and a small cash allowance based not on position, but on family size. Many of the institution's needs and those of its faculty and staff were provided from its own farm, bakery, butcher shop, grocery and general store, carpenter and mechanical shops, central steam plant, and logging mill. Thus the need for financial donations was relatively low and the school focused more on promoting its missionary funds than its own financial needs. In fact, by 1972 PBI had distributed a cumulative total of $3.5 million to various faith missions.[59] According to a recent incumbent of the post, the president's responsibility was not to raise finances but to function as the spiritual inspirer and challenger of staff and students.[60] Not until 1990 did the school deliberately and directly begin to solicit finances for its own needs.[61]

This "faith" missionary approach had an enormous impact on evangelical higher education in Canada. A number of other Canadian schools adopted the PBI model quite explicitly while others modified it to greater or lesser degrees. Invariably, however, the practical, ministry training function of evangelical higher education in Canada created a tendency for institutions to raise funds in a manner similar to that of missionary or parachurch organizations. The systematic, long-term approaches employed by staffs of professionals in colleges elsewhere were less in evidence than "missionary" style letters supplemented in recent years by urgent year-end appeals.

58. *With God on the Prairies* (Three Hills, AB: Prairie Bible Institute, c. 1966), pp. 25-27.

59. John G. Stackhouse, Jr., *Canadian Evangelicalism in the Twentieth Century: An Introduction to Its Character* (Toronto: University of Toronto, 1993), p. 21 n. 237.

60. Ted Rendall, PBI president, 1986-1992, interview by author, Three Hills, Alberta, 4 December 1997.

61. Larry McLanahan, V.P. of Finance, PBI, interview by author, Three Hills, Alberta, 5 December 1997.

Over two decades before the founding of PBI, Charles Blanchard, president of Wheaton College, adopted a very different model of fundraising. While concerned, like Maxwell, to train ministers and missionaries, he also argued that Wheaton's mission involved ". . . sending into the world . . . editors, statesmen, lawyers and physicians who are to be most influential in determining the course of society."[62] He challenged the school's constituency to invest in preparing such leaders. Utilizing language strikingly different from Maxwell's missionary terminology, he stated that "a great school is a business enterprise" which needed sufficient finances so that "teachers can be better housed, fed, and set to work when free from anxiety respecting their daily bread."[63] Accordingly, Blanchard systematically and indefatigably visited potential donors from the Midwest to the east coast and even developed contacts in Ontario.[64]

Among American evangelical liberal arts colleges, the "Blanchard" model appears to have been the most commonly followed. A measure of professionalism became evident; by the 1980s CCCU member institutions' development departments grew to include an average of twelve professional staff members, and a number of departments had twenty or more professional staff members.[65] American organizations dedicated to advancing higher education, including private, Christian colleges, have published a considerable volume of material. For example, the Carnegie Commission on Higher Education and the Council for the Advancement and Support of Education publish books such as *Advancing the Small College, Winning Strategies in Challenging Times for Advancing Small Colleges,* and *The Invisible Colleges.* They also hold professional conferences for people involved in development work. Among evangelicals, the Coalition of Christian Colleges and Universities also holds professional meetings to support the work of advancement staff in Christian colleges and has published guides such as *Friends, Funds and Freshmen: A Manager's Guide to Christian College Advancement* and *Advancing Christian Higher Education.*[66]

62. Bechtel, *Wheaton College*, p. 68.
63. Bechtel, *Wheaton College*, p. 69.
64. Bechtel, *Wheaton College*, p. 69.
65. Willmer, "Christian Higher Education Advancement in Overview," Table 1-15, p. 13.
66. Wesley K. Willmer, *Friends, Funds and Freshmen: A Manager's Guide to Christian College Advancement* (Washington, DC: Coalition of Christian Colleges and Universities,

In Canada, even though the missionary model is no longer explicitly followed even by PBI itself, virtually no professional literature on fund-raising exists, apart from several theses and dissertations written by Canadian Bible college administrators.[67] A vice president of development at Briercrest Bible College, Canada's largest Bible college in the 1990s, recently compared Canadian higher education fund-raising efforts with American practices: "Canadian Christian colleges are a little lax on bringing expertise into fund-raising. . . ."[68]

Endowment Funds

Adam J. Morris argues that building a strong endowment has become the top priority for CCCU schools' development offices. It is believed that significant endowments are necessary to provide a "hedge against future uncertainty" brought about by fluctuating gift incomes and potential changes in government scholarship assistance programs.[69] The pursuit of that priority appears to have had an impact on endowment growth. In the five-year period from 1989 to 1994, in which annual donations received by CCCU member schools for operations increased only very slightly to an average of $1.33 million, donations to endowments nearly tripled to an average of $0.92 million.[70] Endowments ranged in size from $0 to $120 million in 1994, with the average just under $10 million.[71] By 1997, that average had risen to $17.5 million, with the highest endowment, Wheaton's, reported at $212 million.[72] One other CCCU institution, Oral Roberts University, reported an endowment in 1995 of over $100 million. Messiah Col-

---

1990); Wesley K. Willmer, ed., *Advancing Christian Higher Education* (Washington, DC: Coalition for Christian Colleges & Universities, 1996).

67. For example, Carlin E. Weinhauer, "Church-Related College Environmental Relations" (Ph.D. diss., University of Alberta, Edmonton, 1979); Budd, "The Financial Future of Canadian Bible Colleges."

68. Roland Rackham cited in "Larger colleges pursue U.S. endowment model," *Christian Week*, p. 8.

69. Morris, "Development through the Eyes of Faith," p. 66.

70. Morris, "Development through the Eyes of Faith," Table 3-10, p. 65, and Table 3-12, p. 67.

71. Willmer, "Christian Higher Education Advancement in Overview," Table 1-6, p. 6.

72. "CCCU at a Glance."

lege, College of the Ozarks, and Abilene Christian University all reported endowments over $50 million in 1995.[73] While significant in their own right, these figures are not particularly impressive when it is noted that in 1995, twelve U.S. institutions reported endowments of over $1 billion and 128 reported endowments over $100 million.[74]

Endowments have not always and everywhere been a top priority of evangelical institutions. Hoge et al. note that "Historically, endowments were commonly rejected by evangelical churches as theologically indefensible. Why store up wealth when there are sinners to be saved and hungry people to be fed now?"[75] Those holding eschatological views stressing the imminent return of Christ felt especially uncomfortable with the concept of piling up endowments and even any kind of "reserve fund," because any money not used in the present might never be put to use for Christ's cause.[76] In addition, the same line of reasoning that discouraged many evangelical institutions from incurring debt has also been used to discourage the accumulation of endowments. Both debts and endowments not only encouraged putting one's trust elsewhere than in the Lord but also violated the view that "Each generation needs to pay its own bills."[77] Finally, some were wary of endowments because it was feared they would encourage a lack of accountability to the supporting constituency.[78]

Not all evangelicals agreed, however, that endowments were undesirable. After all, strong biblical precedent existed for saving up during

73. 1995 figures, as reported by Web CASPAR, were Oral Roberts, $139 million, Messiah, $74 million, College of the Ozarks, $61 million, Abilene Christian, $57 million, Goshen, $44 million, Oklahoma Baptist, $24 million, Calvin, $23 million. According to the "Wheaton College Report of Investments, Fiscal Year 1997," by 30 June 1997, Wheaton was reporting the market value of its "investment portfolio" at $250 million.

74. Web CASPAR 1995.

75. Dean Hoge, Patrick McNamara, and Charles Zech, *Plain Talk about Churches and Money* (Bethesda, MD: The Alban Institute, 1997), p. 106.

76. PBI's practice of holding some reserve funds was somewhat controversial among its generally dispensationalist constituency in the 1950s. Rick Downs, General Education Superintendent, PBI, interview by author, Three Hills, Alberta, 4 December 1997.

77. McLanahan, interview, 5 December 1997; Hoge et al., *Plain Talk about Churches and Money*, p. 114.

78. Mark Dillon, V.P. for Advancement, Wheaton College, interview by author, Wheaton, Illinois, 24 February 1998.

"seven fat years" to tide one over during "seven lean years."[79] Charles Blanchard justified the accumulation of endowments for Wheaton College in business terms, arguing that no merchant wishes to operate "depending upon today's income for today's outgo."[80] By the end of the nineteenth century, Wheaton's endowment stood at $50,000, sufficient to endow three chairs among a faculty of ten. In 1898 the trustees set a goal of increasing it by $100,000.[81]

One suspects, however, that as important as theological arguments regarding endowments were to some people, practical realities, as much as any other factor, influenced their size and existence. For years, too many evangelical colleges simply faced too many urgent, immediate demands in the form of operational expenses, campus expansion, student assistance and, frequently, debt, and thus were in no position to actively pursue the accumulation of endowment funds. Usually only the more financially stable colleges could afford to divert time and money from immediate needs to future needs. Most CCCU institutions are relatively less well established and, as recently as 1970, fewer than one-quarter of the colleges currently in the CCCU had endowments over $1 million. Of those, only the College of the Ozarks, at $38 million, and Wheaton, at nearly $10 million, were particularly large.[82]

No Canadian evangelical schools, whether Bible Colleges or Liberal Arts institutions, possess significant endowment funds. Rather, debt for capital and sometimes even for operations has posed severe problems for numerous colleges. Canadian evangelical liberal arts institutions in particular are relatively young and are perhaps at similar stages of development, in terms of endowment funds, to that of large numbers of CCCU institutions approximately a quarter century ago.[83]

---

79. Genesis 41; Hoge, *Plain Talk about Churches and Money*, p. 110.
80. Cited in Bechtel, *Wheaton College*, p. 69.
81. Bechtel, *Wheaton College*, pp. 68-69.
82. Web CASPAR 1970.
83. In a surprising development, in light of its past financial policies, PBI is rapidly building one of the stronger endowment funds among evangelical institutions in Canada. The relatively large number of elderly people in its aging constituency have provided it with nearly $3 million in investment funds. McLanahan interview and PBI financial reports.

Conclusion

While no one would deny that Christian institutions of higher education need far more than finances to be successful, higher education is nevertheless an enormously costly enterprise. Pessimists might note that American evangelical colleges are not particularly large and impressive, have not always been successful in meeting their financial needs, and have not always survived. This study highlights, however, that in the United States evangelical colleges operate in an environment that is, comparatively speaking, conducive to achieving financial stability through tuition and fees, donations, and endowment income. A relatively widespread high regard in American culture for liberal arts education, combined with considerable respect and privileges accorded private and confessionally based institutions, has made it possible to attract relatively large numbers of tuition-paying students. Numerous government programs and regulations not only further enhance students' abilities to pay high tuition rates and fees but also reinforce patterns of significant voluntary contributions to higher education. A number of increasingly well-established evangelical institutions, with growing numbers of successful and loyal alumni and other supporters, have been able to accumulate significant endowments, further ensuring financial stability.

A far more pessimistic picture has been painted here of the ability of Canadian evangelical institutions, especially liberal arts colleges and universities, to raise the necessary finances. At every point of comparison, the Canadian evangelical institutions find themselves at a disadvantage with their American counterparts. It has also been noted at various points, however, that the Canadian context has been changing. Since the 1960s the demand for higher education has been growing, and during the 1990s financially pressed governments have granted some additional privileges to the private sector. It remains to be seen whether such changes will lead to something similar to the more open system of higher education prevailing in the United States. It also remains to be seen if Canadian evangelical institutions will be able to respond successfully to the changes taking place and begin to gain the measure of financial stability necessary to accomplishing their mission.

CHAPTER II

Technological Changes and Monetary Advantages: The Growth of Evangelical Funding, 1945 to the Present

BARRY GARDNER

Tell the sons of Israel to raise a contribution for Me; from every man whose heart moves him you shall raise My contribution. And this is the contribution which you are to raise from them: gold, silver, and bronze.

EXODUS 25:2-3 (NASB)

In examining the history of how contemporary evangelical organizations are financed, there are three elements that provide the financial underpinning of religious nonprofits: earning the money, asking for the money, or letting God ask for the money. Each organization chooses its own — frequently unique — mix of these techniques. Interestingly, the particular mix chosen by an organization is sometimes viewed and passionately defended almost as a statement of religious virtue rather than being seen as a preference of style. Is there only one biblical model of Christian fund-raising? Evangelicals disagree.

This is a revised version of a response originally given at the ISAE conference from which this volume derives. Although it is informal, the editors felt it offered such insights into the mechanics of contemporary evangelical fund-raising that it should be included in this collection of research essays.

Other chapters presented in this book demonstrate the decisions that led one ministry or another to choose their "financing mix." Interestingly, the China Inland Mission's proclaimed foundation on faith did not preclude preoccupation with money. Rather, to read Alvyn Austin's chapter on that mission, funding was a constant concern for some years. Perhaps faith and worry are not so mutually exclusive as I had once supposed. Michael Hamilton's chapter presents abundant statistics that demonstrate remarkable growth for evangelical nonprofit organizations during this fifty-year period. Part of this increase reflects growth in the nonprofit sector while still other parts reflect a shift in evangelicals' giving to evangelical ministries instead of other nonprofit organizations. In this chapter I am going to try to explain how and why evangelical funding grew.

Why Funding Grew

Demography

The first and most potent explanation among evangelicals would be that God has provided the resources, in a manner, amount, and timing known only to Him. This is, of course, the only explanation complete unto itself, or as mathematicians say, both necessary and sufficient. But beyond that, other worldly changes have worked to give special impetus to this time in the growth of the church.

Demographic changes were important. To start with the obvious, the money available to evangelical causes grew as the number of evangelicals grew. Hamilton cites sources to document that the percentage of non-Catholic Christian church attenders who identified themselves as evangelical changed from ⅓ in 1945 to ½ in 1985. The exact proportion or timing of the change is not nearly as important as its direction. But in addition to growing in fractional terms, the population of the United States itself was growing.

To a person with my background in finance, the parallel for recent evangelicals would be somewhat like that of today's personal computer companies — it is like a business growing in market share at the same time the overall market is growing. So the growth in funding can be partly explained by the increase in the percentage of the population identified as evangelical in a country that itself has an expanding population. But there's more. All this is multiplied by the higher fraction of income that is given by now-converted evangelicals, as documented by Dean Hoge and Mark Noll's chapter. But what I think is the most interesting part of the growth of evangelical organizations is how the distribution of money has shifted from denominations to independent organizations, and from a more concentrated focus on preaching the gospel to a broader emphasis on working out the gospel.

Postwar psychology was also important. World War II exposed millions of returning GI's to a world overseas and so had put a decisive end to the isolationism of the 1930s. People in far-away places were neither unimportant nor unreachable. They mattered to God, and Christians could and should preach Christ to them. Living overseas became more imaginable for a host of prospective missionaries. Mission Aviation Fellowship, for example, developed as a direct result of the desire of ex-fliers to use their wartime skills. Far Eastern Broadcasting Company was formed by ex-GI's returning to countries they'd seen during the war.

Technology

However, as important as those demographic and cultural changes have been, I am going to focus on the impact that technological innovation has made on the financing of American evangelicalism. Perhaps you recall the two PBS series by science popularizer James Burke, "Connections" and "The Day the Universe Changed." Similar to his thesis, I believe that technological changes affected the growth of evangelicalism and its ability to attract funding. In particular, I think that developments in communications technology, the widespread adoption of computers, the development of direct mail, and the expanded use of the telephone have had profound impact on evangelical organizations and their funding.

Technological Changes in Communications

Recall the state of mass communications at the end of World War II. Local newspapers and radio — more specifically, network radio — were the principal forms of national communication. Then, within a few short years, communication changed dramatically: the development of television; the growth of the big three television networks out of their radio antecedents; the onset of FM radio; the expansion of television to include independent and educational channels; the development of UHF-based broadcasts; the increasingly sophisticated nature of audio recording technologies; the origination and maturation of cable TV (otherwise known as 500 channels and still nothing on); the creation and refinement of video cassette recording; the lessened import of network broadcasting; the Internet — global, available twenty-four hours a day, customized to whatever you wish to learn about or monitor. The amount of communication available is growing, and at the same time it can cater more economically to narrower and narrower interests.

This change in the volume and focus of communications has been mirrored in how evangelicals addressed their audiences. Earlier evangelists such as Sam Jones, cited in the chapter by Charles Hambricke-Stowe, used newspapers as a crucial source of free publicity in the 1880s. In 1945, newspapers were still important. Billy Graham benefited at a key time when newspaper mogul William Randolph Hearst gave the famous order to "puff Graham" at the time of his Los Angeles campaign.

Evangelicals quickly adapted to the new communication media of television. Billy Graham, for example, was a progressive student of communications, moving to television as that medium came of age. As satellite technology matured, he pioneered remote location broadcasts, bringing the world's corners a little closer for Christians too.

Television brought a new immediacy with the needs and ministries around the world. If Vietnam was the first war brought into America's living rooms, that same technology made it possible to bring successful evangelism like Graham's "Hour of Decision" or the latest Crusade to all corners of America. It made it possible for Stan Mooneyham of World Vision to demonstrate the material needs of the world's children to America's Christians.

Individualization Triggered by Communications Technology

But here is the most significant implication of changing technology for independent or parachurch organizations: *Individual evangelicals started to be addressed directly without having to go through the intermediation of the lo-*

cal church. While this phenomenon had occurred before — as Alvyn Austin points out in his chapter on CIM, there was Spurgeon's mailed sermon circulation of 300,000 in the 1870s, and China Inland Mission's circulation of 20,000 in North America — it now became much easier to develop the eventually ubiquitous "mailing list" and speak to one's audience directly.

Fund-raising during this period became more and more attuned to the needs and interests of individual donors. Recently I interviewed some retired personnel from a major mission agency, and when asked what triggered this change, they instantly chorused, "Campus Crusade." You'll recall that Campus Crusade was founded in 1952, near the beginning of the period in question. Campus Crusade staffers were taught to obtain their funding from their circles of friends. While individual major donors have always been key funders of religious causes going back to Jesus' time (e.g., Joseph of Arimathea), the application was now broadened to givers at a lower dollar level. Whereas mediating institutions like denominations and churches had always been important before, they became less so after 1945.

This development did not go unnoticed by churches and elicited strong emotional responses. My interviewees described ministerial reactions to this development with phrases like, "going behind the pastor's backs" and "picking the pockets of the congregation." The words they chose communicated the emotion they felt during this shift, brought on by a new technology and methodological focus.

This development was matched by Christian radio. Parallel to network radio, there were only a relative handful of national Christian radio programs at the beginning of this era. Programs current at the time included Charles Fuller's "Old-Fashioned Revival Hour," "The Chapel of the Air," and "The Radio Bible Class." My interviewees reserved a special opprobrium for Ed Epps's "Back to the Bible Broadcast" from Lincoln, Nebraska, which they felt was particularly pushy in asking for donations that were apart from obligations to (and by inference, instead of) the local church. At the start of this period, agencies of all kinds communicated through bulletin stuffers, sent en masse to churches and distributed largely at the whim of the local pastor. But by the end of this period, agencies — both independent and denominational — could send their own publications directly to the homes of church members and other interested parties.

Technological Changes in Printing

To do this economically required another technological innovation, the computer. Because of the cost and scale of this contraption, changes brought by computer occurred at the middle or end of this period. Consider how the computer was adopted and used.

At the end of World War II, Thomas Watson, Sr., Chairman of IBM, rejected his executives' interest in developing computers because he thought the world market for such devices was limited to perhaps five such machines. Needless to say, he eventually came around to a new opinion. By the late 1950s and early 1960s, computers started to be installed in businesses as a way of automating routine clerical jobs such as billing customers and tracking inventory.

Because of the high cost of early computers, and perhaps in contrast to the modest cost of low-paid staff or free volunteers, religious agencies were perhaps a bit slower to find computers cost-effective solutions. But in Wheaton, Illinois, an agency called Christian Service Brigade had a good-sized computer whose services were sold to a number of other local agencies, thus enabling smaller groups to have access to the benefits of automated data processing. Typically, as in business, computers were introduced as accounting cost-reductions. But where computers had their greatest financial impact was in the efficient utilization of automating mailing labels.

Imagine the amount of manual labor involved in mailing out 300,000 copies of Spurgeon's weekly sermons. It must have been a Herculean task. But as machines were developed to automate mailing tasks, religious agencies of all sizes could now more easily perpetuate their direct contact with individual donors. In 1945, the machine used to automate the addressing of envelopes was the addressograph, really a small-scale, single-purpose printing press that used embossed metal plates to make a printed impression on an envelope. If the 1945 state-of-the-art mimeograph necessitated starting missionary letters "Dear brothers and sisters," the 1960s brought us letters with our names on them. Working off a paper tape, much like a player piano, it allowed a worker to manually insert the name at the top of the page. The electronics revolution started making innovations in this area in the 1970s. I was working in a religious agency in 1975 that bought — actually, perhaps because of the cost, leased — a device called an IBM memory typewriter. Its memory held fifty pages. One could do much more than simply type an address. By setting stopping points in a letter, the operator could insert names from a list, gift amounts, or call the donor by a nickname and then start the machine again on its automatic typing path. Multiple-page letters could be efficiently generated by cleverly combining the personalized first page with a mimeographed second sheet that utilized the same ubiquitous Courier type font.

All of you know that is no longer necessary. The mail merge feature of word processing software makes bulk personalized letters a matter of a few keystrokes. But as technology made "personalized" junk mail available to virtually all agencies, the number of pieces sent increased and the effectiveness of each mailing eventually dropped. Direct mail effectiveness peaked sometime around the mid-1980s and, though still effective, the net amount raised after costs of printing and postage has declined.

Technological Changes Improved Targeting of Appeals

But the key to effective direct mail fund-raising lies in yet another technological development brought by the computer age. That development is the donor database. Fund-raisers back to Dwight Moody — and probably the apostle Paul — knew that certain causes struck more resonance with particular donors. While early fund-raisers relied on handwritten notes to recall the interests of certain donors, the computer automated that data collection and retrieval. Contemporary donor database software has fields for recording birthdays, initial contacts with the organization, hobbies, and relationships to relatives and friends, all in addition to the more mundane information about what type of appeal triggered their gift and the size and regularity of their giving.

Now, if a mailing were sent that appealed to helping children or focused on one's ethnic country of origin, donors who previously responded to such appeals could be targeted. The end result is that practitioners of direct mail have struggled to maintain its overall effectiveness by raising its efficiency. For the more savvy students of the art, the sloppy shotgun method of the late 1970s and early 80s has been replaced by the rifle shot of the 90s.

Interestingly, the *Chronicle of Philanthropy* recently announced the dawn of a "new" effective fund-raising weapon: the handwritten personal letter. The philanthropic community has come full circle to where Dwight Moody left it, with the technique he called "begging letters." All donors, no matter the size of their gift, desire to feel important to the cause. Over the period 1945-95, it became easier to personalize appeals, to the point where only by receiving a handwritten letter can one be convinced of a truly personal appeal!

Technological Change Brought Appeals From a Broader Geographic Area

While national broadcasting on TV and radio brought us appeals from a wider geographic region, another fund-raising technique that came of age during this period was the telephone. Interestingly, while technological advances played a role, as the digital revolution was adapted to telephony, increasing use of telecommunications by charities was largely driven by a change in the legal environment.

As the country installed telephones during the 1920s and 30s, the federal government granted monopoly powers to American Telephone & Telegraph (AT&T), the large New York-based phone giant. Though each state had its own local Bell operating company, subject to state regulation, the national telephone giant controlled the interconnections of these firms and, thus, long distance communication. In a piece of social engineering intended to universalize telephone service, the federal government mandated that local rates be kept low through subsidies from much higher long distance rates.

Long distance calls were inevitably heralded by the cry, "It's ———, calling long distance!" This not only meant that the call was important; it meant that the recipient should hasten in order to minimize the relentless tick of the metering clock. In fact, many people developed an instinctive dread of long distance calls, which all too frequently signaled an accident or death, news of which was too urgent to wait for the mail.

While it was possible and affordable to use the telephone within cities, long distance remained a luxury good (even subject to "excise tax"). That situation changed, however, as the Justice Department eventually sued AT&T for abuse of its monopoly powers. In 1984, under court order, AT&T was broken up into seven smaller (though hardly small) companies, and other competitors like MCI and Sprint rapidly expanded the heretofore lucrative long distance market. Long distance rates plummeted. The end result of this was that calling donors long distance need not be restricted only to major donors, whose large gifts could easily be assumed to offset the cost of calling. Now, donors of more modest means could, too, be targeted.

Fund-raisers developed the "telethon," a system whereby entire rooms of people with telephones would dial lists of past or potential donors. In an attempt to standardize (and usually upgrade the quality) of the funding pitch, callers would read from pre-rehearsed scripts. Sophistication rapidly included the computer as well. The script could be on a computer terminal for the operator. Telemarketers could plug in the called party's response to generate logical branching replies carefully orchestrated to respond to virtually any answer from the potential donor. Computers started doing the dialing. Not only was the computer faster and more accurate, the computer could listen for a person to answer before switching the potential donor to a waiting telemarketer, thus avoiding the delays of awaiting rings, busy signals, and no answers.

Was This Technology Unique to Evangelicals? What Explained the Growth?

David Paul Nord of Indiana University, in critiquing this chapter, asked if this appropriation of technology was something unique to evangelicals. Surely the technology discussed was available to secular and religious charities alike. But, it did seem that evangelical funding grew at a rate greater than did secular charities. What could explain the differential growth rate between the two?

The reason I believe that evangelical organizations grew at their rapid rate was that they were racing to attain a position of parity with their larger, long-established secular counterparts. There are a number of conjectures I can make that could serve as the basis for future work on the part of academics. Consider the situation of the secular charity. Imagine the consequences on fund-raising effectiveness if the American Cancer Society had raised contributions by giving its literature and appeals through doctors of oncology. Pretend its brochures were sent in bundles to doctors who placed them in their waiting rooms or gave them to patients as they traipsed through. Imagine how handicapped the American Cancer Society would be if it had no information about its donors aside from that provided by the doctors.

Substitute the word "pastor" for "doctor" and "church" for "waiting room" and you'll see that this analogy is exactly how many nonprofits were funded through churches prior to the changes I've chronicled here. I believe it is reasonable to assume that indirect presentation of appeals is an impediment to fund-raising effectiveness. Compared with the alternative of going direct, I think it likely that indirect methods of approaching donors would yield lower per-capita giving from its prospective donor base (though this statement is a conjecture that would benefit from more rigorous examination and proof).

Secular nonprofits have nearly always been agencies that dealt directly with a mass donor base, whereas evangelical ones were usually handicapped in effectiveness by having to go through intermediaries. Evangelical agency growth rates could seem to accelerate vis-à-vis secular ones because this limitation in their fund-raising approach had been removed. One can also argue that evangelical organizations were belated in adopting technology. If automation in charitable funding follows the same pattern it does in business, its application is probably a function of scale. Large national charities like the Red Cross, the American Cancer Society, and the March of Dimes were economically able to utilize expensive computer technology earlier than smaller organizations.

Increasing Appeals Brought Other Types of Costs

I argue, however, that many of these changes in fund-raising technology have been implemented in ways that have had unfortunate consequences for the Christian cause. Many leaders of Christian organizations, driven by a sincere belief in the urgency of their cause, had a hard time restraining themselves from gorging on the fruits of fund-raising. One religious fund-raising consultant rather uncharitably described his customers like this: he said that some leaders of his acquaintance were like the monkeys used in experiments about drug addiction. If the monkey learned that pushing a button would release the desired reward, the monkey would press the button at an ever faster pace until no more rewards came down the chute or until the monkey collapsed.

Some Christian leaders kept increasing the frequency of their various appeals — first every six weeks, then every five weeks, then monthly, then monthly plus holidays, and so forth — until no more reward came down the chute. Recipients of those appeals experienced "donor fatigue," a phrase derived from World War II's "combat fatigue."

By the late 1990s, evangelical Christians were faced with an ever-increasing bombardment of information about needs around the world. They were deluged with direct mail. Dinnertime was interrupted by the nightly ringing of telephone appeals. Religious television and radio stations conducted telethons and phonethons, and "infomercials" made the case for individuals supporting organizations involved in relieving one injustice or another. There have been non-financial (but nonetheless real) costs in this collective change in methods of fund-raising, the full implications of which are still not appreciated.

First of all, the aforementioned "donor fatigue" means that evangelicals now tend to guard their hearts as they try to guard their wallets. The typical reaction of any organism to over-stimulation is to dull its response to the stimulus. It tries to become acclimated to noise, pain, darkness, or a host of other annoying stimuli. Appeals for money for Christian causes can become just another annoying stimulus. But the implication of this kind of reaction for evangelicals would mean a retreat from considering the appeals presented. Direct mail ends up going directly in the garbage, unopened and unevaluated. Telemarketers are disdained, regardless of whether they represent sellers of aluminum siding or the local adoption counseling service. Because of the volume of appeals, we end up listening to none of them. The side effect of donor fatigue may be a spiritual malady: hardness of heart.

A second danger to the change in evangelical funding is more subtle. When churches played the role of intermediary, there was some screening of appeals. Whether the screening was adequate or sufficiently performed would be an interesting topic beyond this brief analysis, but a denominational or church screening tended to at least somewhat vet the appeals that came to church members from the outside. As appeals "leaked" around the church, those appeals were unscreened and unscrutinized. Individuals, therefore, had an increasing responsibility to evaluate the multiplying funding appeals even more closely than before.

And the responsibility to evaluate is not a light burden. Andrew Carnegie is said to have complained that giving away his money wisely was much more difficult than making it in the first place. Whereas philanthropists like Carnegie always understood the need to carefully examine funding requests, the mass audience of evangelicals may not fully comprehend or be equipped to accomplish an examination of the need. The burden of evaluation is not one to be taken casually by Christians seeking to be good stewards.

Summary

In my brief essay, I have tried to illustrate that the donor patterns evangelicals have exhibited since 1945 were made possible by changes in technology. As parachurch organizations could broadcast their messages to national audiences without using the mediating services of the church, communicate to donors using lower-cost mailing technology, and personalize their requests to donors by mail and telephone to maximize their appeal, it should be no surprise that donations increased. If one adds these factors on top of an increasing North American population that was itself increasingly evangelical, you can understand the financial results seen in the post–World War II era.

The people I interviewed were unanimous in asserting that both denominations and churches lost importance as financial intermediaries over the period. Whether this was good or bad could be debated, but it certainly changed the nature of fund-raising. Individual donors could do little more than trust nonprofit agencies to be responsible stewards of their funds. After all, it is uneconomical for any individual donor to conduct much examination when one's contribution might be $1,000 yearly or less. From a missionary's perspective, for example, the process of assembling financial support from a collection of small donors takes longer at the outset, requiring greater financial and time resources. Lastly, this reliance on diverse funding sources increases the amount of travel required to maintain personal contact when missionaries return from the field. The loss of intermediation has costs, some of which are being addressed as fund-raising continues to change.

The growth for evangelical organizations was impressive, but also needs to be put in secular perspective. According to Paul Nelson, President of the Evangelical Council for Financial Accountability, the organization's members together have budgets totaling about $5.5 billion. While that is a lot of money, a company with that income would be only number 287 on *Fortune* magazine's 1998 list of the 500 largest industrial firms. Collectively, they approach the size of a single firm like wood products company Boise

Cascade (#288) or the West Coast grocery chain, Fred Meyer (#289), each with about $5.49 billion in sales.

While not all evangelical organizations belong to the ECFA, it does have a substantial share of the parachurch movement. So the scale of evangelical funding from 1945-1995 (apart from church donations) remains important but still modest on the larger world stage. Adding in denominational and church giving would significantly increase this number, but a lot of that money is used simply to maintain church staffs and buildings.

One of my interviewees was from the Conservative Baptist movement, a group that started in 1943. The Conservative Baptists arose in Northern Baptist — now American Baptist — churches because of concerns that denominational missionaries were no longer required to be orthodox and because their work was becoming too socially oriented. As this man and I discussed the growth of some of the largest evangelical organizations like World Vision, Compassion, Food for the Hungry, and MAP International, he told me that a friend of his still in the American Baptist Church had looked at him and remarked that, fifty years later, it seemed that evangelicals had come full-circle — to incorporate a substantial social witness.

The book of James challenges Christians to show their faith by their deeds (James 1:22 and 2:18). Leaders of evangelical charities, in spite of their public infirmities, remain motivated to do good in the name of the Lord. Perhaps what the record of the years 1945-1995 has shown is that evangelical donors have taken that challenge seriously, no matter what name they write on the payee line of their checks.

CHAPTER 12

Money Matters: *The Phenomenon of Financial Counselor Larry Burkett and Christian Financial Concepts*

LARRY ESKRIDGE

The wicked borrow and do not repay, but the righteous give generously.

PSALM 37:21 (NIV)

"The purpose of this study is to help clarify God's perspective on finances."[1] Thus began the introduction to *Your Finances in Changing Times,* a 1975 book by Larry Burkett, a little-known Atlanta-based staff member of Campus Crusade for Christ. Self-published on the strength of $25,000 borrowed from friends, Campus Crusade added the volume to its publication and materials catalog but sales were hardly impressive. Indeed, they reflected Burkett's experience in trying to interest seminars and Sunday School classes on the topic of Christian financial management: most pastors, he found, were not much interested in clarifying "God's perspective on finances." Nonetheless, sure that this was the task God wanted him to do, Burkett and his wife Judy in 1976 took the step of incorporating their own nonprofit ministry, Christian Finan-

1. Larry Burkett, *Your Finances in Changing Times* (San Bernardino, CA: Campus Crusade for Christ, 1975), p. v.

311

cial Concepts (CFC), running it out of the basement of their suburban Atlanta home.[2]

These less-than-spectacular beginnings stand out in stark contrast to the success Larry Burkett enjoyed by the late 1990s when he had achieved the status of evangelicalism's financial "answer man" on everything from balancing a checkbook to balancing the national budget. A prolific author, Burkett has written over seventy books, booklets, workbooks, organizing systems, and — even — novels that have almost single-handedly created "money" and "finance" sections in the nation's Christian bookstores. An influential figure within evangelical radio broadcasting since the early 1980s, Burkett's daily syndicated five-minute feature "How to Manage Your Money" had grown by 1998 to include over 1100 outlets, and his half-hour daily call-in show "Your Money Matters" could be heard on over 300 stations.[3] Christian Financial Concepts (CFC), the organization that once consisted of Larry and Judy Burkett was, by that same year, operating on an annual budget of over $8.5 million and employed 135 staff members at its Gainesville, Georgia headquarters.[4] Besides managing the organization's print offerings and broadcasting department, CFC reportedly fielded over 35,000 telephone, mail, and e-mail queries per month, as well as provided oversight to 40 volunteer seminar speakers and 1,100 referral counselors across North America.[5] In addition, it superintended a dizzying array of products and financial teaching aids designed to educate various substrata of the evangelical populace. Its Life Pathways division offered advice on career planning and decisions as well as offering aptitude and interest tests to thousands of individuals a year.[6] "LB Software Tools" provided home-computing resources that assisted evangelicals in everything from

2. Larry Burkett, interview by author, telephone, 2 November 1998; "Interesting Events Mark CFC's History," *Money Matters* (May 1996): 2.

3. The figure for Burkett's "Money Matters" program comes from Christian Financial Concepts website (http://www.cfcministry.org/radio); the figure for "How to Manage Your Money" comes from "Christian Financial Concepts," a portfolio of information on CFC (Gainesville, GA: Christian Financial Concepts, ca. Summer 1998), p. 4.

4. Christian Financial Concepts, Catalog (Fall/Winter 1998), p. 1; Christian Financial Concepts, Financial Statement for 1997, p. 3.

5. "Christian Financial Concepts" portfolio, p. 5; Christian Financial Concepts Catalog (Fall/Winter 1998), p. 1.

6. Burkett's organization claims that since Life Pathways' founding in 1990 it has provided "assessment services" to over 50,000 individuals; "Life Pathways History" in "Christian Financial Concepts" portfolio, p. 14.

managing their checking accounts to tracking their investments online.[7] A "Money Matters for Kids" and "Money Matters for Teens" series (featuring a bespectacled "Larry the Cat" logo) offered materials that taught children and adolescents how to think about, manage, and make money.[8] And a Spanish-language division made Burkett's financial advice available to Latin America and the United States' growing Hispanic population through the translation of his books like *Usando su Dinero Sabiamente (Using Your Money Wisely).*[9]

Burkett's emergence in the 1970s and the subsequent growth of CFC during the 1980s and 1990s is an interesting phenomenon within the development of American evangelicalism in the last quarter of the twentieth century. Certainly, it is an example of the movement's penchant for creating "baptized" alternatives for nearly every aspect and function of the

7. Among "LB Software Tools" programs are "Snap Shot 20/20," a program designed to analyze one's debts with an eye to their elimination; "Larry Burkett's Money Matters Financial Calculators," featuring desktop, mortgage, and interest calculating functions along with a "daily calendar of biblical financial principles"; and "Larry Burkett's Money Matters," a multi-functional program with checkbook and account management features, check-writing capabilities, and online investment tracking and report capabilities (Christian Financial Concepts, Catalog [Fall/Winter 1998], pp. 5, 12-13).

8. The series aimed at children and adolescents has largely been overseen by Burkett's son Allen (executive vice president of CFC) and his wife, Lauree Burkett. Among the titles in the "Money Matters for Kids" series are Lauree Burkett with Christine Bowler, *Money Matters for Kids* (Chicago: Moody Press, 1997); Lauree and L. Allen Burkett, *50 Money Making Ideas for Kids* (Nashville: Thomas Nelson, 1997); Larry and Lauree Burkett, *What If I Owned Everything?* (Nashville: Thomas Nelson, 1997). In the "Money Matters for Teens" series the titles include L. Allen and Lauree Burkett with Marnie Wooding, *Money Matters for Teens* (Chicago: Moody Press, 1997) along with a pair of age-graded workbooks (Chicago: Moody Press, 1998). CFC also offers other helps for teaching children about finances, including a plastic "My Giving Bank" for ages three and older with three sections: church, store, and bank. In addition, it offers "Larry Burkett's Money Matters" board game ("recommended for ages 7 to adult"), which is somewhat similar in concept to Milton Bradley's "Life" (Christian Financial Concepts, Catalog [Fall/ Winter 1998] pp. 4, 18-21).

9. Larry Burkett, *Usando su Dinero Sabiamente* (Spanish House, 1997) is one of six major translations of Burkett's books (see the Fall/Winter 1998 CFC catalog, p. 44). CFC's Hispanic ministry is headed up by Andrés Panasiuk and seeks to "eventually train Spanish-speaking Christians as volunteer budget counselors in every important city in the Western Hemisphere — from Canada to *Tierra del Fuego*" ("Christian Financial Concepts" portfolio, p. 9). Burkett is also seeking to establish a similar Russian-language ministry ("Outreach," *Money Matters* [May 1996], p. 8).

larger culture.[10] More importantly, however, Burkett's rise to prominence and the fact of his organization's widespread influence within conservative Christian circles provide a unique window to contemporary evangelicals' perceptions and thoughts on a wide variety of economic and financial realities. Anyone interested in knowing the future direction of evangelical attitudes on matters of stewardship — to say nothing of evangelicals' relation to the overall economic apparatus of American society — would be wise to study the teachings and influence of Larry Burkett and Christian Financial Concepts.

But another dimension of Burkett's influence also warrants study. Since the 1991 publication of his best-selling book, *The Coming Economic Earthquake,* Burkett has been an increasingly important voice within the realm of conservative evangelical political opinion.[11] As the leading authority on things financial within the evangelical community, his criticism of the federal government's fiscal policies ties into the wider phenomenon of evangelical involvement in conservative political causes. In this light, Burkett and his organization may prove representative of something much more fundamental than an evangelical equivalent to secular financial advisors such as Sylvia Porter or Jane Bryant Quinn.[12] It may be that Burkett's rise — as well as that of the so-called "Religious Right" itself — is fundamentally a corollary of evangelicals' "economic arrival" in an American society that has basked in unprecedented prosperity and affluence since the end of the Second World War. Within this context, Burkett's message that the guiding principles for functioning as a modern, American economic being can be found in the Bible serve as an enlightening example of how evangelicals have addressed their changing socio-economic circumstances and status in light of their beliefs and subcultural values.

10. This penchant of contemporary evangelicalism to produce a sanctified version of nearly every aspect of the larger American culture from Christian bookstores to Christian nightclubs to "Christian Yellow Pages" is given particularly good attention in Carol Flake's 1984 book, *Redemptorama: Culture, Politics, and the New Evangelicalism* (Garden City, NY: Anchor Books).

11. Larry Burkett, *The Coming Economic Earthquake* (Chicago: Moody Press, 1991).

12. Much of Burkett's practical financial advice would be in line with what one hears from sound, conservative secular financial advisors. See for example Sylvia Porter, *Sylvia Porter's Your Finances in the 1990s* (New York: Prentice-Hall, 1990), and Jane Bryant Quinn, *Making the Most of Your Money* (New York: Simon and Schuster, 1997).

Background: Larry Burkett

Larry Burkett was born in March 1939 in Winter Park, Florida, the fifth of eight children born to Warren "Levi" Burkett and his wife Nuna Boatwright Burkett.[13] Burkett's father, originally from the backwater west-central Florida town of Chassahowitzka, supported his family on an electrician's modest income.[14] Burkett recalls that they dwelt in a section on the fringes of Winter Park — known as a wealthy enclave for "snowbird" émigrés — which was "somewhere between poor and very poor."[15] Despite their lean circumstances, however, Burkett looked back on his childhood and adolescence in central Florida in the late 1940s and 50s with fondness, viewing it as representative of the hard work, values, and common decency that made the 1950s, in his opinion, "the height of America's spirituality in this century."[16]

Burkett's own childhood spiritual training, however, was minimal. He vaguely remembers his maternal grandmother having been a devout member of a Pentecostal Holiness congregation. In his own household, however, churchgoing and formal religious dogma were apparently touchy subjects. According to Burkett, his mother claimed she went forward at a Pentecostal Holiness revival when three months pregnant with her first child; Burkett's father, so the story goes, would not speak to her until after the child was born.[17] Whatever the case, Burkett recalls that he was raised without much religious input from either of his parents: "We were just neutral. . . . Christ was never discussed in my home."[18]

What did seem to get his attention from an early age was the allure of success. According to Burkett, owning a business and becoming a success became his ambition as early as his elementary school years. The example of Warren, his oldest brother, provided something of a trail to follow. Warren Burkett had served in the Army Air Force in World War II and

---

13. Rob Dilbone, "Faithful on All Accounts," *The Christian Businessman* (Jan. 1998): 23; Burkett, interview, 2 November 1998.

14. Burkett, interview, 2 November 1998.

15. Larry Burkett, *Whatever Happened to the American Dream?* (Chicago: Moody Press, 1993), p. 28; Burkett, interview, 2 November 1998.

16. Burkett, *Whatever Happened to the American Dream?*, p. 28.

17. Burkett, interview, 2 November 1998.

18. Burkett, *Hope When It Hurts: A Personal Testimony of How to Deal With the Impact of Cancer* [originally titled *Damaged But Not Broken*] (Chicago: Moody Press, 1996, rev. ed., 1998), p. 103.

after the war attended college on the GI Bill, ultimately becoming the first college graduate in his family. After spending a few years as a high school teacher and coach, he landed a good paying job with IBM. This made quite an impression on young Larry: "Right out of college he was making more money than my father ever had. The signal that sent me was to work hard, get a good education, and . . . opportunities will abound."[19]

Upon his graduation from nearby Orlando's Lakeview High School in 1958, Burkett followed his brother's example and joined the Air Force. Serving as an electronics technician, he was assigned to work on radar and bomb systems with a Strategic Air Command unit based at Pease Air Force Base in Portsmouth, New Hampshire.[20] Burkett did not make the move north alone; shortly before starting basic training he wed his high school girlfriend, Judy Morgan, who was not yet seventeen. The daughter of a fairly prosperous native Floridian family, with a Titusville lumber yard and Orlando-area orange groves among her grandparents' assets, she had met Larry Burkett on a blind date. Beset with troubles at home and an alcoholic mother, she saw marriage as a way out of a bad situation. So, after a ten-month teenage courtship she married Burkett and moved with him to New Hampshire.[21] But the cold New England climate began to aggravate a minor back injury he had received playing high school football, and Burkett was given a medical discharge. In early 1960 the young couple returned to Orlando, where Larry began attending classes at Orlando Junior College and worked in a sporting goods store.[22]

19. Burkett, interview, 2 November 1998; Burkett, *Whatever Happened to the American Dream?*, p. 31.

20. Burkett, interview, 2 November 1998.

21. Burkett, interview, 2 November 1998; Dilbone, "Faithful on All Accounts," p. 23.

22. Burkett, interview, 2 November 1998. The early years of their marriage were, not surprisingly, rough both in financial and emotional terms and seem to have inspired Burkett years later to place a special emphasis on preparing young couples to handle their finances. He claims they "survived mostly on peanut butter sandwiches and Sunday dinner at [his wife's] grandmother's house" and that they both would have probably left each other but for the fact that they "had no other place to go, so we stuck it out." (Larry Burkett, *The Complete Financial Guide for Single Parents* [Wheaton, IL: Victor Books, 1991], p. 23; Larry Burkett, *The Complete Financial Guide for Young Couples* [Wheaton, IL: Victor Books, 1989], pp. 15-16). A particular sore spot in the relationship came from the fact of their widely disparate economic backgrounds. Burkett's innate frugality led him to constantly remind his wife to turn off lights, turn down the thermostat, and once to even un-

In the summer of 1961 following his freshman year at college, a friend persuaded Burkett to apply for work at nearby Cape Canaveral. Hired by the Martin Corporation (later, Martin Marietta), he worked on electronics connected to "Matador," an experimental pilotless bomber. About a year later, Burkett moved over to General Electric where he worked on Titan One–related projects and eventually with "QuickLook," an experimental ground station which was the final checkpoint for various key indicators and gauges right before blastoff for the Gemini, and later, the Apollo manned space programs.[23]

This period of Burkett's life, roughly 1962 to 1968, was an exhausting treadmill of full-time work and full-time school. Moving a growing young family roughly thirty miles east to the Titusville area near the Cape, Burkett normally worked ten- to twelve-hour days, six days a week, while attending evening classes — paid for by General Electric — first at Brevard Community College in Cocoa, and then at Rollins College back in Winter Park. Taking any number of courses in electrical engineering to satisfy his employer, he eventually earned a pair of bachelor's degrees from Rollins in marketing and finance — his real areas of interest.[24] Intent on actually running a business, he received his chance in 1968 when Roger Boatman, a young physicist Burkett had originally hired to work at one of the test stations, asked him to become the managing vice president of his new company TestLine, a small firm that specialized in the manufacture of "in-circuit" testing equipment.[25]

Some time that same year, Campus Crusade for Christ workers came

---

screw the lightbulb in the refrigerator to save on electricity should she forget to close the door (Burkett, *Complete Financial Guide for Single Parents,* p. 23). Burkett now pokes fun at himself for having been such a tightwad; he recalls the time in 1979 when he drove a ten-year-old station wagon with well over 100,000 miles for months after his son had destroyed the transmission's reverse capabilities during an ice storm (Burkett, *Debt-Free Living* [Chicago: Moody Press, 1989], pp. 148-49). Said Burkett: "I discovered how many times you pull into a parking space that you have to back out of."

23. "The Road to the Cross," *Money Matters* (May 1996): 4; Burkett, interview, 2 November 1998. Burkett's knowledge of launch procedures and technology is on display in his second novel *The Thor Conspiracy: Seventy Hour Countdown to Disaster* (Nashville: Thomas Nelson, 1995).

24. "Interesting Events,"p. 1; Burkett, *The Complete Financial Guide for Single Parents,* p. 55; Burkett, interview, 2 November 1998.

25. Dilbone, "Faithful on All Accounts," p. 24; "Interesting Events," p. 1; Burkett, interview, 2 November 1998. TestLine was purchased by Packard-Bell in the mid-1970s but went under by the end of the decade.

door-to-door through the Burketts' Titusville neighborhood where Judy Burkett had settled into the life of a "workaholic's widow" as a housewife and mother to four young children. "Witnessing" to her, the Campus Crusade workers walked her through the "Four Spiritual Laws" and Judy underwent a conversion experience. Although much more of a churchgoer with her Methodist family during her childhood than her husband had ever been, Judy had never shown much of a spiritual commitment until that time. Shortly after her encounter with the Campus Crusade team, however, she began to regularly attend Park Avenue Baptist Church, a large Southern Baptist congregation in Titusville. Larry was tolerant of his wife's religious commitment but told her in no uncertain terms not to bother him. Nonetheless, her influence, a steady round of visits from "Bible thumpers" including her pastor Peter Lord, and a Bible study led by a local dentist eventually began to have an influence. After being criticized for his disruptive, cynical attitude, Burkett read through the Gospel of John and underwent his own conversion experience in the autumn of 1971.[26] From that moment, Burkett claims, "God reached down and touched me, and once that happened I knew I was not going to stay in the electronics field."[27]

Even in the months following his conversion, Burkett's ingrained interest in business and finance made that dimension of the Bible his favorite area of exploration. Once at a weekly businessmen's Bible study Burkett mentioned he had found over one hundred verses that dealt with financial matters. Another attendee disputed his findings, arguing that God was not much interested in the subject. To prove a point, Burkett sat down in the following weeks with a yellow highlighter and marked every biblical passage that dealt with financial matters. When he was done, he found that he had over 700 verses, which he subsequently organized into a "financial concordance" under topics such as "tithing" and "borrowing."[28] Armed with this resource and growing opinions about the subject, Burkett was soon advising people: "By default, I became the financial counselor in my church. When somebody had a question about money, they would call me."[29]

26. Burkett, *Hope When It Hurts*, pp. 106-10; "The Road to the Cross," pp. 4-5; Burkett, interview, 2 November 1998.

27. "The Road to the Cross," p. 5.

28. "The Road to the Cross," p. 5; Burkett, interview, 2 November 1998. Burkett's original list of Bible verses later served as the basis for a concordance-like volume (Larry Burkett, *The Word on Finances* [Chicago: Moody Press, 1994], see pp. 11-12).

29. Dilbone, "Faithful on All Accounts," p. 24; "The Road to the Cross," p. 5.

In 1972 Burkett was introduced to Campus Crusade leader Bill Bright at a conference at Lake Yale near Eustis, Florida. After hearing Burkett talk about the need for some sort of a financial-based ministry, Bright told Burkett that he was interested in creating just such an effort within Campus Crusade and that he should "come on staff." Increasingly convinced that he should utilize his business talents in the service of a Christian organization, Burkett resigned from TestLine in early 1973 and joined Campus Crusade.[30]

What he did not know until after he was hired, however, was that the "financial ministry" Bright had been speaking of was a deferred giving and estate-planning department. This was not what Burkett had envisioned at all — he profoundly disliked asking people for money. To compound his discomfort, Burkett soon found himself a frequent flyer (something he dreaded due to claustrophobia, stemming from a childhood incident when he nearly drowned in an underwater cave).[31] To relieve some of the burden of frequent travel, the Burketts relocated to the Atlanta area.[32]

However, there was no relief from the job itself. Less than a year after joining Campus Crusade Burkett resigned, to pursue at least temporarily a growing opportunity to present the results of his study of biblical financial principles to Sunday School classes and home Bible studies. Learning of Burkett's departure, Bright eventually contacted him as to why he had left and what he was trying to do. Burkett explained: "[Bright] asked me what I really wanted to do, and I told him I wanted to teach people God's principles of handling money." Intrigued by his vision for a ministry that taught "average" Christians how to manage their finances, Bright rehired Burkett, allowing him to work out of Campus Crusade's Atlanta-area offices as he developed lectures and materials that dealt with biblical financial principles.[33]

During 1974 Burkett worked on his presentation and materials and eagerly accepted whatever opportunities came his way, including his first advertised seminar in the backroom of the Cornerstone Bookstore in At-

30. Burkett, interview, 2 November 1998; Dilbone, "Faithful on All Accounts," p. 24; "The Road to the Cross," p. 5.

31. Larry Burkett, *Women Leaving the Workplace: How to Make the Transition From Work to Home* (Chicago: Moody Press, 1995), pp. 112-13.

32. Burkett, interview, 2 November 1998; "The Road to the Cross," p. 5; Dilbone, "Faithful on All Accounts," p. 24.

33. Burkett, interview, 2 November 1998; "The Road to the Cross," p. 5; Dilbone, "Faithful on All Accounts," p. 24.

lanta.[34] A particularly validating experience came when he was asked to speak on the rudiments of budgeting and the financial dimensions of managing a church to a class of graduating seniors at Dallas Theological Seminary. Afterwards, as he sat around over lunch with faculty members plying him with questions about money-related verses in the Bible and advice on basic budgeting and financial management, Burkett claimed that he thought to himself: "it is really true that in the land of the blind a one-eyed man can become king." From this point on he was convinced that he indeed had the necessary gifts to reach his fellow believers on financial topics.[35]

The Origins of Christian Financial Concepts

Sometime during 1974 Burkett contacted several evangelical publishers about his idea for a Christian guide to personal finances. Although he received no interest whatsoever, Burkett still wanted something in print his students could take away from his seminars, and so began work on a book.[36] To finance the project, Burkett made the rounds among friends who included the Atlanta Falcons' Greg Brezina. By early 1975 he had raised $25,000 to cover the costs of editing, proofreading, typesetting, and printing 5,000 copies of *Your Finances in Changing Times*. Burkett sold the book at his seminars and also contracted with Campus Crusade to carry it in its "Here's Life" catalog of materials, thus giving him some entree to the nation's Christian bookstore networks.[37] However, the response from the people in the industry and the Christian book-buying public — during what was certainly a boom time for the evangelical book market — was decidedly less than earthshaking.[38] Burkett was able to repay those who had

34. Burkett, interview, 2 November 1998.

35. Larry Burkett, "Our Economy in Crisis," audiotape, side 2 (Wheaton, IL: Tyndale House, 1994).

36. Burkett, interview, 2 November 1998.

37. Burkett, interview, 2 November 1998; a complete list of those who helped Burkett raise the money to print *Your Finances in Changing Times* (San Bernardino, CA: Campus Crusade, 1975) can be found on the first edition's dedication page.

38. *Your Finances in Changing Times* appeared during a spectacular boom in evangelical publishing; books such as Billy Graham's *Angels* (Waco: Word Books, 1976) and Marabel Morgan's *The Total Woman* (Old Tappan, NJ: Fleming H. Revell, 1973) racked up enormous sales in both the evangelical and secular book market. Burkett's volume was especially situated in light of a propitious season of evangelical prophetic speculation in

loaned the initial seed money and did provide himself with a little income. But Campus Crusade's sales of *Your Finances in Changing Times* over a five-to six-year period, Burkett estimates, was probably around 30,000 copies.[39]

While *Your Finances in Changing Times* did not make Burkett's a well-known name in evangelical households, the response to the book and his slowly growing seminar schedule was enough to embolden him to resign for a second time from Campus Crusade and formally incorporate Christian Financial Concepts in May 1976. Operating out of the basement of their home in Tucker, Georgia, CFC's early staff consisted of Burkett, his wife who handled the phone calls and helped with secretarial work, and his children who helped him collate materials for seminars. In October 1976, CFC received its IRS exemption as a nonprofit 501(c)(3) organization, and

---

the early '70s, fueled by the events of the Six Day and Yom Kippur Wars and the general chaos that engulfed western and American society in that era. Titles such as Hal Lindsey's *The Late, Great Planet Earth* (Grand Rapids: Zondervan, 1971), Salem Kirban's *666: A Novel* (Wheaton, IL: Tyndale House, 1970), John F. Walvoord's *Oil and the Middle East Crisis* (Grand Rapids: Zondervan, 1974), and David Wilkerson's *The Vision* (Old Tappan, NJ: Spire Books, 1973) could hardly be kept in stock for evangelical readers. For that reason, Burkett's title, *Your Finances in Changing Times,* was more than a little pregnant to the Christian bookstore browser with implications about financial security in a world that looked as if it was heading toward the Tribulation. While Burkett's volume was hardly a survivalist guide, his analysis of the contemporary economic scene nonetheless bowed in the direction of regnant premillennial prophetic speculation, with chapters on "The Cashless System" (19-23), "God's Timetable" (24-38), and a chapter titled "Sign of the Beast — The Number System" (39-43). Such was the tone that the book was sometimes jokingly referred to as "The Late, Great Dollar Bill." Most of this material was edited out of the revised 1982 Moody Press edition of the book, although a remnant of this line of thinking was evident in relation to his thinking on the future of credit cards and banking systems (see 33-36).

39. Burkett, interview, 2 November 1998. Although these sorts of sales numbers are not terribly impressive in light of some of the gigantic numbers being rung up in evangelical publishing in the 1970s, it must be remembered that they were probably still significantly better than that of earlier evangelical expositions on money-related issues in the twentieth century such as David McConaughy's *Money, the Acid Test* (Philadelphia: Westminster Press, 1919), Guy Morrill's *You and Yours: God's Purpose in Things* (New York: Fleming H. Revell, 1922), George M. Bowman's *How to Succeed with Your Money* (Chicago: Moody Press, 1960, rev. ed., 1974), or Frank Laubach's *What Jesus Had to Say About Money* (Grand Rapids: Zondervan, 1969). See Gary Scott Smith, "Evangelicals Confront Corporate Capitalism: Advertising, Consumerism, Stewardship, and Spirituality, 1880-1930," pages 39-81 in this volume, for a comprehensive look into evangelical views in the early part of the century.

in early 1977 began to publish its own newsletter, *Gnosis* (changed in 1981 to *Your Money in Changing Times,* and *Money Matters* in 1992).[40]

At about this time, Scripture Press in Wheaton, Illinois, contacted Burkett about the possibility of writing a book that would address the matter of financial management for a feminine audience.[41] The resultant manuscript contained Burkett's basic teachings about the perils of credit, the benefits of debt retirement, and the need to budget. But, it also reflected Burkett's conviction that women needed to take an active role in family financial matters — often to counterbalance their mates' weaknesses and mistakes — as a key to better marriages and solvent households.[42] When the book was published late that year as a thirteen-chapter study book aimed at the Sunday school curriculum market, however, it was patronizingly marketed as a book aimed at the "little lady." Burkett claims that Scripture Press's marketing department, in an effort to capitalize on Dr. James Dobson's best-selling *What Wives Wish Their Husbands Knew About Women,* titled Burkett's volume *What Husbands Wish Their Wives Knew About Money.* Although Burkett was angered by the title, his second book did tolerably well in the Christian bookstores, garnering a second printing in its first year on the market.[43]

In the late 1970s and early 80s Burkett concentrated largely on seminars and his slowly growing newsletter. His organization during this time had grown sufficiently that he had hired some office help and moved out of his own basement to a small, rented building in Tucker and, in 1979, to a remodeled barn and collection of outbuildings near Norcross, Georgia. By the early 1980s, CFC's Norcross site housed a staff of five or six, including some full-time help for Burkett in sharing the seminar-teaching load.[44]

The year 1982 marked a major turning point for Burkett and CFC.

40. "Interesting Events," p. 2; Burkett, interview, 2 November 1998. Today, CFC estimates that its newsletter has a monthly circulation near 200,000 ("Christian Financial Concepts," portfolio, p. 2).

41. Burkett, interview, 2 November 1998.

42. Larry Burkett, *What Husbands Wish Their Wives Knew About Money* (Wheaton, IL: Victor Books, 1977).

43. Burkett, *What Husbands Wish Their Wives Knew About Money;* James Dobson, *What Wives Wish Their Husbands Knew About Women* (Wheaton, IL: Tyndale House, 1975). From this experience, Burkett claims that he learned the importance of having control over the title of his books in contractual negotiations with publishers (Burkett, interview, 2 November 1998).

44. "Interesting Events," p. 2; Burkett, interview, 2 November 1998.

That year Burkett entered the general book market with *How to Prosper in the Underground Economy,* a volume he wrote with some contributions from William Proctor, editor of the *Church Business Report* newsletter.[45] Published by William Morrow, the book toned down Burkett's usual biblical approach with more generic tips about getting one's financial house in order while developing a barter and exchange network that — useful during normal financial times — would be of extreme importance if the expected economic crash occurred.[46] More significant, however, was a proposal from Moody Press in Chicago about publishing a revised version of *Your Finances in Changing Times.* The revised, more attractively packaged version of *Your Finances* appeared late in 1982 and began to make a very solid showing in evangelical bookstores the second time around, eventually selling over 1,300,000 copies by the late 1990s.[47]

This new success, however, was most likely related to a singularly important development that had occurred a few months earlier — an invitation to appear on Dr. James Dobson's "Focus on the Family" radio show.[48] Dobson, the author of best-selling books like *Dare to Discipline, What Wives Wish Their Husbands Knew About Women,* and *The Strong-Willed Child,* was a

45. Larry Burkett with William Proctor, *How to Prosper in the Underground Economy* (New York: William Morrow and Co., 1982).

46. The book emphasized a "legal underground economy . . . based solidly on a community system of sharing goods and services" (16). While not exactly "survivalist" in nature (Burkett advised his readers that he did not "think it's necessary to store guns, gold, and food and hide out in the mountains in order to survive" [13]), the book was certainly "preparationist," noting that having a three month supply of food on hand might not be a bad idea (92-95). Burkett has been consistently in this "preparationist" mode throughout his ministry. In the wake of OPEC's early 1980s tightening of the oil supply, he once believed "the Israelis" were "very close to a breakthrough" in an inexpensive method to "harness hydrogen for energy uses." When this day came, Burkett intended "to operate our ministry and homes off of hydrogen when we relocate" (Larry Burkett, "Gas," *Gnosis* 41 [Apr. 1981]: 2). In more recent years he also advocated a "preparationist" stance in anticipation of possible disruptions in the flow of goods and services caused by the Y2K problem (see Larry Burkett, *Crisis Control in the New Millennium* [Nashville: Thomas Nelson, 1999]).

47. Larry Burkett, *Your Finances in Changing Times* (Chicago: Moody Press, 1982). Burkett says that Moody has sold a little over 1,300,000 copies of the book. In addition, he notes that the Billy Graham Evangelistic Association gave away somewhere in the vicinity of 200,000-300,000 copies of the book as a promotional item in the mid-'80s (Burkett, interview, 2 November 1998).

48. Burkett, interview, 2 November 1998.

growing presence within evangelical circles. His radio program "Focus on the Family" and the organization that bore the same name had begun in 1977, and by the early 1980s Dobson was heard on several hundred radio stations across the country.[49] Burkett, who was doing a series of seminars in Southern California at the time of the invitation had not met Dobson before, but he meshed well with the child psychologist in the six to seven shows they taped. The subsequent response from Dobson's audience to Burkett's appearance overwhelmed CFC's small Norcross staff with phone calls, letters, and requests for CFC seminars.[50]

Burkett claims that shortly thereafter Dean Sipple, program director at the Moody Broadcasting Network's station in Chattanooga, WMBW, began to "bug [him] to death" about making some radio spots. Having about all he could handle in terms of speaking engagements, Burkett began to think that perhaps radio was "an ideal mechanism . . . a big ol' seminar" that could both get his message across while also bringing some sanity to his own workload. Admitting that he "knew nothing about radio," Burkett recorded several "awful" five-minute programs at a studio in Atlanta which were then broadcast over WMBW. Known as "Your Money in Changing Times," the program soon spread to other stations and within a year was airing on over 150 stations.[51]

The balance of the 1980s proved to be a time of major expansion for Burkett's radio presence. By 1985, Burkett realized that his program had grown to an extent where it was no longer manageable as an organizational afterthought. Hiring a full-time broadcast manager to provide oversight, CFC built its own studios and created its own separate broadcasting department.[52] In January 1988 Burkett's daily financial counsel (re-dubbed "How to Manage Your Money") was joined by "Your Money Matters," a daily half-hour call-in show.[53]

49. Quentin J. Schultze, "The Invisible Medium: Evangelical Radio," in *American Evangelicals and the Mass Media*, ed. Schultze (Grand Rapids: Zondervan, 1990), pp. 173-76; Mark Ward, Sr., *Air of Salvation: The Story of Christian Broadcasting* (Grand Rapids: Baker, 1994), pp. 162-63, 219. James Dobson, *Dare to Discipline* (Wheaton, IL: Tyndale House, 1970); James Dobson, *The Strong-Willed Child* (Wheaton, IL: Tyndale House, 1978).

50. Burkett, interview, 2 November 1998.

51. Burkett, interview, 2 November 1998; Dilbone, "Faithful on All Accounts," p. 24; "Interesting Events," p. 3.

52. "Interesting Events," p. 3.

53. "Interesting Events," p. 3.

In the mid-to-late 1980s and into the early 90s Burkett also stepped up his writing efforts considerably, releasing a number of books that addressed specialized topics and individual segments of his audience.[54] In these volumes Burkett provided basic information, tips, and resources dealing with the nuts and bolts of budgeting, debt-retirement, mortgages, handling taxes, and investments. Throughout, he hammered home the basic principles for a Christian's handling of their personal finances that his seminars, early books, and radio broadcasts had begun to make an increasingly assumed part of the evangelical landscape.

The Basics of Personal Finance

Much of Burkett's counsel on personal finances is pure economic common sense, although his justification usually leads back to the Bible. Burkett strongly urges every individual and family to be firmly committed to drawing up — and following — a budget.[55] To determine the priority and necessity of purchases, Burkett advises a tripartite approach to expenditures that he once referred to as a "Volkswagen/Oldsmobile/Cadillac" strategy of *needs* (food, clothing, housing, job-related expenses, medical care, savings, educational provisions, and other basics), *wants* (choices about quality of goods — steak v. hamburger, new v. used car, etc., etc.), and *desires* (those things that can be afforded only after all obligations — material and spiritual — have been met).[56]

Beyond simple budgeting, however, the cornerstone of Burkett's

54. In 1986 Moody Press published *Using Your Money Wisely: Guidelines From Scripture*. The next year saw the publication of *Answers to Your Family's Financial Questions* by Tyndale House Publishers in Wheaton, Illinois. In 1989, Moody Press published yet another volume entitled *Debt-Free Living*. 1990 saw Thomas Nelson's publication of Burkett's volume for business professionals, *Business By the Book: The Complete Guide of Biblical Principles for Business Men and Women*. In 1991 Victor Books published *The Complete Financial Guide for Single Parents* and in 1992 followed up with *Investing for the Future*, the same year in which Moody Press released his *Preparing for Retirement*. The establishment in 1990 of Career Pathways (later Life Pathways), a vocational aptitude and career counseling service within CFC, led to the publication of *Your Career in Changing Times* (1993), a book Burkett co-authored with Career Pathways' director, Lee Ellis.

55. For example see Burkett, *Your Finances in Changing Times* (1982), pp. 149-72; Burkett, *Debt-Free Living*, pp. 75-80; Burkett, *Women Leaving the Workplace*, pp. 183-96.

56. Burkett, *Your Finances in Changing Times* (1975), pp. 83-84.

counsel is that "God's people should be debt-free."[57] Based on numerous biblical passages including Proverbs 22:7 ("The rich rules over the poor, and the borrower becomes the lender's slave") and Romans 13:8 ("Owe nothing to anyone except to love one another . . ."), Burkett believes that debt is the equivalent of bondage and its eradication should be viewed by all Christians — after providing the basics needed to live — as financial task number one. Reflective of his attitude, no single topic gets as much space in Burkett's writings and radio time as does the problem of debt — his advice about avoiding and getting out of debt usually made concrete by anecdotes of any number of "Paul and Julies" and "Bill and Pams" who foolishly went into debt through careless spending, risky investments, or get-rich-quick schemes and who (the majority of the time) come to their senses and are finally able to get their financial act together.[58]

The only things Burkett is willing to concede that any individual Christian may go into debt for is housing and — if they are willing to do so — an automobile (though he strongly pushes the wisdom of buying used cars). These sorts of items, covered by a payment contract, are permitted as long as one faithfully meets the conditions of the payments. Even then, however, Burkett argues that the goal should be getting out of debt as quickly as possible by the prepayment of loan principal and thus avoiding the squandering of thousands of dollars in interest payments.[59]

57. Burkett, *Business By the Book*, p. 12.

58. So pervasive is Burkett's preaching against debt that it is *the* underlying practical financial theme in his writings. His magnum opus on the topic, however, is *Debt-Free Living*, which weaves Burkett's teachings and tips throughout the debt horror stories of "Paul and Julie," "Ron and Sue," "Jack and Mary," "Bill and Pam," "Andy and Bea," and "Allen and Gladis," respectively.

59. For a thumbnail guide to his views on the general principles of borrowing money see "Borrowing: A Biblical Perspective" in Burkett, *Principles Under Scrutiny* (Dahlonega, GA: Christian Financial Concepts, 1985), pp. 75-76. For an example of his views on home mortgages, see Burkett, "Should My Mortgage Come First?" *Moody* (June 1993): 37; and Burkett, *Answers to Your Family's Financial Questions* (Wheaton, IL: Tyndale House, 1987), pp. 81-83, 91-93. For a look at his views on the problems associated with buying automobiles on credit, see Burkett, *What Husbands Wish Their Wives Knew About Money*, pp. 31, 102-3; and Burkett, *Debt-Free Living*, pp. 146-48. Burkett's views about the imperative of repaying all debts have, however, actually mellowed over the years. For example, in the 1975 edition of *Your Finances in Changing Times*, his was a "take-no-prisoners" approach, telling his readers that "A Christian in debt must stop any expenditure which is not absolutely essential for living (Prov. 21:17)" ["He who loves pleasure will become poor; whoever loves wine and oil will never be rich"] (85). But he is a good deal

In light of Burkett's teachings on debt, it is no surprise that he is no fan of credit cards. For those who are worried about security or the burdens of record-keeping he tolerates them as a convenient way to avoid carrying large amounts of cash or writing numerous checks. However, he sees very little upside in their use. Any failure to keep up with monthly payments is improper and imprudent behavior for a Christian. Consistently through the years Burkett has advocated that at the *first* instance of being unable to pay one's monthly credit card balance they should be immediately destroyed.[60]

For those who are hopelessly mired in debt, Burkett counsels "always run toward your creditors, not away from them" with a written statement outlining one's concrete intentions to repay as much, and as quickly, as is possible.[61] This dovetails, he feels, with the spirit of Christ's advice in Matthew 5:25 ("Make friends quickly with your opponent in the law while you are with him on the way in order that your opponent may not deliver you to the judge, and the judge to the officer, and you be thrown into prison"). Attempts to legally wiggle out of debt that individuals have brought upon themselves is not an option for a Christian in light of Psalm 37:21 ("The wicked borrows but does not pay back, but the righteous is gracious and gives"). For that reason, bankruptcy is normally seen as something to be avoided except in very rare instances.[62]

Beyond getting one's financial house in order and avoiding unbiblical financial behaviors and arrangements, Burkett counsels Christians about investing their money for future needs through books such as his 1992 vol-

---

more relaxed in this regard now, seeming to have conceded that even those on a very tight budget or attempting to climb out of debt need to "cut loose" every now and then; see for example *Debt-Free Living*, pp. 77-80, 178-79.

60. See for example, Burkett, *What Husbands Wish Their Wives Knew About Money*, pp. 32-34; Burkett, *Your Finances in Changing Times* (1982), p. 73; Burkett, *Answers to Your Family's Financial Questions*, pp. 76-77.

61. Burkett, *Debt-Free Living*, p. 175.

62. Burkett, "Bankruptcy . . . Is It Scriptural?" in *Principles Under Scrutiny*, pp. 83-84; Burkett, "A Theology of Bankruptcy," *Moody* (Sept. 1995): 34; and Burkett, *Debt-Free Living*, pp. 175-89. Possible exceptions for bankruptcy — *after* one has taken all reasonable effort to put together a plan to pay back one's creditors — would include those instances where someone may be attempting to absolutely destroy you through legal action, where one creditor is attempting to get at your assets at the expense of other creditors, and in the event of catastrophic medical expenses that threaten to take one's home (see for example Burkett, *Debt-Free Living*, pp. 187-88; Burkett, *Hope When It Hurts*, pp. 211-13).

ume *Investing for the Future.*[63] As the model of a canny speculator he finds his biblical example in Solomon, "The best investor the world has ever known."[64] Burkett views Solomon as embodying the traits of the wise investor in that he diversified his investments (Eccl. 11:2: "Divide your portion to seven, or even to eight, for you do not know what misfortune may occur on the Earth"); invested ethically (Eccl. 12:13: "The conclusion, when all has been heard, is: fear God and keep His commandments, because this applies to every person"); and relied upon good counsel (Prov. 15:22: "Without consultation, plans are frustrated, but with many counselors they succeed").[65] Burkett's counsel to the non-Solomonic "average" investor emphasizes varying investment strategies at different stages of life, as well as guides to the most sound investments (a home, rental properties, mutual funds, insurance, company retirement plans, and government-backed securities) and staying away from what he terms the "investment hall of horrors" (commodities, partnerships, tax shelters, precious metals, gemstones, coins, stocks).[66] Although Burkett is bullish on savings and preparing for the future, he believes that Americans' growing mania for storing up huge amounts of money for a lavish retirement is unnecessary and often works against God's being able to direct individual Christians' use of their funds (see below).[67] Likewise, he believes that extravagant inheritances are problematic, tending to wreck the lives of immature children and grandchildren (as reflected in the Parable of the Prodigal Son).[68]

63. Larry Burkett, *Investing for the Future* (Wheaton, IL: Victor Books, 1992; rev. ed., Colorado Springs: Victor Books, 1997).

64. He says about Solomon: "The Queen of Sheba noted that everything his hands touched prospered. So it would seem logical that if we could glean some investment advice from him we should be able to improve our percentages too" (Burkett, *Investing for the Future*, p. 143).

65. Burkett, *Investing for the Future*, pp. 143-54.

66. Burkett, *Investing for the Future*, pp. 91-104.

67. See for example Burkett, *Your Finances in Changing Times*, pp. 106-7, and Burkett, *Answers to Your Family's Financial Questions*, pp. 202-3.

68. For example see Burkett, *Your Finances in Changing Times* (1982), pp. 108-9, and Burkett, "The Issue of Inheritance," in *Principles Under Scrutiny*, pp. 133-34. Generally, Burkett is of the belief that parents should attempt to help their children and to provide for them, but not to buffer them from all of life's material contingencies. In that spirit, he argues that helping adult children avoid the burden of mortgage debt and helping with the purchase of their first car is a good idea that will also benefit their child's marriage (by reducing the potential strife over money), if the parents can afford such assistance

The Spiritual Meaning of Money

As *the* basic financial truth that undergirds all others, Burkett believes that all Christians should take to heart the lesson of 1 Corinthians 10:26 — "The Earth is the Lord's and all that is therein." All of believers' money and possessions — like their life circumstances, family, and their very lives — belong to God: "God calls each of us to a radical lifestyle — total commitment to Him."[69] Burkett teaches that God uses money in any number of ways in the individual Christian's life — to strengthen their trust in him; to demonstrate his love and power over the world; to develop the believer's trustworthiness and provide direction; and to unite Christians and provide for the needs of others.[70] Money and its uses, Burkett contends, is one of God's primary training grounds for the individual believer (based on Luke 16:11: "If therefore you have not been faithful in the use of unrighteous Mammon, who will entrust the true riches to you?" and the Parable of the Talents in Matthew 25). Indeed, Burkett argues that the "way a Christian uses money is the clearest outside indicator of what the inside commitment is really like."[71]

These beliefs, however, do not parlay into Burkett's advocating that Christians should take a vow of poverty or deny themselves the physical wherewithal for them and their families to live. "I believe God wants us to lead a comfortable life," Burkett maintains.[72] His reading of Paul's description of the gift of giving in Romans 12:5-8 implies to him that in order for Christians to be able to give "there must be a gift of gathering."[73] Convinced that there is no inherent spirituality in being impoverished for poverty's sake, Burkett sees the potential of a dangerously pharisaical streak of pride in those he calls "stoics" who crow too much about a simple lifestyle

(Burkett, "First Homes and Young Couples," *Moody* [May 1990]: 38; Burkett, *Investing for the Future*, pp. 37, 162).

69. Burkett, *The Word on Finances*, p. 17.

70. Burkett, *Your Finances in Changing Times* (1982), pp. 48-50.

71. Burkett, "Christian Commitment . . . What Is It?" in *Principles Under Scrutiny*, p. 42. For an in-depth look at Burkett's views on the individual's responsibilities for godly financial attitudes see Burkett's self-study guide *Caretakers of God's Blessings: Using Our Resources Wisely*, The Stewardship Series, #1, Karen C. Lee-Thorp, ed. (Chicago: Moody Press, 1996).

72. Larry Burkett, *Money Smart: Insights into Your Finances* (Chicago: Moody Press, 1995), p. 34.

73. Burkett, *Your Finances in Changing Times* (1982), pp. 43-44.

and "believe that to follow Jesus a Christian must sell everything and become a pauper."[74] At bottom, it is always the heart's attitude that Burkett feels is God's primary concern as believers evaluate their relationship to mammon.[75]

While he teaches that Christians need not fear being wealthy, Burkett also counsels that such blessings do not provide a license to either hoard money or to spend it on a lavish lifestyle. Every Christian, he feels, should aim for a personal status "Somewhere between the careful ant and the foolish hoarder. . . . God wants us to have some surplus but not an attitude of selfishness or greed."[76] His reading of verses like 1 Timothy 6:17 ("Command those who are rich in this present world not to be arrogant nor to put their hope in wealth, which is so uncertain . . .") provides ample justification to avoid the examples of fellow evangelicals like the Hunt Brothers, whose disastrous 1970s attempt to corner the silver market Burkett points to as a prime example of the wrong motives and uses of one's wealth.[77]

Giving

Burkett goes so far as to argue that the only reason a Christian at any economic level has a relative excess of money is to provide for the needs of the organized church, fellow believers, and destitute unbelievers (2 Cor. 9:8: "And God is able to make all grace abound to you, so that in all things at all times, having all that you need, you will abound in every good work"). In his view, the 10 percent tithe "is a minimum testimony" on one's gross income:

> The tithe was established as a physical, earthly demonstration of man's commitment to God. God understood our greedy, selfish nature and

74. Burkett, *Business By the Book*, p. 43; see also Burkett, "Suffering for Christ vs. Living Like a King," in *Principles Under Scrutiny*, p. 19.

75. The Parable of the Rich Young Ruler is evidence of this, Burkett believes, being the instance of one individual's improper relationship to his possessions (see Burkett, *Your Finances in Changing Times* [1982], p. 45).

76. Burkett, *Answers to Your Family's Financial Questions*, p. 136.

77. Burkett, *Investing for the Future*, pp. 44-45; see Burkett, *Business By the Book*, pp. 29-31, and *The Word on Finances*, pp. 93-94, on the problems of ego and success in business.

provided an identifiable sign of our sincerity. By surrendering some of our physical resources, we testify to our origin, just as the farmer does when he surrenders some of his crop to the earth from which it came.[78]

This "minimum testimony," Burkett teaches, should in most cases be given to one's own congregation. Both he, and CFC, take pains in pointing out that this should be done *before* any money is given to parachurch organizations (including CFC).[79] But the tithe is not the end of the believer's giving possibilities. Burkett measures individual giving in a four-tiered hierarchy: (1) tithe; (2) obedience (giving, as one is able, in direct obedience to God's commands to those needs and needy that one encounters in the course of life); (3) abundance (giving above and beyond in individual use of one's excess to meet needs and speed God's work); and (4) actual sacrifice.[80]

In establishing this hierarchy of giving, Burkett is clear that he is no advocate of "health and wealth" teachings and has nothing but scorn for "the prosperity peddlers" whose teachings he sees as little more than a shield for greed on both sides of the message: "We must give out of agape, simply because we love God and expect no reward," Burkett says.[81] In this spirit, he also sees a dimension of evangelism involved in giving: "we are to be witnesses to non-Christians through our material resources, demonstrating that Christ, not money, is ruling our lives."[82] Contrary to the thrust of most prosperity teachings, Burkett believes that it is in the giving away of one's resources, rather than the accumulation thereof, that Christians have a real evangelistic impact for Christ:

---

78. Burkett, *Money Smart*, p. 102. See also Burkett, *Giving & Tithing* (Chicago: Moody Press, 1991), pp. 29-35, and *Your Money in Changing Times* (1982), pp. 112-14.

79. On CFC's website under the "Supporting CFC" link, the organization reminds potential contributors: "As always, you should consider supporting CFC only after financial obligations to your local church are fulfilled" (CFC website: http://www.cfcministry.org/ministry/support). While Burkett does provide some leeway for those individuals whose churches fall short in various areas (for example, evangelism) of their mission (see Burkett, *Giving & Tithing*, pp. 33-35, 60), he generally advises that holding back from one's church should be in cases of outright deceit, dishonesty, or unbiblical uses of funds (see Burkett, *Answers to Your Family's Financial Questions*, pp. 105-8).

80. Burkett, *Your Finances in Changing Times* (1982), p. 119. Burkett's booklet *Giving & Tithing* is probably the best summary of his thought on one's giving responsibilities.

81. Burkett, *Your Finances in Changing Times* (1982), p. 116; Burkett, *Business By the Book*, p. 43.

82. Burkett, *Your Finances in Changing Times* (1982), p. 123.

I find very few unsaved people who are impressed by a Christian's affluence. They have seen enough affluence in the world around them to be
convinced that godly people aren't the only ones who accumulate
money. What does impress both the unsaved and the saved alike are
those rare individuals who have learned to control their lifestyles and
use the abundance that they have to help others and spread God's
Word.[83]

Church Finances

The proper use of money within the local church has been a major
thrust of Burkett's writing and is an area that CFC has targeted through
the development of materials like *Business Management in the Local Church*
and audio sets such as "The Dollars and Sense of Administration" series.[84] Just as he advises individual families to budget, save, and avoid
debt, Burkett's counsel for local congregations resonates with the same
themes. If anything, however, he believes that the "church comes under
a more stringent judgment from God's Word because of its visible position," in its need for adherence to sound, biblical financial principles.[85]
Indeed, Burkett is leery of a church *ever* borrowing money, balking at the
"Huge sums of God's peoples' money [that] go to meet interest payments," money that "could otherwise be used to further God's Kingdom
rather than Satan's."[86]

Beyond these basic aspects of congregational financial management,
Burkett sees a hierarchy in the distribution of its money. The administration of funds for each church, he teaches, should fulfill a fourfold model
that mirrors the example of both the Old Testament storehouse and the
giving patterns of the New Testament church. In this model the church's
responsibilities include: (1) taking care of the Levites = taking care of pastors and staff; (2) feeding the prophets = taking care of missionaries and
evangelists; (3) feeding Hebrew orphans and widows = taking care of poor

83. Burkett, *Business By the Book,* p. 44.

84. David Pollock, *Business Management in the Local Church* (Gainesville, GA: 1992;
rev. ed., Chicago: Moody Press, 1996); "Effective Financial Ministry," Audio Tapes,
Church & Pastor Finance Series (Gainesville, GA: Christian Financial Concepts, 1994).

85. "Church Borrowing," in Burkett, *Principles Under Scrutiny,* p. 55.

86. "The Church & Money," in Burkett, *Principles Under Scrutiny,* p. 57.

believers; and, (4) feeding gentile widows and orphans = taking care of the nonbelieving poor.[87]

While this is Burkett's understanding of how the church should function, his jeremiads on these topics make it clear that he holds no illusions as to how well contemporary evangelicals fulfill the responsibilities of this model. In light of verses such as 1 Timothy 5:17-18 ("The elders who direct the church well are worthy of double honor. . . . 'Do not muzzle the ox' . . ."), Burkett is irritated by the Church's tendency to expect a lower standard of living for those in "full-time Christian service." "Why shouldn't a pastor have a comfortable salary?" argued Burkett in 1975. "Why shouldn't an evangelist, for instance, live as well as someone who is in business?"[88]

Burkett feels even more strongly about the need for individual churches to return to a New Testament model of caring for widows and orphans and other financially destitute people within the congregational family. In Burkett's view, someone who falls within the care network of the church should never have to tap into welfare or any government programs for basic support. Young widows and divorcees with children should — if they qualify under scriptural qualifications of faithfulness — be able to stay at home with their children until, at the very least, Burkett believes, such time as the children are in school.[89] So seriously does he take this dimension of the church's mission that he states: "Under no circumstances can the qualified needy be ignored. . . . If you find a closed attitude in this area, I would recommend changing to a place of worship compatible with your commitment where you can entrust God's wealth."[90] The "miserable failure on the part of the Church of Jesus Christ" to come anywhere near this standard, however, eventually prompted Burkett to write his 1991 book, *The Complete Financial Guide for Single Parents*, and has led him to tout alter-

---

87. Burkett, *Answers to Your Family's Financial Questions*, pp. 107-8.

88. Burkett, *Your Finances in Changing Times* (1975), p. 146.

89. Larry Burkett, "Is Welfare Scriptural?" *Fundamentalist Journal* (Apr. 1985): 21-23; Burkett, *Answers to Your Family's Financial Questions*, pp. 197-98. See also Burkett, *The Complete Financial Guide for Single Parents*, pp. 81-86. Burkett, to say the least, looks dimly on the usefulness and success of government-based remedies for poverty: "Single parents don't need welfare; they need friends who care. The only long-term solution to the dilemma of single parents is a good job with adequate pay" (Burkett, *The Complete Financial Guide for Single Parents*, p. 33).

90. Burkett, *Your Finances in Changing Times* (1982), pp. 122-23.

native ways for churches to meet these needs, such as day care centers, summertime "latchkey" programs, and Big Brother programs.[91]

Family Finances/Working Mothers

"The husband is the final authority in the home, but God has also assigned some responsibility and authority to the wife."[92] Burkett's teachings, as reflected in this statement from his 1989 book *The Complete Financial Guide for Young Couples,* line up with conservative evangelical views on the hierarchical relationship of men and women. Nonetheless, it is clear that Burkett's perceptions of contemporary financial realities and dynamics places a strong emphasis on women as legitimate, functioning economic beings within the family, the church, and the overall economy who frequently bear the brunt of financial victimization at the hands of males.[93] In most cases, Burkett sees men — ignorant of the most basic financial acumen, rationalizing oversights and neglected deadlines, prone to impulse and big-ticket spending, lured by their greed into get-rich-quick schemes — as the likely culprits in family financial troubles.[94] To remedy this tendency,

91. Burkett, telephone interview, 2 November 1988; Burkett, *The Complete Financial Guide for Single Parents,* pp. 81-86.

92. Burkett, *The Complete Financial Guide for Young Couples,* p. 68.

93. The economic role of women within the household and in the marketplace has been an enduring theme of Burkett's work down through the years. Early on in his ministry, his growing awareness of the need for women to be involved in family financial decisions as well as his concern for the safeguarding of widows and divorcees provided the material for his 1977 volume *What Husbands Wish Their Wives Knew About Money.* His conviction that financial problems are the lurking saboteur in most young marriages led him to write his 1989 book, *The Complete Financial Guide for Young Couples.* The growth of single-parent households (usually working mothers) and Burkett's despair at the church's lack of response to their needs stimulated him to write *The Complete Financial Guide for Single Parents* in 1991 and begin a new emphasis within CFC to address that issue in the form of budgeting seminars targeted at that group ("Christian Financial Concepts" portfolio, 4). And the desire to help those women who were seeking financial advice about a return to the role of homemaker prompted his 1995 volume, *Women Leaving the Workplace.*

94. Burkett, *The Complete Financial Guide for Young Couples,* p. 36. See also most any of the anecdotes Burkett uses in his books to make his points about bad financial habits; the serial anecdotes in Burkett's *Debt-Free Living* (such as the story of "Paul and Julie," pp. 17-40, 61-81) reflect his views about men's refusal to toe the line of financial responsibility.

Burkett counsels couples to make financial decisions in partnership.[95] He is adamant that couples approach financial record keeping, budgeting, and decisions in tandem, with the husband ready to lean heavily on the wife's advice, even in regards to their jobs and how they run their (the man's) businesses.[96] Indeed, should the man prove himself completely unresponsive to good sense in financial matters Burkett believes — citing the story in 1 Samuel 25 of Abigail's take-charge intercession on behalf of the churlish Nabal — that the woman is entirely justified in taking over the family's financial reins.[97]

As to the question of whether or not it is right for the wife to work outside the home, Burkett has steadfastly stated his belief that this decision be left up to each Christian couple based on their personal sense of mission, need, and propriety.[98] On the issue of working mothers, however, Burkett's concern for the proper rearing of children causes him to advocate strategies that would allow the wife to remain at home. In fact, from the start of their marriages he advises all young married couples to peg their household bud-

95. See for example "Husband-Wife Communication About Finances," in Burkett, *Principles Under Scrutiny*, pp. 133-34.

96. See for example Burkett, *The Complete Financial Guide for Young Couples*, pp. 68-69; Burkett, *Business By the Book*, pp. 85-92; "Financial Authority in the Home," and "The Wife's Role in Business," in Burkett, *Principles Under Scrutiny*, pp. 117-20.

97. Burkett, *Answers to Your Family's Financial Questions*, p. 21.

98. Burkett has pointed out that there is no argument in Scripture against women working outside the home, but that guidelines do exist as far as the wife's priorities including: (1) her husband's approval (Eph. 5:22); (2) her children are well-cared for (Prov. 31:27); (3) she maintains her home well (Prov. 31:15); (4) she can balance dual authority at home and on the job (James 1:8) [see Burkett, *Answers to Your Family's Financial Questions*, pp. 13-14; Burkett, *Your Finances in Changing Times* (1982), pp. 75-76]. Clearly, he feels that the rise in the number of working mothers has contributed to the nation's problems with its wayward youth (see Burkett, *Women Leaving the Workplace*, p. 10). However, Burkett is also of the belief that the national, consumer-driven economy is geared toward two-worker households: "In many ways, working moms are trapped by our current financial system. . . . Today most families face a lower real income than their parents, frequent layoffs, a stagnating economy, high income tax rates that punish married incomes, and inflated prices for homes and cars that practically demand two incomes" (Burkett, *Women Leaving the Workplace*, p. 23; see also p. 51). But he has also become increasingly aware that lofty prescriptions from evangelical leaders advising women to stay at home in light of these problems are pointless unless there is an emphasis on a reduction in consumer expectations and an economic response from the churches (Burkett, *Women Leaving the Workplace*, pp. 10, 57-65, 142).

gets to the husband's salary. In this way, Burkett believes they can not only salt away savings for major purchases such as homes and cars, but soften the financial blow of pregnancy and make a smooth adjustment to living on one income.[99] Should a couple still consider such a move he is careful to point out that the extra costs involved for the working mother's joining the workforce (transportation, clothes, child care, etc., etc.) often makes for a poor net return on the time and energy invested.[100] Ever the financial realist, however, he also cautions those who are considering opting out of a two-worker arrangement about the sacrifices that will be required of them. Except in the most affluent circumstances, he frankly advises couples that a move to a more traditional male-as-sole-breadwinner family model will mean the cutting back or elimination of such perks as eating out, shopping trips, lavish gift-giving, private schools, cleaning and yard help — to say nothing of personal time and privacy.[101]

This dimension of Burkett's analysis sheds light on the larger thrust of his critique of the two-worker household, and is not merely a measure of his support for traditional gender roles within marriage. The tendency of the two-worker model, he says, is to foster a consumerist mentality to the exclusion of the mental, emotional, and spiritual health of the family. Much of this, he contends, stems from a radically impaired inability to distinguish between our actual needs and the ever-accelerating appetite for material goods. In 1985 Burkett wrote:

> It is commonly accepted in our generation that the cost of maintaining and operating a home requires that both spouses work. . . . Currently the payments on the "average" new home would require nearly 70% of the "average" husband's pay. The logical conclusion, then, is that two incomes are needed. The fault with this logic is that it doesn't consider whether or not the "average" family needs the "average" home.[102]

Because of this materialistic emphasis, Burkett feels that far too many working women will one day join their work-obsessed husbands in look-

---

99. "Should Wives Work?" in Burkett, *Principles Under Scrutiny*, p. 116; Burkett, *Answers to Your Family's Financial Questions*, p. 15.

100. Burkett, *What Husbands Wish Their Wives Knew About Money*, pp. 66-67; Burkett, *Answers to Your Family's Financial Questions*, pp. 13-15.

101. Burkett, *Women Leaving the Workplace*, pp. 57-65.

102. "Should Wives Work?" in Burkett, *Principles Under Scrutiny*, p. 115.

ing back with regret at not having spent enough time with their families, having chased "after the Joneses only to discover that, when [they] finally caught up with them, they had refinanced."[103]

Business Ethics and Practice

Burkett's advice for Christians in the business world is at variance with much common practice and conventional wisdom in the contemporary marketplace. Paying too much attention to one's profession, business, or the pursuit of money at the expense of one's family and spiritual life is a prominent part of Burkett's critique of business. While open to the fact that there are exceptions and emergencies, any regular schedule that exceeds forty-eight hours/six days he sees as both wrongheaded and potentially injurious at any number of levels.[104]

Each Christian business owner, Burkett believes, has five priorities: in descending order these priorities are — evangelism (through the impact of Christian principles and behavior on employees, suppliers, creditors, and customers), discipleship (mostly in teaching those under one's authority), funding "God's work," (giving to various Christian ministries but also providing counseling, materials, and even financial help to employees), providing for needs (paying salaries and benefits, paying for supplies and equipment in a timely fashion, and providing a quality product or service at a fair price), and finally, generating profits.[105] In his practical advice for day-to-day business operations, Burkett leaves little "wiggle room" — strict honesty is always his guiding rule. Christians should always refuse to pay or accept any kind of kickback, bribe, or "special incentive."[106] He is also critical of substantial mark-ups that are added simply because a company is able to get extra money and "everybody does it."[107] On the strength of Proverbs 3:27 ("Do not withhold good from those to whom it is due . . ."), Burkett urges Christians not to take advantage of others by sloppy management and cash-flow schemes that delay

---

103. Burkett, *The Complete Financial Guide For Young Couples*, p. 18; "Should Wives Work?" in Burkett, *Principles Under Scrutiny*, p. 115.

104. Burkett, *Business By the Book*, pp. 31-34.

105. Burkett, *Business By the Book*, pp. 52-53.

106. "Business Ethics" in Burkett, *Principles Under Scrutiny*, pp. 97-98.

107. Burkett, *Principles Under Scrutiny*, pp. 181-88.

payments to creditors.[108] Moreover, Burkett's standards for treating customers fairly goes so far as requiring that business owners and salespeople not sell goods or services one knows a customer might not need.[109]

In his counsel concerning personnel, it is clear that Burkett is unusually sensitive to the need to treat employees fairly. Remembering the barriers he saw between enlisted men and officers during his time in the Air Force, Burkett frowns on any attempt in business to maintain social or class barriers between workers and management, particularly in light of its chilling effect on evangelism.[110] "If you find that you can't give the same honor and regard to the lowest-ranked employee in your business, you need to stop right here and resolve it with the Lord," he advised readers of his 1990 volume, *Business by the Book*.[111] Moreover, pointing to Philippians 2:3 ("Do nothing from selfishness or empty conceit, but with humility of mind let each of you regard one another as more important than himself"), Burkett maintains that next to fulfilling obligations to one's creditors, the next highest priority for a business owner — even above paying themselves — is paying their employees, and paying them a livable wage that fairly takes into account their skills, level of responsibility, term of service, and local cost-of-living.[112]

Beyond this, Burkett advocates that every Christian employer should prayerfully consider such things as family size and the special needs of employees when setting pay rates. As an illustration, he recalled how he once hired a printer — "Big Joe" — for CFC who had "a sizable family" and who, on his income, would never be able to send his children "to college or even buy an adequate home." Poorly educated, a "willing and cooperative worker, but not a particularly good printer," Burkett says he "found the Lord was asking" him to "do something totally illogical and economically unsound: give him a raise." He wrestled with his own conscience and argued

---

108. Burkett, *Business By the Book,* pp. 22-24.

109. Burkett, *Business By the Book,* pp. 25-26. Despite his aforementioned stance against the tendencies of many people toward materialism, buying foolish things, and the problems of the two-worker household, Burkett does not seem to have made a concrete connection between those issues and a critique of the market economy in general or a questioning of the inherent necessity of much of our economic activity.

110. Burkett, *Business By the Book,* pp. 24-25.

111. Burkett, *Business By the Book,* p. 24.

112. Burkett, *Business By the Book,* pp. 136-48; "Paying a Fair Wage," in Burkett, *Principles Under Scrutiny,* pp. 99-100.

with himself that God would not require such "an absurdity," but "ended up giving Big Joe a raise of nearly five hundred dollars a month." Burkett believes this was a test from God about his willingness to obey and watch over those who had been put under his care.[113] Based on Matthew 20:1-16 (the laborers in the vineyard) he views this sort of preference as fair, and sees it as particularly valid in light of struggles experienced by single-income families: ". . . if I know that an employee is the sole provider for his or her family, I will always lean (emotionally) toward paying that person more. . . . Is that totally fair? I believe so. . . . As long as everyone is paid fairly, and what was promised, it's acceptable to pay some workers more generously. Union leaders might not agree, but single-income families sure do."[114]

The problem of when it is just to fire an employee is a nettlesome question in Burkett's mind. He seems especially soft-hearted in cases of incompetence, implying by anecdote that the employer should bend over backwards to find an alternative position within or outside the company for the individual.[115] In fact, Burkett asks the Christian employer to be open to the idea that God has brought a troublesome/incompatible person into their company to serve as "heavenly sandpaper" in the employer's life. In this case, the individual is to be tolerated and the employer is to seek to try and refine those personal weaknesses which that person brings to the fore.[116] Overall, he insists that taking the step of dismissal be approached with gravity and an attitude of clemency:

> When in doubt about what to do, lean heavily to the mercy side. In situations where an employee must be dismissed, the dismissal should be carried out in an attitude of love and concern. . . . Be sensitive to God's leading about helping those you dismiss, even for valid cause. Several times I have felt God's leading to assist ex-employees financially, even though I would never have considered them for rehire.[117]

---

113. Burkett, *Business By the Book,* p. 139.

114. Burkett, *Women Leaving the Workplace,* p. 104.

115. The chapter on firing employees is easily the longest in his *Business By the Book* (see pp. 104-25).

116. Burkett, *Business By the Book,* p. 124.

117. Burkett, *Business By the Book,* p. 120.

The Public and Political Larry Burkett

By the late 1980s Burkett began to branch out from his strictly finances-related persona as he increasingly spoke up on matters pertaining to national economic policy and social and cultural questions. A staunch Republican, his involvement in such causes grew steadily as he became increasingly appalled at the nation's moral state, Reagan's inability to corral the national debt, and George Bush's refusal to toe the line of fiscal austerity. Burkett became involved in organizations such as the Alliance Defense Fund, a legal defense team he co-created in 1994 along with Bill Bright, James Dobson, Florida-based pastor D. James Kennedy, and conservative media watchdog Donald Wildmon to counteract the efforts of the American Civil Liberties Union in religious freedom cases.[118] He has addressed the national convention of Beverly LaHaye's Concerned Women of America, the conservative counter to the National Organization of Women.[119] On the state level, Burkett was also a player in the campaigns of Republican candidates for statewide office as well as the Georgia Public Policy Foundation, a "non-partisan research and education organization" that "actively supports private enterprise, limited government, and individual responsibility."[120] It was the publication of his books The Coming Economic Earthquake (1990, rev. 1994) and Whatever Happened to the American Dream? (1993) on national fiscal policies and the harmful impact of governmental policies, however, that has brought Burkett his greatest success and influence.[121] The subsequent publication of a trio of briskly selling futurist/apocalyptic novels has cemented his role as an influential voice within the so-called "Religious Right."[122]

118. Chuck Thompson, "Legal Wars," Money Matters (Feb. 1998): 4-5, 8; "The ACLU Finally Meets Its Match," fund-raising letter from the Alliance Defense Fund (ADF), ca. Summer 1998. For an example of the ADF's analysis of the nation's moral state and its connection to the legal status of religion see the videotape featuring ADF president, Alan Sears "1995, Incredible Battle for Religious Freedom in America" (Coeur d'Alene, ID: Koinonia House, 1996).

119. Concerned Women of America, 1993 National Convention brochure.

120. Georgia Public Policy Foundation webpage (http://www.gppf.org); Burkett, interview, 2 November 1998. Burkett served as the honorary treasurer for the 1998 gubernatorial primary run of Burkett family friend, Nancy Schaefer.

121. Larry Burkett, The Coming Economic Earthquake (Chicago: Moody Press, 1991; revised and expanded edition, 1994); Burkett, Whatever Happened to the American Dream?

122. Larry Burkett, The Illuminati (Nashville: Thomas Nelson, 1991); Burkett, The Thor Conspiracy; and Larry Burkett, Solar Flare (Chicago: Moody Press, 1997).

An admirer of the Austrian libertarian economist Ludwig von Mises, Burkett has consistently pointed to the problem of the National Debt — exacerbated by the continual spiral of consumer debt — as the overriding problem of the American economic scene.[123] In line with most conservative and free-market analysis of recent American economic and political history, he traces the nation's troubles in this regard to the introduction of Keynesian policies and the expansion of the national debt during the New Deal.[124] This, he argues, represented the death of the free-enterprise system in the United States, ushering in our present system which Burkett believes is a "government controlled and privately owned" arrangement which is technically, in his opinion, "a fascist economy."[125]

While the implementation of these policies might be merely questions of economic philosophy or constitutional legalities to many secular conservative ideologues, for Burkett they carry the additional odium of being a virtual repudiation of God's guidelines for economics. Putting a uniquely economic spin on the "Christian heritage" beliefs which are popular in some conservative evangelical circles, Burkett views the free-market system, free of government controls, as a faithful embodiment of biblical guidelines on finances. William Bradford's implementation of a those-who-will-not-work-will-not-eat policy (based on Paul's admonitions in 2 Thess. 3:10) in the Plymouth Bay Colony, Burkett believes, was the birth of self-initiative and the free market on this continent — principles of freedom that were ingrained within early American society and government for the most part until the twentieth century.[126]

It was with the coming of World War I and the exposure of "millions of American GIs . . . to the amoral values of the European countries," which "spread like a virus" throughout the nation as evidenced in "the ef-

---

123. Burkett, *The Coming Economic Earthquake* (1994), pp. 50-51. Ludwig von Mises (d. 1973) is the patron saint of many modern free-marketers and libertarians (see his *Human Action: A Treatise on Economics* [New Haven: Yale University Press, 1963] and *Omnipotent Government: The Rise of the Total State and Total War* [New Haven: Yale University, 1944]). Burkett's views on the national problems with overspending have been a constant since the first 1975 edition of *Your Finances in Changing Times* (see pp. 15-16).

124. Burkett, *Your Finances in Changing Times* (1975), pp. 15-16; Burkett, *The Coming Economic Earthquake* (1994), pp. 43-51; Burkett, *Whatever Happened to the American Dream?*, pp. 21-22.

125. Burkett, *Whatever Happened to the American Dream?*, p. 56.

126. Burkett, *Whatever Happened to the American Dream?*, pp. 41-48.

fects of . . . immorality [on] the generation of the twenties," that America began to depart from all kinds of biblically based standards of behavior.[127] With the coming of the Great Depression, Americans' growing materialism and greed would not allow them to settle for losing the prosperity they had enjoyed in the 1920s. As a result, much like the children of Israel who sought a strong ruler to save them and ended up with King Saul, Americans elected Franklin Roosevelt and his policies of government control. To Burkett, New Deal policies and subsequent government overspending were a clear departure from the "Christianomics" he believes this country had practiced prior to that time.[128]

This process, Burkett believes, intensified with World War II even as the war served to "spread the immoral values of the European community to millions more American soldiers."[129] After a short "spiritual interlude" in the postwar years, both American society and the economy, which reflects its spiritual state, have been on a decades-long downward spiral. The enormous proliferation of government programs during Lyndon Johnson's "Great Society" and since has both reflected and enhanced the nation's degraded moral condition.[130]

On a financial level, Burkett believed the Reagan administration presented an opportunity to reverse this situation, but failed due to Congress's refusal to match tax cuts with promised spending reductions and its failure to honor the Gramm-Rudman Act.[131] Unhappy with George Bush's failure to live up to his predecessor's policies, Burkett is appalled by Bill Clinton — in any number of ways.[132] In terms of economic impact, however, Burkett

127. Burkett, *Whatever Happened to the American Dream?*, pp. 11-12.

128. Burkett, *Whatever Happened to the American Dream?*, pp. 11-12, 21-22; Burkett refers to the early American free enterprise system and lean government as "Christianomics" on p. 41.

129. Burkett, *Whatever Happened to the American Dream?*, p. 12.

130. Burkett, *Whatever Happened to the American Dream?*, pp. 28-29; Burkett, *The Coming Economic Earthquake*, pp. 63-79.

131. Burkett, *The Coming Economic Earthquake*, pp. 71-72, 119-23.

132. Part of this was in response to his perception that Clinton was intent on instituting all sorts of new government spending, including his failed first term attempt at reforming the nation's health care system (see Burkett, *The Coming Economic Earthquake* [1994], "revised and expanded," as its cover proclaims, "for the Clinton Agenda"). But Clinton's social policies ("Certainly pornographers will receive more tolerance than Christians in the Clinton justice department" [203] and personal behavioral problems (". . . adultery is no longer an issue in national politics . . ." [*Whatever Happened to the Amer-*

likened the '92 election[133] and Clinton's backtracking on promises of a tax cut in favor of raising taxes to "the American people decid[ing] they didn't like 'Captain' Bush [and] elect[ing] 'Captain' Clinton who has been airlifted onto the *Titanic* and is now steaming full speed toward the mid-Atlantic ice pack."[134]

A committed "cyclist" after the theories of the early twentieth-century Russian economist Nikolai Kondratieff and influenced by the contemporary speculations of popular "gloom and doom" economist Ravi Batra, Burkett was sure by the mid-1990s that the U.S. was headed for a major recession by the turn of the century or sooner.[135] Feeling that our having dodged the Batra-predicted "crash of 1990" was something of a lucky break, Burkett told his readers in *Whatever Happened to the American Dream?*:

> I honestly don't have any objective way to know how long we can continue without a major economic crisis. It is my personal conviction that we will *not* resolve the problems and, therefore, are on a collision course with a major economic and social collapse. . . . Based on the 1992 elections and the promises made by President Clinton (assuming that he actually implements them), I would project five to seven years. . . .[136]

---

ican Dream?, p. 12]) also came into play. Perhaps his attitude toward Clinton was best revealed in a public speech where he mentioned one of his favorite bumper stickers: "Bill Clinton: God's Man for America — Repent!" (Larry Burkett, "Our Economy in Crisis," side 1 [Wheaton, IL: Tyndale House, 1994]).

133. Burkett believes that the 1991 first edition of his book *The Coming Economic Earthquake,* which sold nearly 550,000 copies, played a role in costing Bush the presidency in 1992 (see Burkett, *The Coming Economic Earthquake* [1994], pp. 7-8).

134. Burkett, *The Coming Economic Earthquake* (1994), p. 8.

135. Burkett, *The Coming Economic Earthquake* (1994), pp. 91-102. Nikolai Kondratieff was a 1920s Russian economist whose theories about fifty- to sixty-year cycles have been applied to everything from recessions to waves in fashion and popular music (see his *Long Wave Cycles* [New York: Richardson & Snyder, 1984]). Ravi Batra, a professor of international economics at Southern Methodist University and follower of Hindu philosopher P. R. Sarkan, achieved some notoriety for a string of popular books that predicted imminent financial meltdown (see particularly Batra's *The Great Depression of 1990* [New York: Simon & Schuster, 1987]).

136. Burkett, *Whatever Happened to the American Dream?*, p. 48; Burkett noted that he received much of the information on which he based parts of the book from Republican congressmen Dan Burton of Indiana and Tom Delay of Texas (7).

Given the decline in America's moral climate, Burkett viewed the social, cultural, and political prospect of a major economic downturn as potentially catastrophic. "Just consider the anger, frustration, and potential violence," Burkett wrote, "if millions of Americans see their lifetime dreams evaporate [as] they lose their jobs, their homes, and even their retirement savings." In such a scenario, Burkett envisioned that "the flame of resentment" would probably be lit "by the inner-city poor who see their subsidies cut to the bone and inflation rob them of all hope." But worse yet was the "anger of middle-class America." These people, Burkett argued, "may not riot . . . they may vote in a 'dictator.'"[137]

It was here that Burkett forecast the possibility of a particularly dangerous future awaiting America's evangelical Christians. Seeing the expansion of the federal government's control over the economy, over the states, and into such areas as education and the environment, Burkett envisioned the abolishment of religious organizations' tax-exempt status as nearly inevitable.[138] But this could be born-again believers' least problem. "I fear that we are in the early stages of class persecution," he says. "The liberal 'left' sees us as the greatest impediment to 'social progress.' . . . In a time of great trial, scapegoats are usually in demand. . . . We are the only politically 'incorrect' minority left in America."[139]

This is the scenario that fueled the plots of Burkett's popular novels, *The Illuminati* and *The Thor Conspiracy*. In *The Illuminati*, evangelical Christians become the target of government persecution in the wake of an economic crash brought on by decades of government deficits and over-regulation of the business and environment. Behind the scenes, a supernaturally evil group known as "The Society" controls the President and many other high-ranking officials in its quest to implement a one-world government and a cashless, computer-controlled economic system. "Fundamentalists," unpopular in light of their regressive views on these matters and such things as abortion and homosexuality, are framed for the assassination of three Supreme Court justices and many are rounded up and sent to detention camps. Meanwhile, Atlanta Pastor John Elder, head of a Christian Coalition-like group called the Constitutional Rights Committee, seeks to combat the conspiracy with the aid of computer genius

137. Burkett, *Whatever Happened to the American Dream?*, p. 49.
138. Burkett, *Whatever Happened to the American Dream?*, pp. 72-76.
139. Burkett, *Whatever Happened to the American Dream?*, p. 37.

Jeff Wells.[140] In *The Thor Conspiracy,* Wells returns a decade later to crack a massive government cover-up of a 1960s-era weapons test gone bad. In this instance, The Society is using the ozone hole in the atmosphere as an excuse to manipulate a worldwide environmental crackdown that throws the United States into a new nightmare of social and economic havoc.[141] Only Wells's computer savvy and insider knowledge, along with the help of a states-rights regime in a Wyoming populated with several million of Elder's self-relocated evangelical followers, stands in the way of national calamity. Both novels sold extremely well, and on the strength of *The Illuminati* as well as the continued sales of *The Coming Economic Earthquake* the Christian Booksellers' Association named Burkett its 1992 "Author of the Year."[142]

140. In an article in the *Christian Century* ("New World-Order, Old World Anti-Semitism" [Sept. 13-20, 1995]: 844-49) an Episcopal priest, Ephraim Radner, in an exposition of Pat Robertson's controversial book *The New World Order* (Waco: Word Books, 1991) also looked at Burkett's *Illuminati* as an example of the widespread conspiratorial mindset present within conservative evangelical circles. Although Burkett used the "Illuminati" imagery in his title, Radner did admit that Burkett's "use of the conspiracy theory actually lies closer to Hal Lindsey's ambivalent philo-Israeli apocalypticism than it does to Robertson's sources" (845), which he flatly condemned as anti-Semitic. To be fair to Burkett, upon a thorough reading of his materials I can find no trace of anti-Semitism; his attitude on these questions is probably better depicted as the enthusiastic philo-Semitism frequently found in evangelical premillennial circles.

141. Burkett is an outspoken critic of the radical environmentalist movement and the Environmental Protection Agency. While applauding early efforts to clean up water and streams (see Burkett, *Whatever Happened to the American Dream?*, p. 57), he feels the EPA has gone beyond all good sense in their policies of wetland preservation and their "Superfund" penalties (see pp. 91-103). More serious, however, are the radical "greens" whom Burkett views as dangerous elitists with an "I've got mine" attitude that are out to depopulate the globe through their efforts to ban DDT and CFCs as part of their quest for a pristine Earth. As of the early 1990s, Burkett believed there was little, if no, scientific evidence for global warming or the problem with the ozone layer (see pp. 108-38), a stance he still maintained in late 1999 (Burkett, telephone interview, 16 September 1999).

142. "Burkett, Larry," s.v. in *Contemporary Authors,* vol. 140, p. 62. Burkett's 1997 novel *Solar Flare* offered a somewhat different emphasis than his first two novels and, within an apocalyptic setting, embodies a rather traditional Jeffersonian, Southern nostalgia for a return to local, rural community. The novel's plot envisions the aftermath of a massive solar burst of energy that — after warnings are unheeded by smug government agencies — destroys almost all human capacity to generate electricity. Bereft of almost all our modern manufacturing, technology, communication, and transportation, the United States is immediately thrown — understandably — into chaos. The crisis is gradually

Seemingly at the zenith of his influence, Burkett was diagnosed with renal cell carcinoma in March of 1995 and underwent two painful surgeries that saw the removal of one of his kidneys and his left shoulder blade. Rejecting the often-destructive results of chemotherapy in his particular type of cancer, he opted for an alternative strategy that combined immuno-therapy (at the time available only in the Czech Republic) with nutritional treatment. Although his disease went into remission, Burkett now lived with chronic pain from his ordeal. Nonetheless, he saw this as an opportunity to counsel fellow believers in similar circumstances with spiritual comfort and information on cancer and treatment resources and strategies in his 1996 Moody Press book *Damaged But Not Broken* (retitled *Hope When It Hurts* in 1998).[143]

Conclusion

Untouched by major controversy or by scandal in his more than two decades as a Christian financial counselor, Larry Burkett and Christian Financial Concepts is today a major component in the armada that is the evangelical parachurch. Far and away, he is the preeminent evangelical voice on money and finance, and with his connections to James Dobson and other leaders of the Religious Right he is the most recognized and authoritative spokesperson for conservative government fiscal policies in the eyes of the evangelical public. Burkett — his health cooperating — and Christian Financial Concepts — with or without Burkett — would appear to be set as

---

overcome as the U.S. Government implements a plan that relocates the populations of cities and suburbs to hundreds of giant cooperative farms where they must work together to raise their own food, educate their children, and maintain internal order and external security against roving bands of — usually — urban thugs. Revivals break out in the camps and many Americans, viewing the crisis as God's judgment, are converted to an evangelical faith. After a period of about a year (when the effects of the original solar phenomenon have finally abetted and the electrical infrastructure can be restored) many Americans have found that they enjoy the rural, agricultural life — free from the intrusion of television and mindless consumerism and characterized by the local autonomy and religious good-feeling each "camp" had enjoyed — feel that their new lot in life is better and decide to remain in the countryside.

143. Larry Burkett with Michael E. Taylor, *Damaged But Not Broken: A Personal Testimony of How to Deal With the Impact of Cancer* (Chicago: Moody Press, 1996).

an organizational force within the evangelical subculture for years to come.

Burkett's rise to prominence — as well as that of subsequent authors with similar emphases on financial management and counseling that have arisen in his wake[144] — is an interesting development in the seemingly limitless expansion of America's underlying evangelical infrastructure. Within the context of that long-running phenomenon, Burkett surely represents the cutting edge of a new layer of the evangelical parachurch's increasing reach into what was once, or had become, purely secularized turf. However, the response to Burkett's particular message on financial management is indicative of factors and realities that lead one deeper into the historical trends and trajectories of evangelicalism.

One of the most intriguing aspects of Burkett's emergence in the 1970s is the manner in which it seemed to reflect new financial realities about evangelicals themselves. In concert with the great riptide of postwar prosperity, evangelicals certainly shared in the bounty of a generally climbing standard of living. Fueled by the giving and purchasing power of their prospering constituencies, evangelical denominations, parachurch organizations, schools, and dependent "industries" such as the Christian bookstore and music sector experienced tremendous growth in the 1960s and, especially, the 1970s and 1980s.[145]

At the same time, it was apparent that many evangelicals were trying to figure out how to handle all this new-found prosperity. The 1970s saw the advent of books like Harold Hill's *How to Live Like a King's Kid* and the growing popularity of the "health and wealth," "name it and claim it"

144. Probably the best known of these other financial counselors is executive and financial planner Ron Blue; see his *Master Your Money: A Step-By-Step Plan for Financial Freedom* (Nashville: Thomas Nelson, 1986; rev. ed., 1997). See also Austin Pryor, *Sound Mind Investing* (Chicago: Moody Press, 1996).

145. For a look at the growth in evangelical publishing and the Christian Bookstore scene in the 1970s and 1980s see John P. Ferré, "Searching for the Great Commission: Evangelical Book Publishing Since the 1970s," in Schultze, ed., *American Evangelicals and the Mass Media*, pp. 99-117. See also Colleen McDannell, *Material Christianity: Religion and Popular Culture in America* (New Haven: Yale University Press, 1995), pp. 246-69. For insight into the growth of the "Christian Contemporary Music" scene see Paul Baker, *Contemporary Christian Music: Where It Came From, What It Is, Where It's Going* (Westchester, IL: Crossway Books, 1985); and William D. Romanowski, "Rock 'n' Religion: A Socio-Cultural Analysis of the Contemporary Christian Music Industry" (Ph.D. diss., Bowling Green University, 1990).

brand of prosperity teaching as touted by figures like Kenneth Copeland and Robert Tilton.[146] At the same time, the new affluence provided grounds for much soul-searching as evidenced by the impact of books like Ronald Sider's *Rich Christians in an Age of Hunger*.[147] Larry Burkett's writings and radio broadcasts addressed both aspects of this dilemma and provided a safe middle ground where God honored hard work and expected us to live a decent, comfortable life — even as all one's possessions belonged ultimately to Him and were thus expected to further kingdom work and help those in need.

But as Burkett provided a way for evangelicals to conceptualize the meaning of money and how they should relate to it as Christians, his counsel also provided very practical guidance in navigating the treacherous uncertainties of the economy and maintaining or bettering one's position therein. During a historical period marked by varying periods of double-digit inflation, skyrocketing interest rates, ever-expanding sources and methods of obtaining credit, and an apparent fundamental shift in the very nature of the American economy from an industrial base to one oriented towards service and information, a lot of Americans were "standing in the need" of financial information and advice — to say nothing of prayer. From the success of Burkett's advice materials and radio broadcasts, it is clear that many evangelicals were included in that number.

Here it is important to remember the social and economic demographics that have marked the evangelical subculture within this century. Much has been made in the two-decade-plus resurgence of scholarship on evangelicalism of the ways in which evangelicals are a representative slice of American culture. This was, in part, a response — justifiably so — to the dismissive Menckenesque perceptions of scholars such as Stewart Cole, Norman Furniss, and Richard Hofstadter, which tended to brand all "fundamentalists" as rural, backward, poverty-stricken, mostly

146. See Harold Hill, *Live Like a King's Kid* (Plainfield, NJ: Logos Publishing, 1974); Kenneth Copeland, *The Laws of Prosperity* (Fort Worth, TX: Kenneth Copeland Publications, 1974); Kenneth Hagin, *How God Taught Me About Prosperity* (Tulsa, OK: Kenneth Hagin Ministries, 1985). While these sorts of teachings enjoyed a major resurgence in the 1970s and 1980s, their roots lay deep in the "positive confession" teachings of nineteenth-century healer E. W. Kenyon (see Bruce Barron, *The Health and Wealth Gospel* [Downers Grove, IL: InterVarsity Press, 1987], pp. 60-63, 119).

147. Ronald J. Sider, *Rich Christians in an Age of Hunger* (Downers Grove, IL: InterVarsity Press, 1977; 2nd ed., 1984; Waco, TX: Word Books, 3rd ed., 1990; 4th ed., 1997).

Southern, anti-intellectual regressives having a difficult time making the adjustment to modernity.[148] While the "new" scholarship on evangelicals has done much to expand and clarify who evangelicals are and what they have been all about, it may also to some degree reflect the wounded sensibilities of a portion of evangelicalism that wanted to insist that, just like "mainstream America," their twentieth-century story was middle-class, urban/suburban, and Northern.[149] While this "new" dimension of the story is valuable, perhaps it is time to revisit — without the reliance on old, pejorative stereotypes — the socio-economic class dimensions involved in understanding the historic and contemporary dimensions of twentieth-century evangelicalism. Indeed, the majority of individuals bearing the "fundamentalist," "pentecostal," and even "evangelical" label in this century tended to fit into one or more of the following categories: Southern or rural Midwestern, and poor/working class. And even though those evangelical inhabitants of recent decades may have been

148. See Stewart G. Cole, *The History of Fundamentalism* (New York: Richard Smith, 1931); Norman F. Furniss, *The Fundamentalist Controversy, 1918-1931* (New Haven: Yale University Press, 1954); Richard Hofstadter, *Anti-Intellectualism in American Life* (New York: Alfred A. Knopf, 1962). One might argue that there is a more refined spin on this argument in recent years, which casts conservative American Protestants to one degree or another "at war" with contemporary American culture (see the four volumes put out under the auspices of The Fundamentalism Project, Martin Marty and R. Scott Appleby, editors [Chicago: University of Chicago Press, 1989-1994]).

149. While a recent wave of scholarship on evangelicalism has transformed the field, the thrust of some of the most outstanding volumes have concentrated on urban-based, largely Northern and Midwestern networks within the fundamentalist and developing evangelical networks, particularly the "Moody-Wheaton-NAE-Graham-Fuller" nexus (see for example George M. Marsden, *Fundamentalism and American Culture: The Shaping of Twentieth-Century Evangelicalism* [New York: Oxford University Press, 1980]; Marsden, *Reforming Fundamentalism: Fuller Seminary and the New Evangelicalism* [Grand Rapids: Eerdmans, 1987]; and Joel A. Carpenter, *Revive Us Again: The Reawakening of American Fundamentalism* [New York: Oxford University Press, 1997]) — a grouping that in terms of sheer numbers and cultural presence pales in comparison to the South's Baptist-Pentecostal-Holiness-Church of Christ evangelical networks. An attempt to redress this balance in explaining the contemporary role of Southern cultural and political dynamics in evangelicalism's recent history is the so-called "Shibley Thesis" (see Mark Shibley, *Resurgent Evangelicalism in the United States: Mapping Cultural Change Since 1970* [Columbia, SC: University of South Carolina Press, 1996]; for a position opposing this argument see Christian Smith, David Sikkink, and Jason Bailey, "Devotion in Dixie and Beyond: A Test of the 'Shibley Thesis' on the Effects of Regional Origin and Migration on Individual Generosity," *Journal for the Scientific Study of Religion* 37, no. 3 [Sept. 1998]: 494-506).

more likely to be an accountant in Kansas City, a car salesman in Akron, or a teacher in San Bernardino, it's highly likely that they were, respectively, born in Atoka County, Oklahoma; had parents who came from Cambria, Michigan; or had a father that gave up on life as a farm laborer in east-central Mississippi.

In this regard, it may be easier to understand the important role that a Larry Burkett and his organization provided within the context of the recent history and development of evangelicalism. Given the swirling maelstrom of American economic life, Burkett provided a valuable service to many evangelicals who, by dint of their socio-economic position, family background, and/or life experience found the problems associated with mortgages, credit cards, taxes, saving for children's college educations, and investing for retirement not only complicated, but strange new territory. Better yet, Burkett provided not only basic information about nearly every aspect of one's finances, but did it all with an eye to what God thought about the whole thing. You might say that while the people at First Congregational were naturally inclined to listen when E. F. Hutton spoke, the folks at Antioch Baptist or Evangel Nazarene wanted to listen to someone like Larry Burkett.

Beyond his influence in the individual economic lives of evangelicals, however, Burkett and his message(s) may also be instructive to those who are concerned about the class dynamics of evangelicalism as a movement and its relationship to the larger culture and matters of public policy. Burkett's apocalyptic scenarios of imprudent fiscal policy, budgetary collapse, and attendant moral anarchy, so well-received by many evangelicals, may tell us as much about how evangelicals perceive themselves and their position within American culture and society as it does about their inclination toward conservative Republican politics. Having achieved a tenuous hold on prosperity, they now find themselves under assault not only by a society whose moral and cultural values they believe are contrary to God's guidelines, but one that rejects His views on finances as well.

CHAPTER 13

Levels of Contributions and Attitudes toward Money among Evangelicals and Non-Evangelicals in Canada and the U.S.

DEAN R. HOGE AND MARK A. NOLL

Every man according as he purposeth in his heart, so let him give; not grudgingly out of necessity: for God loveth the cheerful giver.

2 CORINTHIANS 9:7 (KJV)

All recent evidence agrees that evangelicals give more money to their churches than do other Christians. This is true whether contributions are measured in dollars per household or in the percentage of family income given. The evidence comes in two forms: data reported by denominational offices, and nationwide surveys that asked people how much money they donated to their churches in the previous year. Both forms are credible for comparing one set of denominations with another or comparing evangelical believers with others.

The best analysis of denominational reports has been done by John and Sylvia Ronsvalle.[1] They compared giving in eight U.S. denominations belonging to the National Council of Churches and eight belonging to the

---

1. John L. Ronsvalle and Sylvia Ronsvalle, *The State of Church Giving through 1994* (Champaign, IL: Empty Tomb, 1996). Also see John and Sylvia Ronsvalle, *Behind the Stained Glass Windows* (Grand Rapids: Baker, 1996).

National Association of Evangelicals. In 1994 the average giving per member in the former was $443; in the latter it was $630.[2] As a percentage of per capita income it was 2.93 for the former and 4.16 for the latter. The Ronsvalle team also reported that the percentage of contributions going for benevolences, rather than congregational finances, was greater for the evangelicals. In 1994 it was 18 percent for the evangelical denominations and 13 percent for the mainline.

The best survey data comes from two studies. First is the General Social Survey, an annual sociological survey of the U.S. population sponsored by the National Science Foundation. It asked about religious contributions in 1987 to 1989. Second is a 1988 Gallup survey. Both sets of data were analyzed by Hoge and Yang in 1994.[3] They found that evangelical and conservative denominations (combined) had somewhat higher levels of giving than mainline denominations in the late 1980s. The percentage of household giving was clearly higher for the evangelicals and conservatives.

Later Hoge, Zech, McNamara, and Donahue made a detailed study of five denominations — Catholic, Presbyterian, Lutheran, Southern Baptist, and Assemblies of God.[4] They found, in agreement with other research, that giving among the more strictly evangelical denominations — the Assemblies of God and Southern Baptists — was somewhat higher than among the Lutherans and Presbyterians. Catholics were lowest of the five. To our knowledge, higher giving by evangelicals has been found in every research study.[5]

The reason for evangelicals' higher giving has been repeatedly discussed. The answer is certainly not some factor specific to evangelical members' finances. Rather, it is related to members' religious commitments, since all research shows giving to be highly associated with a person's level of participation in church life. Hoge and his colleagues, in their

2. Ronsvalle and Ronsvalle, *The State of Church Giving*, p. 32.

3. Dean R. Hoge and Fenggang Yang, "Determinants of Religious Giving in American Denominations: Data from Two Nationwide Surveys," *Review of Religious Research* 36, no. 2 (Dec. 1994): 123-48.

4. Dean R. Hoge, Charles Zech, Patrick McNamara, and Michael J. Donahue, *Money Matters: Personal Giving in American Churches* (Louisville: Westminster/John Knox, 1996).

5. For an analysis of giving to British Columbia churches see Robert K. Burkinshaw, *Pilgrims in Lotus Land: Conservative Protestantism in British Columbia, 1917-1981* (Montreal: McGill-Queen's University Press, 1995).

study of five denominations, found that financial contributions to one's church correlated .38 with frequency of church attendance and .27 with number of hours volunteered per month to help the church.[6] This means that as involvement with the church increases, so also does the level of giving. Clearly, giving forms one part of members' involvement in their churches.

In the five-denomination study the evangelical congregations were higher not only in their financial giving, but in their attendance and volunteering as well. For example, the percentage of members reporting at least once weekly was 93 for the Assemblies of God, 87 for the Southern Baptists, 79 for the Catholics, 60 for the Presbyterians, and 55 for the Lutherans.[7] The average number of hours that members volunteered for church tasks in the month prior to the survey were 5.6 for Baptists, 5.3 for Assemblies of God, 3.6 for Presbyterians, 3.1 for Lutherans, and 2.2 for Catholics.[8] On all three measures, evangelicals were highest.

Hoge and his colleagues assessed numerous factors to find the main determinants of high financial giving. For the Assemblies of God they found four:

1. High family income (statistically a strong factor).
2. High level of involvement in the church (a strong factor).
3. Planning one's giving by the year — tithing or pledging.
4. Spouse attends the same church.

For the Southern Baptists they found seven:

1. High family income (a strong factor).
2. High level of involvement in the church (a strong factor).
3. Evangelical theology.
4. Planning one's giving by the year — tithing or pledging.
5. Spouse attends the same church.

6. Dean R. Hoge, Charles Zech, Patrick McNamara, and Michael J. Donahue, "The Value of Volunteers as Resources for Congregations," *Journal for the Scientific Study of Religion* 37, no. 3 (Sept. 1998): 470-80.

7. Hoge et al., *Money Matters*, p. 187. These figures are higher than figures obtained from random surveys of members, due to bias in the persons who returned lay questionnaires, yet the comparison of denominations is reliable.

8. Hoge et al., *Money Matters*, p. 55.

6. Age about forty to sixty-five.
7. The congregation uses canvassing (a weak factor).[9]

In light of this evidence, the question of why evangelicals give more needs to be rephrased: it becomes the question of why evangelicals are higher in church *commitment* more broadly, rather than just why they give more money. Hoge and his colleagues pursued a series of case studies and found that financial giving was higher in churches which are clearly oriented toward evangelistic outreach in theology, which preach strong biblical authority for guiding one's life, which have altar calls in worship services, and which de-emphasize social witness (except on divorce, pornography, abortion, and homosexuality). Most churches with higher giving preach abstinence from alcohol, gambling, and extramarital sex. They emphasize tithing or proportional giving.

This research team also reported that evangelical churches often preach reciprocity with God, in that a Christian who tithes and supports his or her church can expect blessings from God in return. Numerous sermons cited Malachi 3:10, saying that God will reward a tither with overflowing blessings.[10] Evangelical and Pentecostal churches include this emphasis in their teaching more than do mainline or liberal Protestant churches, who tend to be circumspect in their teaching about rewards from God for financial gifts. Evangelicals commonly trust in God when they make large contributions, and they often say that God will not let anybody down. In this research, they affirmed that tithers will be blessed and cared for in ways that nobody can foresee.

This chapter reports the findings in new high-quality survey data on the United States and Canada. It describes evangelical and non-evangelical religious giving and attempts to explain the differences. Interpretation of this new data comes partly from the survey and partly from the earlier research by Hoge and his colleagues.

9. Hoge et al., *Money Matters*, pp. 91-92.
10. The passage reads, in the New International Version, "'Bring the whole tithe into the storehouse, that there may be food in my house. Test me in this,' says the Lord Almighty, 'and see if I will not throw open the floodgates of heaven and pour out so much blessing that you will not have room enough for it.'"

Data and Measures

In 1996 Wheaton College's Institute for the Study of American Evangelicals (ISAE) was part of a research group that undertook a large survey of the United States and Canada. In October of that year the Angus Reid Group of Toronto completed 3,000 phone interviews in the U.S. and 3,000 in Canada, using random dialing, and weighing the data to fit national population statistics.

Although most of the survey concerned political questions, several items concerned money and giving. Our first task for understanding the results was to identify the evangelicals in the sample. For this task we used two methods: first, identifying denominations that are predominantly evangelical, and second, identifying persons with evangelical commitments regardless of denominational affiliation.

Categorization of Denominations

The survey asked three pertinent questions. (1) "Do you ever think of yourself as part of a religious tradition? For example, do you consider yourself as Christian, Jewish, Muslim, other non-Christian, agnostic or atheist, nothing in particular, or something else?" (2) Everyone who answered "Christian" was asked a second question: "What *specific* denomination is that?" Note that the word "member" was not included in these questions. (3) Later in the interview the respondents were asked a third question: "Do you consider yourself to be any of the following: A charismatic Christian? A pentecostal Christian? An evangelical Christian? A fundamentalist Christian? A liberal or progressive Christian?" The respondents could respond "yes" or "no" to each of the five.

Is the third question useful? We checked on the validity of the self-definitions in the third question by comparing its responses with the respondents' denominational membership. For example, do any mainline Protestants such as Episcopalians or Methodists consider themselves to be evangelicals or fundamentalists? The answer is yes. We found that the self-definitions were quite independent of denominational membership. To take an example, the percentage of Presbyterians who said they were evangelical was 19 in the United States and 14 in Canada. The percentage saying they were pentecostal or charismatic was 18 in the United States and 12 in

Canada. The percentage of Catholics who said they were evangelical was 12 in the United States and 10 in Canada, and the percentages saying they were pentecostal or charismatic were 18 and 14. For our analytic purposes these self-definitions did not seem reliable, and we did not use them.[11]

Next, we divided the respondents in each nation into ten categories, based on their self-reported denominational affiliations: evangelical Protestants, mainline Protestants, other Protestants, Catholics, Eastern Orthodox, Mormons, Jews, Christians uncertain about their denomination, members of non-Judeo-Christian religions, and secular persons. Most persons who said they were Christian knew which denomination they belonged to, but some responded in vague descriptive terms, such as "fundamentalist" or "charismatic." We used these terms interchangeably with denominational names in making the categories.

To classify all the denominations we followed earlier researchers in identifying groups that were most clearly evangelical or mainline.[12] This left us with many respondents who did not know their denominational identity or who had none, plus some who belonged to denominations not easy to classify (for example, Jehovah's Witnesses). To keep the evangelical and mainline categories as undiluted as possible, we assigned persons in unclassifiable denominations to two other categories: "other Protestants" and "Christian but don't know which denomination." In assigning the correct places for borderline groups we inspected the theological beliefs of the groups' members as a help. For example, we looked at the specific beliefs of members of Brethren, Mennonite, and non-denominational Protestants, and on the basis of their responses categorized Brethren and Mennonites in the "other" category.

Using this procedure, our evangelical category included Alliance, Baptist, charismatic, Church of Christ, Church of God, evangelical, fundamentalist, holiness, non-denominational, and pentecostal groups. The mainline category included Anglican, Congregational, Episcopalian, Lutheran, Methodist, Presbyterian, Reformed, and United Church denomi-

---

11. For perceptive research that studies individuals and networks that self-consciously use the term "evangelical" for themselves, see Christian Smith, *American Evangelicalism: Embattled and Thriving* (Chicago: University of Chicago Press, 1998).

12. Lyman A. Kellstedt, John C. Green, James L. Guth, and Corwin E. Smidt, "Grasping the Essentials: The Social Embodiment of Religion and Political Behavior," ch. 10 in *Religion and the Culture Wars,* ed. John Green et al. (Lanham, MD: Rowman and Littlefield, 1996), pp. 174-92. Also see Hoge and Yang, "Determinants."

TABLE 1 **Distribution of Main Religious Traditions (in percents)**

	Canada	U.S.
N=	(3,000)	(3,000)
Evangelical Protestant	6%	23%
Mainline Protestant	19	16
Other Protestant	2	4
Catholic	33	23
Jewish	1	2
Orthodox Christian	1	*
Latter-Day Saints	*	1
Christian but don't know which	7	9
Non-Judeo-Christian Tradition	7	8
Secular or non-religious	24	15
*Less than ½ percent	100	101

nations. (In the U.S., United Church meant the United Church of Christ, and in Canada it meant the United Church of Canada.)

The "other Protestant" category included Adventists, Brethren, Quakers, Jehovah's Witnesses, Mennonites, Unitarian-Universalists, and unspecified "Protestants." The "secular" category included persons who said they are agnostic, atheist, nothing in particular, or "don't know." These people are not necessarily militant secularists; some are merely uncommitted to any specific religious tradition.

Table 1 above shows the percentages of the population of the United States and Canada in each of these categories. Note that the percentage of evangelicals is much lower in Canada than in the United States (6% versus 23%), and the percentage "secular or non-religious" is much higher (24% versus 15%). The Canadian culture in general is less evangelical.[13]

13. The number of evangelicals discovered in the Angus Reid survey, when defined by denominations, corresponds closely to the number found by other researchers using the same criteria on other data sets. For the United States, see Kellstedt et al., "Grasping the Essentials," p. 182; for Canada, see Reginald W. Bibby, *Unknown Gods: The Ongoing Story of Religion in Canada* (Toronto: Stoddart, 1993), p. 35. On U.S.-Canada comparisons see Mark A. Noll, *A History of Christianity in the United States and Canada* (Grand Rapids:

TABLE 2 **Religious Traditions of the Main Ethnic Groups in the U.S. (in percents)**

	White	Black	Hispanic
N=	(2,276)	(203)	(277)
Evangelical Protestant	23%	51%	8%
Mainline Protestant	20	8	2
Other Protestant	3	3	8
Catholic	22	8	42
Jewish	3	0	0
Orthodox Christian	*	0	0
Latter-Day Saints	1	0	0
Christians but don't know which	9	3	10
Non-Judeo-Christian Tradition	6	13	11
Secular or non-religious	14	13	19
*Less than ½ percent	101	99	100

Race

We did not consider the respondent's race when making our categories, yet race is an important factor in church involvement. In the U.S. sample, 76 percent of the respondents were white, 7 percent were black, 9 percent were Hispanic, 2 percent were Asian, 3 percent were multiethnic, and the rest were of another race or didn't know. The Canadian sample was more homogeneous; 90 percent were white, 2 percent were black, less than 1 percent were Hispanic, 3 percent were Asians, 2 percent were multiethnic, and the rest were "other" or didn't know. The Canadian sample lacked enough minorities for making a reliable breakdown, but we broke the United States sample into three major categories, as shown in Table 2 above. The percentage of American blacks who are evangelical is much higher than the percentage of whites or Hispanics — 51 percent of the sample, compared with 23 percent of the white sample and 8 percent of the Hispanic sample. The mainline Protestant category is disproportion-

Eerdmans, 1992), and John G. Stackhouse, Jr., *Canadian Evangelicalism in the Twentieth Century* (Toronto: University of Toronto Press, 1993).

ately composed of whites; 20 percent of the whites belong to the mainline churches, compared with 8 percent of the blacks and 2 percent of the Hispanics.

Categorization of Individuals

Our second method of identifying evangelicals was expressed through individuals' beliefs. Tables 3 and 4 (on pp. 360, 361) depict the questions asked in the interviews, and it gives the responses for each of six religious traditions. Table 3 contains seven traditionally Christian (or Judeo-Christian) behaviors and beliefs, and Table 4 contains three contrary beliefs. On Christian doctrinal beliefs the members of evangelical denominations in both nations rank higher than anyone else. These people also attend church more often than anyone else (Table 3, line 1). For example, in Canada 49 percent of the evangelical members attend weekly, compared with 34 percent for the "other Protestants" (the next highest group) and 22 percent for the mainline Protestants. In the U.S., 56 percent of the evangelicals attend weekly or more often, compared with 47 percent of the "other Protestants" and 39 percent of the mainliners. This survey agrees with earlier research in finding higher church attendance in the U.S. than in Canada — for all religious groups. The most dramatic patterns in Table 3 are on the items about the literal interpretation of the Bible (fifth item), the self-report that one is a converted Christian (sixth item), and the importance of converting non-Christians (seventh item). In all three, the members of evangelical denominations are far ahead of the mainline Protestants. Also, the gap between evangelicals and mainliners is consistently greater in Canada than in the U.S.

Table 4 depicts three non-Christian attitudes, and it shows the percent *disagreeing* with each. The data have the same pattern as in Table 3: members of evangelical denominations disagree the most, while Jews and secularists agree the most. To identify evangelical persons, we constructed a summary "Evangelical Beliefs Index" composed of six items:

1. "I feel that through the life, death, and resurrection of Jesus, God provided a way for the forgiveness of my sins." (Agree)
2. "I believe the Bible is the inspired word of God." (Agree)
3. "I have committed my life to Christ and consider myself to be a converted Christian." (Agree)

TABLE 3 Attitudes and Behaviors of Major Religious Groups

	Canada						U.S.					
	Evan-gel.	Main-line	Other Prot.	Cath.	Jew	Sec-ular	Evan-gel.	Main-line	Other Prot.	Cath.	Jew	Sec-ular
N=	(180)	(580)	(71)	(993)	(35)	(710)	(685)	(491)	(110)	(682)	(65)	(436)
Church Attendance												
Apart from special occasions, how often did you attend religious services or meetings in the last 12 months? Once a week or more.	49%	22%	34%	27%	5%	2%	56%	39%	47%	45%	17%	7%
Beliefs												
Do you consider religion to be an important part of your life, or not? Yes.	84	69	79	72	60	18	92	87	77	88	63	36
I feel that through the life, death, and resurrection of Jesus, God provided a way for the forgiveness of my sins. Agree.	94	76	86	76	9	29	98	93	83	93	5	50
I believe the Bible is the inspired word of God. Agree.	91	76	80	78	41	33	97	88	89	89	40	52
I feel the Bible is God's word, and is to be taken literally, word for word. Agree.	64	36	52	27	19	11	79	52	62	51	26	29
I have committed my life to Christ and consider myself to be a converted Christian. Agree.	79	41	65	42	1	9	87	71	71	53	5	20
I feel it is very important to encourage non-Christians to become Christians. Agree.	65	34	56	27	5	6	81	63	66	42	4	21

TABLE 4 Beliefs of Major Religious Groups

	Canada						U.S.					
	Evangel.	Main-line	Other Prot.	Cath.	Jew	Secular	Evangel.	Main-line	Other Prot.	Cath.	Jew	Secular
Non-Christian Beliefs												
Human beings are not special creatures made in the image of God; they are simply a recent development in the process of animal evolution. Disagree.	84%	59%	76%	65%	47%	27%	90%	79%	74%	79%	39%	41%
In my view, Jesus Christ was not the divine son of God. Disagree.	96	79	84	82	22	44	95	90	88	88	18	59
All the great religions of the world are equally good and true. Disagree.	61	30	51	23	19	29	61	41	57	27	21	33

4. "I feel it is very important to encourage non-Christians to become Christians." (Agree)
5. "Human beings are not special creatures made in the image of God; they are simply a recent development in the process of animal evolution." (Disagree)
6. "In my view, Jesus Christ was *not* the divine son of God." (Disagree)

How many people agreed with the first four and disagreed with the last two? Such people we call "highest," and Table 5 depicts the percentage scoring highest in each nation and in each religious group. In general, this table reveals that the level of evangelical beliefs is much higher in the U.S. than in Canada. Contrary to our expectations, however, the percentage of those who rank "highest" does not approach 100 percent in any denominational category, even in evangelical Protestant denominations. The highest percentages are for members of evangelical Protestant denominations and the Latter-Day Saints. The main reason why the figures for evangelical Protestants in Table 5 are not higher is that the Evangelical Beliefs Index includes the statement "I feel it is very important to encourage non-Christians to become Christians," and not all members of evangelical denominations agree. As Table 3 shows, only 65 percent of the members of evangelical groups in Canada and 81 percent of their counterparts in the U.S. agree with this statement. Apparently some evangelically inclined persons are unsure about evangelizing non-Christians. If that statement were not a part of the index, the figures in Table 5 (on p. 363) would be higher.

An important lesson from this table is that theological beliefs do not follow denominational lines very closely. Persons with evangelical beliefs are found in a wide variety of denominations. For this reason analysts must be careful to notice where observers apply the word "evangelical" to individuals and where they apply it to denominations.

Do the regions of Canada or the U.S. vary in evangelical beliefs? We looked at regional variations on the Evangelical Beliefs Index in Canada and found only small variations. The top-ranked regions in percent "highest" on an evangelical scale were the prairie provinces (Saskatchewan and Manitoba) at 25 percent, followed by the Atlantic region at 22 percent. Lowest were Quebec (12%), Ontario (14%), and British Columbia-Alberta (17%). By contrast, in the U.S. the regional differences were substantial. The top-ranked region was the South (49% scoring highest), followed by the Midwest (45%). Lowest were the Northeast (25%), Pacific (27%), and

TABLE 5 **Percent Scoring Highest on the Evangelical Beliefs Index (Strongly agree or agree on all six items)***

	Canada	U.S.
N=	(3,000)	(3,000)
All	16%	39%
Evangelical Protestant	60	69
Mainline Protestant	16	48
Other Protestant	41	48
Catholic	14	26
Jewish	1	3
Orthodox Christian	14	45
Latter-Day Saints	65	58
Christians but don't know which	36	55
Non-Judeo-Christian Tradition	4	15
Secular or non-religious	2	6

*Strongly disagree or disagree on two reversal items.

Mountain regions (36%). For purposes of further analysis we divided the Evangelical Beliefs Index measure into three levels — low, medium, and high.[14] We used it in analyses which we will explain shortly.

Influences on Financial Giving

We now look at financial giving by evangelicals as compared with others, using both methods of identifying evangelicals, that is, as members of evangelical denominations and as individuals with certain beliefs. The sur-

14. In constructing the Evangelical Beliefs Index we looked only at responses by Protestants, Latter-Day Saints, and Christians unsure of their denomination. We did not consider other respondents, since the index was intended for use mainly in distinguishing types of Protestants and others influenced by Protestant teachings. The first four items were scored Strongly agree = 5, Agree = 4, Don't know = 3, Disagree = 2, and Strongly Disagree = 1. The last two were scored in reverse. The mean of the six was the index score. When we divided the index into low, medium, and high levels we used cutting points which produced three maximally equal-sized groups.

vey asked about annual household income before taxes, and also about the percentage of total household income the respondent gives "to churches and other religious organizations."[15] It did not ask how many *dollars* the household contributed. The approximate average incomes of the six main religious groups are given in Table 6 (on p. 365), first line. In Canada the difference between the evangelicals and the mainline Protestants is small, but in the United States, the evangelicals reported lower income (41.7 thousand) than the mainline Protestants (50.2 thousand). In both countries the Jews have higher incomes than any other group. The percentage of income given to religious organizations is shown in the second line of Table 6. In the total sample, 11.9 percent did not respond to the question or did not know, and of those who *did* respond, 37.9 percent reported giving nothing at all. (People not responding are excluded from Table 6, but those contributing nothing are included in the average figures.) In agreement with past research, Table 6 shows that evangelicals give a higher percentage to religious organizations than any others.

Reported giving is much higher in the U.S. than in Canada, and it is higher than earlier researchers found, indicating that the Angus Reid survey contains an upward bias. We are certain that such a bias exists in the data, and we believe that it was partly caused by asking respondents about the *percent* of their income they contributed, rather than about the dollars they contributed. Consider the interview situation. For a respondent it is easier to report the amount given than the percentage of income given. For the latter the respondent needs to make a quick calculation, and this will inevitably give rise to approximation and an upward bias. Nevertheless the existence of bias does not greatly harm our analysis, since the amount

15. The question about family income asked the respondent to choose one of six categories: Less than $20,000; between $20,000 and $39,999; between $40,000 and $59,999; between $60,000 and $79,999; between $80,000 and $99,999; and $100,000 and over. When computing the mean we set each category at its midpoint; the lowest category we set at $15,000 and the highest at $120,000. A total of 9.3 percent refused to answer. On the question about religious giving, 33.4 percent reported no giving at all, and an additional 11.9 percent did not answer. A few respondents reported incredibly high percentages given. Thirty persons reported giving 30 percent or more of their income, and among them, six reported giving 100 percent of their income. These high percentages are probably errors or special circumstances, therefore we deleted all thirty cases from the analysis. When we report mean percentages given, the figures include persons who did not give at all.

Levels of Contributions and Attitudes toward Money

TABLE 6 Responses by Major Religious Groups

	Canada						U.S.					
	Evan-gel.	Main-line	Other Prot.	Cath.	Jew	Sec-ular	Evan-gel.	Main-line	Other Prot.	Cath.	Jew	Sec-ular
N=	(180)	(580)	(71)	(993)	(35)	(710)	(685)	(491)	(110)	(682)	(65)	(436)
Average household income (approximate, in thousands)	$50.3	52.2	42.6	48.3	53.7	48.8	41.7	50.2	39.3	46.7	69.5	41.1
Percentage of total household income given to churches and other religious organizations	6.2	2.7	4.2	2.1	2.2	0.7	7.2	5.4	4.7	4.6	3.0	1.1
Percent who will make a claim for charitable donations on this year's tax return	72	75	75	57	76	52	49	56	49	54	66	39

of bias is probably similar in various categories of respondents, thus it does not greatly affect our breakdowns.

The figure for Jews in Table 6 is misleading in that Jews have high levels of philanthropic giving, but money going to Jewish organizations is not always considered by Jews as giving "to religious organizations." Many Jews give to United Jewish Appeals and to Israel and consider it non-religious giving. Hence the Jewish figure in this research, as in earlier surveys, is unduly low. Total giving to Jewish organizations is much higher, probably higher than any other category in Table 3.[16] Also in agreement with past research, Catholic giving is lower than Protestant giving, although not by a large margin in this study. All other studies reported a wider gap between Protestants and Catholics.[17]

We looked at regional differences in percent of income given (not shown in Table 6) and found that in both Canada and the U.S., giving was highest in the regions where evangelicalism is the strongest. In Canada giving was highest in the Atlantic region (3.4%) followed by the Prairie provinces (3.2%). Lowest were Quebec (1.3%), British Columbia-Alberta (2.2%), and Ontario (2.4%). In the U.S., giving was highest in the South (5.9%) and the Midwest (5.3%). It was lowest in the Pacific region (3.7%), the Northeast (4.0%), and the Mountain region (4.0%). The last line in Table 6 shows the percentage of respondents who said they will make a claim for charitable donations on their tax return. The numbers are higher in Canada than in the U.S., almost certainly because of the difference in tax laws. In the United States it pays to itemize deductions for charitable giving only if donations exceed the standard deduction (in 1997, $4,150 for individuals, $6,900 for married couples). By contrast, in Canada a percentage of all charitable donations can be counted as a deduction from the tax liability itself (in 1998, 17% of the first $200 donated and 29% of total donations above $200).

Attitudes regarding Money

Table 7 (on p. 367) depicts responses to six questions about attitudes toward money. The first statement, "I want to live a spiritual life, more than I

16. For details on Jewish philanthropy see Barry A. Kosmin and Paul Ritterband, eds., *Contemporary Jewish Philanthropy in America* (Savage, MD: Rowman and Littlefield, 1991).

17. See Hoge et al. *Money Matters*, ch. 1.

TABLE 7 Attitudes of Major Religious Groups

	Canada						U.S.					
	Evangel.	Mainline	Other Prot.	Cath.	Jew	Secular	Evangel.	Mainline	Other Prot.	Cath.	Jew	Secular
N=	(180)	(580)	(71)	(993)	(35)	(710)	(685)	(491)	(110)	(682)	(65)	(436)
Attitudes toward Money												
I want to live a spiritual life, more than I want to be rich. Agree.	90%	67%	77%	67%	44%	44%	92%	88%	88%	81%	62%	58%
People who love God and work hard will always have enough money. Agree.	42	31	32	29	13	14	51	34	43	43	11	27
I feel that churches put too much emphasis on asking for money. Agree.	52	52	65	54	41	67	53	50	54	56	50	74
Churches and religious organizations should spend more money on helping the poor. Agree.	86	81	86	84	95	85	87	83	84	86	84	85
If churches and other religious groups find that they have received money that has been obtained through crime or illegal business practices, they should give the money back. Agree.	90	82	86	86	72	80	82	80	78	80	83	71
I think churches and other religious organizations should be required to pay income and property taxes. Agree.	22	32	28	34	53	52	16	19	25	26	35	44

want to be rich," finds more agreement among evangelicals than anyone else. In Canada the difference between evangelicals and everyone else is large, while in the U.S. it is small. In both countries the Jews and secular persons are the least likely to agree with the statement.

The second statement, "People who love God and work hard will always have enough money," again finds most agreement among the evangelicals and least among the Jews and secularists. The third statement, complaining that churches put too much emphasis on asking for money, finds more agreement among secular persons than among churchgoing persons. Otherwise denominational differences are small. The fourth statement, saying that churches should spend more to help the poor, receives assent from most respondents, with no denominational differences. The fifth statement similarly has few denominational differences.

The last statement in Table 7 asserts that churches should pay taxes, and the percent agreeing is higher in Canada than in the U.S. In both countries, Jews and secular persons were the most likely to agree, and evangelicals were the least likely.

Next we looked at individual evangelicals identified by their beliefs, not a comparison of different denominations. We made tables similar to Tables 6 and 7, in which we compared individual Protestants and Catholics (regardless of denomination) scoring high, medium, or low on the Evangelical Beliefs Index. Persons high on the index clearly gave a higher percentage of their money to their churches. In Canada, the percentages were 7.0 for persons scoring high, 3.4 for those scoring medium, and 1.2 for those scoring low. In the U.S. the corresponding figures were 8.0, 4.9, and 2.3. In addition, the persons scoring high much more often agreed that "I want to live a spiritual life, more than I want to be rich." We give more details below.

Influences on Protestant Giving and Attitudes About Money

The remainder of this chapter looks into what factors influence Protestants to give more, or less, money to their churches and to have distinctive attitudes about money. Table 8 (on p. 369) shows three factors that clearly predict levels of giving and attitudes about money. Since the focus of the analysis here is on Protestants, Table 8 reports responses for Protestants only (including Latter-Day Saints and Christians unsure of their denomina-

TABLE 8 Three Factors Affecting Giving and Attitudes About Money (Protestants Only)

		Canada			U.S.		
		Percent Given	Spiritual Life	Have Enough	Percent Given	Spiritual Life	Have Enough
All		3.6	73%	33%	6.4	90%	43%
Evangelical Beliefs:	Low	1.6	57	20	3.2	74	24
	Medium	3.7	85	48	5.2	86	41
	High	8.0	97	48	8.4	98	52
Church Attendance:	Weekly or More	7.5	90	47	9.0	96	48
	Monthly, Few/Month	3.4	78	34	5.7	89	43
	Several Times a Year	1.9	69	27	3.1	84	37
	Never	0.7	50	22	1.6	71	29
Do you consider religion to be an important part of your life?							
	Yes	4.5	83	39	6.9	93	45
	No	0.9	45	14	2.1	65	29

tion). The table has three columns for each country. The first column shows the percentage of household income given to churches, the second has the percent of respondents agreeing with "I want to live a spiritual life, more than I want to be rich," and the third has the percent agreeing with "People who love God and work hard will always have enough money."

The second item (lines 2, 3, and 4) in Table 8 merits special attention. It depicts the very strong impact of evangelical beliefs on church giving. In Canada the percentage of income given varies from 1.6 percent to 8.0 percent, and in the U.S. it varies from 3.2 percent to 8.4 percent. The third item shows the strong impact of church attendance. The influence of church attendance is the strongest of all. The fourth item, about how important religion is to the person, is an additional strong influence.

The relationships in Table 8 do not prove anything about causation. We do not know what causes what, or whether an outside factor causes them all. All this data proves is that beliefs, churchgoing, and giving are strongly *associated*. Yet it is reasonable to believe that somehow they influence each other. Compared with these three items, the other variables we studied — age, education, and family income — were weak, and they are not shown in Table 8.

Table 8 shows the influences not only on financial giving but also on attitudes about money. The second and fifth columns show the correlates of "I want to live a spiritual life, more than I want to be rich," and the third and sixth show the correlates of "People who love God and work hard will always have enough money." The latter statement is ambiguous in that it speaks of both love of God and hard work, and the two may or may not go together. We understand it to mean that *both* are needed if a family is to be financially secure. As the table shows, people with evangelical beliefs are more likely to agree with both statements, as do people who attend church regularly and consider religion to be important in their lives.

In preparing Table 8 we also looked at the impact of marital status and found that married people give more than persons who are single. This finding is ambiguous, since it is partly a matter of age. We did not look at gender differences, since the survey asked about household giving, not individual giving.

Table 9 (on p. 371) answers the question of whether denominational grouping or evangelical beliefs are more important in influencing giving. It breaks the Protestants and Catholics into three levels of evangelical beliefs, then looks at giving in the resulting twelve cells. When we compare the

TABLE 9 **Percent of Family Income Contributed,
Broken Down by Religious Tradition
and the Evangelical Beliefs Index**

		Evangelical Protestant	Mainline Protestant	Other Protestant	Catholic
Canada					
Evangelical Beliefs:	Low	1.8	1.7	1.5	1.4
	Medium	5.3	3.7	*	3.2
	High	8.5	6.8	7.9	4.9
U.S.					
Evangelical Beliefs:	Low	2.8	3.5	2.6	3.1
	Medium	5.8	4.3	4.6	5.3
	High	8.6	7.9	6.8	7.5

*Data are not reported for cells with fewer than 20 cases.

columns and rows we see that evangelical beliefs are more strongly related to giving than is denomination. Denominational differences in giving seem to reflect the different levels of belief and participation that characterize them. Thus, both the beliefs of those who make up the denominations and the institutional factors supplied by the denominations themselves must be understood in an analysis of why denominations have different levels of giving. In general, the religious beliefs are the more important.

Table 10 (on p. 372) depicts the correlates of levels of giving. It is limited to Protestants only. The larger the number, the stronger is the relationship. Weak associations (weaker than .15) are not shown at all. Note that three factors are strong influences on giving. Most important is the frequency of church attendance; the correlations are .61 in Canada and .57 in the U.S.[18] Also important are evangelical beliefs and seeing reli-

18. The measure of church attendance in Table 10 is based on attendance per year. But since this measure is highly skewed, we experimented with taking its square root to see if it would portray the true relationship more clearly. This occurred, so we used the square root of times per year. A person who attended weekly has the score of 7.21, which is the square root of 52.

TABLE 10 Correlates of Percentage of Household Income Given to Religion (Protestants Only)

	Canada	U.S.
Age	—	— *
Family Income	—	—
Level of Formal Education	—	—
Frequency of Church Attendance (Sq. Rt.)	.61	.57
Evangelical Beliefs Index	.52	.42
I consider religion an important part of my life.	.36	.30
I want to live a spiritual life, more than to be rich.	.32	.28
People who love God will always have enough money.	.20	—
Churches should spend more money on the poor.	—	—

*Correlations weaker than 0.15 are too weak to show. All those shown are significant at the .01 level.

gion as an important part of one's life. A fourth factor is slightly less important: wanting to live a spiritual life rather than wanting to become rich. These are the principal determinants of Protestant giving, and evangelicals are higher than others in all of them. These variables largely explain the high levels of evangelical giving. By contrast, other variables in Table 10 have no effect. Age, level of family income, or level of education are unimportant.

The last variable in Table 10 probes for any relationship between level of giving and feelings about whether churches should spend more money on the poor. We found no relationship in either Canada or the U.S. As Table 7 (line 4) tells us, evangelicals are no different from other Christian denominations in their feelings on this question.

Conclusions

The findings of the 1996 Angus Reid survey confirm what historians have been saying about evangelicals. There are more evangelicals in the U.S., on average, than in Canada, and present-day U.S. culture is more suffused with evangelical faith. The level of churchgoing is higher in the U.S. than in

Canada.[19] Evangelicals in both countries, compared with other Protestants, attend church more frequently, consider religion to be more important in their lives, believe more firmly in the gospel promises, believe strongly in biblical authority, and feel more of a desire to evangelize non-Christians.

An often neglected fact that this survey affirms is that "evangelicals," as defined by beliefs, are not all found in the denominations that scholars usually classify as evangelical. Conversely, some of the persons affiliated with evangelical denominations do not display traditional evangelical beliefs. For some questions, such as the relation of religious beliefs and practices to financial giving, one must remember the different (and yet valid) ways of defining what it is to be "evangelical."

All research agrees in showing that evangelicals give much more to their churches than other Christians. The Angus Reid survey agrees, and it helps us understand why. From the evidence of this survey, three factors are foremost. First, evangelicals are more involved in their churches, and church involvement is the strongest single predictor of giving. Second, evangelicals hold to strong beliefs in Bible truths, and this is a strong predictor of giving. Third, evangelicals disproportionately consider religion important in their lives, and this is a predictor of giving. Evangelicals' faith includes belief in God's promises that God will take care of the faithful, and it gives higher priority to a spiritual life than the material life. From the survey evidence, these are the prime explanations for impressively high evangelical giving, rather than any background factors such as education, age, or occupation.

19. It is a challenge for historians to interpret Canada's lower level of church attendance since, as late as 1957, the Gallup Poll showed higher levels of churchgoing in Canada than in the United States. See Bibby, *Unknown Gods*, p. 6.

CHAPTER 14

"Too Good to Be True": The New Era Foundation Scandal and Its Implications

THOMAS C. BERG

Lay hands suddenly on no man. . . .

I TIMOTHY 5:22 (KJV)

In May 1995, a Philadelphia-based charity called the Foundation for New Era Philanthropy collapsed and declared bankruptcy, revealing a fraudulent financial scheme that had taken more than $350 million from hundreds of individuals and charitable organizations during the previous four years. The victims of the fraud had been convinced to deposit money with New Era because the foundation supposedly had a group of wealthy anonymous donors who would match the deposits, producing a doubling return, within six months. Although many organizations received "matching gift" payments from New Era, the operation was eventually revealed to be a pyramid or "Ponzi" scheme: there were no anonymous donors, and payments were made out of new deposits attracted by the scheme.

Among the victims of the charity fraud — the largest in American history — were more than two hundred evangelical Christian organizations, including colleges, relief organizations, evangelistic ministries, and even denominations and local churches. Some were threatened with losing money they had deposited; others faced having to repay money they had received from New Era — money that they had already spent on their ministries — on the ground that it was tainted by the fraud. In either case, organizations that had leaned heavily on New Era to bring in funds now faced the prospect of halting expansion campaigns, laying off workers, or even going out of existence. And they faced a fight among themselves and with a host of secular charities over how the available assets would be distributed among claimants.

In the end, however, the charities involved avoided lengthy litigation by reaching a settlement over how money would be repaid and distributed. The settlement, which was spearheaded by the bloc of evangelical organizations, produced a return of more than 85 percent of the deposits that were made with New Era — a kind of silver lining in the cloud of the scandal.

This chapter has two chief purposes beyond chronicling the New Era story. First, it discusses and evaluates the factors that made it possible for a scheme such as New Era to steal so much money from so many reputable organizations, especially evangelical Christian colleges and agencies. In particular for this project on "The Financing of American Evangelicalism," what does the New Era episode reveal about the attitudes of American evangelicals toward money in the latter decades of the twentieth century?

The second purpose of the article is to describe the process by which hundreds of charities, led by evangelical nonprofits, settled potential claims against each other over the distribution of New Era money. The settlement is an important part of the New Era story, for it too reflects, at least in part, how evangelicals view money and how they seek to witness to the world in matters concerning money.

The New Era Scheme

The New Era Foundation was created in the late 1980s by John Bennett (b. 1936), a former alcohol-rehabilitation counselor turned nonprofit investment advisor.[1] Bennett had a record of financial troubles, but after he

---

1. For a fuller description, see Tony Carnes, "New Era's Bennett to Prison," *Christianity Today*, 27 Oct. 1997, p. 86; *United States v. Bennett*, 161 F.3d 171 (3d Cir. 1998) (review of Bennett's criminal fraud sentence), petition for certiorari denied, No. 98-1957 (Oct. 4, 1999).

joined an evangelical church in Philadelphia's wealthy suburbs he made a number of contacts that helped propel him forward in the nonprofit world. Dynamic and self-assured, he gained the endorsement of several prominent financiers and philanthropists and began to operate and publicize a program called New Concepts in Philanthropy. Under the program, organizations would deposit funds with New Era, and in six months the deposit would be returned with a matching gift from a small group of wealthy, anonymous donors. These donors, Bennett claimed, were extremely secretive but were grateful for the blessings they had received from God and wished to share them with others. Not only could charities themselves seek matching gifts, but individuals and for-profit companies could make a deposit and designate that it, together with the matching gift, would go to a particular charity.

New Era operated largely among two groups of charities quite different in nature. The first included major blueblood organizations in the Philadelphia area, such as the Museum of Arts, the Philadelphia Orchestra, and the University of Pennsylvania, and extended to major establishment educational institutions like Harvard and Yale. The second group was a large network of evangelical Christian entities, including colleges, relief and welfare agencies, evangelism ministries, religious broadcasters, and even denominations and local churches. The roster included many of the largest and most respected evangelical institutions in the nation, including Focus on the Family, Gordon College, Moody Bible Institute, Wheaton College, World Vision, and others.

New Era began taking deposits and making payments in 1990. As organizations began to receive payments on their deposits and other organizations suddenly received unsolicited double gifts, the word began to circulate and others became anxious to sign up. That, of course, is the essence of a pyramid or "Ponzi" scheme (named after Charles Ponzi, a 1920s Boston con artist): the payments attract more deposits, but they are funded by nothing more than those later deposits. Each month the incoming money must expand more and more to fund the increasing number of maturing obligations, but at some point the pyramid cannot continue expanding and it crashes down. For example, in the first four frantic months of 1995 before New Era declared bankruptcy, it raised almost $120 million; and Bennett, desperate for funds, announced a new program under which depositors could almost triple their money in a few months. When the foundation declared bankruptcy on May 15, 1995, those organizations that had deposited money and not received a corresponding gift were left with the losses. As a result, some faced the prospect of financial ruin; most others were confronted with the likelihood of cutting back on their operations and payroll, or at least postponing new ventures.

Although the Ponzi scheme was bound to crash eventually, two events precipitated its end. Prudential Securities had operated as an advisor to Bennett, holding the money received from depositors in an account and from 1994 on loaning money to New Era against that collateral — and thus arguably contributing to the success of the scheme, as will be discussed below. Prudential eventually determined that New Era could not repay its commitments, and it seized $44 million in deposits. In May 1995, Prudential filed suit, forcing New Era's bankruptcy.

At the same time, the U.S. Securities and Exchange Commission closed in on Bennett, acting on a tip from Albert Meyer, a young professor of accounting at the evangelical Spring Arbor College in Michigan. Meyer, who also balanced Spring Arbor's books, had noticed two years earlier that the college had deposited $294,000 with New Era. Suspicious of the arrangement, he raised questions with Spring Arbor's president and board members but was rebuffed because the college had received its promised matching payments and could find no proof that New Era was fraudulent. Meyer persisted and became more aggressive in the spring of 1995. He obtained copies of New Era's financial statements, including its 1993 tax forms. The 1993 tax Form 1990 showed a mere $34,000 in interest earnings on over $41 million in income, proving that New Era had not invested deposited funds but simply paid them out to cover maturing matching-grant obligations. With this evidence in hand, Meyer contacted the government. His efforts and his eventual vindication make up one of the most interesting stories in the New Era affair.[2]

John Bennett was obviously a con artist of the first order. According to federal prosecutors, he began the matching-gifts scam simply as an effort to cover an earlier check-kiting scheme. Assessing all his motives, however, is a bit more complicated. He took a large amount (as much as $6 million) out of New Era funds for himself and his various other businesses, but perhaps not as much as he might have were he simply a swindler. Some have suggested that in addition to his more venal motives, he had a sort of

---

2. On Meyer's story, see Peter Michelmore, "On the Trail of a Fraud," *Reader's Digest* (Mar. 1996): 110-15.

"addiction to giving." Bennett claimed that he had become mentally and religiously unbalanced, had believed the anonymous donors actually existed, and had held imaginary meetings with them. After the scandal broke, he was charged with eighty-two counts of mail fraud, wire fraud, money laundering, and lying to government regulators. After the federal judge refused to allow defenses of mental illness and "religious fervor," Bennett pled guilty. In September 1997 he was sentenced to twelve years in prison without parole — half the maximum sentence — which the judge said reflected the seriousness of Bennett's crime but also the fact that he had voluntarily made restitution of about $1.5 million.

Why the Scheme Succeeded

In hindsight, New Era's offer to double organizations' money in only six months should have raised more serious suspicions than it did. As many pundits remarked after the scandal broke, the lesson was an old one: "If it's too good to be true, it probably is." Yet New Era was remarkably successful in inducing reputable organizations to hand over large sums of money. This section considers why that was true, and in particular what the episode indicates about the attitudes of evangelical ministries toward money and stewardship in the 1980s and 1990s.

To begin with, it is worth noting that the New Era scandal did not (except in a few questionable instances) involve fraud or corruption by the officials of evangelical organizations. Columnist Cal Thomas complained that New Era showed that the desire for money was "eclipsing [many ministries'] purpose and diluting the power of their message."[3] But in almost all cases, the leaders of organizations that invested money with New Era did so in good faith to raise money to pursue their ministries. In this sense, New Era differed from many of the other highly publicized charity scandals of the 1980s and 1990s: the revelations of fraud and illicit sex among the leading televangelists; the diversion of organizational money to personal uses by the presidents of the United Way, the National Baptist Convention, Mississippi College, and Adelphi University; and the use of NAACP funds by the organization's executive director to settle a sexual harassment suit against him. Each of those cases involved corruption within

3. Cal Thomas, "New Era, Old Trick," Denver Post, 21 May 1995, p. D4.

the organization, while the conduct by most entities caught up in New Era was at most careless.[4]

Nevertheless, any negligence by charities in handling donated funds is a serious matter as well, for it too can have a significant effect on the public's confidence. Moreover, the misjudgments in New Era were widespread throughout the charitable community; they were not simply the actions of a few marginal organizations. They seemed to reflect systematic rather than isolated problems.

In assessing the actions of those who invested with Bennett, it is also important to remember that New Era was a carefully designed fraud. The matching gift vehicle, as he obviously knew, is common in the nonprofit and religious world; among other things, it offers a way of confirming for the potential donor that the charity has other support and is a worthy recipient. Nor was the anonymous nature of the supposed gifts uncommon; donors often prefer to remain secret for various reasons. And of course, the scheme was all the more tempting because organizations were receiving large matching-gift payments from New Era. Could an official of a charity say no to such a potential return when other organizations — including those in the same line of mission — seemed to be benefiting so handsomely?

New Era did differ from most matching-gift arrangements because the organizations had to turn over control of their money. This raised red flags for many observers. However, even here Bennett had answers: the deposits were necessary in order to provide funds for New Era to invest (in safe instruments, everyone was assured) to cover its operating expenses. Bennett also cleverly argued that for an organization to surrender control over its money was actually a safeguard, because it effectively limited the organization to contributing reserves and endowment funds rather than actual operating funds.

Most important, Bennett arranged for the organizations to deposit their money not with New Era, but with Prudential Securities in what were billed as "quasi-escrow" or "custodial" accounts invested in safe in-

---

4. A scent of corruption among ministries rose from the activities of some evangelical leaders who worked vigorously to enlist smaller ministries in pooled deposits that would reach New Era's $500,000 minimum. Some such intermediaries received what were referred to as "thank offerings" from the ministries that they had signed up. In these cases, association with New Era dovetailed with individuals' financial interest (although the fees were usually donated to the intermediaries' designated charities, and the intermediaries generally lost money in New Era investments as well).

struments like treasury bills. A depositing organization could phone Prudential and receive information concerning the T-bill numbers and the date they were purchased. This arrangement led many organizations to treat their deposits as simple fund-raising vehicles, or at least as safe rather than risky investments.[5] In fact, however, the deposits were commingled in one account, to which Bennett had access, and against which Prudential later began loaning New Era money — both features inconsistent with the custodial status that Bennett represented to depositors.

A civil lawsuit later brought against Prudential by thirty-one New Era depositors — one of four such suits — accused the brokerage firm of fraud and recklessness for maintaining these arrangements with Bennett in the face of evidence of New Era's problems, and for contributing to the plaintiffs' false belief that their deposits were safe. According to the organizations' complaint, the Prudential broker had early on sent a letter to depositors representing that their accounts were custodial, and the company committed fraud by never correcting that misimpression.[6] Prudential denied any negligence or misstatements, and the cases were settled in 1997 without any judicial determination concerning Prudential's role. But the Prudential account and the procedures for confirming it did contribute to New Era's appearance of credibility. So did a favorable report from an IRS audit — which Bennett secured by concealing the matching gifts program from the auditors and by giving them fabricated minutes of New Era board-of-directors meetings (in reality, New Era had no board).[7]

Another important boost to New Era's credibility came through Bennett's ability to secure the support and testimonials of several prominent financiers and philanthropists, including Laurence Rockefeller, former treasury secretary William Simon, former Goldman Sachs chairman John Whitehead, and Sir John Templeton. In fact, Rockefeller, Simon, and

---

5. Bob Andringa, Coalition of Christian Colleges and Universities, interview by author, telephone, 10 March 1998; Paul Nelson, Evangelical Council for Financial Accountability (ECFA), interview by author, telephone, 13 March 1998.

6. Complaint in *Houghton College et al. v. Prudential Securities, Inc.*, Civil Action No. 96-CV-3554 (E.D. Pa., filed May 7, 1996), pp. 21-28. The plaintiffs, nearly all of them evangelical organizations, included colleges and seminaries such as Houghton, Messiah, and Fuller, and mission organizations such as Scripture Union and Mission Aviation Fellowship. Each had deposited more than $500,000 with New Era, although some had received partial returns in matching payments.

7. See *United States v. Bennett*, 161 F.3d 171, 187-88 (3d Cir. 1999).

Whitehead each donated large sums to New Era ($4.3 million in Rockefeller's case); and although Templeton was not named as a donor, many people assumed he was among those providing the anonymous matching gifts. In addition, New Era gained a reputation for educating nonprofit executives in management and fund-raising techniques, holding popular seminars at Templeton's Institute for Religious Non-Profit Excellence.[8] An organization's executive might be invited to such a seminar, be told there how selective New Era was in choosing organizations to participate in its matching-gifts program, and then several months later receive a letter with the flattering news that his organization would be allowed to participate. (This sense of privilege at being allowed into the circle also made many organizations reluctant to irritate Bennett by raising any concerns.) As Paul Nelson of the Evangelical Council for Financial Accountability (ECFA) put it, Bennett "set the bait and hook" extremely well.[9]

Nevertheless, New Era's success in fooling evangelical leaders cannot be attributed solely to the cleverness of Bennett's scheme. The fact that many organizations received payments was, of course, no guarantee of New Era's soundness, since such early bounties are the essence of a Ponzi scheme. Although a number of organizations investigated New Era for precisely that reason, many others did not. Checking out New Era would still leave an organization with several reasons to worry. For example, there was no assurance that different organizations' deposits were being held in separate accounts — which would have quickly revealed any unauthorized payouts — rather than in one commingled account (as turned out to be the case). In addition, New Era had a spotty record with its financial statements and regulatory filings: it did not register with Pennsylvania until 1992; it did not file the required federal tax Form 990 until 1993; and its financial statements were never audited.

The widespread nature of the New Era disaster can be attributed in part to two systemic characteristics of the nonprofit sector, particularly its large evangelical component. Neither of these features is unique to the evangelical sector, as is demonstrated by the fact that many non-evangelical organizations became embroiled in New Era. But these factors may be espe-

8. For a description, see Ludmilla Lelis, "End of a Fund-Raising Era," *Asbury Park (NJ) Press,* 23 July 1995, p. A1. Sir John Templeton maintained that he was not aware of all the ways in which his name was being used by Bennett. Carnes, "New Era's Bennett to Prison," p. 86.

9. Paul Nelson, interview by author, Herndon, VA, 17 February 1998.

cially strong within evangelical entities, which may explain why New Era touched so many of them.

1. The first characteristic of the nonprofit sector that New Era reveals is the increased pressure on nonprofit organizations, including evangelical ones, to raise money. Michael Hamilton's contribution to this volume details the significant growth of the nonprofit sector and its evangelical component over the last two generations. Hamilton also explains how among evangelical organizations, the desire to spread the gospel and expand various ministries has produced increased pressure to raise money: "The mindset now locked into place in the evangelical parachurch world is the assumption that 'more net income . . . translate[s] directly into more ministry.'"[10]

At the same time as ministries grew and were pressed to grow even more, certain external factors in the 1980s made fund-raising more difficult and competitive.[11] Many nonprofit agencies were hit hard by Reagan-era federal budget cuts, which reduced government subsidies while placing greater reliance on private charities to handle social welfare problems (not all religious agencies received subsidies, but nearly all were affected by the increased need for their services). Although the government expressed support for private charitable initiatives, tax reforms in the 1980s weakened incentives for giving, and for this and other reasons, major corporate philanthropy declined after 1986.[12] As a result, gifts to charities, while still increasing in absolute amounts over the last decade, have fallen as a percentage of national income. As one observer sums up: "Our nonprofit organizations find themselves caught between reduced government funding and donor burn-out, yet face high demand for their services."[13]

Religious charities, including evangelical ones, have felt some of the

10. Michael S. Hamilton, "More Money, More Ministry: The Financing of American Evangelicalism Since 1945," pp. 107-8 in this volume (quoting Lars B. Dunberg, president of the International Bible Society).

11. See summary in Peter Dobkin Hall, "Historical Perspectives on Nonprofit Organizations," in *The Jossey-Bass Handbook of Nonprofit Leadership and Management* (San Francisco: Jossey-Bass, 1994), pp. 3, 27-28. See also Peter Dobkin Hall, "Business Giving and Social Investment in the United States, 1790-1995," *New York Law School Law Review,* 41 (1997): 789-93; Evelyn Brody, "Institutional Dissonance in the Nonprofit Sector," *Villanova Law Review* 41 (1996): 433.

12. Hall, "Business Giving and Social Investment in the United States," pp. 792-93. He traces the decline of conservative ideological arguments which question the legitimacy and effectiveness of corporate giving.

13. Brody, "Institutional Dissonance in the Nonprofit Sector," p. 466.

same limits on fund-raising. According to the research center Empty Tomb, gifts to congregations declined as a percentage of members' income for ten straight years from 1986 through 1995, overall, dropping from 3.1 percent of income in 1968 to less than 2.5 percent in 1995. Among evangelical churches the totals dropped from 6.1 percent in 1968 to 4.1 percent in 1995.[14] Over the same period, congregations — which are one of the largest sources of contributions to parachurch charities — have significantly limited those contributions. According to Empty Tomb, support of non-congregational religious agencies in several major denominations was less in constant dollars in 1995 than it was in 1968, and during that period dropped more than 40 percent as a percentage of members' income.[15]

Perhaps as a consequence, the world of charitable and religious fund-raising has become extremely fast-paced and sophisticated, relying more and more on high technology, carefully targeted direct-mail campaigns, and "innovative" development opportunities. The nonprofit economy has become more like the for-profit world, and in both, increasingly, innovation is crucial and "[t]he rules are never quite clear."[16] This represents a major culture shift for some evangelical groups, as the *Philadelphia Inquirer* described in an article about Messiah College. The small Brethren-oriented liberal arts school outside Harrisburg had placed $2 million into New Era — an unusually aggressive and worldly move for an institution in the Brethren tradition, where, as Franklin Littell of Temple University commented, "[u]ntil recently even the stock market was anathema according to official church teaching." But, as Littell added, "[W]hat do you do with an endowment in the modern world? You invest it."[17] In the words of an editorial in *Christianity Today,* "For harried development directors and ministry leaders, New Era was a dream come true."[18]

14. See John and Sylvia Ronsvalle, *The State of Church Giving Through 1995* (Champaign, IL: Empty Tomb, 1997); John and Sylvia Ronsvalle, *Behind the Stained Glass Windows: Money Dynamics in the Church* (Grand Rapids: Baker, 1996), pp. 17, 36.

15. Ronsvalle, *The State of Church Giving Through 1995;* Ronsvalle, *Behind the Stained Glass Windows,* pp. 17, 36.

16. Robert Wuthnow, *God and Mammon in America* (New York: The Free Press, 1994), p. 17.

17. B. J. Phillips, "A Double Blow to a Small College," *Philadelphia Inquirer,* 12 July 1995, p. C1.

18. David Neff, Editorial, "How Shall We Then Give? Lessons from the New Era Debacle," *Christianity Today,* 17 July 1995, p. 20.

Some other evangelical organizations were attuned to the kind of opportunity New Era presented because they were risk-taking by nature. As the *Christianity Today* editorial put it, "[e]vangelicalism is all about having confidence in the face of uncertainty and risk": its theology emphasizes faith in the miraculous saving power of Christ, and its organizations are often "the result of risk-taking, entrepreneurial visionaries [who are] unwilling to wait for slower denominational machinery to act [and who seek] to save, heal, or disciple people in fresh ways."[19] As Rollin Van Broekhoven of ECFA put it, "many Christians looking for a way to expand their ministries might have said, 'After all, I'm a sinner; the gospel is too good to be true; I've taken a chance on it — so why not take a chance on New Era, which might indeed (especially given its well-publicized early successes) be God's vehicle for an expansion of His work?'"[20]

As the quotes in the last few paragraphs show, the concept of trusting in God's provision is ambiguous, as is so much else of the churches' teaching on money.[21] One key ambiguity lies in how one identifies the vehicles for God's provision. One might argue that by committing to New Era's double-your-money offer, organizations were showing a lack of faith in the customary, relatively secure channels of Christian giving. But one might also argue that they were showing a faith in the possibilities of divine movement outside the normal channels.

2. A second feature of the nonprofit sector which the New Era scandal revealed is that the leaders of nonprofit organizations, especially of evangelical ministries, tend to interact extensively with each other. Through his seminars and personal contacts, Bennett easily insinuated himself into the "old boys' network" of wealthy and prominent people — mostly men — who serve as major donors, board members, and trustees of nonprofits. For example, at two major Chicago-area institutions, Wheaton College and Moody Bible Institute, trustees — many of whom are interlocked in business relationships as well — introduced New Era to each other, their institutions and major donors, and other nonprofits in the area.[22]

19. Neff, "How Shall We Then Give?," p. 20.

20. Rollin Van Broekhoven, Chairman of Board of Directors, Evangelical Council for Financial Accountability, interview by author, Herndon, VA, 17 February 1998.

21. Wuthnow, *God and Mammon in America*, pp. 25-28.

22. See Michael Fritz, "Ties That Bind Too Tightly: How Moody, Wheaton Shunned Ponzi Altar," *Crain's Chicago Business* (July 1995): 15.

In many organizations, board members personally vouched for Bennett, helping to overcome doubts raised by the nature of the scheme. Although many organizations did independent "due diligence" research into New Era before depositing, too many took only minimal steps. A Philadelphia nonprofit trustee who questioned New Era's bona fides and called counterparts elsewhere found that they were all "relying on the idea that somebody else had done the investigation."[23] "[T]his whole episode has revealed how incestuous the charitable or philanthropic community is," said ECFA's Paul Nelson, who called New Era "the greatest example of groupthink I've ever seen."[24]

New Era's connections with trustees and major donors meant that the impetus to invest typically came from the highest level within organizations: the president or a trustee board member. As the *Philadelphia Inquirer* noted, it is difficult for an organization's staff to resist the suggestions of board members who not only have power and eminence (often because of their own gifts to the organization) but also sit on the board, in part, precisely in order to bring in fund-raising opportunities.[25]

In gaining the trust of Christian board members and executives, Bennett appeared as a just and godly, missions-minded businessman, a model that has long positive associations for American evangelicals. From the business leaders who funded Dwight Moody's evangelistic campaigns to J. Howard Pew's funding of Billy Graham, there is a venerable tradition of admiration for businessmen who apply their talents to spreading the gospel. Indeed, in popular works such as Bruce Barton's *The Man Nobody Knows,* the gospel itself became a business campaign and Jesus the ultimate warm-hearted, forward-thinking executive.

Despite the scare from New Era, few evangelical or other organizations are likely to reduce their reliance on personal connections or testimonials from board members. Nonprofit entities must seek to develop and exploit personal connections, because there are a limited number of potential major donors for their work. The executive director of the Philadelphia Orchestra, another charity burned in New Era, told a newspaper reporter this story:

23. Nancy R. Axelrod, "Why Charities Were Vulnerable to New Era Scheme," *Chronicle of Philanthropy* (June 1995).

24. Hiawatha Bray, "A Subtle, Seductive Sell," *In Trust* (Autumn 1995): 10; Nelson, interview, 17 February 1998.

25. B. J. Phillips, "It's the Silence of the Shorn," *Philadelphia Inquirer,* 23 June 1995, p. C1.

A New York friend, who has made a ton of money, told me, "Joe, all my life I've depended on other people's judgment, on what they tell me. If I couldn't do that, I couldn't exist. If I'm disappointed once every 10 years, or once every 15 years, then that's the price I pay. You can't set up enough defenses."[26]

And so it goes.[27]

The evangelical network was doubly dysfunctional during the years of New Era's operations: while it worked so efficiently to spread confidence in Bennett, it ironically worked very slowly to spread caution about him. Organizations and individuals that had doubts say they were reluctant to alert others because of the fear of a defamation lawsuit by a then-successful organization. Some skeptics were pressured by New Era and at least one was permitted to keep its New Era money in its own escrow account while being strongly urged not to tell anyone else about the special arrangement.[28]

A final question raised by New Era is whether it reflected a failure of the regulatory framework in the religious nonprofit world. Government regulation of religious fund-raising is limited by the First Amendment, which prevents the state from looking into allegedly fraudulent claims about spiritual matters,[29] but Bennett's claim that there were anonymous donors was the kind of "this world" falsehood that could constitutionally be the basis for a fraud prosecution (like Jim Bakker's assertion that he was using PTL "Prayer Partners'" contributions for the ministry instead of for gold-plated bathroom fixtures in his house[30]).

On the state level, the lack of regulatory resources was the major problem. The Pennsylvania state charities bureau, which had jurisdiction over New Era, had no policy for investigating a charity unless and until someone complained. However, in the early stages of a Ponzi scheme, typ-

26. David Boldt, "Trying to Shake New Era Gloom," *Philadelphia Inquirer,* 4 Aug. 1995, p. B1.

27. For information on another questionable scheme involving several agencies of the Christian Reformed Church in which scores of individual denomination members have lost money in a failed (though not necessarily fraudulent) investment plan operated by two respected and well-connected CRC laymen, see Chuck Fager, "Real Estate Investment Failure Hurts Churchgoers," *Christianity Today,* 16 Nov. 1998, pp. 30-32.

28. Bray, "A Subtle, Seductive Sell," p. 11. Discusses Biola University.

29. *United States v. Ballard,* 322 U.S. 78 (1944).

30. See *United States v. Bakker,* 925 F.2d 728 (4th Cir. 1991) (upholding Bakker's conviction).

ically everyone is satisfied. Thus New Era did not register in Pennsylvania until 1993, after it had been operating for several years and running the matching-gifts scheme for at least a year. Even then, it did not file audited reports, and of course Bennett told the same lies to state regulators that he did to the IRS. After New Era, the Pennsylvania bureau hired more investigators and began conducting random audits of charities.[31]

Policing in the charitable world is done in large part by private and self-regulatory organizations, and for evangelical ministries the most important is the Evangelical Council for Financial Accountability (ECFA). Although ECFA received praise for organizing the successful settlement in the bankruptcy case, it took criticism for not having blown the whistle on New Era, especially since more than 100 of the council's 800 members were involved as depositors or grant recipients. An article in the *Chronicle of Philanthropy* asked, "Why didn't the council warn its members — who must meet numerous financial and management standards — to steer clear of the foundation, since council leaders had serious reservations about the New Era deal?"[32] Other observers questioned whether ECFA's structure — it is financed largely by dues from the member organizations it oversees — limited its ability to be a vigorous watchdog.[33]

ECFA's officials had developed doubts about New Era by the fall of 1994 but had decided not to do a formal investigation or report. They gave several reasons.[34] Because New Era itself was not an ECFA member, the council had no power to compel New Era to provide any more financial records than any depositor could. Without any detailed evidence, ECFA worried, like others, that making public accusations would expose it to legal action. Most fundamentally, ECFA regarded a member organization's participation in New Era as a matter of business judgment; ECFA maintained it could not feasibly expand its mission from evaluating its mem-

31. Stephanie Ebbert, "Bureau That Oversees State Charities Audits Big 33 Foundation," *Harrisburg (PA) Patriot-News,* 17 Aug. 1997, p. A1.

32. Debra E. Blum, "Shepherding Christian Charities," *Chronicle of Philanthropy* 12 (Dec. 1996): 39.

33. Blum, "Shepherding Christian Charities," p. 39. For a generally positive assessment of ECFA's performance, see Geoffrey P. Goldsmith, *Self-Regulation of the Financial Disclosure of Evangelical Not-for-Profit Organizations* (UMI Dissert. Serv., 1996).

34. See Blum, "Shepherding Christian Charities," pp. 41-42; Letter from Rollin Van Broekhoven to Members of ECFA and United Response, 4 April 1996, pp. 3-4; Nelson, interview, 17 February 1998; Van Broekhoven, interview, 17 February 1998.

bers' fund-raising representations and financial accountability into judging the riskiness and advisability of their investments. Council officials did make informal contacts with members they knew had invested in New Era — they claimed they were later surprised by how many more of their members were actually involved — and advised those organizations to be careful in making the decision to deposit.

After New Era, ECFA's president Nelson says, the council gave only brief consideration to becoming involved in reviewing its members' investment decisions.[35] But ECFA did acknowledge that unwise, costly investments could undercut the credibility of its member agencies almost as much as fraudulent fund-raising or money management. It therefore began to give members more public advice about investment decisions and more public warnings about particular questionable investments. For example, a spring 1997 issue of ECFA's newsletter raised doubts about Lifeline, a marketing campaign for long-distance phone service under which new subscribers could designate a charity which would then receive a rebate on its service. The article advised boards to ask certain questions about Lifeline but added, in bold print, that "ECFA has no information that would indicate that Lifeline is doing anything illegal."[36] Another ECFA newsletter in early 1998 contained an article on "investing funds wisely" and a set of guidelines for drafting an investments policy.[37] In writing these and other notices, ECFA conceded that whatever its formal jurisdiction, its role has in practice expanded, that it "increasingly . . . has been viewed as a protector of sorts of the Christian community."[38]

The Bankruptcy Settlement

If the collapse of New Era and the revelation of the fraud were disasters for the evangelical charitable world, the impending bankruptcy process threatened to "add insult to injury," in the words of ECFA's Paul Nelson.[39]

35. Nelson, interview, 17 February 1998.

36. "Making a Decision About Lifeline?" *Focus on Accountability* 17, no. 3 (May/ June 1997): 1, 3.

37. Dan Busby, "Investing Ministry Funds Wisely: Are Your Policies Up-to-Date?" *Focus on Accountability* 18, no. 1 (Jan./Feb. 1998): 1.

38. Busby, "Investing Ministry Funds Wisely," p. 1

39. Bray, "A Subtle, Seductive Sell," p. 8.

The original filing stated that New Era had more than $550 million in liabilities and only $80 million in assets. Although that figure was quickly adjusted, it certainly appeared that New Era's creditors, including religious depositors, would soon be fighting each other over a limited pot of money. Such litigation would likely dissipate the available assets, ensuring that charities would indeed lose all that they had deposited. A Pennsylvania newspaper editorial warned that "it's possible that lawyers will walk away with money originally donated in good faith to worthy institutions."[40] At the least, ongoing litigation would produce long delays before any money was repaid, while many of the charities that had lost New Era deposits needed the money to continue their operations. Moreover, the spectacle of legal fights between evangelical organizations would do further damage to the Christian witness, already damaged by the scandal itself.

There was, however, a chance for a more amicable settlement and a speedier, and perhaps even much larger, repayment to depositors, if those organizations that had received money from New Era would voluntarily repay it so that it could be distributed to those who had lost. Such a plan emerged as a result of ECFA's efforts and a group it formed of evangelical charities involved in New Era.

Two days after the bankruptcy filing, ECFA and a few large evangelical charities formed a group called United Response to New Era. United Response was originally intended to serve as a network for evangelical organizations involved in the scam and as a spokesman for their interests in the bankruptcy case. In the latter role, United Response played a major role in electing the permanent bankruptcy trustee, who had the task of collecting all of New Era's money (including debts owed to New Era) and distributing it to creditors. The power of these evangelical organizations (United Response was the largest single bloc of creditors in the proceeding) helped secure the election of Arlin Adams, a prominent Philadelphia lawyer and former federal judge who, although Jewish, also had connections with and an appreciation for the evangelical world.[41]

Within a few weeks, United Response and ECFA asserted a more ac-

40. Editorial, "Poor Stewardship of Funds," *Somerset (PA) American,* 12 June 1995.
41. Joseph A. Slobodzian and Daniel Rubin, "Group Wants Ex-Judge for New Era Job," *Philadelphia Inquirer,* 26 June 1995, p. A1. Among other things, Adams had co-written a book on church-state law with an evangelical lawyer from Wheaton College. Arlin Adams and Charles Emmerich, *A Nation Dedicated to Religious Liberty: The Constitutional Heritage of the Religion Clauses* (Philadelphia: University of Pennsylvania Press, 1990).

tive role in the proceedings, proposing the outline of a settlement that would avoid litigation among the charities. Within the evangelical community, it was presented as resting on biblical teachings of stewardship, compassion, and witness. All the New Era-related funds, United Response said, were "held in trust, bounties that were God's alone"; Christian charities had to cooperate, rather than fight, in allocating the money; and the settlement must take compassionate account of all involved, not only those who had lost money but those who had received funds in good faith and for whom repayment would be difficult.[42]

The proposed settlement distinguished between two basic groups of charitable organizations that had deposited money with New Era. Those who had received more in various matching-fund payments from New Era than they had deposited were referred to as "net positives"; they had a basic obligation to return the money, since it was tainted by fraud. Other organizations, referred to as "net negatives," had put more on deposit with New Era than they had received. These organizations should be reimbursed as much as possible, but the terms were to be mitigated by the Golden Rule: "do unto others as you would have them do unto you." For example, some net positives who could not repay immediately and continue their operations were instead requested to pay as much, and as soon, as they could. As the chairman of ECFA's board of directors explained, the plan sought to strike a fair balance "between law and grace," acknowledging the legal claims of those defrauded by New Era while taking into account the equitable stake of those who had received and spent money in good faith.[43]

However, the organizations that agreed to return payments they had received would not be acting purely from altruism — they likely had a legal obligation to repay anyway. The bankruptcy law provides that certain transactions made by a person or organization within at least a year (and possibly up to three years) before it declares bankruptcy can be voided, and any money the bankrupt paid out must be returned to the trustee for distribution to creditors.[44] This provision serves to protect creditors while stopping a debtor's efforts to hide its assets. Although the law refers to such transactions as "fraudulent transfers," it has expanded to permit the recov-

42. Letter from Rollin Van Broekhoven to United Response Members, April 4, 1996, p. 8.

43. Rollin Van Broekhoven, quoted in "Unusual Settlement in Charity Debacle," *Los Angeles Times*, 31 Aug. 1996, p. B4.

44. 11 U.S.C., section 548.

ery even of money that the debtor paid out in good faith, if the transaction rendered the debtor insolvent and the recipient did not pay "reasonably equivalent value" in return. Since New Era's payments to charities were gifts rather than business exchanges, the recipients would probably be legally required to return the payments.[45]

To be sure, the "net positive" charities could have made legal arguments for their right to keep New Era payments. Some charities argued that they had provided "value" to New Era by temporarily depositing their money; others pointed out that they had received money in good faith and had already spent it (in part, they claimed, because their nonprofit legal status forbade them from accumulating assets and not plowing them back into their operations). Religious charities, in particular, argued that to require the repayment of donations received in good faith and spent on ministries would leave church operations in jeopardy and violate constitutional guarantees of the free exercise of religion.[46] Other charities disputed the particular amount they had received from New Era, or whether their receipts fell within the time period for voidable transactions.

These arguments, if made by scores of organizations, could surely have tied up the bankruptcy proceeding for months or years, during which the net positives would not have had to make repayments. But the net positives would also have paid large legal bills to litigate their position, so the strategy did not promise them much ultimate gain. In the end, moral considerations were certainly one factor that convinced net positives to return their payments, but it would be naive to think they were the only factor.

The settlement, hammered into final form by the spring of 1996, was complex. By "netting" each organization's payments from New Era against its lost deposits, the settlement departed from the typical structure of a bankruptcy proceeding. Normally the trustee collects all money owed to

45. A prominent federal appeals judge in Chicago ruled this way in an unrelated but similar case decided only days after New Era's bankruptcy. *Scholes v. Lehmann,* 56 F.3d 750 (7th Cir. 1995) (Posner, Chief Judge).

46. A similar claim succeeded in federal court in 1996 in circumstances where the religious entity had a much stronger equitable argument: a bankruptcy trustee was barred from recovering tithes that an individual had made regularly in good faith to his local church during the three years before he declared bankruptcy. *In re Young,* 82 F.3d 1407 (8th Cir. 1996). Congress later codified this protection for charities in the Religious Liberty and Charitable Donation Protection Act of 1998, amending 11 U.S.C., section 548(a) (signed into law June 19, 1998).

the estate, including transfers made within the "fraudulent transfer" period, and then distributes the money out to all creditors, so as to follow the bankruptcy statute's complex system of priority among creditors. But here, after satisfying the claims of creditors with legal priority (such as secured lenders and taxing jurisdictions), most other creditors of New Era stood on roughly the same footing: all had given money to the foundation expecting a double return to themselves or to the charities they had designated. Thus it made sense to net these claims in order to reduce the overall amount of money in dispute.

An even more complicated aspect of the settlement involved the donors who had given money to New Era not to receive a double return themselves, but to produce a double gift for the charity they had designated. Again, the settlement sought to reduce the amount of money shuttling back and forth by giving these donors a financial incentive to forego reclaiming their money and instead to "assign" their claims to designated charities (usually the charities they had originally designated). The advantage of this mechanism was that a number of net positive organizations in difficult straits — those who no longer had the money on hand to make a repayment — would be bolstered by receiving assigned claims from donors. Together, the twin mechanisms of netting claims and assigning donor claims reduced depositor losses from more than $500 million to just over $100 million, with approximately $85 million in tainted payments to be returned.

The most protracted settlement negotiations concerned how much would satisfy an organization's obligation to repay its New Era receipts. United Response, as noted above, sought provisions that would allow some leeway — "grace," in its terms — for organizations that had already spent their money. Eventually, the terms provided that a few large organizations would pay 93 percent of their receipts; other organizations would repay 85 percent (those who agreed to do so, and those with small amounts to repay); most others (about 400 in all) would pay 65 percent; and finally, organizations that could show financial "hardship" would be allowed to pay less according to their circumstances.[47]

---

47. The terms of the settlement are summarized in the bankruptcy judge's opinion approving it, *In re Foundation for New Era Philanthropy*, Bankruptcy No. 95-13729F (Eastern District of Pennsylvania, Aug. 21, 1996), which I hereafter refer to as the Court Opinion.

To persuade Judge Adams to agree to these terms — and thereby forego suing net positive organizations for the full amount of their receipts — United Response had to provide evidence that many charities would actually repay more than the minimum the settlement obligated them to pay. Adams, however, refused to join the deal until net positives had repaid some $40 million. That amount was eventually received, much of it from evangelical charities, after United Response repeatedly pleaded with them to take the lead as a form of Christian witness.[48]

Still, there were a number of objections to the proposed settlement, mostly on the basis that it did not seek sufficient repayment from the net positive charities. United Response defended the settlement based on biblical themes of stewardship, peacemaking, and grace; Adams, as trustee, offered a secular version of the same themes. He testified that an immediate settlement, even at some discount, would be more beneficial to the charities involved, even the net negatives, because it would reduce litigation costs and increase the chance that net positives would be willing or able to pay at all. Moreover, he argued that the entire charitable community, including the negatives, would be harmed by continued litigation, which would delay repayments and produce continued bad publicity.

Although most evangelical organizations involved in New Era joined the settlement, the objectors included several evangelical groups. One critic, the Seattle-based Crista Ministries, raised religious and moral objections, arguing that net positives were being allowed to keep some money stolen from others in violation of Christian moral standards.[49] On the other hand, one Christian entity, the Syracuse (New York) Rescue Mission Alliance, seemed to be upset that the settlement reflected Christian morals; the Mission asserted in court that the trustee, by forgiving some repayments owed, had illegally "based his decision in part on the desires of some members of the creditor body which seek to substitute biblical principles for business judgment."[50] The chief objector, Prudential Securities, like-

---

48. Letters from Paul Nelson to United Response Members, 16 January 1996 and 26 February 1996.

49. Randy Frame, "New Era Bankruptcy Case Moves Toward Resolution," *Christianity Today,* 16 Sept. 1996, p. 82. Crista had lost $2 million on deposit with New Era.

50. Court Opinion, p. 45. The Rescue Mission had lost $1.3 million; it eventually signed a separate settlement and later estimated it would get 85 to 90 percent of the money back. James T. Mulder, "A Tremendous Relief: The Rescue Mission Gets Back Much More Money Than It Expected," *Syracuse Post-Standard,* 7 June 1997, p. C1.

wise argued that the settlement "protect[ed] the interests of the religious charities and the charitable community as a whole, rather than the interests of creditors of New Era" as was the trustee's duty.[51]

In August 1996, the federal bankruptcy judge overseeing New Era approved the settlement as a fair method of assuring reasonable payments to creditors in a short period of time, a result beneficial to all concerned. The projected repayment of depositors eventually rose from 65 percent to more than 85 percent as the result of an $18 million payment by Prudential Securities in early 1997 to settle the various lawsuits against it.[52] Distributions of funds were made in December 1996 and August 1997, and a return figure of nearly 90 percent was reached by mid 2000. Judge Adams continued to prosecute a host of small lawsuits against 350 charities which together had received about $10 million from New Era. But the largest share of the dispute was resolved in the settlement initiated by United Response and its evangelical members.

Conclusion

If the New Era scandal inflicted a black eye on the world of evangelical charities, the settlement partly repaired that damage. Most obviously, the settlement saved many evangelical (and secular) organizations from even more severe financial consequences. More broadly, though, the evangelical world's leadership in the settlement process generally spoke well for its level of cooperation and responsibility. The initial revelation that so many ministries had fallen into New Era's trap had conjured up uncomfortable pictures of evangelicals as unsophisticated and gullible — long-standing, pejorative images that still resonate in popular culture.[53] But the settlement partly countered that by showing that evangelicals could draw on sophisticated resources and offer them to the broader society. ECFA, for example, has enjoyed increased opportunities to speak about the nonprofit sector and its regulation to the media, state regulators, and research orga-

51. Court Opinion, p. 68.
52. "Prudential Settles New Era Suit," *Christianity Today,* 6 Jan. 1997, p. 68.
53. Michael Weisskopf, "'Gospel Grapevine' Displays Strength in Controversy Over Military Gay Ban," *Washington Post,* 1 Feb. 1993, p. A1. Describes perception of evangelicals as "poor, uneducated, and easy to command."

nizations.[54] It may not stretch matters too far to see the New Era settlement process as an indicator of how evangelicals, who were alienated in many ways from mainstream American culture earlier in this century, have now come to see themselves as having significant responsibility for the culture.

The evangelical institutional network, a weakness insofar as it helped spread the New Era virus, became a strength insofar as it helped push settlement efforts forward. As I have already noted, all the charities involved, not just the evangelical ones, had practical reasons to reach a settlement. But there can be little doubt that the process was aided by the evangelicals' institutional ties such as ECFA, and by their shared moral framework and vocabulary — with concepts such as law and grace and stewardship — that enabled them to see a larger meaning in the process. Indeed, the New Era settlement offers support for Robert Wuthnow's thesis that religious values can be applied fruitfully to complex financial questions, even if today's churches often fail in this regard.[55]

The relative success of the bankruptcy process may have one disadvantage. Charities that were involved in New Era are likely to be much more careful in their investments for a while, but for others the scandal may not teach as clear a lesson as it would have had the results been worse. Fewer organizations may even have New Era in their minds because the settlement took it out of the media spotlight.

Despite the seriousness of the New Era episode, it seems unlikely that it will have a systemic effect on the way evangelical charities handle money. Many are likely to be more careful about investing in unusual financial vehicles in the short term. But the very success of the settlement may dilute the force of the lessons that New Era offers. Moreover, some of the causes of the debacle are deeply ingrained features of the nonprofit, especially evangelical, world: a constant need to raise money for ministries and a heavy reliance on personal connections and credibility. These factors are not likely to disappear soon, even if executives and board members are more cautious.

54. See ECFA 1996 Annual Report, pp. 3-4.
55. See Wuthnow, *God and Mammon in America;* Robert Wuthnow, *The Crisis in the Churches: Spiritual Malaise, Fiscal Woe* (New York: Oxford University Press, 1997).

PART III

CONCLUDING OBSERVATIONS

CHAPTER 15

Contemporary Evangelicalism and Mammon:
Some Thoughts

JOEL A. CARPENTER

No man can serve two masters: for either he will hate the one and love the other; or else he will hold to one and despise the other. Ye cannot serve God and mammon.

MATTHEW 6:24 (KJV)

An odd set of personal circumstances puts me in a position to speculate at greater length on the broader significance of three chapters in this book. First, I now work at an evangelical college in the United States with close denominational ties to three sister schools in Canada. Second, I was living in Philadelphia in 1995 when the New Era scandal broke, and I was personally acquainted with Jack Bennett. Third, my wife and I took part in a money management seminar sponsored by our home church back in the early 1980s; I think it was with Larry Burkett's group.

The chapters by Larry Eskridge on Larry Burkett and by Thomas Berg on Jack Bennett fit neatly together in that they both address some of the evangelical world's extraordinary traits that have come to the fore as the movement has entered into the brave new world of postwar American consumerist capitalism. For its part, Robert Burkinshaw's chapter, which compares evangelical endeavors in higher education in the United States and Canada, adds another important dimension in deepening our understanding of how very unique the U.S. evangelical scene has become.

In the broader Philadelphia area, there was scarcely a significant non-profit entity, evangelical or otherwise, that was not touched by the New Era scandal. Even among those that did not hand over part of their assets to New Era in the hope of doubling them, surely most heard about the opportunity, and their managers and boards no doubt argued over whether or not to participate. Among the scores of agencies that did get involved, ranging from the Philadelphia Orchestra to the Glenside Bible Church, many anguished moments followed. Endowments and their expected income evaporated. Church building funds disappeared. At Glenside Bible Church, the fund was mostly insurance money to pay for the rebuilding of a fire-ravaged sanctuary. Inner-city community development agencies such as Nueva Esperanza, run by the Hispanic Clergy of Philadelphia, saw their hard-earned cash reserves flying away into thin air.

Particularly frustrating and disillusioning for New Era's evangelical creditors was the fact that Jack Bennett was one of the most visible evangelicals in town. He was an officer in the Philadelphia Christian Leadership Foundation, a partnership of business people and urban ministry leaders linked via an annual Prayer Breakfast event. Bennett was also the chairman of the finance committee for the 1992 Billy Graham Crusade in Philadelphia. He was also well known at the Union League, the old-money men's club in downtown Philadelphia. What made his scam especially insidious, however, is that his organization, the Foundation for New Era Philanthropy, had a legitimate existence prior to the Ponzi Scheme. In addition to the Templeton-funded Nonprofit Management Institute that Bennett had organized for urban pastors and ministry leaders, New Era also acted as a grant-making and monitoring agent for a number of individual donors and small family foundations. Some of these benefactors preferred to remain anonymous, so various charities and ministries around town were used to dealing with unnamed donors backing the grants from New Era. It was thus relatively easy for Bennett to set up a credible Ponzi scheme, even in one of the most tightly connected civic and religious networks in the country. Not only did he have the benefit of word-of-mouth referrals, everyone knew him and his work. His widespread reputation as a philanthropist made his scheme all the much more credible.

Unfortunately, the media coverage suggested that the evangelical community was especially vulnerable because it was so idealistic and naive. In my estimation, this characterization is yet another secular stereotyping of the evangelical community. As Professor Berg's chapter shows, some of the savviest fund-raising cultural institutions in town, a number of internationally renowned financiers, and many blueblooded Main Line Philadelphians — in all a very canny group of elites — were also deeply taken in by Bennett. What the story reveals is more what the evangelicals and the mainstream charities shared in common, which is a tendency to work via personal referrals and networks of friendly trust in matters of personal and charitable finances. These otherwise prudent people engaged in a sort of disconnect from what they might do at their Center City offices. No bank officer in her right mind would loan money to an organization without seeing its tax returns and audits. But as a board member for a local charity, the same cautious banker might perhaps be swayed by a testimonial: "Mrs. Crenshaw, you know, says he's wonderful." Jack Bennett apparently sensed this vulnerability when it came to charities, and he took advantage of it.

But even if the evangelicals were no more vulnerable than non-evangelical people who had long experience with finances and nonprofits, was there anything particularly revealing in the way they engaged in this affair? I think Professor Berg is right in pointing out that the rapid growth of evangelical parachurch agencies and the insistent demands for raising more money drove the cupidity of the participants. As Mike Hamilton's chapter clearly shows, a multibillion-dollar evangelical parachurch industry has emerged since the Second World War, and while some of the evangelical agencies are much more "commercial" in their revenue structure (i.e., dependent mostly on the sale of goods and services), others depend more deeply on contributions. The whole ethos of postwar evangelicalism is driven by the adage with which Hamilton ends his paper: more money means more ministry. The vast majority of ministry leaders would never subscribe to a prosperity gospel ideology, but they are deeply infused with an American capitalist cultural understanding of the gospel — that God measures success by the numbers, that more money means more ministry, which means more success for God's kingdom. So they tend to measure their own success as disciples and servants of the Lord by the size of their ministry. The ones whose ministries command millions are introduced on the prayer breakfast rostrums as God's "choice servants."

For a biblical people, however, that is an odd measure of one's value in the Kingdom, where Jesus speaks lovingly of the widow's pennies. Such a propensity for financial gigantism, however, is a deeply American trait. It underscores the drive for growth that characterizes American evangelical religion and that tipped the scales in favor of the New Era scheme in the minds of ministry decision makers, from Wheaton College to Nueva Esperanza.

Larry Burkett, as he appears in Larry Eskridge's detailed and nuanced account, could not appear more different from Jack Bennett. Burkett argues for, and apparently lives, a life characterized by careful stewardship, material modesty, and personal moral integrity in financial and commercial dealings. Eskridge's chapter provides much to admire about the man, his ministry, and the commonsense advice he gives people about their finances. Nonetheless, when Burkett turns to the larger social, economic, and political scene, another mode of operation takes over, and he indulges in wildly speculative thinking and rhetoric, promotes conspiratorial thinking, and poses simplistic models of political economy. So we have an unlikely combination, which on the one side features warm piety, resolute biblicism, and commonsensical, expert advice about everyday living in some of its most important dimensions, and on the other side displays some really volatile and simplistic sociopolitical perspectives. Larry Burkett is not alone in displaying these Dr. Jekyl and Mr. Hyde traits. They are very common among the most popular evangelical spokespersons of our day.

So Larry Eskridge's conclusions are convincing. He suggests that the Christian financial stewardship phenomenon is a symptom of *arriviste* middle-class evangelicals' social and economic insecurities and their desire to navigate complicated and strange new financial territory. They are looking for a more secure platform on which to maintain their place in middle-class America. At the same time, says Eskridge, these class dynamics frame evangelicals' willingness to accept Burkett's apocalyptic scenarios about this world's imminent collapse. Their historic commitment to live in the world but not of it is taking on new dimensions, and they continue their awkward, arm's-length dance with it.[1]

1. A similarly ironic dissonance attended some evangelical responses to the Y2K scare. On the one hand, evangelical doom-sayers hailed the dawn of the new millennium in terms of the biblical apocalypse. On the other, they defined the problem strictly in terms of the technological, computer-driven circumstances of a very secular, Western political economy. For a shrewd exploration of that irony, see Susan Wise Bauer, "Y2Krazy," *Books and Culture* (Sept./Oct. 1999): 20-21.

These conclusions, however, can be taken a step further. Postwar evangelicals, by and large, have decided to come in from the sectarian margins of American life. They have decided, for various reasons, that they need to move to some new middle ground, leaving the realm of world-flight, entering the territory of world-engagement, but resisting the temptation to slide all the way over to world-embrace. In that middle ground, which sociologist Christian Smith argues is a vital and energizing center, there will be tensions.[2] I would argue further that much of the angst and contradictory behavior we see in earnest evangelical leaders like Larry Burkett (and to cite another example, James Dobson) arises from the relative absence of consistent Christian perspectival tools. Their move into concerns such as family rearing and finances, which scholars David Watt and James Hunter see as pure secularization or cultural accommodation, I read as something else.[3] Evangelicals are trying to address the agenda posed by the first generation of post-fundamentalist reformers, such as Carl Henry and Harold Ockenga. These leaders criticized fundamentalism's narrowing of the gospel to personal salvation and piety. The "neo-evangelical" reformers called for a holistic gospel that would make a difference in every realm of one's life.[4]

Today's evangelical leaders assume, then, that the gospel is comprehensive enough to deal with family life, finances, cultural values, and politics, too. Dispensational theology and zealous revivalism were fine for a sectarian stance, but they gave conservative evangelicals precious little by way of worldview and constructive principles for answering Francis Schaeffer's question, "How shall we then live?"

But what do today's evangelical leaders use instead? Burkett's instinct is the most common one, to find all the answers via some concordance-driven search of the Bible. Such biblicism has a long tradition. Evangelicals tend to distrust systematic theology and moral and political philosophy; but their method is deficient. Piecemeal readings can provide practical wisdom for discrete circumstances, but what about the big picture? The large

2. Christian Smith, *American Evangelicalism: Embattled and Thriving* (Chicago: University of Chicago Press, 1998).

3. David Watt, *A Transforming Faith: Explorations of Twentieth-Century American Evangelicalism* (New Brunswick, NJ: Rutgers University Press, 1991) and James Hunter, *Evangelicalism: The Coming Generation* (Chicago: University of Chicago Press, 1987).

4. I have tried to portray these assumptions in *Revive Us Again: The Reawakening of American Fundamentalism* (New York: Oxford University Press, 1997), pp. 187-210.

JOEL A. CARPENTER

questions of civilization require a profound synthesis of the Bible's message. This is where evangelical leaders fail, again and again, at the ideological level. What we see, in both Christian Financial Concepts and Focus on the Family, is both the strengths and the limits of biblicism, and the reversion, by default, to the apocalyptic, conspiratorial thinking of fundamentalism whenever the sights are raised from personal holiness to the big picture. In times like these, when evangelicals are insisting on being culturally engaged, principled and architectonic thinking is required for society, politics, economics, and culture. Christian theologies that have engaged in this kind of thought — such as found supremely in Augustine's *City of God,* and then in several Roman Catholic and Reformed traditions — have much to offer evangelicals for these times between the times, and in anticipation of the coming kingdom.

Precisely at this point the perspective of Robert Burkinshaw's chapter takes on great importance. Evangelical Christians who serve the kingdom from vantage points outside the United States also have much to offer. As Burkinshaw's chapter shows, very dramatically indeed, even in a Western democracy such as Canada, where Christianity has had a strong traditional role, evangelical Protestants today have nothing like the advantages or centrality they enjoy in the United States. For all the tendency to complain about outsiderhood and disadvantage, and some leaders' outraged thumping on the "Christian American theme," American evangelicals have no idea what marginality really means. The American evangelical scene is a great anomaly. We are so incredibly blessed (spoiled?) here in our country that it warps our outlook. For nearly all the rest of the world, pietist Christian faith simply means marginality. It is utterly amazing, indeed humbling, given these circumstances, to see, all over the world outside of Western Europe and North America, the rise of new evangelical Christian colleges. In such places as Lithuania, Russia, Kenya, South Africa, Nigeria, Argentina, Korea, and the Dominican Republic, evangelical Christians are struggling and sacrificing to build their own colleges of higher learning. In such locations the social, economic, and political situation for evangelicals will be much more like the Canadian scene than like the United States. What this wonderfully informative chapter about the Canadian evangelical efforts to make higher education Christian shows is that the Canadians have more to share with the rest of the world about such endeavors than Americans do. Canadian evangelicals' recent successes in breaking the impasse in cultural attitudes and political controls regarding religiously founded higher education have much to commend them as models to the burgeoning worldwide Christian college movement.

Not to sell ourselves short as American evangelicals, we also should learn from Burkinshaw's chapter that Americans have gained very useful knowledge about how to build, promote, and sustain nongovernmental agencies and develop lively civic and cultural sectors. Not the least among these society-serving and democracy-sustaining institutions are our "uncommon schools," the evangelical Christian colleges. Yet seeing ourselves as others see us deeply illuminates our limitations as well. American Christianity, these chapters remind us, is deeply shaped by our culture of democratic capitalism. American Christians are material creatures, as missions historian Andrew Walls reminds us. We are "uninhibited about money" and have a very large "concern for size and scale." This "materiality," Walls asserts, often gives us a "somewhat stunted appreciation" for the less material dimensions of life, including the realm of the spirit. We tend to translate everything into the technical, material, and pragmatic dimensions we can appreciate. As Walls puts it, we see life as a series of "problems to be solved," as "something that can be all worked out." We approach religion, Walls quips, with "big boots in the Temple."[5] These are historic features of the American religious character, Walls reminds us, as much true in the 1840s as the 1990s. But the chapters in this book demonstrate that in the postwar years these traits have been accentuated. Evangelicals have mastered some of the organizational, financial, and managerial keys, it seems, to achieve a level of institutional takeoff and cruising speed that will sustain the movement's levels of "ministry activity" for a long time. But does more ministry activity mean an advance of the kingdom? To answer that question aright, we Americans need some outside help.

5. Andrew F. Walls, "The American Dimension of the Missionary Movement," in *The Missionary Movement in Christian History: Studies in the Transmission of Faith* (Maryknoll, NY: Orbis, 1996), pp. 222-23.

CHAPTER 16

Money and Theology
in American Evangelicalism

JOHN G. STACKHOUSE, JR.

*So if you have not been trustworthy in handling worldly wealth, who
will trust you with true riches?*

LUKE 16:11 (NIV)

The contrasting economies of heaven and earth collide in Frank
Capra's well-known film, *It's a Wonderful Life*. The hero, George
Bailey, has fallen victim to the financial stupidity of a dotty uncle and faces
ruin and disgrace. Considering suicide, he is rescued by an earnest angel,
Clarence Oddbody. As Clarence tries to convince George that he is a guard-
ian angel and has been sent to help him, George's retort focuses on what
he perceives to be his central need: "You don't happen to have any money
on you, do you?"

Clarence replies that he doesn't have any because money isn't used in
heaven. George looks up at this startling announcement and then
deadpans, "Well, it sure comes in mighty handy down here, bub."

Undaunted, Clarence proceeds to help George see that what really
matters in his life is not his lack of wealth, but his enormous success in
helping others live happy, useful lives. George eventually comes to appreciate that he has had a wonderful life after all.

The movie ends, however, with the economies of heaven and earth coinciding. George, after all, still faces jail if he cannot come up with a large amount of cash. He is rescued by all of the friends he has made through his own sacrifice, diligence, and compassion. They come through for him in his hour of need with an outpouring of donations. And as George beams at the kindness of his community, a bell rings to signal that Clarence the angel indeed has done his job.

As the authors in this volume have considered aspects of how American evangelicals have raised and spent — and, sometimes, thought about — money, no single pattern emerges. There is, to put it mildly, a wide range of views of money within the evangelical tradition in America, as there is in the Christian church worldwide. Money is a powerful symbol; indeed, it bears many and diverse meanings that connect with crucial priorities in the lives of individuals and communities. Our own culture testifies to this fact in its colloquialisms: money is equated with both the staff of life (thus one has lots of "dough" or plenty of "bread") and with odious waste (thus one is "filthy" or "stinking" rich).

Such a potent symbol, not surprisingly, shows up often in the recorded discourse of Jesus Christ. Interpreters of American religion who have no direct access to their subjects' inner lives do well to pay heed to the ancient gospel wisdom of analyzing where the "treasure" is in order to decide where the "hearts" are also. Let us follow, therefore, the way money moves through the life of a typical evangelical donor and a typical evangelical institution.

Such a narrative will illumine a large and complex network of theological issues as the economies of heaven and earth overlap in the lives of Christians who are obligated by Jesus' teaching to render to Caesar what is Caesar's, and to God what is God's. Recognition of the varying ways in which American evangelicals have viewed these theological themes (highlighted in **bold** type) will go a long way to explain why evangelicals have treated money in such different ways. And recognizing just how *many* theological themes — both doctrinal and ethical — are in play when it comes to money helps to explain why evangelical views and practices regarding money may at times be inconsistent: coordinating all of these topics into a coherent theology of money is a daunting task.

Ms. Evangelical, then, goes to **work**. Does she view her work in theological terms, and if so, what terms? Some Christians have endured work as a necessary evil to be eliminated eventually in a paradise of continual ease or, as in the aspirations of mystics, in ceaseless contemplation of

God. Others have seen work as intrinsically good, as God himself is a "worker," and thus to be undertaken as part of representing the *imago dei*. Still others have commended work as something Christians do for the time being to keep a fallen world more or less in functional order so as to preserve the raw material out of which God is fashioning the church.[1]

In each case, there is the question of locating the question of work within a broader sense of **vocation**, of a "calling" by God to do this or that for some divinely approved reason. Does Ms. Evangelical view her work in terms of some kind of hierarchy, and if so, what values inform it? Some evangelical hierarchies, for example, have placed a premium on evangelism, and thus have lionized missionaries who proclaim the gospel at great personal cost, while this sort of hierarchy depreciates business people who are encumbered with making and spending mere money. Other evangelical hierarchies, however, have completely reversed the order, seeing God as the guarantor of health and wealth to all who have sufficient faith. Thus the wealthy are the blessed and the poor are properly suffering for their unbelief. Evangelical intellectuals, not surprisingly, have been tempted to value those whose jobs focus on ideas and "high culture." And, as activistic as evangelicals typically have been, they all tend to glorify the workaholic: "Better to burn out than to rust out," as one modern evangelical hero (Jim Elliott) affirmed. Finally, does Ms. Evangelical view her work as an organic part of her broader calling as a Christian, as a component to be prudently integrated with the rest of her life's relationships (as daughter, neighbor, friend, and church member)? Or does she see herself primarily as "a physician" or "an engineer" or "a salesperson" or "a police officer"?

The situation is more complicated when a Christian understanding of vocation is perverted by less noble motives. The Reformation doctrine of the goodness of all divinely acceptable vocations, for instance, has gone to seed in some episodes of American evangelicalism in which it has been used to justify what is at root simply hedonism. The tension, let alone the conflict, between God and mammon has thus been resolved by seeing the two as partners. God, you see, wants me to succeed in my profession/business/career in obedience to his calling and for his greater glory — so I can

---

1. This last suggestion is perhaps the most uncommon: for a recent articulation of it, see Robert Jenson, "The Church's Responsibility for the World," in *The Two Cities of God: The Church's Responsibility for the Earthly City,* ed. Carl E. Braaten and Robert W. Jenson (Grand Rapids: Eerdmans, 1997), pp. 1-10.

eat my cake and have it, too, gaining both earthly goodies and heavenly glory.

So far, these themes may seem to have little directly to do with money. But in this economy, as in most (but not all: slaves, for instance, work without recompense), there are **earnings** to be expected. Ms. Evangelical's view of earnings may well depend on her view of work. What is the relationship in her mind between her labor and her wages? Are her earnings simply what "her own hand hath gotten her" according to the current market price — thus, her earnings are her own by right? Perhaps instead her earnings are the gracious provision of God for her maintenance and stewardship, and are (strictly speaking) only accidentally related to the work she does. That is, they merely happen to be what the market pays for her work just now, and are not in any sense an objective indicator of the importance of her work nor of her success in it. Ms. Evangelical might take a different view yet and see the amount of her earnings as directly correlated with her obedience to God, as blessings to God's favorites (as in the biblical phrase "he who honors me, I will honor"). Are such blessings primarily for her to spend on her own enjoyment, then, and only secondarily to help others?

Part of Ms. Evangelical's view of the matter here will have to do with her view of **economics**, however articulate or inchoate. Does she see her earnings as her "just deserts" rendered by a market guided by an "invisible hand" of divine providence? Or, does she see her earnings as her not-quite-just deserts, that is, as (at least) what she deserves from a not-so-infallibly-guided market that seems to pay those people over there too much compared to what Ms. Evangelical thinks her own work is worth? Some have said that American evangelicals have tended to treat economic systems as if there were part of the climate or topography: realities simply to be dealt with as given, not as human constructs thus amenable to human revision. Does Ms. Evangelical ever wonder whether the economic system includes some basic inequities for which she should use her money, political influence, and other resources (to compensate)?

How, then, does Ms. Evangelical spend her money? How does she arrive at her financial priorities? Here we have the question of **ethical and theological method**. In an integrated Christian worldview, her management of money will emerge out of her sense of God's call on her life. But where is she to learn about her vocation, and particularly about a Christian view of money? Perhaps she depends most upon the teachings of her pastor or of popular authors she has read — whether Christian or secular.

Surely she is influenced by advertisements, both secular and Christian. But do they clarify her vocation or distract her from it by manipulating her through feelings of guilt or greed? To what extent is her ideal standard of living informed by the lifestyles of her favorite characters on television or in the movies? Her view of money likely depends to a great extent on the values she learned growing up and the churches she has attended. Has she ever processed these models according to her mature Christian commitments? Does she see her responsibility as a Christian steward requiring her to conduct research into the best value for her money, whether reading *Consumer Reports,* or engaging in comparative shopping, or reading Christian newsmagazine accounts of the integrity and efficiency of this or that charity? In sum, the question of ethical method here is how Ms. Evangelical comes to her financial decisions and with whom she deems it valuable to consult.

Let's suppose she now decides to give some of her money away to explicitly Christian institutions. How does she decide how much to give and to whom? In particular, she faces the category of **tithing**. Some Christian communities simply take over from Old Testament legislation the figure of ten percent of income. In our age of income taxes and many other compulsory contributions to the public good, however, is that now 10 percent of net income or of gross? The mention of things Canadian in this volume reminds us that Canadians generally are taxed more than Americans to provide a more extensive social welfare program: so should that affect one's tithe? What we have here is the complicated question of ethical method as it regards the application of the Old Testament law of Israel to the New Testament Christian community, particularly in the light of no direct teaching in the New Testament regarding tithing per se.

Is the tithe owed to the local congregation for its maintenance and ministry? Is it owed, in part, to the denominational family of which the congregation is a part? Or somehow to the church universal? What about Christ's Body as it is active outside the congregational/denominational structures, in so-called (and, in some ecclesiologies, pejoratively termed) parachurch organizations? Some pastors teach that InterVarsity Christian Fellowship, or World Vision, or Evangelicals for Social Action, or Promise Keepers do deserve financial support, but only *after* the congregation/denomination gets its tithe. But is this the best way to understand the nature of the **church**, as if congregations are primary and other Christian institutions are somehow secondary?

Ms. Evangelical has made up her mind and now wants to pay. She might write a check, hand over cash, or authorize withdrawals from her bank account on a regular basis. All of these media, of course, link her with the **world** of commerce, of the state ("Whose inscription does it bear?"), and of society at large. Thus a theology of money will be related to a theology of **culture**. What is the world, what is culture, what are they for, and how ought the individual Christian and the Christian church relate to them in greatest faithfulness to Christ? Is she responsible, for instance, for how her bank invests the money she locates there?

Common evangelical wisdom holds that she should tithe every pay period as her first financial obligation, and then manage her money from there. So should Ms. Evangelical borrow money in order to pay her church or some other Christian organization as well as her bills, whether through a loan per se or (more likely) through a credit card?[2] Some evangelicals have taught that indebtedness is a mark of excessive entanglement with the world, even a sort of voluntary servitude to the world, and is to be avoided at all costs. Is it right for her, then, to take on a student loan or a mortgage, quite apart from the question of making good on her tithe commitments?

As she takes the bills from her wallet or flips open her checkbook, she confronts **money** itself. Some Christians have viewed money as a value-neutral tool, a form of power to be used well or badly but itself neither good nor evil. Others have warned that it is instead a "power" as the New Testament describes such things (Rom. 8:38; Eph. 6:12; Col. 1:16), and to be reckoned with carefully as such. Is it in fact an alternate god, mammon, which competes for the soul's allegiance with the true God? Money is a highly complicated and multivalent symbol, performing a wide range of psychological and sociological functions for various kinds of people. How is Ms. Evangelical to view it?

The money is now dispensed. What does Ms. Evangelical think will be the **return** for her use of money in this way? Has God promised, as health-and-wealth teaching says he has, to reward her with a literally significant financial return? Will the organization she supports in this way

---

2. The question of indebtedness and bankruptcy has come before the American courts of late in regard to a couple who were already in debt and in the process of going bankrupt. They gave money to a church along the way, and creditors sought to get the offerings back to pay the couple's debts. See Randy Frame, "Bankruptcy Tithes Exemption Sought," *Christianity Today*, 8 Dec. 1997, p. 76.

send her a tangible premium of some sort? Does she believe instead that her "mansion" in heaven will be better furnished because of this "investment" in charity here below (Matt. 6:19-33 and par.)? Is she simply to enjoy the temporary, but welcome, relief of the guilt feelings that plague her from time to time, and what is she to make of this motivation as a Christian? And then there is the question of a tax receipt — which raises the interesting question of whether she needs to make sure to give *that* away, too, in order to make sure her tithe of ten percent really *is* donated. . . .

Once the tithe money has reached its destination, beyond the control of Ms. Evangelical, how will it be used? What is the ratio of "overhead" costs to "ministry" expenditures and how is the organization itself to set its priorities? Each organization has to decide how much, if anything, should it put into endowment for future use and a measure of security, how much into promotion and "development," and how much into immediate use, perhaps trusting God to supply day by day. Should new projects be undertaken before capital is at hand in faith that God will cover later costs, or should they be deferred for fear of leaving the "house" half-built, as the parable puts it (Luke 14:28-30)?

How is money to be raised? Executives of such organizations wrestle with how often and how hard to press the panic button to rouse their constituencies, particularly through direct mail campaigns. Others face the question of the morality of their advertising as it resorts to sentimentality, end-of-the-world alarmism, or even criticism of competing "ministries" in order to focus donors' attention on the needs of their organization.

Many missionary societies have required prospective missionaries to engage in "deputation," the practice of raising one's own support from friends, relatives, and churches. While this policy keeps missionaries in touch with their supporters (for all sorts of reasons), its successful practice obviously requires a set of skills in some ways different from those required of, say, a Bible translator or an AIDS counselor. Critics have seen this policy to place an inappropriate burden on such workers and, indeed, to privilege successful fund-raisers over those who might indeed be better suited for the actual work of the agency.

Each organization has to work out the connection between those who donate the money and those who decide how it ought to be spent. To what extent, for instance, do major donors dictate the spending of the organization? As American churches have moved from establishment to denominations to a populist free-for-all, within congregations themselves there can be acute pressure on clergy to kowtow to those members whose financial support seems crucial. (This pressure is all the more obvious in other institutions lacking the biblical aura of the congregation itself: if such organizations are not doing what the people want, the people will move their money elsewhere.)[3] Furthermore, beneath this dynamic in churches is the very relation of pastor to people: To what extent does the perspective of the marketplace shape this relation, so that the pastor is sometimes viewed as nothing more than an employee of the church?

The flip side to this question is the role of leading personalities within the organization — especially if there is a single figure who symbolizes the organization to its public. To what extent do such individuals set priorities by their power to raise funds? To what extent is the organization shaped by the economic dependence of every employee upon the charisma of the leader?[4]

The question of fund-raising interlocks with the question of image, of the way the organization presents itself. Does it make well-heeled donors feel at ease by entertaining them with fine dining and meeting them in tastefully appointed headquarters (that require expensive upkeep as part of basic operational costs)? Or is money spent lavishly on appearances to signify to lower-income donors that God's blessing rests upon it? Does the organization pay for high-quality print and audio-visual promotional materials in order to present its case most vividly and, to be frank, to make it stand out from its counterparts? (This reference to "counterparts" raises, of course, the especially American, "free market" phenomenon of the multitude of independent organizations, which are free to try their hand in Christian service, limited by no denominational hierarchy but instead only by their ability to attract and retain support from sectors of the Christian

---

3. For the historical roots of this question, see Nathan O. Hatch, *The Democratization of American Christianity* (New Haven: Yale University Press, 1989).

4. Harold John Ockenga, champion of the "neo-evangelical" movement of the 1940s and following decades, made clear his views of leadership and money in an interview he gave in his seventy-seventh year: "The pastor should sit on the board of trustees, not as a member, but just as he should sit on the board of deacons, or elders. He ought to know where everything goes. He has to raise the money, therefore he ought to be able to see where it goes. . . . He ought to have a good bit to say about the final disposition of funds. I didn't do that directly; I did it through the boards. I sat on every board that spent a dime, because I didn't want the money to go to the wrong place. It was too hard to raise" ("Harold John Ockenga: Chairman of the Board," *Christianity Today,* 6 Nov. 1981, p. 28).

public.) Does the organization instead convey its commitment to thrift by economizing everywhere it can?

These dovetailed questions of fund-raising, priorities, and image remind us of a long-standing tension in Christian relations with the rich. As the church receives donations — whether from medieval lords, Renaissance magnates, early modern burghers, or Gilded Age robber barons — it seems to be offering approval. Protestants have been scandalized in this regard particularly over the Roman Catholic practice of granting indulgences, but Protestants, too, have often been glad to offer certain laurels to donors possessed of questionable motives. (The Orthodox, whose story does not figure largely in American history, have their own complicated heritage of relations with the powerful.) Ms. Evangelical, that is, might well expect another "return" to motivate her donation: a lovely ceremony lauding her as a fine Christian patron and her name suitably inscribed on this or that monument for later generations to admire.

Beyond the question of relating to the rich is the question of the economy in general — and thus we encounter again the theology of **culture**. To what extent, that is, does the church implicitly or explicitly endorse the economy in which it finds itself, and particular players within it? The most crucial example of this question in American history, of course, is the defense of the slave trade. In the century-and-a-half since then, however, Christians have continued to engage in other economic controversies, whether the rise of the free market domestically and internationally, the threat of communism, the emergence of the welfare state especially since the New Deal and expanded through the Great Society, the furor over Reaganomics, and so on. It is easy, with hindsight, to spot nineteenth-century evangelicals exploiting Scripture to justify the slave-based economy of the South. Such exploitation, however, can hardly be presumed to have vanished since.

Again, we return to most American Christians, and perhaps evangelicals in particular, treating the economy as they have the weather: complaining about it, but generally simply taking it for granted. (This attitude might well have been more true of white evangelicals than of black or Hispanic, of course, given the violent history of the latter groups' encounter with American economic forces.)[5] Evangelical holdings in church build-

5. See Clifford A. Jones, Sr., "How a Christian African-American Reflects on Stewardship in a Consumer-Oriented Society," in The Consuming Passion: Christianity and the

ings, schools, missionary societies, advocacy organizations, and other institutions, however, amount to hundreds of millions of dollars, quite apart from evangelicals' personal domestic and business properties, investments, and so on. Clearly, evangelicals have had a significant financial presence in America. Yet one has to look northward to Canada, to Social Credit and the Cooperative Commonwealth Federation (now the New Democratic Party), to find broad-ranging movements, let alone political parties, devoted to economic reform with Christians at their core.

However the money comes in to this organization then, how should the employees be paid and otherwise benefited? Some Christian organizations have paid everyone the same, while most have employed differentiating criteria, whether seniority, qualifications, experience, need, function, and so on.[6] What constitutes an appropriate standard of payment in this institution — what parallels with what other institutions, if any, will be sought to peg remuneration in this one?[7] Clerical salaries have long been used by historians as measures of a church's self-image vis-à-vis the broader culture, whether farmer-preacher Baptists or highly educated and professional Episcopalian priests. Every other institution faces similar questions. Will a Christian college, for instance, compare its scale with

---

Consumer Culture, ed. Rodney Clapp (Downers Grove, IL: InterVarsity Press, 1998), pp. 151-66; and Calvin O. Pressley and Walter V. Collier, "Financing Historic Black Churches," in *Financing American Religion*, ed. Mark Chaves and Sharon L. Miller (Walnut Creek, CA and London: AltaMira, 1999), pp. 21-28.

6. Speaking of the zone I know best, namely, Christian higher education in Canada, I note that at least three approaches to faculty remuneration have been formulated that break with typical North American patterns. Prairie Bible Institute in Alberta for most of its history paid all staff members similarly, regardless of function, allowing only for marital status and dependent children. Ontario Theological Seminary in Toronto (now Tyndale Theological Seminary) had no ranks among its faculty members (everyone was a "professor" of his or her field) and paid everyone the same. And Regent College, Vancouver, did employ the typical North American ranks of assistant, associate, and full professor, but paid one salary per rank, regardless of years already spent in that rank (that is, there were no "steps" in the pay scale). For more on the ethos of these institutions, see my *Canadian Evangelicalism in the Twentieth Century: An Introduction to Its Character* (Toronto: University of Toronto Press, 1993).

7. One is reminded of Billy Graham's long-standing policy of having his Board pay him a fixed salary — regardless of income received by the Billy Graham Evangelistic Association — that was pegged to the typical salary of the pastor of a large urban American congregation (see William Martin, *A Prophet with Honor: The Billy Graham Story* [New York: William Morrow, 1991], p. 139).

other Christian colleges in its region, or in the country, or in North America? Will it compare itself with secular schools? Will a missionary society compare itself financially with a secular charity or with a government agency? With the organization of labor in modern times comes the question of unions — even in Christian "ministries." How ought Christians, whether labor or management, workers or owners, to consider collective bargaining? Some see unions as disruptive of organizational harmony and therefore particularly to be avoided in Christian ventures. Others see them as necessary tools for promoting justice and restraining evil. Answering all of these questions, then, will depend upon consideration of the interlocking theological themes of **providence**, **vocation**, **mission**, **stewardship**, **community**, and more.

Christians with a well-developed doctrine of **sin** will exercise an appropriate hermeneutic of suspicion toward theological justifications of any financial policies. Such Christians might inquire, for instance, whether the practice of paying everyone the same low salary truly exemplifies Christian community, or is instead a rationalization for poor fund-raising and woolly-minded administration. They might, to pick a different example, ask whether the structuring of an organization in parallel with secular bureaucracies is a mark of worldly wisdom, or just sheer worldliness that privileges élites at the expense of others.

In regard to the ever-present temptation to rationalize, historian James Bratt speaks of the "seductive powers of economies of scale" that tempt evangelical institutions to think that "bigger is better." He also warns of economic necessity being turned into evangelical virtue: thus cooperating with other groups merely in order to survive becomes a splendid venture of ecumenical good will, or refusing to file proper tax information is defended as keeping God's money out of the hands of worldly powers.

One can observe theology being used to justify all sorts of economic situations and decisions. But, as theologian John Mulder has argued, it isn't equally good theology in each case.[8] Sometimes, of course, the theology is sheer hypocrisy. Often, however, the case is that the theological ideas used to consider money are sound enough, but there are not enough of them: not enough to provide theological and ethical balance and thus prevent easy and extreme decisions. The typical evangelical impulse toward prag-

8. John M. Mulder, "Faith and Money: Theological Reflections on Financing American Religion," in *Financing American Religion*, ed. Chaves and Miller, pp. 157-68.

matism, evangelism, and activism — and away from systematic theological reflection — has not served evangelicalism well in this respect.[9]

A related dynamic in evangelical history has been the invocation of secular wisdom to solve Christian financial disputes. "Each generation should pay its own debts" has justified a refusal to take out long-term loans, while "each generation should pay its own way" has warranted a refusal to seek endowment funds. Both of these proverbs have been solemnly intoned as if they were Proverbs. Again, the fundamental question appears of which values, which wisdom, even which language, have Christians used to think about, and therefore make use of, money.

Finally, all of these themes need to be seen in the light of the **Christian Story** of Creation, Fall, Redemption, and Consummation. Where have we been, where are we now, and where are we going? Jesus frequently discusses money as if there are two realms distinguished both spatially (earth and heaven) and chronologically (this world and the next). And his consistent message is to view money and make financial decisions with this twofold reality in mind. How is this cosmology and teleology, as it were, to be understood and applied in our day?

If Christ is returning imminently to establish an entirely new heaven and earth upon the eradication of the current cosmos, then to invest in long-term projects would be a waste of valuable and urgently needed resources. If instead there is to be a lot of continuity between this world and the "new earth" to be inaugurated, then some kinds of investments in, say, environmental stewardship are indeed justified in the very long haul. We would, that is, be cooperating with God in his ongoing project of redeeming the planet. What, then, is the church's **mission** in the world in the light of this vast Story? Is it primarily evangelism, primarily justice-seeking, primarily charity to the needy, primarily worship, primarily living out the values of the kingdom of God as "proleptic community," or perhaps some combination of these?

Answering such questions brings to the fore the question of **value** and what counts as success. By what standard does the individual believer and the Christian organization rightly measure success in the service of God? What is, in short, the good life? Money is all-too-convenient a symbol, whether in terms of income, expenditure, savings, or investments.

9. Mark A. Noll, *The Scandal of the Evangelical Mind* (Grand Rapids: Eerdmans, 1994).

This individual is blessed by God: one can tell by how much money she has — or has given away. That organization is failing to please God: one can tell by its small donor base — or by its sponsorship by rich Christians. Where does the sense of value and worth (as in "net worth" or "worthy service") come from for Christians?

Money is a complicated symbol psychologically, and it is bound up with a daunting range of theological themes.[10] It is hardly surprising, therefore, that evangelicals have disagreed with each other over it, and even found it hard to treat it consistently by their own lights. Whatever the theological tradition and conviction, however, it seems fair to suggest that at least Christians should think and act in regard to money in a way consistent with their convictions about fundamental theological themes. Indeed, a well-formed theology should act as a sort of razor: properly honed, it should help Christians, whether individuals or institutions, make decisions about money.

Ironically, one can look at the money/theology relationship the other way. In doing so, one can claim dominical authority for concluding that theology, whether well formed or not, has indeed affected evangelical decisions about money. For as one observes how American evangelicals have raised, spent, and thought about money in history, one sees what Christ himself encouraged one to see: that where their treasure has been, there their hearts — and minds — have been also. Reading back from behavior to motivation, as historians and social scientists sometimes try to do, is a delicate business, and never more so than in financial matters in which layers of rationalization and aspiration, worldliness and sanctification, rarely separate out nicely. But Christ's teaching assures the diligent observer that looking at the history of evangelicals and finance is worthwhile. For while money may not have been evangelicals' only value, it is a strong indication of what they have in fact valued.

10. For recent reflections by a Christian psychologist, see David G. Benner, *Money Madness and Financial Freedom* (Calgary: Detselig, 1996).

Contributors

ALVYN AUSTIN is an assistant professor of history at York University in Toronto, Canada.

THOMAS C. BERG is a professor of law at the Cumberland School of Law at Samford University.

ROBERT BURKINSHAW is an associate professor of history and political science at Trinity Western University in Canada.

JOEL A. CARPENTER is a historian of American religion and provost of Calvin College.

LARRY ESKRIDGE is the associate director of the Institute for the Study of American Evangelicals (ISAE) at Wheaton College.

BARRY GARDNER is a financial consultant for businesses and non-profit organizations and lives in Wheaton, IL.

PETER DOBKIN HALL is a research scientist for the Program on Non-profit Organizations at Yale University where he also lectures on Church and Society.

CHARLES E. HAMBRICK-STOWE is a United Church of Christ clergyman and an adjunct professor of history at Lancaster Theological Seminary.

MICHAEL S. HAMILTON is an assistant professor of American history at Seattle Pacific University.

DEAN R. HOGE is a professor of sociology at the Catholic University of America in Washington, D.C.

ROBIN KLAY is a professor of economics and business administration at Hope College.

JOHN LUNN is a professor of economics and business administration at Hope College.

MARK A. NOLL is the McManis Professor of Christian Thought at Wheaton College and Senior Advisor of the ISAE.

TED OWNBY is an associate professor of history and Southern Studies at the Center for the Study of Southern Culture at the University of Mississippi.

GARY SCOTT SMITH is a professor of sociology at Grove City College.

JOHN G. STACKHOUSE, JR. is the Sangwoo Youtong Chee Professor of Theology at Regent College in Vancouver, British Columbia.

SUSAN M. YOHN is an associate professor of history at Hofstra University.

Index

(BGEA), 100, 101; statistics, 119. *See also* Graham, Billy

BIOLA (Bible Institute of Los Angeles), 263-64, 265, 271

Blanchard, Charles, 107, 293, 296

Blue, Ron, 116

Borden, William, 226-27, 228, 234

Boll, R. H., 248

Bradford, William, 341

Briercrest Bible College, 294

Bright, Bill, 134, 319, 340

Broomhall, A. J., 212

Broomhall, Benjamin, 219-20

Budgeting, 70-71, 70-71n.149, 325-27

Burkett, Judy, 311-12, 316, 318

Burkett, Larry, 116-17, 137, 402-4; as author, 311, 320-21n.38, 322, 323; and beginnings of Christian Financial Concepts, 311-13, 320-25; on business ethics, 337-39; on church finances, 332-34; on credit, 326-27; on debt, 325-27; early life, 315-18; on environment, 345n.141; on giving, 331-32; influence on evangelicals, 312-14, 348-50; on lifestyle issues, 329-30; on personal finances, 325-28; political involvement of, 340-45; on responsibility to poor, 333-34; on women and finances, 326, 333, 334-37

Burroughs, Nannie Helen, 183, 190, 198-99, 206; and African-American Woman's Convention, 200, 201; and National Baptist Convention, 202-3; and National Training School for Women and Girls, 200, 201, 203, 204

Bush, George, 340, 342, 343, 343n.133

Business Methods, evangelicals' adaptation of, 16, 23, 24-26, 72-74; and technology, 298-310; and women's missions organizations, 187, 191

Buswell, J. Oliver, 266

Campbell, Joe, 240

Camping, 127-28, 130, 267

Campus Crusade for Christ, 134, 302, 311, 317-18, 319, 320-21; statistics, 119. *See also* Bright, Bill

Canada, evangelicals in, 355, 356, 357, 358, 359-63, 364, 404-5. *See also* Education

Capitalism, 341, 343, 408-9; and Church of Christ metaphors, 248; and Protestant women, 197-98, 204-6; and Southern Pentecostal critiques, 243-47. *See also* Economy, United States

Carnegie, Andrew, 168, 169-70, 171

Catholics. *See* Roman Catholics

Chicago, as post-war evangelical capital, 259-60

China Inland Mission, 207-34; core principles, 210; as model for other evangelical missions and organizations, 209; North American branch, 207, 209, 221-33; statistics, 211, 213n.15, 219, 224, 224n.46, 228-33, 270-71, 302. *See also* Faith Missions, and Overseas Missionary Fellowship (OMF)

China's Millions, 210, 212, 213, 223, 225, 228, 233

Christian Action Council (CAC), 128

Christian Booksellers Association, statistics, 122

Christian Broadcasting Network, statistics, 122

Christian Camping International, 128

Christian Coalition, 129, 130

Christian Financial Concepts (CFC), 312-13, 321-25, 404. *See also* Burkett, Larry

Christian Life, 259

Christian Parenting, 124

Christian Service Brigade, 303

Christianity Today, 383, 384

Christianity Today, Inc., 123

Chronicle of Philanthropy, 387